To my Mother and Father

KARL JASPERS AND THE ROLE OF "CONVERSION" IN THE NUCLEAR AGE

Gregory J. Walters

UNIVERSITY
PRESS OF
AMERICA

Lanham • New York • London

Copyright © 1988 by

University Press of America,® Inc.

4720 Boston Way
Lanham, MD 20706

3 Henrietta Street
London WC2E 8LU England

Printed in the United States of America

British Cataloging in Publication Information Available

Library of Congress Cataloging-in-Publication Data

Walters, Gregory J., 1956–
Karl Jaspers and the role of ''conversion'' in the nuclear age.
Bibliography: p. Includes index.
1. Jaspers, Karl, 1883–1969. 2. Nuclear warfare—Moral and ethical aspects.
3. Conversion. I. Title.
B3279.J34W32   1988   172'.42   87–31466 CIP
ISBN 0–8191–6836–X (alk. paper)
ISBN 0–8191–6837–8 (pbk. : alk. paper)

All University Press of America books are produced on acid-free
paper which exceeds the minimum standards set by the National
Historical Publications and Records Commission.

TABLE OF CONTENTS

BIBLIOGRAPHY OF WORKS CITED 277

PREFACE

For the sake of convenience Jaspers's major works are referred to in this work either by their German or English title, and most frequently, by abbreviations in the case of book-length works and frequently cited monographs and articles. Although we cannot here take up the question of the translation-- and thus interpretation-- of Jaspers into English by his major translators, E.B. Ashton and Ralph Manheim,/1/ to whom we must now add the names of Edith Ehrlich, Leonard H. Ehrlich, and George B. Pepper,/2/ this study primarily uses existing English translations of Jaspers's major works and articles where available. Where necessary for clarification or emphasis, we have checked them against the original German. Where other foreign language sources are cited the translation is our own unless otherwise indicated.

Following the practice of Jaspers's English translators, we have not translated or underlined the term "Existenz"-- a truly "technical" term in his philosophizing (though Jaspers sought clarity and a non-technical use of language)-- which he appropriated directly from Kierkegaard's Danish. We use the term existential (_existentiell_) primarily as the adjective of Existenz, unless the context clearly suggests the adjectival form of (physical) existence in the sense of _Dasein._ Where necessary, we have attempted to clarify the translation and definitions of terms used by Jaspers, mindful of the fact that any terminological approach to his philosophizing leads to pseudo-insights and violates the spirit and method of his transcending thinking./3/

The use of the terms "intellect," "reason," "consciousness-as-such," and "conversion" deserve special mention here. Because Jaspers takes his basic philosophical vocabulary from Kant, he appropriates Kant's use of _Verstand_ for the Latin _intellectus_ and _Vernunft_ for the Latin _ratio_ (Fr. _raison_)./4/ This distinction between the "intellect" and "reason" in Kant's thinking, between the faculty of cognition and the faculty of thinking, has been argued at length by Jaspers's student, Hannah Arendt,/5/ and frequently the major works in English on Jaspers's thinking use "intellect" and "reason" for the German _Verstand_ and _Vernunft._

Linguistically distinct from _Verstand_ or "intellect" is Jaspers's use of _Bewusstsein überhaupt_ which has been variously translated as "consciousness in general," "consciousness at large," and "consciousness-as-such."/6/ We use the latter term following the recent helpful translations by E. Ehrlich, L.H. Ehrlich, and G.B. Pepper. "Intellect" and "consciousness-as-such," are used virtually synonymously by Jaspers./7/

The role of humanity's "redirection,"/8/ "transformation," (Verwandlung), "turn about" (Umkehr), "turn around" (Umwendung) or "change" (Veränderung) in our way of thinking-- what we speak of throughout this study as "conversion"-- is central to Jaspers's philosophical thinking. These German concepts, of course, are not to be equated with the specific idea of religious conversion in the sense of the German Bekehrung./9/ There are, however, precedents in existing English translations for the use of "conversion" to convey Jaspers's concept of Verwandlung or Umkehr./10/ The reason for our use of the term "conversion" will become clear in the final chapter. In the spirit of Jaspers's quest for communication we have tried to use inclusive language throughout.

This work owes it realization to numerous others. From the outset, I would like to acknowledge the generous assistance of the Social Sciences and Humanities Research Council of Canada, without whose financial support this project would have never been completed.

To Rev. Dr. André Guidon, o.m.i., Professor of Moral Theology at Saint Paul University, Ottawa, Ontario, I owe a great debt for his personal encouragement and support in the early 1980s while researching the psycho-spiritual aspects of nuclear developments on the family, children and adolescents in the United States. That earlier research, and the questions and problems it raised, help set the stage for this study.

Dr. Kenneth R. Melchin and Dr. James Pambrun both read earlier versions of the manuscript, and helped me to see the importance of methodological rigour and the value of studying a foundational thinker like Jaspers on the nuclear problem. Dr. Melchin was a vital conversational partner throughout, particularly with respect to many of the social, political, economic, and military issues raised by the arms race and militarism.

Rev. Dr. Dale Schlitt, o.m.i., offered many helpful and illuminating suggestions regarding both method and substance in reading an earlier version of the text, and in noting numerous Hegelian influences in Jaspers's thinking even though Jaspers himself was opposed to the idea of system building.

Professor George B. Pepper, co-founder of the Karl Jaspers Society of North America, provided invaluable guidance through oral and written correspondence, and challenged me to clarify an earlier version of Chapter Eight.

A sincere expression of gratitude is due to Rev. Dr. Benoît Garceau, o.m.i. It was his insightful questioning and life lived out of an encompassing philosophical reason that helped lead to this study and to a deeper awareness of the limits of knowledge and the meaning of faith, particularly faith in "the other."

Mrs. Irene Williams took time and care in reading my English translations of Jaspers's German prose, while Mr. Charles Williams frequently assisted in the role of caregiver with my son Joel.

The names of colleagues and friends who work for the Biblical vision of Shalom and justice and who have provided spiritual support in base christian community during the years of labour invested in this work are too numerous to mention here. Their agapic praxis has sustained and encouraged my reflection from the outset.

The dedication of this book to my mother and father expresses an indebtedness of a fundamental nature. To my wife, Sonia, who helped labour with proof-reading and the compilation of the Index, and whose love daily teaches me the importance of "conversion" to a new mode of thinking and doing in the nuclear age, I am eternally grateful.

1. On the problem of existing English translations
   of Jaspers's German works, see Charles Wallraff,
   "Jaspers in English: A Failure of Communication," Philosophy and Phenomenological Research
   37 (1977), pp.537-548, and the response by Adolph
   Lichtigfeld, "Jaspers in English: A Failure Not
   of Communication But Rather of Interpretation,"
   Philosophy and Phenomenological Research 41
   (1980/81), pp.216-222.

2. Karl Jaspers: Basic Philosophical Writings,
   Selections, edited,, translated, with
   introductions by Edith Ehrlich, Leonard H.
   Ehrlich, George B. Pepper (Athens, Ohio and
   London: Ohio University Press, 1986). This
   helpful work appeared shortly before completing
   Chapters Six and Seven of the thesis. We have
   nonetheless made use of the new translations
   where possible.

3. Ludwig B. Lefebre has provided a useful glossary
   of translations and definitions of terms used by
   Jaspers; in Schilpp, pp.xvi-xxvi.

4. E.B. Ashton, "Translator's Note," PHT I, p.xv:
   "The word Verstand [...] comes from the verb
   verstehen, to understand, and has therefore been
   'technically' translated time after time as 'the
   understanding.' But the German word for
   understanding is Verstandnis, something
   altogether different from Verstand-- which to
   German laymen and philosophers from Kant to
   Jaspers means precisely what we mean by
   'intellect'."

5. Hannah Arendt, The Life of the Mind, one volume
   edition (New York and London: Harcourt Brace
   Jovanovich, 1978), pp.13-14 and p.57, where
   Arendt notes that the distinction between the
   faculty of thinking and cognition, "on its most
   elementary level and in Kant's own words, lies in
   the fact that 'concepts of reason serve us to
   conceive [begreifen, comprehend], as concepts of
   the intellect serve us to apprehend perceptions"
   ("Vernunftbegriffe dienen zum Begreifen, wie
   Verstandesbegriffe zum Verstehen der
   Wahrnehmungen"). In other words, the intellect
   (Verstand) desires to grasp what is given to the

senses, but reason (<u>Vernunft</u>) wishes to understand its <u>meaning</u>."

6. E.B. Ashton, "Translator's Note," PHT I, p.xv, notes that the former translations of <u>Bewusstsein</u> <u>überhaupt</u> will do for Kant, but not for Jaspers "who needs to distinguish not only the Kantian concept from an individual consciousness, but consciousness 'as such' from such post-Kantian psychological phenomena as sub-consciousness and the 'unconscious.' Besides, he has so refined the concept that generality is now only one of its aspects, and not the most important one in today's world." Cf., E. Ehrlich, L. H. Ehrlich, G. B. Pepper, eds., <u>Karl</u> <u>Jaspers</u>, pp.146-149.

7. This distinction has been clarified by Professor Leonard Ehrlich in his discussion of the use of "intellect" for <u>Verstand</u> in Jaspers's thinking: "All thought is determinative by virtue of the forms of thought which are explored in formal sciences such as logic and the theory of knowledge. Jaspers, like Kant, calls this 'consciousness as such'. Some human thinking fulfills the requirements of the universal forms of thought, for other human thought the forms of thought are as inadequate as they are un-avoidable. Instances of the former are scientific knowledge and everyday experience. It is this that Kant and Jaspers call 'Verstand' and Locke and Hume, for example, the 'understanding'. However, 'understanding' has too many uses, particularly when speaking of Jaspers in the English language." He goes on to note precedents for the use of 'intellect' for <u>Verstand</u>, including Thomas Aquinas and Anselm's "<u>fides</u> <u>quaerens</u> <u>intellectum</u>." <u>Karl</u> <u>Jaspers</u>: <u>Philosophy</u> <u>as Faith</u> (Amherst: University of Amherst Press, 1975), p.240, n.19.

8. Professor Ehrlich prefers to speak of the important, indeed central, role of "redirection" in Jaspers's thinking: "redirection [...] makes itself felt in his call to purification in the Post-World-War-II discussion of German guilt; it becomes explicit in his exploration of the role of reason and of the individual in the political situation engendered by the dual threat of atomic annihilation and totalitarianism; and again in his warning against the political lethargy of the German people with respect to past transgressions

and renewed threats to political freedom [...]
Jaspers's own conception of redirection is that
of philosophizing as continuous learning to die,
which is Plato's simile for the constant task of
'rebirth to a true life'." Karl Jaspers:
Philosophy as Faith, p.122.

9. On this point, see also Alan M. Olson,
    Hermeneutics and Transcendence: An
    Interpretation of the Philosophy of Karl Jaspers
    (The Hague, Boston, London: Martinus Nijhoff,
    1979), p.7: "What one might term a "trans-
    cending-transformation" of the consciousness of
    self-Being is not the result of a leap out of the
    world or away from the world but always within
    and through the world. It is [...] the qualified
    immanence of Jaspers's notion of Transcendence
    which distinguishes the conversion of con-
    sciousness to which he refers from that which is
    usually claimed as the source of so-called
    'religious' conversions."

10. E.g., Ralph Manheim, WW, p.60; EDP, p.58. Also
    Norbert Guterman, ABR, p.50; HS, p.165. (N.B.
    Abbreviated entries separated by a semicolon (;)
    correlate the English and German sources.
    Throughout this work, this method is used most
    frequently with references to FM and AB).

INTRODUCTION

"Philosophizing starts with our situation."/1/
Although our knowledge of the human situation is
inevitably limited by a given historical horizon, few
would deny the great challenges confronting humanity at
this juncture of history. Looming alongside the
problems of world hunger, the population explosion,
environmental deterioration, and the social, political,
and economic costs of global militarism ($1.3 trillion
Cdn or $2.4 million a minute in 1986),/2/ stands the
possibility of nuclear war. Victor F. Weisskopf,
Institute Professor of Physics, emeritus, at the
Massachusetts Institute of Technology and the former
director general of the European Center for Nuclear
Research in Geneva, explains the potential for nuclear
war:

> If any human beings are alive 50
> years from now, they may look back on
> today's situation as a virulent case of
> collective mental disease that gripped
> humanity [...] More than 50,000 Soviet
> and U.S. nuclear warheads are now de-
> ployed, with a total explosive power of
> 6,000 times the amount of explosives
> used in World War II. A mere few hun-
> dred of today's warheads are enough to
> destroy Western and Eastern civili-
> zation. If this is not a symptom of
> mental derangement, what is?/3/

Culturally, Yale University psychiatrist, Dr.
Robert J. Lifton, has in recent years advanced the idea
of the "nuclear image,"/4/ an image of possible human
extinction, which has come to represent a societal
boundary, a limit of mundane human experience and
imagination in the present. Historians of philosophy
point to a rise in apocalypticism, whether of the
christian "triumphant" variety which associates nuclear
holocaust with the second coming of Christ, or of the
secular "catastrophic" type which sees apocalypse as
coming from the hands of human beings rather than
God./5/ Moral philosophers and theologians debate the
problems of militarism, nuclear weapons use, and
deterrence. We are told the possibility of massive
nuclear destruction forces upon us "changes in our
religious symbolism and in the frames of reference
within which we make our value judgements and moral
choices."/6/ Bishops and church leaders address the

moral issues of war, peace, and strategic military policy in a way unparalleled in the past./7/

Politically, East-West relations are marked by a new Cold War as reflected by public policy debates during the past few years concerning the U.S. nuclear weapons freeze campaign, cruise missile testing in Alberta, the 1979 NATO decision for the Euromissile deployment, a comprehensive test ban, the U.S. abandonment of the SALT II treaty, and the on-going debate over the moral, legal, economic, political, strategic, and technological ramifications of space-launched nuclear weapons, space-based anti-ballistic missile systems, and anti-satellite weapons (or "Star Wars"). Militarily, the combined nuclear arsenals of the United States and the Soviet Union are larger today than they have ever been both in terms of the total number of strategic warheads and the equivalent megatonnage of those warheads./8/ And future trends indicate that large numbers of nuclear warheads will continue to be produced by the super-powers and other nations, even though weapons development is toward greater miniaturization, accuracy, and lower yields./9/

Over a generation has passed since the U.S. bombings of Hiroshima and Nagasaki, and Einstein's sober admonition: "The unleashed power of the atom has changed everything save our modes of thinking, and we thus drift toward unparalleled catastrophe."/10/ But after decades of peace plans, proposals, arms control negotiations, test bans, and treaties it appears that our modes of thinking have not been changed, but skewed in the direction of technocracy and instrumental reason. The "technological imperative" (Anatol Rapoport)/11/ frequently forces new scientific discoveries into the service of militarism, and continues unabated in the service of a reductionist rationality. Try as we may to dismiss the problems of the nuclear arms race and the human future with classical labels such as "apocalyptic rhetoric," "utopian protest," or "millenarian fervor," none seem to square precisely with our knowledge of scientific and technological possibility today.

Karl Jaspers (1883-1969), physician, psychiatrist, and preeminently philosopher, was one of the first Western thinkers to take up Einstein's challenge for a "new" mode of thinking commensurate with the demands of the atomic age. In _Die Atombombe und die Zukunft des Menschen: Politisches Bewusstsein in unserer Zeit_ (The

Future of Mankind), which won the German peace prize in 1958, the philosopher presented a searching analysis of the nuclear problem in terms of the twin possibilities of nuclear annihilation and totalitarianism. "By one, we lose life," he wrote, "by the other, a life that is worth living."/12/ The "new" mode of thinking to which he appealed was an "encompassing" rational thinking distinguished from intellectual or abstract thinking. Echoing Einstein, Jaspers avowed that an altogether novel situation had been created by the advent of atomic weapons. The bomb represents an essentially "new fact" since it poses the possibility of human self-destruction: "Either all mankind will physically perish or there will be a change in the moral-political condition of man."/13/ The needed change or "conversion" begins first with the individual.

> This inner change could spread through mankind like a wave-- not just of alarm, not just of outrage at all agents of perdition, but of rational will. This would lead to a re-examination of the whole of our humanity, of our lives, our motives. The eternal source could yield a new beginning of what we should be, to be worthy of life. It is only if consciousness of the new fact came to influence our lives that conventional politics, its interests and objectives, could be transformed into a new politics that might cope with the threat of extinction./14/

Jaspers's call for an inner change or "conversion" of humanity constitutes the leitmotiv of the book and runs throughout all of his writings on the nuclear problem during the decade of the original Cold War. He argues that the needed moral-political change of humanity cannot follow from a "new politics," but is instead the very condition of possibility of world peace. A "new politics" commensurate with the demands of the nuclear age will take its "suprapolitical" (überpolitische) guidance from the power of the ethical idea, sacrifice, and an encompassing reason. The "conversion" without which humanity will continue along the lines of the old politics-- and thus to nuclear destruction or total rule-- also demands a "conversion" within the realms of science and religion. His thesis may be summarized in terms of a threefold "conversion:" (1) from intellectual thinking to a "new" rational thinking and a continual "will to truth" (Plato); (2) from individual and collective bondage to existential and political freedom; and (3) from exclusive and narrowly dogmatic faith-- whether Marxist or Christian-- to "philosophical faith" (philosophische Glaube) lived out of "the Encompassing" (das Umgreifende). And while the problem has no lasting "solution," this threefold "conversion" of humanity realized in daily Lebenspraxis could provide a new basis of hope in the nuclear age.

Jaspers's thesis has not stood without criticism. As Werner Schneiders notes, his political thinking has been the most discussed aspect of his philosophizing, and many commentators-- primarily academic philosophers and political scientists-- have been anxious to assess the political implications of his philosophical method./15/

The most common line of criticism levelled against Jaspers's thesis questions his characterization of the nuclear problem as an ostensible alternative between two evils: that is, between human annihilation on the one hand, and subjection to the tyranny of totalitarianism, on the other hand. Robert Spaemann, for example, criticizes Jaspers for his "apparent attempt to morally justify the total annihilation of humanity as the ultima ratio of democracy," and for his consideration of "universal democracy as the only alternative, as the necessary prerequisite of world peace."/16/ The historian and political scientist Golo Mann also asks whether Jaspers "has not demonized the Russian state a bit too much," and whether the assertion that an atomic war "must inevitably and immediately lead to the Apocalypse" is not in fact "too absolute" given the existing military situation. The Russians must also be trusted as human beings with possibilities for change, and he is not absolutely convinced that Jaspers's treatment of the totalitarian world is merely a hypothetically constructed case. If he agrees that Jaspers exposes "coexistence" as a trick and an illusion, Mann asks: "Could not even the friendly illusion be helpful-- and assume reality?"/17/ In the same vein, and more radically, Julius Ebbinghaus charges Jaspers for presupposing the alternatives between annihilation and totalitarianism in such a way "that a victory of Russia would necessarily mean the dehumanization of all humanity."/18/ By casting the alternatives in terms of an either/or, he feels Jaspers makes a moral choice impossible. We are left with only one choice between two means of human annihilation: totalitarianism or the atom bomb.

The second thrust of critical analysis levelled against Jaspers's is that his appeal to a moral-political change or "conversion" of humanity is guilty of neglect and misrepresentation. Ebbinghaus chides Jaspers for the idea that a change of conviction can come about as a result of anxiety over the atom bomb. A human transformation or change based upon fear of atomic death-- however warranted the fear-- is simply not a "moral" change. Similarly, Robert Spaemann has challenged Jaspers for his attempt to fuse politics and morality, lamenting that "to base peace upon a general turn about in conviction, would be for the politician to say that the probable could be grounded upon the completely improbable."/19/

Tübingen professor, Richard Schaeffler, echoes criticism against both Jaspers's putative view of the Russians and the idea of an existential "conversion." With respect to the Russians, Schaeffler points to an ostensible inconsistency in his assessment. He asserts that Jaspers wants, on the one hand, to deny a "total process" of reality which would exclude human freedom; while, on the other hand, he implies that a total loss of freedom could in fact become a reality as a result of totalitarianism. Thus for Jaspers, Schaeffler writes, "the atomic danger is not primary, since it is only a derived form of totalitarian danger. Only from the totalitarian state is the unleashing of atomic war to be feared."/20/ With respect to Jaspers's idea of a moral-political "conversion," Schaeffler charges him with turning the salvation of humanity into an "objective" criterion of morality in the nuclear age. This contradicts his earlier philosophical thinking. Rather than grounding morality in the "unconditional" and non-objective reality of "possible Existenz" as he does in his earlier works, he maintains Jaspers fixes upon, or falls prey to, the prevailing, "objective" universal opinion in his book on the atom bomb. In short, he laments the way in which his existential elucidation has given way to a view of the present as an "eschatological hour."

Georg Mende, in his recension on the atom bomb book, asserts that Jaspers has "in the name of peace, directly and indirectly aided and abetted war preparations [...] by not professing the abolition of the atom bomb and thus the peoples' right to legalize the means of politics." He feels Jaspers reveals his true colors insofar as he would provisionally halt the atom bomb, even though this action would be a threat to peace. He also asserts that "Jaspers goes in for the reunification [of East and West Germany] with atomic weapons." According to Schneiders, these are blatant misunderstandings of Jaspers, even though Mende actually comes close to the kernel of Jaspers's problematic when he writes that "Jaspers approves the politics of the atom bomb, especially of West Germany, even as he spreads the hope in a miracle."/21/ However, Mende interprets the content of Jaspers "miracle" not in terms of a moral-political transformation of humanity, but as the collapse of the Socialist camp, which Jaspers, himself, never believed would happen. In the final analysis, Mende believes Jaspers's book only propogates suicide as the freedom of anti-socialism.

Summarizing the foregoing criticisms, Schneiders suggests that Jaspers's hope for the "conversion" of humanity and its possibilities in the socio-political realm remain unclear for three reasons. First, he believes the concept of a moral-political "conversion" remains _indeterminate_ with respect to its content. Secondly, Jaspers makes politics and legal order overly dependent upon _individual_ morality. Thirdly, and with respect to Jaspers's view of the Soviets, the concept of an existential "conversion" remains unclear because-- given the philosopher's presuppositional framework-- "conversion" can only happen in the West. Schneiders is led to the conclusion that "if the East is free enough to change existentially," then Jaspers's "presupposition of opposition to an absolute evil at any price also falls."/22/ In short, the price that Jaspers is prepared to pay for an ordered society remains problematical in Schneiders's estimation.

These criticisms by political scientists and philosophers of Jaspers's thesis concerning a moral-political "conversion" of humanity raise a host of questions. Does Jaspers indeed establish his problematic in terms of an either/or, annihilation or totalitarianism? Does he make socio-political morality and freedom overly dependent upon existential freedom? Is his call for a moral-political "conversion" of humanity indeterminate? If so, is this a peculiar failure of his book on the atom bomb, or merely a function of his philosophical method? Is his call to human "conversion" consistent with his philosophizing as a whole? In short, what is living and what is dead in the philosopher's analysis for our new Cold War situation today, particularly for those seeking to follow Christ in the nuclear age?

These general questions provide a point of departure for the three focal questions we bring to the meaning, value, and limits of Jaspers's thesis in the light of our own situation and faith: (1) What is his understanding of and "solution" to the nuclear problem? (2) What value does he assign to the role of "conversion" within science, morality and politics, and religion? And (3), what are the possibilities and limits of his understanding of "conversion" in the light of christian faith and the present situation? Our "hypothesis" is that while Jaspers's understanding of "conversion" is important, influential, and indeed necessary, it is insufficient for the boundaries of our present situation as seen in the light of christian faith. We speak of "hypothesis" rather than thesis in order to acknowledge, with Jaspers, that all knowledge is tentative and stands within a particular horizon or circle of meaning.

The aim of this work is twofold. First our descriptive analysis, which follows from questions (1) and (2) above, seeks to listen carefully and honestly to the philosopher in order that his understanding of the nuclear problem and the role of "conversion" in science, morality and politics, and religion be brought to light. It will take all of the chapters to reveal the depth of his transcending method, and to situate properly his clarion call for a moral-political "conversion" of humanity within the broader context of his philosophical thinking as a whole. While we attempt to let the philosopher speak as much as possible, analysis inevitably betrays a particular interpretation. This is a sympathetic one insofar as we acknowledge the necessity of human "conversion" within our present situation. The faithful articulation of Jaspers's own position, therefore, constitutes the primary aim of the study.

Secondly, we want critically to examine the possibilities and limits of Jaspers's understanding of human "conversion" in the light of our present situation and christian faith. His call for human change is incomprehensible apart from his idea of philosophical faith. Thus this work, conceived as an "experiment" in Christian Social Ethics, must truthfully and openly examine what Jaspers's thesis entails for our own christian worldview. We must determine to what extent we are able to walk with the philosopher from our own faith perspective. Thus a concluding critical discussion of the possibilities and limits of Karl Jaspers's understanding of the role of human "conversion" in the nuclear age constitutes our secondary aim.

Two limits of the study warrant mention here. First, while we are primarily interested in Jaspers's thesis of "conversion"-- and thus the possibilities and limits of faith in the nuclear age-- we cannot avoid ranging through various aspects of his historical, foundational, scientific, ethical, political, and religious thinking. Jaspers insists that philosophizing must not be limited to "departmentalized" thinking, especially when the "solution" to the nuclear problem "lies at a depth of human existence which man achieves by no special knowledge, by no special activity, [but] only by himself."/23/ Conversely, it is impossible to analyze fully all aspects of his thinking on the problem. Hence methodological limits concerning the use of Jaspers's sources are stated at the outset of each chapter. For the most part, we have avoided Jaspers's early scientific, psychiatric, and psychological studies as well as his later German political writings in order to limit the sources and give primacy to the thesis of his book on the atom bomb and the future of humanity. Though we must inevitably range through various concepts, foundations, directions, and even tensions of insolubility in his thinking, this movement of thought should not distract us from the ultimate question of the possibilities and limits of the role of "conversion" in the nuclear age.

Secondly, though we speak of the relevance of Jaspers's philosophical faith for christian faith and the present situation, we pretend neither to speak for "christian faith," nor to analyze systematically our contemporary situation. Both christian faith and the present situation, however, are as necessary to this study as they are limited by our own understanding and knowledge.

Structurally, then, **Chapter One** begins with an introductory treatment of Jaspers's earnest turn to political philosophizing after the Second World War, and his major biographical developments as a whole since all philosophizing, he tells us, is intimately connected with the life of the philosopher.

Because all philosophizing begins with one's historical situation and because Jaspers saw the twin threats of nuclear annihilation and totalitarian mass movements as <u>symptomatic</u> of the spiritual "crisis" of humanity in the modern age, **Chapter Two** provides the <u>historical</u> background to the nuclear problem as defined by its two most recent and decisive epochs, the "Axial Age" and the age of modern science and technology. This chapter takes up Jaspers's characterization of modern science, its boundaries, domains, and origins, and the nature and limits of modern technology. It also analyzes what Jaspers understands as the present "crisis" situation of humanity, and the trends toward socialism, world unity, and faith.

Chapter **Three** provides the <u>epistemological</u> framework within which Jaspers situates the problem by taking up his "foundational thinking" (<u>Grundgedanken</u>) and transcending methodology. It takes up the Kantian background of Jaspers's basic questions, illuminates the subject-object dichotomy of human consciousness and the idea of "the Encompassing" and its various modes within which the nuclear problem and the role of "conversion" must be illuminated, and introduces the role of philosophical faith as life lived out of the Encompassing and barrier against the false hypostatization of truth.

In **Chapter Four** we turn to a synthetic analysis of Jaspers's understanding of the nuclear problem during the original Cold War period, and his threefold thesis concerning the role of "conversion" in science, morality and politics, and religion in the light of his historical and philosophical foundations.

Chapter Five analyzes the role of "conversion" in science as a turn towards an encompassing reason, the distinction and alliance between his philosophy of reason and science, and Jaspers's critique of positivism, anti-science, and scientific Marxism. The chapter concludes by summarizing the "conversion" to reason in science as a turn to the "will to truth."

Chapter Six takes up the meaning and implications of the "conversion" to existential and political freedom. It elucidates the "suprapolitical" foundations for humanity's moral-political "conversion" in terms of the relationship between freedom and will (the "grand will"), conditional and unconditional action, and existential communication and political intercourse. The meaning of political freedom is elucidated in the light of Jaspers's understanding of the rational community, the idea of democracy, and the role of authority and force in politics. Jaspers's appropriation of Weber's "ethic of responsibility" and Kant's idea of "perpetual peace" is discussed.

Chapter Seven concludes the analysis by treating the philosopher's call for the "conversion" to philosophical faith. The primacy of faith for his philosophizing as a whole is set forth in terms of philosophical faith's foundational conflict with religion over knowledge and authority, faith's relation to truth, the antithesis of reason and "catholicity," and Jaspers's transcending metaphysics, i.e., his theory or ciphers. Philosophical faith's understanding of revelation, ritual and community, sacraments, prayer, theology, and the cipher of the Incarnation are analyzed, as are the implications of Jaspers's call for a "conversion" from "formal religion" to "Biblical Religion."

In **Chapter Eight,** a "critique"-- where "critique" is understood to mean showing what one believes in Jaspers's sense of faith-- we argue the "hypothesis" that Jaspers's understanding of the role of "conversion" in science, morality and politics, and religion is indeed necessary, but insufficient for the exigencies of the present situation. At the same time, we believe our treatment refutes those critics who see Jaspers's thesis of "conversion" in the atom bomb book as "indeterminant," and as having moved away from his earlier philosophical thinking. First, we offer a third term beyond Jaspers's distinction between the scientific intellect and reason which draws upon the idea of belief in and knowledge of "the other." Secondly, the possibilities and limits of Jaspers's construction of the nuclear problem are argued in the light of present nuclear capabilities, moral discourse, and christian faith. Finally, in a "Concluding Theological Postscript," five lines of "critical" analysis are set forth in response to Jaspers's call for a "conversion" to philosophical faith as set forth in his atom bomb book and in his final treatment of the relationship between philosophical and religious faith. This section takes up the question of the relationship between religious and philosophical faith by drawing upon previous criticisms of Jaspers's religious philosophizing by Soren Holm, Paul Ricoeur, Fritz Buri, Dorothee Sölle, and Alan Olson. The postscript also sets forth a preliminary statement of a christian understanding of "conversion" which draws upon the new movements in political and liberation theology.

The chapter concludes with a summary of the importance of the idea of "conversion" for the <u>whole</u> of Jaspers's philosophizing, and an appreciation of the relevance of philosophical faith in the nuclear age. In the final analysis, then, our "critique" is actually understood as a "loving struggle" between two faiths that need each other for self-clarification. And we are convinced that it is in the "conversion" to "the other" that both philosophical and christian faith can work together for freedom and liberation before the nuclear boundary today.

NOTES

1. PHT I, pp.43-45. Cf., MMA, pp.23-32.

2. Ruth Leger Sivard, World Military and Social Expenditures 1986, quoted in The Ottawa Citizen, 24 November, 1986, p.A2. At the time of Jaspers's analysis of the nuclear problem in 1958, world military expenditures were calculated at a quarter of a billion dollars daily (FM, p.60). According to Ernie Regehr, the annual arms trade in Canada in 1986 was $50 billion; "Canada and the Arms Trade," The Ploughshares Monitor VII (1986), p.13, excerpt from Arms Canada: The Deadly Business of Military Exports (forthcoming, James Lorimer and Co., Toronto).

3. Victor F. Weisskopf, "The Task for a New Peace Movement," Bulletin of the Atomic Scientists 43 (January/February 1987), p.26.

4. Robert J. Lifton, The Broken Connection: On Death and the Continuity of Life (New York: Simon and Schuster, 1979), esp., Part III, "Death and History-- The Nuclear Image," pp.283-387.

5. Richard H. Popkin, "The Triumphant and Catastrophic Apocalypse," in Nuclear Weapons and the Future of Humanity: The Fundamental Questions, ed. by Avner Cohen and Steven Lee (Totowa, N.J.: Rowman & Allan, 1986), pp.131-150. Popkin identifies Salem Kirban's, Guide to Survival (1968) and Hal Lindsey's, The Late Great Planet Earth (1970) as representative versions of the "triumphant apocalypse" today, and Bertrand Russell, Albert Schweitzer, Karl Jaspers, Jonathan Schell, and Robert J. Lifton as representative of the "catastrophic apocalypse."

6. Gordon Kaufman, Theology for a Nuclear Age, (Manchester and Philadelphia: Manchester University Press and the Westminster Press, 1985), p. 9.

7. United States Conference of Catholic Bishops, "The Challenge of Peace: God's Promise and Our Response," Origins 13 (May 19, 1983), pp.1-32. World Council of Churches, "Statement on Peace and Justice," in Gathered for Life, Official Report, VI Assembly of the World Council of Churches, Vancouver, Canada 24 July-10 August

1983, ed. by David Gill (Grand Rapids: W.B. Eerdmans and Geneva: World Council of Churches, 1983), pp.130-138.

8. Ground Zero, Nuclear War: What's In It For You? (New York: Pocket Books, 1982), app., C.

9. Nuclear Weapons Databook, Vol.I, U.S. Nuclear Forces and Capabilities, ed. by Thomas B. Cochran, William M. Arkin, and Milton M. Hoenig (Cambridge, Ma.: Ballinger, 1984), Table 1.7, "Projected Nuclear Warhead Production, 1983-1990s," p.16.

10. Otto Nathan and Heinz Norden, eds., Einstein on Peace (New York: Schocken, 1968), p.376.

11. Anatol Rapoport, "The Technological Imperative," Paper delivered at the University of Waterloo Conference on Philosophy and Nuclear Arms, September 28-30, 1984 (Mimeographed).

12. FM, p.4; AB, p.22.

13. FM, p. vii; AB, p.5.

14. FM, p.5; AB, p.23.

15. Werner Schneiders, Karl Jaspers in der Kritik (Bonn: H. Bouvier, 1965), pp.90-106 at p.91. For a sympathetic treatment of the major reactions to the political implications of Jaspers's works as a whole, see Godfrey Robert Carr, Karl Jaspers as an Intellectual Critic: The Political Dimension of His Thought, European University Series, Series XX, Philosophy, vol.125 (Peter Lang: Frankfurt am Main, 1983), esp., pp.116-136.

16. Robert Spaemann, "Zur philosophisch-theologischen Diskussion um die Atombombe," Hochland 51/3 (1958/1959), p.214: "die totale Vernichtung der Menschheit als ultima ratio der Demokratie ins Auge fasst und sittlich zu rechtfertifen sucht und als einzige Alternative die universale Demokratie als notwendige Bedingung des Weltfriedens gelten lässt." Quoted in Schneiders, Karl Jaspers in der Kritik, p.105.

17. Golo Mann, "Strategie und Philosophie der Atombombe," Merkur 12/12 (1958), pp.1188-1189:

"den russischen Staat ein wenig überdämonisiert"
[...] "müsse unvermeidlich und augenblichlich zur
Apokalypse führen" [...] "Kann nicht auch der
freundliche Schein hilfreich sein-- und
Wirklichkeit annehmen?" Quoted in Schneiders,
Karl Jaspers in der Kritik, p.99.

18. Julius Ebbinghaus, "Die Atombombe und die Zukunft
des Menschen," Studium generale 10/3 (1957),
p.149: "dass ein Sieg der Russen notwendig die
Entmenschung aller Menschen zur Folge haben
müsse." Quoted in Schneiders, Karl Jaspers in
der Kritik, pp.104-105.

19. Robert Spaemann, "Zur philosophisch-theologischen
Diskussion um die Atombombe," p.214: "Den
Frieden auf einen allgemeinen Gesinnungswandel
gründen wollen, heisst aber für den Politiker,
das Wahrscheinlichere auf das ganz
Unwahrscheinliche gründen wollen." Quoted in
Schneiders, Karl Jaspers in der Kritik, p.105.

20. Richard Schaeffler, "Philosophische Überlieferung
und politische Gegenwart in der Sicht von Karl
Jaspers," Philosophische Rundschau 7 (1959),
p.277: "Die Atomgefahr ist nicht die erste, denn
sie ist nur eine abgeleitete Form der totalitären
Gefahr. Nur vom totalitären Staat ist die
Entfesselung des Atomkrieges zu befürchten [...]"
Quoted in Schneiders, Karl Jaspers in der Kritik,
p. 101.

21. Georg Mende, Bookreview in Deutsche Zeitschrift
für Philosophie, 6/6, 1958, p.998, 1000, 1001:
"im Namen des Friedens mittelbare und
unmittelbare Kriegsvorbereitung begunstigt, [...]
die Atombombe zu einem unabschaffbaren und somit
volkerrechtlich legalisierten Mittel der Politik
erklart" [...] "Jaspers tritt für
Widervereinigung mit Atomwaffen ein" [...]
"Jaspers befürwortet die Atombombenpolitik,
insbesondere auch Westdeutschlands, indem er die
Hoffnung aug ein Wunder verbreitet." Quoted in
Schneiders, Karl Jaspers in der Kritik, p.94.

22. Schneiders, Karl Jaspers in der Kritik, p.106.

23. FM, p.10; AB, p.30.

1.0 INTRODUCTION

In the introduction to his 1956 Philosophische Autobiographie Jaspers remarked that "all philosophy--because it is an activity of the human spirit-- is, in its themes as well as its causes, intimately connected with the life of the person who is philosophizing."/1/ If the connection between thinking and life experience is true for Jaspers's philosophy as a whole, then it is true, a fortiori, for his political thinking. For just as contemporary "political" and "liberation" theologians would remind us that theology is essentially critical reflection on praxis, so too Jaspers would remind us that it is precisely in its politico-practical appearance that a philosophy shows what it is. This insight became clear to him as a result of his twelve years under Nazi totalitarianism:

> No great philosophy is without political thought, not even that of the great metaphysicians, not that of Plotinus, not at all that of Spinoza, who even went so far as to take an active, spiritually-effective role. From Plato to Kant, to Hegel, to Kierkegaard and Nietzsche goes the grand politics of the philosophers. What a philosophy is, it shows in its political appearance. This is nothing incidental, but of central significance. It was no accident that National Socialism, as well as Bolshevism, saw in philosophy a deadly spiritual enemy./2/

For Jaspers, then, philosophy and political theory and praxis are inextricably linked. As Elisabeth Young-Bruehl has noted, Jaspers "ascribes to political thinking an importance that is different from those philosophers who distinguished the political from the theoretical life-- the bios politikos and the bios theoretikos."/3/ For him the interrelation between philosophy and politics is not "bound to the tradition in which philosophy is virtually identified with contemplation-- the tradition which Kant both participated in and destroyed: for Jaspers, 'thinking is as the thinker does.'"/4/ And as he had stated the matter already at the outset of his Philosophie, "philosophical thinking occurs in movements that accomplish and confirm an ethos so that the effects of the philosophical thought extend into our private and political lives, thus showing what it is." To this he added that all thinking proves true only "if it encompasses our everyday actions as well as those of the exalted moment of its birth."/5/

In this chapter we want to look more closely at the major biographical developments in Jaspers's life and works which stand before and after his turn to political philosophy proper after the Second World War. Obviously a detailed biography of the man and his political endeavours is neither possible nor desirable here./6/ However, a brief survey of his life and major works will not only allow us to comprehend the significance with which he came to esteem political thinking, but it will also provide us with the broader context within which to situate his thinking on the problem of the atom bomb and the future of humanity. For clearly, after the second world war, philosophical reflection and political thinking became to him as inseparable as life and breath.

Jaspers's life and major works may be historically divided into three periods which provide the structure for this chapter: from his birth to the outbreak of the first world war (1.1); from 1914 to the end of National Socialism and Hitler's totalitarianism in 1945 (1.2); and finally, the remaining two and one-half decades of his life from 1945 until his death at eighty-six years of age on February 26, 1969 (1.3). This final period marks Jaspers's turn to political philosophy, proper, in which he dedicated his thinking primarily to a study of the great philosophers and to both German and global politics. This third period also marks an increased interest in the relationship between philosophical and revelational faith.

1.1 THE EARLY YEARS: 1883-1914

Karl Jaspers was born on 23 February, 1883, in Oldenburg, Germany near the North Sea coast. He attended Gymnasium in the village, and from 1901 onwards studied law in Heidelberg (two semesters) and Munich (one semester in 1902) and medicine in Berlin, Göttingen, and Heidelberg (1902-8). His experimentation with different universities is a telling witness of a restless and searching existence as a student. In 1907, at Heidelberg, he met his wife to be, the Jewess Gertrude Meyer, whom he married three years later in 1910. In 1908 he passed the state medical exam, completed his dissertation on homesickness and crime ("Heimweh und Verbrechen"), and met the indomitable Max Weber for the first time. He eventually received his Medical degree from Heidelberg in 1909. From 1909-1915 he worked as a voluntary assistant in the psychiatric hospital at the University of Heidelberg. In 1913 he habilitated with his Allgemeine Psychopathologie (General Psychopathology) as Privatdozent under Windelband in Psychology, a department under the auspices of the Philosophy Faculty at Heidelberg.

Jaspers's early life was exceptional in many ways. His father and mother both hailed from a long line of merchants and farmers, and provided him with a spirit of courage and determination in a loving home. Led by the authority of his father, he was brought up "with a regard for truth and loyalty, for achievement and reliability, yet without church religion (except for the scanty formalities of the Protestant confession)."/7/ Already at the Gymnasium he showed his independent spirit when, in a loving struggle with an authoritarian headmaster, he refused out of conviction to join a "fraternity." "These groups," he maintained, "made distinctions on the basis of the social status and occupation of the parents and not on that of personal friendship."/8/ This was not to be the last time that he would stand alone for upholding a principle.

Jaspers's protean lifestyle as a university student during the years 1901-2 reflects his discontent with himself and society. Contemplation and solitude during this time were often painful for him, a lonely, melancholic, and overly self-conscious individual. While he did undertake to study philosophy simultaneously with his law courses, he always found himself at odds with the instructors. "Against philosophy professors," he recounts, "I had an antipathy because they did not treat what really mattered most to me. As persons they appeared arrogant and opinionated."/9/ It was not until he embarked on the study of medicine in 1902 that his aimless way of life came to an end, and the search for the "knowledge of facts and of man" began./10/

Nietzsche's dictum that life experiences which do not kill one actually make one stronger applies well to Jaspers. Only in his nineteenth year was he correctly diagnosed as suffering from "bronchiectasis with cardiac decompensation"/11/-- a lung condition which theoretically gave him only fifteen years to live. Throughout what turned out to be an ironically long life, this condition forced him to forego the normal diversions of youth, limited his mobility, and gave many the impression that he was aloof and indifferent. At the risk of health, his work always demanded a concentrated and relaxed lifestyle. His health posed a fundamental boundary throughout his life, and one cannot but speculate that his prolific writings grew from a resolute will to overcome this basic physical condition, as well as from inherent talent. Moreover, it seems likely that Jaspers's admiration for Max Weber, "the greatest German of our age,"/12/ sprung partially from an empathy with Weber's physical, or more accurately, psychical afflictions.

Jaspers's work during this early period is represented by various articles on intelligence, hallucinations, delusions, and the development of diseases illustrated by case study. Much of this was produced during the years 1908-15 while he worked as an assistant at the psychiatric hospital in Heidelberg, which was under the direction of the famous neuro-pathologist Franz Nissl, successor to Emil Kraepelin. The intellectual and methodological confusion in psychiatry at that time was the motivating force behind his Allgemeine Psychopathologie in 1913 (General Psychopathology). The young Jaspers set out in this work to determine the various conditions determining cognition in the psychological realm. Both Husserl's phenomenology, which Jaspers appropriated except for its development into "essences" (Wesensschau), and Dilthey's "descriptive and analytical psychology," which he termed "verstehende Psychologie," provided the study with its method. Jaspers's differentiation of "explanation," as empirically existing cause and effect relationships, and "Verstehen," as a non-causal, yet meaningful relation of psychological phenomena, has been acclaimed by one commentator as one of the most fruitful clarifications this remarkable first work brought to the field of psychology by the barely thirty year old Jaspers./13/

Jaspers's seven-year experience (1908-1915) as a voluntary assistant in the psychiatric hospital at Heidelberg deserves to be cast into sharper relief, since it was this experience which stood directly behind his move from psychology to philosophy. It was

4

during this period that he had to contend with everyday
"practical" tasks, rather than living in the world of
ideas and strictly philosophical thinking. Although he
enjoyed working with the many distinguished physicians
on the staff, his position in the tightly knit group
was abnormal. His lung condition limited his
opportunity to become a regular staff assistant, and he
neither took his meals at nor lived in hospital.
Despite his condition, however, Jaspers's general
epistemology of psychopathology was well received,
particularly by Nissl, who had earlier given him an
excellent mark on his dissertation and had agreed to
let him work in his hospital. It was Nissl who
encouraged him to habilitate with the famous Kraeplin
in Munich and Alzheimer in Breslau, since there were no
openings in medicine at Heidelberg in 1913. And yet
because of his love for Heidelberg, he turned both
opportunities down. Instead, he chose to habilitate
himself in the psychology department of the
philosophical faculty with the hope of returning to
Nissl's hospital as soon as a position was opened for
him.

It was this habilitation which partially resulted
in his transfer from medicine to philosophy. The other
factor, yet again, was his health. For during the
first World War he had been asked to replace Nissl,
himself, who had taken a research posting in Munich.
Jaspers and his wife decided that, even with an
apartment in the hospital, this would be physically
impossible. The decision was a painful one. The
prospect of pursuing the spirit of formal research as a
physician seemed more attractive than a life confined
merely to books and an academic teaching career. But
in retrospect he came to see the events of this period
as linked to his own possible Existenz.

> In looking back it all seems
> remarkable. What at that time was
> enforced by my illness and was done
> reluctantly, viz., the definitive
> choice of the philosophical faculty,
> was indeed leading me to the road for
> which I was destined. From early youth
> on I had been philosophizing. Actually
> I had taken up medicine and
> psychopathology from philosophical
> motives. Only shyness in view of the
> greatness of the task kept me from
> making philosophy my life's career./14/

There is no evidence, then, to suggest that
Jaspers was directly concerned with politics during
this early period of his life. The lacuna is not
accidental. For while his grandfather, father, and two
brothers were all state representatives in Oldenburg,
he was apolitical for the first thirty-one years of his
life. As revealed in his Nachlass, Jaspers admitted
that as a student he "felt little responsibility for
the course of [political] events as a whole."/15/
Instead, he saw himself as devoted to purely academic
tasks. The only two exceptions to this rule were the
ridicule he felt for Kaiser Wilhelm's "pompous bombast
of words and his provocative actions," which led
eventually to the First World War, and the terror he
felt in 1908 upon the flight of the dirigible Zeppelin
and the nationalistic "intoxification" it provoked
among the people./16/

1.2 FROM WWI TO THE END OF GERMAN TOTALITARIANISM:
1914-1945

Although Jaspers's earnest turn to political
thinking came about as a result of World War II, his
non-political stance was to undergo inevitable
transformation with the outbreak of the war in 1914.

Everything which seemed long to
have been secure with one stroke
appeared threatened. We felt that we
had gotten into an irresistible, opaque
process [...] This our human fate I
sought from then on to comprehend, not
as the knowable necessity of a dark
supernatural process of history, but as
a situation whose results--on the basis
of what is properly knowable, which is
always something specific--are
decisively determined by our human
freedom./17/

From the war's outset Jaspers's political thought
took guidance from Max Weber who at the time was
critical of both Kaiser Wilhelm and, in 1917,
Ludendorff for their political "stupidity." Weber's
understanding of nationalism,/18/ and a Germany
different from both Russian and Anglo-Saxon hegemony
influenced Jaspers up to 1933. And yet, he was always
skeptical of both Weber's Prussianism and his high
regard for Bismarck, even if it was from both a Kantian
and Weberian foundation that Jaspers would later
develop the two fundamental principles of his political

philosophy: first, political freedom exists only in accordance with the freedom of all; and secondly, there is "no peace without freedom, but no freedom without truth."/19/

Despite the profound impact of Weber's political thinking on Jaspers, the early years of this second period were characterized again primarily by continued attention to his academic tasks. From 1914 until 1 April, 1922, at which time he received an appointment by Heinrich Rickert to full professorship in philosophy at Heidelberg, Jaspers gave lectures on the psychology of character-types, sense perceptions, memory, fatigue, pathography, religion and morals, and, the epistemology of psychology. These lectures culminated in his Psychologie der Weltanschauungen (1919) which, on Jaspers's own admission, truly marked his turn to philosophy from psychology, and the foundation for his later thinking. It was here that Jaspers first developed the idea of the subject/object dichotomy-- yet here as a distinction between Weltanschauungen qua attitudes (subjective) and Weltanschauungen qua world-views (objective)-- which figures so predominantly in his later philosophical writings. The work also elaborated his notion of ideal and spiritual psychological "types", the latter of which included his understanding of values and "boundary situations."/20/

Apart from a pathographic study on Strindberg und Van Gogh in 1922 and Die Idee der Universität in 1923 (both revisions of earlier manuscripts), Jaspers published nothing else for a decade during the period of his intentional public silence (1923-31). It was during this period that he prepared his three volume Philosophie, with its Kantian order of ascent from the world (World-Orientation, vol.I), to self (Existenz-elucidation, vol.II), to God (Metaphysics, vol.III). This work, which always remained closest to his own heart, was eventually published in December of 1931. It contains foundational political ideas concerning an individual Existenz's claim in society and state,/21/ and the limits of "purposive" technological and political action. The possibility of human self-destruction, which he would come to see as an "intellectual" probability twenty-five years later in his book on the atom bomb and the future of mankind, was already alluded to in this work when he wrote that "some day man will be capable of exploding the planet and reducing it to cosmic dust."/22/

7

While Jaspers was not directly involved in politics during this silent period it would be erroneous to say that he had no political existence, even if such involvement was narrowly circumscribed to the university. On the university Senate as a <u>Privatdozent</u> in 1919, for example, he refused to sign a petition which had been called for all German universities by the rector of the University of Berlin. The petition opposed the conditions of the peace-treaty of Versailles. He objected to the petition not because of its unjust peace conditions, but because he felt that the petition, in principle, compromised the intellectual freedom of the university. Its task he always regarded, like that of the church, as being supranational.

A similar incident occurred again in 1924 when he defended a statistics lecturer by the name of Gumbel against the wrath of nationalist professors at Heidelberg. An avowed pacifist, Gumbel both opposed the re-establishment of the German military and decried the loss of soldiers during the war. Patriotism ran high and Gumbel, who was seen as dishonoring the war dead, became the victim of actions which sought the termination of his teaching responsibilities. Jaspers defended him not because Gumbel was a pacifist, but because he knew that the conditions of academic freedom were at stake.

> If today, because of political pacifist convictions and because of actions disclosing a political breach of treaty (even if that breach be that of the Versailles dictate of peace) an instructor can be reprimanded under the guise of an insult to national honor which carefully veils those facts, then tomorrow another one (may suffer this same fate) because of his atheism and day after tomorrow still another because of his nonconformity to the existing regime of the state./23/

He always upheld the freedom of the university as one of the most important conditions for authentic political freedom.

Jaspers's first serious involvement with "political" thinking came in 1929 when he was commissioned to write a work for the Goschen-Series on the spiritual "movements" of the time. As Dolf

Sternberger has written, however, his _Die geistige Situation der Zeit_ (_Man In the Modern Age_) was not so much an analysis of the German political situation as it was an analysis of an "epochal consciousness" which had become detached from being, of the moral-spiritual situation of the time, and thus only indirectly a statement of the possibility of politics in the age of technology and mechanization./24/ The book was completed in September 1930 at the same time as the successful election to the _Reichstag_ of National Socialism, whose madness Jaspers saw as "impossible" and certain to pass.

When the _putsch_ came in 1933 in all its horror, Jaspers was incredulous./25/ Hannah Arendt asked him at the time what he would do given the "election." He responded simply that the event was an "_operette_" and that he would not play the hero therein./26/ And when Ernst Mayer told him in the summer of 1933 that the Nazis would "'one day bring us Jews into barracks and set the barracks on fire,'"/27/ he thought the idea was simply insane. Reflecting on the event at the end of his life in 1969, however, he could confess that "'at first I deceived myself. I think of it with shame. I still did not think of the extreme consequences [of the _putsch_]. [I considered] a rapid change of the nonsense and a coup of the government possible. I wanted the fear not to have the likeness of truth.'"/28/

Jaspers's work and life experience from 1933 to 1945 forms a chapter by itself. Events moved from bad to worse, and eventually became unbearable: from 1933 on he was excluded from the university administration whose Nazification had become completed in the early summer of 1935; in 1937 he was no longer allowed to teach; by 1938 he was forbidden to publish by the Nazi censorship board, the _Reichsschrifttumskammer_./29/ In the meantime he had written _Vernunft und Existenz_, 1935 (_Reason and Existenz_), his books on Nietzsche (1936) and Descartes (1937),/30/ as well as the _Existenzphilosophie_, 1938 (_Philosophy of Existence_). He also made numerous attempts at emigration./31/ Though banned from the university and from publishing, his interior self-discipline allowed him to continue working until 1941. Though he and his Jewish wife had to live under grim circumstances, they worked together intensely. Jaspers revised his _Allgemeine Psychopathologie_, prepared the first of a one-thousand page volume (_Philosophische Logik_) on truth (_Von der Wahrheit_, 1947), and worked on various past

9

philosophers for his history of "the great
philosophers."

He was certain that events in Germany-- if not
since 1933 then certainly after 1939-- spelled the end
of the country, finis Germaniae. Two political ideas
were foremost in his mind during the twelve long years
of Nazi totalitarianism. The first was the meaning of
being German, which he defined in terms of "language,
home, and heritage." Secondly, there was the meaning
of Germany as a political entity, which he then saw as
no longer capable of being "grounded either morally or
spiritually upon restoration tendencies, nor upon the
memories of the last century and a half."/32/ He knew
Germany would have to be created anew after the
catastrophes of the two wars and Hitler's totalitarian
fascism. The positive ideas of a supranational court
of law and of "world citizenship", and the negative
myths of non-interference and absolute sovereignty--
the latter of which Jaspers would systematically
deprecate in his later writings-- had their
insemination under the tyrannical rule of Hitler.

In 1941 Jaspers defined his life task as being
consigned to his work on logic and a universal history
of philosophy as the fundament of a Weltphilosophie.
He saw both as complementary in thought, and opposed to
a "system" in which Being and truth could be made
clear./33/ But his three volume Logik was never to be
completed. The intensity of his totalitarian
life-setting changed his thinking. The dangerous years
that followed eventually sapped his ability to work and
finally made any work impossible. He and his wife were
even scheduled to be taken from Heidelberg to a
concentration camp on 14 April, 1945. The American
forces liberated the city on 1 April, 1945. "After
1945," he writes, "the problems of the day supervened,"
but "the philosophical work remained in the
background."/34/ His turn to political philosophy had
had its definitive birth. Philosophizing from this
point forward would be historico-political
thinking./35/

1.3 THE TURN TO POLITICAL PHILOSOPHY AND WORLD
       CITIZENSHIP: 1945-1969

Dolf Sternberg writes in his treatment of Jaspers
and the state that "the dictator had changed us all,"
and that after 1945 "another Jaspers emerges from the
seclusion of oppression."/36/ Shortly before the end
of the war Jaspers had written in his diary that

10

"whoever survives the war, to him a task must be established for which he ought to be consumed the rest of his life."/37/ And the chaotic political situation of Germany under the Allied government soon demanded all his energy, attention, and thinking. As he concluded in the preface to "Die Wandlung" after the war in 1945: "We want to and must try to find our way as thinking people in the unprecedented distress."/38/ During the early postwar years, Jaspers had the hope that he could with others find language as a political writer for Germans who could, with the help of the allies, still build a new state./39/ He knew that the focus of German writers at the time could not be political events per se, since all power lay in the military government. It was, rather, the "inner, spiritual-moral state of affairs as the condition of politics"/40/ which he understood as the writer's true task.

He undertook this new political task in his first major publication after the war in 1946, Die Schuldfrage (The Question of German Guilt), and in numerous shorter articles written during the first phase of his writing on German politics (1945-47)./41/ That he saw his task during this time as spiritual and moral, rather than political, is reflected by his initial remark in his lectures on German guilt: "I want to speak to you about our situation, and so I shall constantly skirt the immediate actuality of concrete politics, which is not and should not be our theme. Yet what we want to ponder is a condition precedent for our judgement in politics as well."/42/ This all important condition was seen as the "purification" (Reinigung) of the soul. As an "inner process," purification is never ended, but demands a repeated "conversion" whereby "we continually become ourselves. Purification is a matter of our freedom."/43/ Without it there is no political freedom.

A revealing example of Jaspers's personal transformation is the first speech he made just three months after the war on the occasion of the solemn reopening of the School of Medicine at the University of Heidelberg on 15 August, 1945. In his treatment of the renewal or regeneration of the German university, "Erneuerung der Universität,"/44/ from within a political situation best epitomized by the ancient cry "Vae victis" (woe to the vanquished), he sounded the possibilities for renewal of the university, science and humaneness, the freedom and dignity of humanity, the soul, and faith in God. Only after an admission of personal guilt and culpability for the atrocities committed under National Socialism, however, could such a healing regeneration take place.

> As our Jewish friends were taken away we did not demonstrate in the streets, we did not shout until in turn we, too, were destroyed. We chose to survive on the weak but correct ground that our death would amount to nothing. Our guilt is to be still alive. We know before God what has happened to us. During these twelve years we have gone through what one may call the remolding of our very being. We have been cudgeled by the devils who dragged us along into confusion and left us stupefied. We have won insights into the reality of world and man and of our own selves--insights which we shall never forget and whose consequences for our thinking cannot be measured./45/

On the occasion of his speech, Jaspers betrayed his own "metaphysical guilt," one of the four types along with "criminal," "political", and "moral" guilt differentiated in his analysis of the question of German guilt. He identified metaphysical guilt as that which inevitably results from the solidarity that exists among human beings. Metaphysical guilt reminds us that we are all, as human beings, co-responsible for human injustice committed against others. In contrast, crimes committed in one's presence or with one's knowledge, or atrocities committed against others inevitably weighs upon the survivor as indelible guilt. Jurisdiction in criminal, political, and moral guilt rests with a judge, the power and will of the victor, and our conscience and friends respectively. With metaphysical guilt, alone, does jurisdiction rest with God. The presence of metaphysical guilt for Jaspers, if properly perceived, ushers into a self-consciousness transformation before God, a "conversion" in which pride and arrogance are broken./46/

Another of Jaspers's most important "political" texts during this first phase of his writing on German politics was the lecture, "Vom Europäischen Geist," delivered on 13 September, 1946, in the course of the "Rencontre Internationales de Genève."/47/ Before the European intellectual community he set out,/48/ still amidst the ashes of the war, to answer the great question: "Is this indeed Europe's decline, or is it a crisis of rebirth?"/49/ Both being possible, he emphasized the shaking of the century's foundations as a result of the technology which had transformed the conditions of modern life. Now "every people must either come to terms with technology and its results or become extinct."/50/ Here Jaspers identified the spiritual aims of a European self-consciousness along three lines so characteristic of his later "political" writings: the broadening of the idea of Europe into the idea of humanity, preserving the best of the European historical soul, and the transformation and reappropriation of "Biblical religion" in the churches.

During the years 1945-47, marked by the absence of the Federal Republic, Jaspers also helped establish the journal, "Die Wandlung," with the help of Werner Krauss and Alfred Weber. The journal was conceived as a forum for moral and political renewal. With contributing authors such as Arendt, Brecht, Mann, Buber, Eliot, Auden, Sartre and Camus it maintained a high standard until its termination in 1949./51/

Jaspers was apparently one of the clearest and most respected voices for Germany after the war, even though he craved neither publicity nor fame. But the tide soon changed. Eventually he became saddened by what he understood as the "missed turn about" (verpasste Umkehr) of Germany's political path. In a letter dated 31 January, 1947 referring to Die Schuldfrage and his various political writings, he wrote, "what I write is virtually ignored."/52/ He also underwent a form of character assassination when the German press considered his move to the University of Basel in 1948 as a "betrayal" and "desertion" of Germany, not unlike the experience of his colleague Gumbel at the University of Heidelberg many years earlier. A rebuttal was in order. In an open declaration in the "Rhein-Neckar-Zeitung" on 24 March, 1948, he spoke of his philosophical duty as being "fulfilled in the service of an absolutely supranational task," stating that his previous stay in Heidelberg had not been a "profession of ultimate loyalty", in the same way that his move to Basel was not to be understood as such./53/ The move to Switzerland was marked by the publication of Der philosophische Glaube 1948, a work whose unliterally translated title by Ralph Manheim (The Perennial Scope of Philosophy) nonetheless reveals that Jaspers's understanding of philosophy is inextricably linked to the idea and content of "philosophical faith." This faith has as its foundation the will to boundless communication./54/

The task of a universal history of philosophy, for which Jaspers had conceived the design in 1937, materialized in part in 1949 with the publication of Vom Ursprung und Ziel der Geschichte (The Origin and Goal of History). It was predominantly the unforgettable years of National Socialism, Hitler's tyranny and Holocaust, which led him to grapple with a schema of world history in this work. Finis Germaniae had meant the end of an historical epoch, and raised for him anew the fundamental questions of world history and Germany's place therein./55/ Moreover, there remained the philosophical task of clarifying for himself, both in this work and his later political writings, "the moral presuppositions and the real conditions of politics" as well as orienting his political thinking "on the anticipatory standpoint of the world citizen."/56/ To reiterate, it was Jaspers's life experience at a boundary during the reign of Nazi terror, which revealed an insight that was to guide him throughout the remainder of his life: "What a philosophy is, it shows in its political appearance. This is nothing incidental, but of central significance."/57/ He had come to feel that it had taken his political experience and involvement to make his thought "fully conscious, down to its metaphysical roots."/58/ The close relation between personal existence and politico-historical reality, including future possibilities, is well summarized in his autobiographical thinking on political ideas:

> The decisive (point) is this: there is no law of nature and no law of history which determines the way of things as a whole. The future depends upon the responsibility of the decisions and deeds of men [...] upon each individual. By his way of life, by his daily small deeds, by his great decisions, the individual testifies to himself as to what is possible. By this, his present actuality, he contributes unknowingly toward the future./59/

The remainder of Jaspers's life and work reveals that his turn to political philosophy was never to be reversed, even as he pursued his lifelong interest in a philosophy of world history through the great

14

philosophers. Throughout the decade of the fifties and even after his retirement from the University of Basel in 1961, he prolifically produced nearly one major work a year./60/ By 1963 his German works had been translated into some sixteen foreign languages comprising 160 different editions./61/ The historico-political concentration of his major works, when considered along with the many articles he penned during this last period of his life, corroborates his passionate concern with both German and global politics after the war.

Of Jaspers's political writings during the Cold War 1950s, his outstanding contribution came from his reflection on the atom bomb and the twin possibilities of annihilation and totalitarianism made possible by the unleashed power of the atom and the technological "mass-order" characteristic of our century. In the Origin and Goal of Human History in 1949 he had already identified the "completely different vista" technology opened up in the shape of the atom bomb and its perils for mankind on the path to a world order./62/ In 1950 he took up the subject again in, "Das Gewissen vor die Bedrohung durch die Atombombe."/63/ This text marks the beginning of his concentrated analysis of the moral, political, and existential problems raised by the invention of the atom bomb during the decade of the original Cold War.

Six years later, in the Fall of 1956, he delivered over German radio his lecture on "The Atom Bomb and the Future of Man."/64/ It was due to the controversy raised by this lecture that Jaspers felt behooved to pen Die Atombombe und die Zukunft des Menschen, 1958 (The Future of Mankind), which he understood as an answer to the many "objections, questions, and imprecations" the lecture elicited from his German radio audience./65/ As mentioned in the Introduction, this monograph won him the peace prize of the German book trade in the same year, and his acceptance speech upon its conferral provided him with the opportunity to note the fundamental interrelationship between truth, freedom, and peace./66/

The political Left in Germany reacted strongly to his analysis of the atom bomb and the future of mankind. As Hans Saner notes, Jaspers was criticized as being "the philosopher of NATO, the henchman of class enemies, and as giving expression to a middle-class decadence."/67/ Although it was only for a short time, the book was popular with the political

Right; and in 1959, at 76 years of age, Jaspers was even nominated as a candidate for the presidency of the Federal Republic, which he lost in the election to Heinrich Lübke.

A negative and critical response to Jaspers's specifically German political writings was firmly established with the publication of <u>Freiheit und Wiedervereinigung</u>, a work that brought together writings originally published in the summer of 1960 in "Die Zeit." The work also included the text of Jaspers's television interview with Thilo Koch, wherein he argued that any historical legitimation of German reunification was both politically and philosophically unrealistic. Jaspers identified the threefold priority of political tasks as he understood them at the time. First, echoing the thesis of the atom bomb book, he advocated the idea of world peace grounded in freedom and established by means of a world confederation. Secondly, he addressed the issue of the self-determination of the West and the development of freedom against the danger of total rule, which is both an outer and <u>inner</u> threat. Thirdly, he took up the idea of the German state, the Federal Republic, which he understood as being able to rightly take its place in the West and the whole of mankind only by virtue of maintaining a democratic lifeform in a postwar world./68/

The book drew many threats and insulting letters. One anonymous letter decried Jaspers as "the traitor of the fatherland--the henchman of Communism--the political pig."/69/ According to Hans Saner, it was not so much the criticism of the German politicians in power at the time that made Jaspers critical toward the West German state, as it was their resistance to accept the historical reality of a divided Germany-- a division which he saw as necessarily following from the consequences of the war and Germany's culpability therein./70/

If the coals of political ostracism were warmed by Jaspers's analysis of freedom and reunification within the context of a post-war Germany, the flames of criticism nearly engulfed him after the appearance of his <u>Wohin treibt die Bundesrepublik</u>? (<u>The Future of Germany</u>) in 1966. Hannah Arendt considered this to be politically the "most important book to appear in Germany after the Second World War,"/71/ and it was indeed the political bestseller throughout the year of its publication. Jaspers's main thesis was that the

16

Federal Republic of West Germany had for years been moving toward an "oligarchy of parties" which spelled the end of parliamentary democracy. He saw the emergency laws proposed at that time as laying the political groundwork for a "dictatorship of politicians."/72/ The book was met by a united opposition from both the Right and the Left. The press portrayed Jaspers as a man bitter against his nation, without a political and philosophical foundation from which to write, and as acting without political or scientific responsibility. It apparently succeeded in turning an important part of the academic world against him. Jürgen Habermas, for example, came to regard Jaspers's political writings as merely the "fruits of an intelligent newspaper reader."/73/

Ironically, Jaspers received a more favorable response, including a lengthy 13-page letter in June 1966 from East German President Walter Ulbricht, from East Germany where the sale of the book was banned. Jaspers confirmed the letter, but was hesitant to respond at length out of fear that his correspondence could be used for propaganda purposes. It was in his 1967 Antwort: Zur Kritik meiner Schrift "Wohin treibt die Bundesrepublik?", that he would set forth a response to the many critics of his analysis of Germany's failure in democracy and its implications for the future. Jaspers wrote this against those who would not admit that the German state in 1933 was criminal.

> [1933] was a breakdown--or a revelation of the character of the German majority. Considering the facts everyone could see, it was possible only if one would either deny the facts or treat them as non-existent. It took criminal untruthfulness. To fail to be absolutely, unreservedly anti-Nazi in view of the criminal facts, one had to be unimpressed by lawlessness and crime wherever apparent. Without profound inhumanity it was not possible./74/

As if to signal his final falling out with the political situation in Germany, Jaspers also applied for and was granted citizenship status by the Swiss government and canton of Basel in 1967. Although his political writings frequently reflect a high regard for the exemplary political principles manifested in the history of Switzerland, he nonetheless wrote in his

Nachlass with reference to Switzerland that he was "just a pilgrim without a fatherland."/75/

The breadth of Jaspers's political writings during the last few years of his life seems remarkable when one considers the medical problems he encountered. After 1965 his lung condition had become quite serious. He experienced bleeding from the intestines, and a spreading arthritis in his hands, arms, and legs. Eventually he needed assistance in walking--requiring first one, then two canes, and finally a walker. In August 1968 he suffered a stroke which was followed by two others in September and October, after which time his physical condition grew quite severe. Hans Saner recounts how once, during these last few months of his life, when visitors tried to change the conversation to politics Jaspers said bluntly: "it has no more meaning for me. Let's speak about philosophy."/76/

On the evening of the 16th of February, 1969, Jaspers suffered yet another stroke which debilitated both his speech and comprehension. On his birthday, 23 February, he received friends for the last time, mentioning that he did not have long to live. Two days later pneumonia brought on a severe fever. On 26 February, 1969--the 90th birthday of his wife-- he died at 1:45 p.m., relinquishing his spirit to death's ultimate boundary.

* * *

As this brief survey of Jaspers's life and major works has shown, he underwent a radical transformation of thinking as a result of his experience under the thumb of Nazi totalitarianism. Because "philosophizing always begins with our situation,"/77/ it is understandable why he was behooved to think through the moral presuppositions and conditions of political life within the larger context of a world history from this time forward. Hitler's tyranny with its resultant Holocaust had shocked the world. Europe was in shambles both inwardly and outwardly, and had come to assume an intermediate position on the global scene between Russia and America. The United States exploded the first atomic bombs against Hiroshima and Nagasaki just three months after Germany's defeat. With the Japanese bombings a new situation had arisen in history. For Jaspers, the development of the atom bomb came to represent a fundamentally "new fact" which had led "mankind to the possibility of total self-destruction."/78/

18

NOTES

1. PAT, p.5. Cf., WW, p.134.
2. PAT, p.70.
3. Elisabeth Young-Bruehl, Freedom and Karl Jaspers's Philosophy (New Haven and London: Yale University Press, 1981), p.42.
4. Ibid., p.39.
5. PHT I, p.13.
6. For a listing of biographical works on Karl Jaspers, see Hans Saner, Karl Jaspers in Selbstzeugnissen und Bilddokumenten (Reinbeck: Rowohlt, 1970), p.171. Our indebtedness to Saner's work will be apparent throughout this chapter. For discussions concerning Jaspers's turn to political philosophy after the war and attempts to discern critically the essence of his political thinking, see, Dolf Sternberger, "Jaspers und der Staat," in Klaus Piper, ed., Werk und Wirkung (Munchen: R. Piper, 1963), pp.133-141; Werner Schneiders, Karl Jaspers in der Kritik, pp.91-134; and Godfrey Robert Carr, Karl Jaspers as an Intellectual Critic: The Political Dimension of his Thought, pp.36-92.
7. OMP, p.159.
8. PAT, p.6.
9. PAT, p.9.
10. OMP, p.159.
11. PAT, p.9.
12. LDW, p.189.
13. Ludwig B. Lefebre, "The Psychology of Karl Jaspers," in Schilpp, p.478.
14. PAT, pp.23-4.
15. Karl Jaspers, Nachlass, quoted in Hans Saner, Karl Jaspers, p.43: "Als Student spürte ich keinnerlei Mitverantwortung für den Gang der Dinge."
16. PAT, p.55, 58.
17. PAT, p. 55.
18. Cf., LDW, p.206.
19. Karl Jaspers, "Wahrheit, Freiheit und Friede," in HS, p.176: "kein Friede ohne Freiheit, aber keine Freiheit ohne Wahrheit."
20. Ludwig B. Lefebre, "The Psychology of Karl Jaspers," in Schilpp, pp.489-91.
21. PHT I, pp.318-339.
22. PHT II, p.147.
23. PAT, p.50.
24. Dolf Sternberger, "Jaspers und der Staat," in Klaus Piper, ed., Werk und Wirkung, p.134: "das Berühmte Göschen-Bändchen betraf doch wiederum

nicht eigentlich die politische, sondern eben
die, "geistige" Situation der Zeit, und sein
mächtig wirkender Appell rief nicht zur Rettung
der Republik, sondern zum Aufschwung der Person,
zum, 'Selbstsein.'"

25. Cf., SchW, p.35.
26. In Saner, Karl Jaspers, p.43.
27. Karl Jaspers, quoted in Saner, Karl Jaspers,
    p.44:   "Man wird uns Juden eines Tages in
    Baracken bringen und die Baracken anzünden."
    Cf., SchW, p.35.
28. Karl Jaspers, quoted in Saner, Karl Jaspers,
    p.44:   "Am Anfang machte ich mir in der Tat
    Illusionen. Ich denke daran mit Beschämung. An
    die äussersten Konsequenzen dachte ich überhaupt
    noch nicht, hielt eine schnelle Wandlung des
    Unfugs und einen Umsturz der Regierung für
    möglich.   Ich wollte das Fürchterliche nicht
    gleich wahrhaben."   Cf., P, p.159.
29. Cf., Saner, Karl Jaspers, p.44ff.
30. Nietzsche: Einfuhrung in das Verstandnis seines
    Philosophierens; Descartes und die Philosophie.
    Walter Kaufmann sees Jaspers's interpretation of
    Nietzsche in 1936 as tragically failing to mute
    the Nazi version of Nietzsche a la Baumler.
    Jaspers's interpretation helped, he maintains,
    "to reduce to relative ineffectiveness a
    philosophy which was unalterably opposed to the
    forces which have determined recent German
    history." Walter Kaufmann, "Jaspers' Relation to
    Nietzsche," in Schilpp, p.432.
31. These eimigration attempts included the
    possibility of working in Zurich in 1936, in
    Istanbul and America (Princeton) in 1938, Paris
    (Caisse Nationale de la Recherche Scientifique)in
    1939, and Basel in 1941 (Kuratorium der Freien
    Akademischen Stiftung).   Saner, Karl Jaspers,
    p.46.   On Jaspers's chances of emigration and
    diary accounts of his and his wife's dangers from
    1939-1942, see further SchW, pp.143-62, and the
    recent diary translations by Edith Ehrlich,
    Leonard H. Ehrlich, and George B. Pepper, eds.,
    Karl Jaspers, pp.535-543.
32. PAT, p.65.
33. OMP, p.184.
34. OMP, p.185. Cf., PAT, p.66.
35. Cf., PWT, pp.298-299.
36. Dolf Sternberger, "Jaspers und der Staat," in
    Klaus Piper, ed., Werk und Wirkung, p.134: "Die
    Diktatur hat uns alle verwandelt. Ein anderer

Jaspers trat aus der Verborgenheit der
Unterdrückung hervor."

37. Karl Jaspers, Tagebuch, quoted in Saner, Karl
Jaspers, p.51: "Wer es überlebt, dem muss eine
Aufgabe bestimmt sein, für die er den Rest seines
Lebens verzehren soll."
In accordance with our speaking of a turn in
Jaspers's thinking to a more explicit concern
with political philosophizing as a result of the
war, F. H. Heinemann writes: "In the years of
his retirement [i.e., dismissal from the
university by the Nazis], which lasted until the
end of the Second World War in 1945, he went on
with his work. This limit-situation which he
himself had to experience and to suffer gave him
not only time to study the prophet Jeremiah, but
brought about a change in his attitude which
allows us to speak of a second period."
Existentialism and the Modern Predicament (New
York: Harper & Row, Harper Torchbook, 1958),
p.71. We prefer to speak of this change in terms
of a third period.

38. Karl Jaspers, quoted in Saner, Karl Jaspers,
p.51: "Geleitwort für die Zeitschrift 'Die
Wandlung' 1945: "So wollen und müssen wir
versuchen, wie wir uns denkend in dieser
ungeheuren Not zurechtfinden." Cf., HS, p.30.

39. Karl Jaspers, quoted in Saner, Karl Jaspers,
p.53: "[...] als politischer Schriftsteller mit
vielen anderen die Sprache zu finden für die
Deutschen, die jetzt [...] mit Hilfe der
Alliierten [...] einen neuen Staat bilden
würden." Cf., SchW, p.37.

40. Ibid.: "allein auf die innere geistig-sittliche
Verfassung als den Boden der Politik." Cf., HS,
p.19.

41. See, HS, pp.27-53.

42. QGG, p.11.

43. QGG, p.120. Cf. HS, p.142.

44. Karl Jaspers, "Erneuerung der Universität," in
HS, pp.31-40. The German original first appeared
in Die Wandlung 1, Nr.1, Heidelberg (L.
Schneider), pp.66-74.

45. Karl Jaspers, "The Rededication of German
Scholarship," trans. by Marianne Zuckerkandl, The
American Scholar 15 (Spring 1946), pp.181-2.
This address represents the first time Jaspers
was able to raise his voice again since he had
been barred from teaching in 1935, and since the
ban on his publications in 1939.

46. QGG, p.32, 71-2.

47. In L'Esprit Européen, Rencontres internationales de Genève, trans. by Jeanne Hersch (Paris: La presse française et étrangère, O. Zeluck, 1947), pp.291-323. The German original is in RA, pp.275-312.

48. Present at this meeting along with Jaspers were Benda, Bernanos and Guehenno (France), de Salis and de Rougemont (Switzerland), Georg Lukacs (Hungary), and Stephen Spender (Great Britain). Spender has reported his experience of the meeting, including the famous controversy between Jaspers and Lukacs. According to Spender, Lukacs attacked Jaspers from a "social-realist" critique, "saying that Jaspers was a 'broken man' representing the point of view of a bankrupt individualism." Stephen Spender, "The Intellectuals and Europe's Future," Commentary III (1947), pp.7-12. For Lukacs understanding of the situation of the European spirit after the war, see his "L'Esprit Européen devant le Marxisme," La Nef 3 (November 1946), pp.39-41.

49. Karl Jaspers, "Is Europe's Culture Finished?", trans. by E. B. Ashton, Commentary IV (1947), p.519.

50. Ibid., p.520.

51. Saner, Karl Jaspers, p.54.

52. Karl Jaspers, Briefe, quoted in Saner, Karl Jaspers, p.55: "was ich schreibe, fast ignoriert wird."

53. Karl Jaspers, "Offentliche Erklarung." "Rhein-Neckar-Zeitung" am 24. Marz 1948, quoted in Saner, Karl Jaspers, p.56: "Ich möchte meine Pflicht dort, wo ich bin, erfüllen im Dienst einer schlechthin übernationalen Aufgabe. Mein Hierbleiben wäre kein Bekenntnis wie auch mein Fortgang nach Basel kein Bekenntnis ist."

54. Leonard H. Erhlich, Karl Jaspers: Philosophy as Faith, p.8, has argued how integral Jaspers's notion of philosophical faith is to the whole of his thinking. He understands Jaspers's treatment of philosophical faith as an "act of synthetic openness" which always leads one back to his foundational ideas, i.e., his philosophy of freedom, Being and the subject-object dichotomy, the transcendental method, his "ingenuous synthesis," periechontology, and the idea of a general fundamental knowledge. See also below, Chapter Seven.

55. This meant nothing else for Jaspers than that the knowledge of man had to undergo a change, even if Nazi totalitarianism was not so much new in its

roots (i.e., tied to the evil possibilities of man), as it was new in appearance. Cf., PAT, p.60 and OGH, p.148.

56. PAT, p.69.
57. PAT, p.70.
58. Karl Jaspers, "Philosophical Memoirs," in PWT, p.278.
59. PAT, p.69-70.
60. Of the period from 1950-69 Jaspers' most important works included: Einführung in die Philosophie (The Way to Wisdom) and Vernunft und Widervernunft in Unserer Zeit (Reason and Anti-Reason in Our Time) both published in 1950. Rechenschaft und Ausblick, 1951 (Existentialism and Humanism); Lionardo als Philosoph, 1953 (Leonardo as Philosopher); Die Frage der Entmythologisierung, 1954 (Myth and Christianity); Schelling: Grösse und Verhängnis, 1955; Die grossen Philosophen, vols.I and II, 1957 (The Great Philosophers); Die Atombombe und die Zukunft des Menschen, 1958 (The Future of Mankind); Philosophie und Welt (Philosophy and the World); Freiheit und Wiedervereinigung, 1960; Der philosophische Glaube angesichts der Offenbarung, 1962 (Philosophical Faith and Revelation); Nikolas Cusanus, 1964 Kleine Schule des Philosophischen Denkens (Philosophy is for Everyman) and Hoffnung und Sorge in 1965; Wohin treibt die Bundesrepublik?, 1966 (The Future of Germany) and a lengthy response to its critics in Antwort; Zur Kritik meiner Schrift "Wohin treibt die Bundesrepublik?", 1967; his autobiographical writings in Schicksal und Wille, 1967; Aneignung und Polemik (a collection of his lectures and essays on the history of philosophy), 1968; Provokationen (13 dialogues and interviews), 1969; and finally, his posthumously published, Chiffren der Transcendenz, in 1970.
61. Klaus Piper, ed., Karl Jaspers: Werk und Wirkung, p.14.
62. OGH, pp. 206-10.
63. In RA, pp. 370-77.
64. Translated by Norbert Guterman in the Evergreen Review 2 (1958), pp.37-57. The German original is in HS, pp.153-172.
65. FM, p.v.
66. Karl Jaspers, "Wahrheit, Freiheit und Friede," in HS, pp.173-185.
67. Saner, Karl Jaspers, p.60.
68. FW, p.13.

69. Cited in Saner, <u>Karl</u> <u>Jaspers</u>, p.61.
70. <u>Ibid.</u>, pp.61-2.
71. Hannah Arendt, "Forward," in FG, p.v.
72. Among the proposed German emergency laws to which Jaspers strongly reacted were plans for the construction of civilian bomb shelters which were justified then by an appeal to the "Red menace." Although he had supported such a view of the Russians in the early and mid-1950s, in 1966 he had come to a different perspective: "Today the threat is a mirage." FG, p.36.
73. Jürgen Habermas, "Deutschland--wohin?", <u>Die</u> <u>Zeit</u>, 13 May 1966, quoted in Saner, <u>Karl</u> <u>Jaspers</u>, p.63.
74. FG, p.167.
75. Karl Jaspers, quoted in Saner, <u>Karl</u> <u>Jaspers</u>, p.64: " [...] bloss Wanderer zu sein und kein politisches Vaterland zu haben."
76. <u>Ibid.</u>, p.67: "Es hat für mich jetzt keine Bedeutung mehr. Wir wollen von der Philosophie sprechen."
77. PHT I, p.43.
78. FM, p.4; AB, p.22.

2.0 INTRODUCTION

Jaspers's turn to historico-political thinking had had its definitive birth after 1945, even though he had conceived the design for both a philosophical logic and a universal history of philosophy as early as 1937. After 1945 the development of his philosophical logic remained in the background as witnessed by the fact that his two other projected volumes were never realized. His understanding of the nuclear problem, however, became situated within the horizon of his historico-political thinking and quest for a Weltphilosophie. If the nuclear problem forces us to know "what we want, how we would wish to live, [and] what we must be prepared for,"/1/ it also requires that we perceive it within the larger horizon of past and present human history. For thoughts about the twin threats of annihilation and totalitarianism "only acquire their full insight as elements of a total conception of history."/2/ In order to analyze the nuclear problem from within Jaspers's own terms of reference, therefore, we must first make a detour through his understanding of past and present history.

Linking the nuclear problem to the broader spiritual situation of the age when speaking on "Das Gewissen vor der Bedrohung durch die Atombombe" in 1950, he wrote,

> A world in which faithlessness grows, divorce increases, a scattered life in immediate pleasures takes precedence over a concentrated life in historical continuity, the old, secretive wickedness is considered to be standard, the so-called realist position stands as the epitome of a reason that claims to be free of illusions-- in this world are such terrors as the atom bomb only a consequence and therefore a mere symptom./3/

Although he speaks in this text of the development of the atom bomb as representing a fundamentally new step in the meaning and consequences of war, its terror was nonetheless seen as only one of many precarious manifestations of the present spiritual situation of

humanity. And as early as 1931, in Die geistige
Situation der Zeit, he had identified this malaise as
having the proportions of a "world crisis."/4/ In 1947
he spoke boldly of the post-war situation as "the most
profound caesura in human history to date."/5/   Again
in 1949 he epitomized the European spiritual situation
as a "disintegration of the connecting western spirit,"
a "chasm" epitomized by that monstrous symbol of
unspeakable horror: "the Nazi concentration camps with
their tortures, at the end of which stood the gas
chambers for millions of human beings."/6/   Hannah
Arendt, perhaps Jaspers's most insightful political
interpretor, affirms that it is against the background
of present "political and spiritual realities [...]
that one must understand his new concept of mankind and
the propositions of his philosophy."/7/

Jaspers's experience of exclusion under the
terrors of National Socialism was essentially
responsible for the transformation of his interest in
history. The year 1937-- and his dismissal by the
Nazis from his professorship at Heidelberg-- signalled
the beginning of his design for a world history of
philosophy./8/ Two questions which helped establish
the idea for his work on the great philosophers arose
out of his experience at that time.   The first
concerned the positive way in which past philosophers
had both created and protected that philosophical
spirit capable of resisting political terror.   The
second asked, conversely, how philosophers have
contributed to this terror by their very thinking.
With respect to the second question Jaspers writes in
his autobiography,

Totalitarianism meant the most
radical rupture of communication from
person to person and therewith, at the
same time, the end of man's being
himself.   It became clear that the
rupture of communication in favor of
violent wilfulness is always not merely
a threat to personal existence and the
real danger of losing oneself, but that
this alternative finds its expression
in the great powers of history./9/

In response to this new historical rupture of
communication, then, he embarked upon a project for the
possibility of universal communication by means of a
world history of philosophy.   His search for Vom
Ursprung und Ziel der Geschichte (The Origin and Goal

of History) became by 1949 the framework for such
communication. This work, his treatment of "the great
philosophers," the Philosophie, and his early work on
the spiritual situation of the time are all essential
to his understanding of the historical situation./10/

Foundationally, Jaspers's approach to history
contrasts Historie and Geschichte. He considers
knowledge of the past which has been methodically and
critically tested as historical science, while this
same knowledge converted into present existential
self-understanding constitutes the meaning of
"philosophy of history."/11/ Both represent arcs of
the hermeneutical circle: historical science is vital
for historical understanding, and the philosophy of
history is vital for history's meaning as the
illumination of Existenz which presupposes an
encompassing search for history's aim and
structure./12/ Philosophy of history searches for that
consciousness of "historicity" (Geschichtlichkeit) "in
which the self becomes aware of its historicity as the
only reality it has."/13/ In short, Jaspers
understands the philosophy of history as the
transformation of historical science into existential
self-understanding by way of appropriation. As he puts
it, "to express the historic consciousness of an
Existenz that grows aware of its present by way of
knowing the past-- this is what we call philosophy of
history."/14/

What matters most in his approach to history is
his understanding of present temporality and the
"cipher" status of Geschichtsphilosophie. "By making
history our own," he writes, "we cast an anchor through
history into eternity."/15/ His philosophy of history
relates all time to present Existenz. The past never
becomes a "rounded whole," but is always open via the
present, while the future always "remains a possibility
without turning into an inescapable necessity."/16/
Because all historical facts and future possibilities
latent in the present are to be read as possible
"ciphers" of the unity of Existenz with its
Transcendence, his search for a contemporary philosophy
of "world history" must be seen as provisional, valid
only to the present, and continually subject to
alteration by the future./17/ "A picture of history as
a whole, from beginning to end, appears as the cipher
of transcendent being,"/18/ he tells us. He ventured
this universal and cipheric history of humanity, on the
one hand, for the sake of universal communication in a
world threatened by the possibilities of "world empire"

and atomic annihilation, and, on the other, for a world in search of new forms of economic and socio-political thinking, world order, and faith.

In this chapter, then, and in keeping with Jaspers's supposition that all philosophizing begins with the historical situation, we focus upon his view of history as defined by its two most recent and decisive epochs, the "axial age" (Achsenseit) (2.1) and the age of modern science and technology (2.2). In turn, we will illuminate the present "crisis" situation of humanity within which Jaspers situates the genesis of potential nuclear annihilation and the reality of political totalitarianism (2.3), and the present tendencies toward socialism, world unity, and faith.

2.1 THE AXIAL AGE

Since his philosophy of history demands the tools and methods of historical science, it must seek empirical foundations for its understanding. This is especially the case today, in an age in which the "universal scientific approach" has transformed all traditional thinking./19/ It is therefore a fundamental premise that a philosophy of world history must obtain from an empirical "fact."/20/ This "fact" is identified by his thesis of the "axial age" of human history./21/

Central to his axial thesis is the insistence that its meaning is capable of being adopted as a common basis of communication for all of humanity beyond all differences of creeds./22/ In contrast, "traditional" views of history suffer from the problem that they are not sufficiently universal, since they derive exclusively from a Christian Weltanshauung which presupposes an "absolute view" of world history./23/

> It is a Christian idea that the course of mankind with its decisive events--the Creation, the Fall of Man, the Incarnation, the End of the World, and the Last Judgment--is strictly singular. The Christian knows about the whole [...] It was the transformation of this Christian view of history which brought forth the philosophy of history as total knowledge of human events. The line of descent from the Christian idea runs from Herder, Kant, Fichte, Hegel, Marx

to Nietzsche. The central premise is always a vision of the whole./24/

If this Christian view has dominated the western understanding of history up until at least the sixteenth century, it is no longer adequate for the communicative demands of the twentieth century according to Jaspers. For "the Christian faith is only one faith, not the faith of mankind."/25/ Whereas Hegel saw the appearance of the Son of God as the axis of history,/26/ Jaspers tilts this axis backwards to the period from 800 to 200 B.C. It was the extraordinary events and spiritual flowerings which arose independently and virtually simultaneously in the West, India, and China during this period that have guided humanity up until the present age.

> Confucius and Lao-tse were living in China, all the schools of Chinese philosophy came into being [...] India produced the Upanishads and Buddha and, like China, ran the whole gamut of philosophical possibilities [...] in Iran Zarathustra taught [...] in Palestine the prophets made their appearance, from Elijah by way of Isaiah to Jeremiah to Deutero-Isaiah, Greece witnessed the appearance of Homer, of the philosophers--Parmenides, Heraclitus and Plato--of the tragedians./27/

Jaspers insists that the miraculous rise of new spiritual and sociological realities during this time arose simultaneously in all three cultures. What is spiritually "new" about the axial age is that human consciousness in all three areas of the world became aware of itself. Humanity became that humanity which has characterized human existence up to our present age. "Man becomes," Jaspers writes, "conscious of Being as a whole [...] of his limitations [...and] experiences absoluteness in the depths of selfhood and in the lucidity of transcendence."/28/

With the birth of the great world religions, the age produced the basic categories of our religious and philosophical thinking. One witnesses a step by humanity "towards the universal," while the age of radical mythology came to an end./29/ Instead, logos battled against mythos and, in turn, myth became transformed into parable. There also arose a corresponding birth in ethical consciousness. The "spiritualization" of existence is dramatically witnessed by the rise of the "paradigmatic individuals," i.e., Socrates, Buddha, Confucius, and Jesus, the breakdown of the subject/object dichotomy, and the rise of the unio mystica in speculative thought./30/ One also witnesses the struggle for liberation and redemption in the world. The search was the same in all three cultures whatever form it took. Jaspers speaks of this liberation primarily in spiritual categories such as "an ascent to the Idea; or in ataraxia--passive resignation; or by immersion in thought; or in the knowledge of himself and the world as Atman, the Universal Self; or in the experience of Nirvana; or in harmony with the Tao--the cosmic order; or in surrender to the will of God."/31/

He also finds remarkably parallel sociological conditions in China, India, and around the Mediterranean during the axial age. Each region is characterized within by small city-states struggling against each other for power and domination. Reciprocal communication through travel and trade led to the founding of schools and academies for the intellectual life, with the parallels between the politico-philosophical thinking and activity of Confucius and Plato being one obvious example. For the first time, human existence became the object of reflection as "history", whether conceived negatively as a cycle of decline or positively as one of ascent. Indeed, it is from the axial age that history has received the only structure and unity that has endured until the present. But when the creative energy that had been bound up with the incredible transformations in art, religion, and law was lost, a similar phenomena took place. A "petrification of dogmas" and a "general levelling" developed. More significantly, the earlier creative "spiritualization" process gave way to an order of "technological and organizational planning" in the great, universal empires (i.e., the Tsin-Shi-Hwang-Ti dynasty in China, the Maurya in India, and the Hellenistic empires and Imperium Romanum in the West). These attempts at total planning, he suggests, spelled the end of democracy in the self-governing Greek city-states./32/

In order to complete Jaspers's "schema" of world history, we must recall that the axial age is only one of four ages within which humanity has started out anew upon the basis of fundamentally changed conditions. Prior to the axial time, and primordial, there was the age of pre-history or, what Jaspers terms after the Greek god Prometheus, the "Promethean age," characterized by the invention of tools, crude language, and the use of fire. It was during this age that "man became man in distinction to a purely biologically defined human species, of which we can scarcely conceive."/33/

The Promethean age was followed by that of the ancient high civilizations, the Sumerian, Egyptian, Aegean, pre-Aryan Indian, and the archaic Chinese cultures, as well as by isolated developments in Mexico and Peru or what contemporary anthropologists would call the "New World." Characteristic of this period, "history" proper, were socio-political organization, the discovery of writing (which led the way to a common language, culture, and mythology), the domestication of the horse, and the first rise of "world-empires." These ancient civilizations established the economic, political, intellectual, and religious pre-conditions of life upon which the axial age was grounded. All of the ancient civilizations were brought to an end by the axial age, which either levelled, assimilated, or forced them out of existence./34/

2.2 THE AGE OF MODERN SCIENCE AND TECHNOLOGY

Since the axial age there has been only one entirely new "spirtually and materially incisive event," according to Jaspers's schema./35/ This is the historical "dividing-line" represented by the age of modern science and technology. Having arose at the end of the Middle Ages, it had its theoretical foundations laid in the seventeenth century, developed rapidly in the last century during the industrial revolution, and has grown at its most remarkable pace in this century. The following description of the age is scarcely surprising since it was written after the U.S. bombings of Hiroshima and Nagasaki, and the very year that the Soviet Union tested its first atomic bomb (1949).

> During the last few centuries a single phenomenon that is intrinsically new in all respects has made its appearance: science with its consequences in technology. It has revolutionized the world inwardly and outwardly as no other event since the dawn of recorded history. It has brought with it unprecedented opportunities and hazards [...] New

31

foundations for the whole of existence
have now been inescapably laid./36/

Thus in order to interpret accurately the present
age from which the nuclear problem has developed as one
"symptom" of the human condition among others, it is
imperative that we see the radically new elements in
modern science and technology clearly.

2.2.1 Characterization of Modern Science

Jaspers has repeatedly characterized that which is
peculiarly new to modern science in virtually identical
terms in various of his essays and books. By science,
he means "the conquest of an existence <u>independent</u> <u>of</u>
<u>the</u> <u>knowing</u> <u>subject</u>. It is motivated by the urge to
know what applies always and everywhere, regardless of
changes in time and in historic individuality-- to know
what will be valid even beyond man, for any possible
rational being."/37/ He takes its three indispensable
traits to be its (1) methodical structure, (2)
compelling certainty, and (3) universal validity. It
is by scientific method that we can both explain how we
gain knowledge and demonstrate its limits.   Because
science is cogent certainty, we also know uncertainty,
probability or improbability by it.   And finally,
because the insights of science can be experienced by
every intelligence, unanimity and universality are its
hallmarks.   These   three   criteria have   been
characteristic of western science ever since the
pre-Socratics. But modern science has purified and
transformed the classical Greek sciences which had "the
appearance of something completed," and for which "the
notion of progress was not essential."/38/ Only in its
bare essentials was science developed in China and
India.

Seven features characterize the uniqueness of
modern science for Jaspers. We present them here in a
composite form./39/

(1) In contrast to the science of antiquity,
modern science is <u>universal</u>. There are no limits to
inquiry and research. "Nothing shall be hidden, nothing
shall be silent, nothing shall be secret" to it./40/
Religion and every kind of authority is subject to its
investigation. Jaspers distinguishes the ideal of <u>a</u>
universal science, as a universal method, from the
universality of science's concerns. The "universal
scientific approach" has destroyed both a single

universal science and philosophy's claim (e.g. by Descartes and Hegel) to such universality as well./41/

(2) Inspired by a belief in progress, modern science presses constantly onward, and is thus by definition <u>unfinished</u>. Cognition is forever incomplete, though everything that exists is to be understood. And yet, presuppositions always give way to new, more comprehensive presuppositions. "Through the infinity of the existent it is directed toward Being, which, however, it never reaches-- and it knows this through self-criticism."/42/

(3) To modern science <u>nothing</u> <u>is</u> <u>indifferent</u>. Having sprung from a love of nature in the natural sciences and the love of the classics in the intellectual sciences, it searches out all that can be known. It was always a joy in the realities of the world that spawned the will to know. However, whenever modern science abandons the "philosophical substance" which inspires research, it loses its ground. It becomes "bustle, technique, and consumption of philological data."/43/

(4) Whereas the ancient sciences remained scattered, modern science strives to be integrated into a universal framework. It also acknowledges, at the same time, that there is no single universal method, but rather that there is a <u>plurality</u> <u>of</u> <u>methods</u>. "Though a true world-system is no longer possible," he writes, "a cosmos of the sciences is still conceivable."/44/ Systematics are necessary, albeit temporary, "if knowledge is not to be scattered into disconnected and indifferent parts."/45/ And while we do not know the ultimate reason why all knowledge belongs together, this very fact makes us seek knowledge for its own sake./46/

(5) The radical form of modern scientific <u>doubt</u> and inquiry is today unparalleled by the past. The thinking that contradicts appearances-- such as that which began in antiquity with astronomy-- has culminated today in a physics beyond imagination, working even through "non-perceptual mathematics."/47/ Scientific doubt calls into question established doctrine, and sets forth new hypotheses which give way to new possibilities and insights. Descartes was right in this respect. But if daring everything and the freedom of experiment are aspects of the scientific tradition, of "the passion for novelty," Descartes went

wrong in transferring this passion to philosophy where it does not belong./48/

(6) Modern science is marked by a _plurality of categories_ for which "infinity" and "causality" are only two among many. It tries to use every form and object that appears mathematically, physically, biologically, hermeneutically or speculatively possible. "The results are a world of categories capable of limitless expansion and a corresponding unclosed theory of categories."/49/

(7) Finally, science has given rise to the attitude of a universal scientific approach or "scientificity" (_Wissenschaftlichkeit_)./50/ This attitude, imbuded with reason, is only realized by those willing to question, discuss, investigate, test, and criticize everything conceivable. It is diametrically opposed to "scientific dogmatism." It stands aloof from sects, cults, creeds, articles of faith, and societies of like-minded individuals. Instead, it distinguishes between what is and what is not logically compelling, and desires to know the method by which each object of knowledge has been obtained. Human veracity is determined by this attitude once science has become truly scientific. "When we enter into its sphere," Jaspers avows, "we have the sensation of breathing clean air, of leaving behind us all vague talk, all plausible opinions, all stubborn prejudice and blind faith."/51/

2.2.2 The Boundaries and Domains of Modern Science

In order to survey the domains of science-- which Jaspers determines according to three basic forms of "cogency" (_Zwingenden_)-- we must first recall his distinction between scientific and philosophical "world orientation."/52/ Scientific world orientation consists in the empirical search by the intellect for objectively verifiable facts. It flows from certain principles and is guided by methods whose application results in a cogent body of information or world-image. This empirical world orientation which gears itself toward both _real_ objects-- like nature and the Rosetta stone-- and _ideal_ objects-- like the Pythagorean theorem and the law of gravity-- is never complete but remains an infinite process. Here we always come up against "endlessness," though true science will point to a unity of what can be known and will deal with data in a systematic whole.

Philosophical world orientation, on the other hand, never fuses research results into a unified world-image (<u>Weltbild</u>), but looks instead "for <u>what</u> <u>is</u> <u>doubtful</u> in factual world orientation."/53/ It functions essentially as a <u>critique</u> of any ostensibly "scientific" totality. Philosophical world orientation discloses two <u>boundaries</u> of science proper, as well as its own orientation. The first boundary appears to scientific world orientation because whenever we take up a "pure object" we must always "<u>abstract</u> <u>from</u> <u>something else,</u> from something we had to eliminate so as to come to generally valid truth."/54/ According to Jaspers this process is an <u>abstraction</u> <u>from</u> <u>the</u> <u>subjective,</u> which scientific world orientation regards as a source of error. It desires to get beyond subjective distortions of perspectives, arbitrary appraisals, and mere standpoints. It omits these from its view, and relegates them to mythological, religious, and philosophical history. In the process, however, subjectivity is inevitably objectified, robbed of its inner being, and falsified as an object of empirical investigation./55/ The very success of science depends upon its ability to suspend or bracket questions pertaining to an all-encompassing world-view. To the extent that scientific world orientation forgets this and absolutizes a particular claim to validity, it turns into "scientific positivism" which erroneously "equates being with what the natural sciences know [...] being and objective being become one and the subject-object split dissolves into a principle of uniform objective being."/56/

Acceptance of the positivist conclusion negates what Jaspers sees as the authentic basis of scientific insight, namely, the transcending quest for an experience of world not as a mere object, but as an <u>intelligible</u> <u>unity.</u> Where the empirical positivist falsely levels everything in the name of the object, the absolute idealist schematizes everything in the name of the subject. For both, the <u>transcending</u> quest toward a never finally obtainable unity is lost by their respective reductionisms.

The second boundary appears to philosophical world orientation, whose orientation is not to round out a self-sufficient and self-explanatory natural world, but to show how the limits of scientific knowledge make such an intention untenable. It seeks to point to truth that transcends merely cogent truth, however important this has become in the modern age. The boundary appears in its experience of <u>imperfectibility.</u>

In Jaspers's words, in philosophical world orientation, "I acquire cogent insight, but the cogency does not become absolute. I prevail over endlessness, but it also remains unconquered. I attain unities, but not the unity of the world."/57/

Authentic science, then, arises out of a quest for unity and the experience of being bounded. Both scientific and philosophical world orientation have their limits. But they are limits, as Jaspers would say, which are relevant for possible Existenz. For they demonstrate that the world "cannot be rounded into being-in-itself-- in other words, that <u>cognition</u> <u>is</u> <u>not</u> <u>exhausted</u> <u>with</u> <u>cognition</u> <u>of</u> <u>the</u> <u>world</u>-- and that the scientific meaning of world orientation comes from a source not subject to scientific cognition."/58/ Philosophical world orientation tells us that we cannot account for subjectivity and open ourselves to Transcendence unless we break through a conclusive empirical world orientation. This "breakthrough to subjectivity" shows that there is room for philosophizing in existential elucidation and speculative metaphysics, that the meaning and purpose of science can only be grasped from a point of view outside science, and indeed, that the clarification of science, perhaps the most difficult form of cogency to obtain, is essentially a philosophical task.

Given Jaspers's distinction between scientific and philosophical world orientation we must ask, as Jaspers does at the outset of his treatment of the limits of world orientation: what is the "pure object" of world orientation, independent of individual subjectivity? His response is simply that object which cogently exists for the intellect or consciousness - as - such. <u>Cogency</u> is Jaspers's summary way, as Sebastian Samay has pointed out, of including or implying all of the requisite features of scientific knowledge./59/ The <u>domains</u> of scientific knowledge are composed essentially of judgments which are bound by those who accept them as cogent. And the bounds of this knowledge are determined by three forms of cogency:

(1) cogent thoughts of mathematics and formal logic;

(2) cogent reality of objective experience in the empirical, natural and intellectual sciences; and,

(3) phenomenological cogency or the compelling "visuality" (<u>Anschauung</u>) of "categories, essences, and possibilities of objective being."/60/

Each form of cogency differs in its source and methods, but they are all inextricably linked in the "knowledge" yielded by world orientation. The cogent knowledge of empirical reality (2) is impossible without the other two (1) and (3), which are "psychologically impossible" without empirical experience. Let us look briefly at each domain.

Within <u>mathematics</u>, Jaspers distinguishes between what would today be called pure mathematics and intuitive mathematics. Both are based on axioms which serve as indubitable first principles for a hypothetico-deductive method. Like formal logic, these axioms state nothing but the <u>form</u> of certainty in mathematics. In pure math, these axioms are postulated arbitrarily and lead on <u>ad infinitum</u> like a form of play in non-Euclidean geometry. In contrast, the postulates of intuitive mathematics "lead to things which are originally evident but heterogeneous in kind." Intuitive math overlaps with the third domain of cogency, like the axioms of Euclidean geometry. In both cases, however, knowledge is "hypothetical." It is the hypotheses, whether arbitrary or self-evident, which give the form of cogency and constitute a valid "world." But this world still does <u>not</u> comprehend all of being. Mathematical cogency is of interest because its knowledge is so compelling, "but at the same time it is a matter of complete indifference if it remains unsubstantial."/61/

The <u>empirical sciences</u> deal with the vast domain of reality in contrast to mathematics and logic which deal simply with forms. In this domain, no reality is completely subject to cogent knowledge. Here we begin with the observations of <u>facts</u>. But facts themselves need to be determined by the selection of relevant factors in the event under observation. What makes facts accessible is not pure sense perception, but "reflective apperception." Our awareness of the method with which we bring "facts" to mind is the critical test of whether and in what sense they are facts. In other words, our very <u>selection</u> <u>and</u> <u>observation</u> of data over time, in its recurrent or non-recurrent patterns, requires a hypothesis or <u>theory</u> which seeks to explain the phenomenon in question. In turn, this theory provides a unified world-view which will be valid or invalid for a similar phenomenon in such a way that science eventually makes predictions of unobserved phenomena. A hermeneutical circle is operative here: the finding of facts depends upon an anticipatory theory, while the verification of the theory or hypothesis is grounded on the facts as found. And the boundary of the cogency of any given theory is that it never applies to the whole of reality.

The third domain of cogency concerns an intuitive phenomenology of the doctrine of categories. In this field "there is the visual presence of objects that are possible if not real; what happens here is that identical, unmistakable, undefinable, but visualizable elements and structures of world orientation are circumscribed, explicated, and made conscious as the framework in which, for us, the objective world exists."/62/ Phenomenological cogency exists as a given when we intuit a certain value, discover a certain relation, or directly apprehend a gestalt.

The compellingness of phenomenological cogency, however, is limited first of all by its "communicability." For apart from "the possibility of empty talk, of mouthing words instead of visualizing contents, I can never be quite sure that I and another are thinking about the same thing."/63/ Here we are up against the problem of saying what we essentially mean and meaning what we essentially say. An "essence" can certainly be called by the same name, but visualized differently by different people. Secondly, a limit of phenomenological perception lies in "systematics and completeness." Phenomenological cogency never reaches as far as the organization of the given. To use an example given by Charles Wallraff, whether or not Max Scheler was correct in thinking that he had made a thorough phenomenological investigation of the world of value, the immediacy of this intuition could not prove the four levels at which he placed what he intuited./64/ Neither in communication nor organization is an intuition cogent, except in the particular. We are always confined to orientation whereby "the universal limit of this cogency is that as something determinate it always refers to something else."/65/

What the domains of science reveal for Jaspers, then, is that modern science is inseparable from its limitations. From the limits of science we regain an approach to authentic philosophizing in the present situation. These limits, of course, follow from his own suppositions: first, that scientific cognition of

things is not a cognition of "being itself." Precisely
by means of its knowledge of determinate objects,
science produces a most decisive "non-knowing"
(Nichtwissen). It constantly reminds us of what we do
not know. Secondly, scientific understanding cannot
give us goals for life. It gives us no direction with
respect to values. It cannot tell us, as Kant
attempted with his categorical imperative, how to act
so as to treat ourself and others as an end and never
as a means./66/ Finally, science can give us no answer
to the question of its own meaning which is freedom.
Human freedom is not an object of science, but belongs
to the field of philosophy proper./67/

2.2.3 The Origins of Modern Science

The unique characteristics, boundaries, and
domains of science owe their character to those sources
which constitute the origins of modern science. These
sources stem from a complex concatenation of
sociological conditions which have sprung up since the
seventeenth century, and from the state of mind and
impulses that have their historical roots in "Biblical
religion."/68/

With respect to the diverse sociological
conditions which gave birth to the new science, Jaspers
points to the freedom of states and cities, the leisure
of the aristocracy and middle class, the cultural
contacts between Europe and alien cultures after the
crusades, the spiritual conflict between Church and
State, and the dissemination of ideas that followed the
advent of the printing press. But if these
sociological investigations can point to the
interconnection between the old and the new science,
they cannot account for the motives that led to modern
science. To be distinguished here are the two
interpretations that modern science springs from either
a "will to power" or from a will to know which
naturally desires to unravel the processes of nature.
Jaspers adamantly rejects the view that sees the
impulse behind the will to know as a form of
aggression. Nonetheless, the reality of the Nazi
concentration camps made him only too aware of the
scientist's will to power and destruction which
manipulates science "for purposes of aggressivity in
speech, action, and practical application."/69/
Whenever this happens true science is lost.

"Biblical religion," and especially Scripture's
demand for truthfulness, also played a crucial role in

the formation of modern science. God does not allow knowledge to be played with like a game. Life and death are often at stake here. Moreover, the world as God's creation, as something that is good, has led to the idea that knowing is a reflection upon God's thought. Whereas the Greeks (Aristotle and Democritus) stayed imprisoned in their closed universe, the Logos of "Biblical religion" demanded through its counterpart, the alogon, a drive toward repeated destruction in order to gain itself anew in a different form. In the Logos lies the origin of what Jaspers esteems to be the dialectic between reason and anti-reason. "The continuous, unceasing reciprocal action of theory and experiment" in science, he notes, is the "great example and symbol of the universal process that is the dialectic between Logos and anti-Logos."/70/

Finally, the fact that the world is filled with cruelty and horror also shores up a dialectical tension between scientific knowledge and faith. The God who refuses to be known through illusion or a false consciousness demands, to use the expression of Paul Ricoeur, a "hermeneutic of suspicion"/71/ with respect to all that exists. God insists upon knowledge, even if this should indict God's existence in turn. Like Job, the modern scientist cannot take comfort in dogmas or sophism. She or he must invite a self-criticism which, in turn, becomes productive by breaking-down former hypotheses as new data no longer fit a theory. Conversely, therefore, science becomes degraded when discussion is shunned, when individuals "imprison themselves and their ideas in a milieu of like-minded savants and become fanatically aggressive to all outside it."/72/ A continual danger is always that the scientist, in search of cogency, will "compel the certainty of things" that he or she deems important./73/

2.2.4 The Nature and Limits of Modern Technology

Although Jaspers can affirm that a new scientific attitude, a "universal methodological consciousness,"/74/ has transformed the nature of knowledge in our age, he sees the nature and limits of technology as the cardinal theme for the comprehension of our present situation. It is the question of what technology may make of humanity in the future, and the radically new conditions technology poses which constitute the urgent challenges to present reflection./75/

He understands the nature of technology as that process whereby certain means are introduced for the attainment of a given end. Technology exploits the intellect in order to calculate these means and their possibilities in terms of "quantities" and "relations." Most importantly, technology is based on knowledge as a form of power. And through the power of knowledge, technology attempts to master the power of nature by setting the natural forces of nature against themselves. Technology as power is thus "an ability whose procedure in relation to the aim is external;" as such, its ability "is one of fabrication and utilisation [and thus] not of creating and causing to grow."/76/

As a form of "purposive action,"/77/ about which we shall have more to say in Chapter Six, technology comes up against real limits. First, there are material limits. We cannot make things, like God, ex nihilo. Secondly, there are quantitative limits of given substances and forces, such as the speed of light. Thirdly, technological activity is limited by human existence, and the need for food, air, sleep, etc. Jaspers also sets off technological action, as the exploitation of "unorganic nature," from the realities of the life, soul, and the mind. The latter cannot be technologically made, but are conditionally influenced. Contemporary genetic engineering may refute Jaspers's claim. But his primary concern is with that "intermediate area" between the technological control of things and the positive possibilities of human action which are not bound, generally speaking, by mechanical means. For this is the space wherein universal communication between Existenzen must take place today./78/

2.3 THE PRESENT "CRISIS" SITUATION OF HUMANITY

As other thinkers before him,/79/ Jaspers refers to the present situation as a "decline of the West," a world "crisis," "the most profound ceasura in history to date."/80/ And yet, the radically new conditions established by modern science and its technological consequences for the working methods, lifestyle, modes of thought, and religious symbols inherited from the axial age cannot be reduced to these factors alone. Two foundational suppositions are operative in his understanding of the present "crisis" situation, and they will bear directly upon his later analysis of the atom bomb and the future of humanity.

First, there can be no total understanding of the
contemporary situation just as there can be no total
knowledge of being. Although to exist means to be in
situations, our attempts to grasp completely situations
within which we stand are doomed to be shipwrecked,
since situations are continually changing./81/ To cite
one of Jaspers's favorite mental images, humanity today
is voyaging upon "uncharted sea, unable to reach a
shore from which a clear outlook on the whole would be
attainable."/82/ To state it differently, we can only
know situations in a schema, "veiled as typically
general," though never wholly surveyable./83/ This is
especially true in our present situation in which the
loss of self-understanding remains hidden in the bustle
of mass life with its "eruption of unchained
instincts."/84/ And yet, to confront a given situation
directly is the crucial first step in coming to terms
with it, since to scrutinize a situation arouses a will
to modify its being./85/

Secondly, the totality of human existence in
economic, sociological, and political situations would
all have to be considered in an attempt to define the
situation of human existence in the present age. It is
certainly no coincidence that Jaspers simultaneously
published his foundational three volume Philosophie
with Die geistige Situation der Zeit, since his
analysis of the spiritual situation of humanity in 1930
was incomprehensible apart from his philosophical
foundations./86/ In this early piece he emphasized
that a truly encompassing, yet limited knowledge of a
given situation demands the search for being in terms
of world (as scientific and philosophical
world-orientation), self (as freedom working in
communication, historicity, and unconditional action)
and God (as a cultural metaphysics of faith and belief
in society that ultimately allows one to interpret
human life as a manifestation of Transcendence)./87/
His coupling of these two early works warns one against
attempting any simple description of the general
"crisis" of the present situation or of the twin
problems of annihilation and totalitarianism apart from
his philosophical foundations.

If the present "crisis" situation cannot be neatly
identified two things are certain. First, having been
wrought by western science and technology, the "crisis"
is first and foremost a European one. Secondly, it
represents a critical "turning-point" of world history
given the experience of two world wars./88/ Jaspers
summarized the disillusionment of the European spirit

which followed upon the aftermath of the Second World
War in this way.

> We have no more confidence in
> humanism. But we love it and we wish
> to do everything to preserve it.
> We have no more confidence in
> modern civilisation, in science and
> technique. But we grasp its
> significance for world history, we do
> not wish to give it up, but with all
> our strength to develop it and give it
> a significant form.
> We have no more confidence in the
> society of Germano-Latin nations in
> their political balance of power. But
> we wish to save the idea of a unity of
> independent free European nations.
> We have no more unconditional
> confidence in the Christian churches.
> But we hold fast to them as being the
> most precious vessels of irreplaceable
> tradition./89/

Jaspers characterized the post-war "crisis" by
both changed external and internal conditions.
Externally, Europe and the world have been transformed.
European expansion and colonialization during the past
four centuries has ceased along with emigration.
Space, raw materials, and population now essentially
determine the reality of power. Europe stands in an
intermediary position between the superpowers, while
"the one-time colony comes to be master over
Europe."/90/ Until the end of the nineteeth century
all history had remained Western history. But the
Second World War inaugurated the true beginning of
world history, since the First World War was still a
European war. As a result of communications
technology, the possible "unity of the planet" has
arrived, and thus new perils and opportunites
characterize what is henceforth "a situation of
mankind."/91/

The present "crisis" is also accompanied by an
even more significant inner transformation. With the
Christian conquest of the world at a standstill, "the
absolute certainty of Christianity is no matter of
course."/92/ China and India confront us as autonomous
spiritual entities. They now have the same problem as
we in the West: "how to find in our technical
tradition our new spiritual form."/93/ The radical

43

transformation wrought by technology in daily life has made humanity homeless by forcing both work and society into "the channels of mass-production," and the planet "into a single great factory."/94/ Human existence has come to be _mass_ existence.

Whether understood as an "easily influenced majority" of a given population or the "average in a nation," Jaspers sees "the masses" as decisive for the present historico-political process. Today it is the subject, though ironically more powerless than ever before, who participates in a "mass will" and shapes the course of history. This mass will is guided by the propaganda of leaders who frequently act for profit or power. The danger is that the mass will, as happened in Hitler's Germany, shall fall prey to a party or a tyrannical "Pied Piper" who leads them down the path to the annihilation of freedom./95/ The important question in this situation of mass existence is to what extent the individual can give birth to new beginnings leading to the recovery of authentic humanity. One thing is certain: "the way to the future leads through the individual, through each individual."/96/

Jaspers characterized the present "crisis" situation in 1931 by more than simply mass-rule and the dominion of a technological apparatus which reduces the individual to a mere cog-in-a-wheel. _Traditional values_ have also crumbled. Leadership has given way to efficiency within the system or with the methods of technology. The sanctity of marriage has yielded to license, divorce, and the "technisization" of sexual life which contribute to the disruption of the family. Joy in life and work have given way in the "rationalisation and universalization of the life-order" to dread and anxiety. Even sport, which allows for a healthy "soaring and refreshment," had come to represent something of an _ersatz_-transcendence for both player and spectator alike./97/

Religious authority, community, and tradition have also been transformed by the age of modern science and technology. The "crisis" of religious and sacral authority has profoundly stripped us of an integral part of our inner being. The age manifests a "catastrophic descent to poverty of spirit, of humanity, love and creative energy."/98/ Spiritually, humanity "still lives among stage props left from other times," but they have "ceased to set the stage" for our lives./99/ In the past, authority had its locus on a sacral landscape for China, India, and the West alike.

The new authority of the present has been established through "the organization of technological labour."/100/ Authority is no longer based on a person's substance, but rather on their ability to consume and produce in response to labour's obligation to perform. In such a situation individuals easily yield to violence or scientific superstitions, even as they cease to seek honest refuge in either the Church or philosophical thinking./101/ The present loss of religious authority has broken the link between social conditions and religion. Everyday life and religious belief have given way to a loss of faith among the masses, secularization, and the retreat of faith into privatization./102/

And yet, because humanity is "incapable of living without faith,"/103/ the present crisis is not merely manifested in the decline of traditional faiths. Faith itself has become manifested in cults, narrowly dogmatic and intolerant creeds, demonology, the deification of man, and, most dramatically, nihilism. Nihilism has led in the past two centuries to "pseudo-scientific" total conceptions in Marxism, psychoanalysis, and racial theory. "Simplification" is the defining trait of these many programs of salvation to which substitute faiths attach themselves. Here slogans, universal theories that explain everything, and absolutes hold sway./104/

Finally, ideology is yet another typical manifestation of the dissolution of faith and authority in the present era of crisis.

An ideology is a complex of ideas or notions which represents itself to the thinker as an absolute truth for the interpretation of the world and his situation within it. It leads the thinker to accomplish an act of self-deception for the purpose of justification, obfuscation, evasion, in some sense or other to his own advantage./105/

Self-reflection, of course, the pre-condition of all truthfulness, is derelict in ideological thinking because it prevents the "unmasking" of one's own prejudices. And even worse, when the thinking that "unmasks" becomes itself ideological, as in the case of Marx, Engels, and Freud, authentic self-reflection and truth is invariably lost.

45

Nietzsche and Kierkegaard are farthest from ideological thinking in the present age. They foresaw the "crisis" of modernity better than any other modern thinkers. Both spelled the end of tradition by proclaiming the "death of God" and the death of "Christendom." The affinity of both thinkers for Jaspers lies primarily in their questioning of reason and their recourse to individuality and freedom, to Existenz./106/ Both opposed the reduction of reality to methodical correctness or system-building, and understood authentic knowing as a hermeneutical endeavour. While the small "stream" of thinking which flows from them in the present age is vastly different from that much broader "stream" flowing from the natural sciences, it is by no means less important. Indeed, Jaspers insists that both "streams" must be merged in a "ingenuous synthesis" in the present epoch if truth-- and not ideology-- is to be allowed free movement./107/

Essentially, the struggle between "ideologies" is one in which rational communication and truth is lacking. One simply attacks all views which do not fit with one's own ideology. If Jaspers saw the totalitarianism of Stalin and Hitler as the most insidious forms of political ideology in this century, it must be emphasized that totalitarian ideology cannot be reduced to a specific form. Totalitarian ideology can appear in the future in other forms as well./108/

2.3.1 Present Tendencies:
Socialism, World Unity, and Faith

When Jaspers ventured a "prognostic" forecast for the future of humanity in 1949 with a view to a universal world history,/109/ it rested upon the primary goal of political freedom.

> We speak of political freedom, social freedom, personal freedom, economic freedom--religious freedom, freedom of conscience--freedom of thought, freedom of the press, freedom of assembly, etc. Political freedom occupies the foreground of discussion./110/

The basic positive tendencies of the present, along with their negative counterparts, included the possibilities of socialism versus socio-political and economic oppression through total planning; a new world order versus a totalitarian world empire; and faith versus nihilism. He understood socialism, world order, and faith as "signposts" of the basic questions confronting any meaningful prognosis of the future, and he was convinced that they could converge only in the accomplishment of existential freedom./111/

Jaspers's positive acknowledgement of socialism is often overlooked by those critics who group him with apolitical and asocial forms of existentialism and judge him to be an essentially conservative thinker./112/ In fact, he accords great significance to socialism as "the universal tendency of contemporary mankind toward an organisation of labour and of participation in the products of labour that will make it possible for all men to be free [...] it is the basic trait of our time."/113/ Jaspers does not dispute the demands for all to be supplied with basic human necessities. It is a matter of justice that there be an equal distribution of the burdens of labor and its products. His concern is not with a justification for socialism, but rather with the manner of its implementation; not with the necessity of planning for the needs of all, but with the dangers of total planning.

Nonetheless, it must be admitted that he frequently links the direction of modern socialism to "scientific communism" and Marxism conceived as a total knowledge of the course of history and human affairs, and a skewed self-understanding of science. Marxism sees power in the hands of the dictatorship of the proletariat and planning on the basis of science as the two requirements of its ostensible goal toward the establishment of justice and liberty. But in its claims to need nothing else, Marxism ends up being dogmatic, doctrinal, and ideological.

In his evaluation of power and planning in modern socialism, and in his own positive understanding of the socialist ideal, Jaspers tries to steer a course between the extremes of power as an unchecked violence and planning as total planning. If socialism is to truly "win liberty in justice," then it "must unite with the forces that save man from violence--both from the arbitrary will of the despot and from the [...] masses in temporary majorities."/114/ And just as social and juridical legality must hold violence in check, so too the law must check ad libitum accumulation of capital which makes monopolies possible. Jaspers was opposed to economic monopolies which lead to power over consumers, workers, and employees alike by means of control over the entire labor field. But he was equally opposed to the idea of total planning which is only possible through the agency of the state: "in its planning the State either confines itself to the ordering of free initiative by means of laws, or it embarks itself upon undertakings that bear a monopoly character a priori; in the latter case, the limit is reached when the State, in principle, assumes control of everything in total planning and by unlimited force or power."/115/

Given the extreme possibilities of power as antinomial violence and total planning in the technological age, Jaspers appeals to law as the path between the extremes, and to an encompassing reason as the way of handling the limits of socio-political planning. Positively, this means that the socialist ideal sets itself against individualism as caprice, against capitalism as unchecked private ownership of the means and mode of production, and against liberalism as a form of indifference toward the evils which develop out of the free market interplay of forces. Negatively, there is the corresponding danger that each hypothesis may become absolutized in such a way that the individual is denied all rights, that all private property is abolished, and that planning is transformed into total planning. When this happens, socialism becomes an ideology and the possibilities for political freedom become lost amidst the power necessitated by state total planning./116/

World unity is also essential from the perspective of a universal history. Because communications technology has brought about the unification of the globe, now more than ever before has humanity been united by a single destiny. The pressing question for Jaspers is the direction in which the unitary world order will move, whether toward "world empire" or "world order." In the former instance, world peace is the static peace of despotism, maintained by the use of force, terror, and total planning imposed through censorship and propaganda. In the latter case, world peace is based on majority decision and legal negotiation in the light of the natural law,/117/ with sovereignty based on that of humanity as a whole and the relinquishment of the veto and force. Here the old concept of the State gives way not to the idea of a "World State," but to a federalism grounded upon the idea of world citizenship.

Jaspers makes an analogy between the present historical situation and the end of the axial age in which creative political activity gave way to extended empires and despotic forces.

> All the phenomena of the present have the appearance of a preparatory struggle for the points of departure of the final battle for the planetary order. Contemporary world politics are seeking a basis for the ultimate settlement, whether this is to be reached by military or peaceful means [...] the present appears as a transition to this final planetary order, even if the exact opposite develops first: e.g. the radical interruption of communication on earth for the majority of people by totalitarian regimes./118/

He understands the present historical situation as one in which humanity is again to pass critically through the formative circumstances which confronted the ancient high civilizations with their technological planning and organization. "Possibly," he speculated just a few years before his death, "mankind will pass through such gigantic organizations to reach a new Axis period, still very far away from us, still invisible and as yet unimaginable to us, an Axis period of development into the true, the real human being."/119/

Finally, given the loss of traditional moorings in the substance of a common faith, humanity is confronted anew by the question of "the authentic origin of faith in man;" the alternative is either nihilism or love. But the specific question of the future, "which conditions and includes everything, is how and what man will believe."/120/ While we shall have more to say about faith below, suffice it to say here that faith is essential to Jaspers's foundational thinking. Faith cannot be discussed in the same terms as socialism and world unity because it is neither a matter of the goal of the will or of a thinking that manifests itself in purposes and programs.

> [Faith] is the [Encompassing] by which socialism, political freedom, and world order must be borne along their path, because it is from faith alone that they receive their meaning.

Without faith there will be no guidance
from the fountainhead of humanity, but
a falling prey to that which has been
thought, conjectured and imagined, to
doctrines, and then, as a result, to
chaos and ruin./121/

* * *

For Jaspers, then, the present historical
situation demands humanity's "conversion" to a
universal communication and faith upon which freedom,
socialism, and world order might be grounded, and thus
human annihilation and political totalitarianism
avoided. He once wrote that the thesis of his
philosophizing is simply that "the individual cannot
become human by himself. Self-being is only real in
communication with another self-being."/122/ He
believes it is possible to gain a historical foundation
common to all humankind by appropriating the facts of
the axial age. The age stands as a challenge to
"boundless communication," and can provide an assurance
for the future in an age where the great question is
whether or not the coming course of historical
evolution will indeed remain open./123/

1. FM, p.4; AB, p.22.
2. EH, p.35.
3. GBA, p.375: "Eine Welt, in der die Treulosigkeiten wachsen, die Ehescheidungen sich ständig vermehren, ein in Augenblickssensationen sich zerstreuendes Leben den Vorrang hat vor dem sich konzentrierenden Leben in geschichtlicher Kontinuität, vieles Niederträchtige heimlich für selbstverständlich erachtet wird, die sogenannte realistische Betrachtung für den Gipfel illusionsloser Vernunft gilt, da sind solche Schrecken wie die Atombombe nur eine Konsequenz und damit ein blosses Symptom."
4. MMA, p.83.
5. Karl Jaspers, "Our Future and Goethe," in EH, pp.35-6.
6. Karl Jaspers, "Premises and Possibilities of a New Humanism," in EH, p.74, and OGH, pp.147-50.
7. Hannah Arendt, "Jaspers As Citizen of the World," in Schilpp, p.541.
8. PAT, pp.81-84.
9. PAT, p.82.
10. In this chapter we are following Jaspers's philosophy of history as set forth in MMA, PHT I, pp.204-226, 284-294, PHT II, pp.104-133, 342-357, PHT III, pp.159-161, OGH, WW, pp.96-109, 132-144, GPT I, pp.3-6, and PFR, pp.186-196.
11. PHT II, p.346; PH II, p.397: "Wissen, als Wissen methodisch-kritisch geprüft, ist Historie als Wissenschaft; verwandelt in existentielles Selbstverständnis, ist es Geschichtsphilosophie."
12. Cf., OGH, pp.xiii-xvi, 219, 264-5. WW, p.96-109.
13. PHT II, p.104-105; PH II, p.119.
14. PHT II, p.121.
15. WW, p.109.
16. PHT II, p.122. Jaspers's has a limited notion of future unlike other contemporary thinkers such as Heideggar, Sartre, Teilhard de Chardin, Bloch, Moltmann, and Rahner, for whom the future designates the primary dimension of time and the ground of meaning in the present. On this point, see Norbert J. Rigali, "A New Axis: Karl Jaspers' Philosophy of History," International Philosophical Quarterly 10 (1970), p.445, n.34. One might add political theologian, Johann B. Metz to Rigali's grouping. For Metz-- at least the early Metz-- past and present are wrongly conceived without reference to the future. Cf., Metz, "The Responsibility of Hope," Philosophy

<u>Today</u>, X (Winter, 1966), p.282. In his more recent attempt to work out a practical fundamental theology, however, Metz has emphasized past and present "memory," "narrative," and "solidarity" as categories of critique against "post-theological" theories of history and society. In contrast to Jaspers's emphasis on communication, he emphasizes <u>justice</u>. The problem Metz sees with both liberal and Marxist views of history is that "the dialectical version of these theories remains firmly tied to the historical unity of mankind, but gives a relative value to the idea of universal justice that qualifies this unity. It does so by applying this universal justice exclusively to future generations and not to the dead and the sacrifices of history." <u>Faith in History and Society: Toward a Practical Fundamental Theology</u>, trans. by David Smith (New York: Seabury Press, 1980), p.75.

17. OGH, p.262-63.
18. PHT II, p.348.
19. PFR, pp.50-51.
20. It would be erroneous to suggest that Jaspers's thesis of an axial age is, itself, an empirical fact. Rather, it "rests" on empirical facts. OGH, p.10. For Jaspers's definition of an empirical "fact" and the bounds of its cogency, see, PHT I, p.124.
21. OGH, pp.1-21, 51-60. For a critical treatment of Jaspers's axial age thesis which brings together much of the contemporary Christian criticism, see, Gabriel Simon, SS.CC., <u>Die Achse der Weltgeschichte nach Karl Jaspers</u>, <u>Analecta Gregoriana</u> 147 (Roma: Libreria Editrice dell'Università Gregoriana, 1965).
22. Cf., OGH, pp.19,21.
23. NC, p.61.
24. NC, p.51-2.
25. NC, p.55.
26. WW, p.99.
27. OGH, p.2. Cf., WW, pp.99-100.
28. OGH, p.2.
29. Karl Jaspers, "The Axial Age of Human History," trans. by Ralph Manheim, <u>Commentary</u> 6 (1948), p.432.
30. GPT I, pp.15-96.
31. Jaspers, "The Axial Age of Human History," p.432.
32. <u>Ibid</u>., p.433.
33. WW, p.98.
34. Cf., OGH, p.45-6.
35. WW, p.98.
36. OGH, p.61.
37. PHT I, p.120.

38. Karl Jaspers, "Is Science Evil?," trans. by Irving Kristol, <u>Commentary</u> 9 (March 1950), p.230.
39. For Jaspers's understanding of the age of modern science and technology upon which our present analysis draws, see MMA, p.144ff, OGH, p.83ff, UZG, p.83ff, WW, p.150ff, PGO, pp.95-103, PFR, p.50ff, and LDW, p.125ff. Also, Karl Jaspers, "Philosophy and Science," trans. by Ralph Manheim, <u>Partisan Review</u> 16 (1949), p.873ff; "Is Science Evil?," p.230ff.; and "Truth and Science," trans. by Robert E. Wood, <u>Philosophy Today</u> 6 (Fall 1962), p.200ff.
40. Karl Jaspers, "Is Science Evil?," p.230.
41. PFR, p.50.
42. OGH, p.84.
43. PFR, p.52.
44. Karl Jaspers, "Philosophy and Science," p.874.
45. PHT I, p.177.
46. Cf., PHT I, p.187.
47. OGH, pp.86-87.
48. LDW, p.133.
49. OGH, p.87.
50. PGO, p.95, PFR, p.50. In the OGH, pp.87-88, Jaspers speaks simply of the present age's "scientific attitude." Cf., UZG, "wissenschaftliche Haltung," p.116.
51. Karl Jaspers, "Philosophy and Science," p.875.
52. On the three domains of science for Jaspers, we are following PHT I, pp.68-71, 99-127; PH I, pp.28-31, 61-93. See also, Chapter Five.
53. PHT I, p.69; PH II, pp.29-30: "Philosophische Weltorientierung fasst nicht letze Ergebnisse der Wissenschaften zu einem einheitlichen Weltbild zusammen, sondern zeigt die Unmöglichkeit eines solchen gültigen Weltbildes als des einen und absoluten; sie sucht die Fragwürdigkeiten der faktischen Weltorientierung."
54. PHT I, p.121.
55. Cf., PHT I, pp.121-122.
56. PHT I, p.222.
57. PHT I, p.122.
58. PHT I, p.123.
59. Sebastian Samay, <u>Reason Revisited</u>, p.89.
60. PHT I, p.123; PH I, p.89.
61. PHT I, p.124.
62. PHT I, p.123.
63. PHT I, p.125.
64. Charles Wallraff, <u>Karl Jaspers: An Introduction to His Philosophy</u> (Princeton, New Jersey: Princeton University Press, 1970), p.49.
65. PHT I, p.126.

66. Cf., GPT I, p.292.
67. Cf., Karl Jaspers, "Is Science Evil?," p.231. This position is close to the Second Vatican Council's Pastoral Constitution on the Church in the Modern World, Gaudium et Spes (para.57), which acknowledges both the limit and positive value of science and technology within its treatment of the relationship between faith and culture. Walter M. Abbot, S.J., ed., The Documents of Vatican II (New York: Guild Press, 1966), pp.263-264.
68. Cf., MMA, pp.15-23. Also, OGH, pp.88-93.
69. OGH, p.90.
70. Karl Jaspers, "Is Science Evil?," p.232.
71. For Ricoeur, of course, psychoanalysis is the paradigm of such a hermeneutic. But a "hermeneutic of suspicion" seems equally applicable to the mental forces which gave birth to modern science out of Jaspers's "Biblical religion." Paul Ricoeur, Hermeneutics and the Human Sciences, ed. and trans. by John B. Thompson (Cambridge: Cambridge University Press and Paris: Editions de la Maison des Sciences de l'Homme, 1981) p.34.
72. Karl Jaspers, "Is Science Evil?," p.233.
73. PHT I, pp.126-7.
74. PFR, p.51.
75. This is the fundamental question which guides Jaspers's reflection in the OGH, pp.96-125.
76. OGH, p.100.
77. Technological, cultivational and educational, and political action constitute the three types of "purposive" action limited by theoretical world orientation. PHT I, pp.145-9.
78. PHT I, p.148.
79. Goethe, Niebuhr, Talleyrand, Tocqueville, Stendahl, and Ranke are all authors who exercised a kulturkritik of a declining Europe. Jaspers synonymously refers to this criticism as the "epochal consciousness." Karl Jaspers, "Our Future and Goethe," in EH, p.45. Cf., MMA, p.11.
80. Karl Jaspers, "Is Europe's Culture Finished?," trans. by E. B. Ashton, Commentary 4 (1947), p.519; MMA, p.83; EH, pp.35-6. In this section we must acknowledge our indebtedness to the work of John F. Kane, Pluralism and Truth in Religion: Karl Jaspers on Existential Truth. AAR Dissertation Series, No.33. Ed. by H. Ganse Little, Jr. (Chico, Ca.: Scholars Press, 1981).
81. PHT II, p.178.

82. MMA, p.33. On the Greek origins of the existential metaphors of navigation, shipwreck, and spectator, see Hannah Arendt, The Life of the Mind, one-volume edition, vol.I, "Thinking" (New York and London: Harcourt Brace Jovanovich, 1971), pp. 129-141, and p.233, n.39.
83. PHT II, pp.177-8.
84. EH, p.66.
85. Cf., MMA, p.24.
86. As Jaspers himself admitted, Die geistige Situation der Zeit "needed the Philosophie as its foundation," PAT, p.60. He did not want Die geistige Situation der Zeit, which was written in 1930, to appear before his Philosophie, however, since it had been nearly a decade since he had published anything prior to this foundational work, MMA, p.v. Even though Jaspers's cultural criticism in 1930 is properly tied to his philosophy with its strict limitations on absolute knowledge and total system building, critics nonetheless fault him for trying to encompass too much in this early diagnosis of the present situation. See, e.g., Jürgen Habermas, ed., Observations on "The Spiritual Situation of the Age:" Contemporary German Perspectives, trans. by Andrew Buchwalter (Cambridge, Massachusetts and London, England: MIT Press, 1984), p.3.
87. MMA, p.29. Having said this, we must recall that in his 1950 Vernunft und Widervernunft in unserer Zeit, Jaspers announced his preference for describing his work as Philosophie des Vernunft rather than as Existenz philosophy. RAT, pp.63-64. Cf., Jaspers's "Reply to My Critics," in Schilpp, p.238.
88. OGH, p.140. Cf., WW, p.24.
89. ES, p.29-30.
90. Jaspers, "Is Europe's Culture Finished?", p.518. Cf., OGH, pp.76-7.
91. OGH, p.127.
92. Jaspers, "Is Europe's Culture Finished?", p.519.
93. ES, p.47.
94. OGH, p.98.
95. OGH, p.130. Cf. MMA, pp.54-8, 108.
96. ES, p.51. Jaspers's specific complaint over the rise of mass society and his emphasis upon the importance of the individual has also not gone without recent criticism. See, Ulrich Preuss, "Political Concepts of Order for Mass Society," in Jürgen Habermas, ed., Observations on "The Spiritual Situation of the Age," pp.89-90.

97.   MMA, pp.54-71.
98.   OGH, p.96-7.
99.   EH, p.66.
100. PFR, p.29.
101. Cf., PFR, p.30.
102. Cf., ES, p.30.
103. MMA, p.152.
104. Cf., OGH, p.134.
105. OGH, p.132.
106. See, Karl Jaspers, "The Origin of the Contemporary Philosophical Situation," in RE, pp.38-9, 48-50.
107. Karl Jaspers, "Nietzsche and the Present," trans. by Ralph Manheim, Partisan Review XIX (1952), p.29.
108. Karl Jaspers, "The Fight Against Totalitarianism," in PWT, p.68,87.
109. OGH, pp.141-213.
110. OGH, p.153.
111. Cf., OGH, p.152 and 172ff. Jaspers's conceptualization of these three tendencies had close affinities with the three ideals of the French Revolution, i.e., "fraternité" (world order), "égalité" (socialism), and "liberté" (faith). See, Godfrey Carr, Karl Jaspers as an Intellectual Critic, p.97.
112. This point has been forcefully argued by Carr, Karl Jaspers as an Intellectual Critic, p.117, in response to the critiques by Theodor Hartwig, Der Existentialismus (Vienna, 1948) and Georg Lukacs, Existentialisme ou Marxisme?, trans. by E. Kelemen (Paris, 1961).
113. OGH, p.172.
114. OGH, p.174.
115. OGH, p.175.
116. Cf., OGH, p.190.
117. Cf., OGH, p.198: "Natural law [...] is the foundation of the rights of man, and in world order would erect an authority that would also protect the individual person from acts of violence on the part of his State, through the possibility of effective legal action under the sovereignty of mankind."
118. OGH, p.196.
119. Karl Jaspers, "The History of Mankind as Seen by the Philosopher," Universitas 6 (1964), p.216.
120. OGH, p.152, 214.
121. OGH, p.214.
122. OMP, p.174.
123. Cf., OGH, p.25, RE, p.49, and FM, p.285.

3.0 INTRODUCTION

In the previous chapter we situated Jaspers's understanding of the nuclear problem in the light of the historical horizons of present and past history, since he saw the terror of the atom bomb as merely a consequence and "symptom" of an age in desperate need of new foundations for a universal basis of communication. While Jaspers states that his philosophical foundations remained "in the background" after his turn to historico-political thinking in 1945, his "foundational thinking" (Grundgedanken) nonetheless informs all of his subsequent thinking, particularly his analysis of the nuclear problem during the decade of the Cold War. This is why his method of approach to the nuclear problem and his thesis concerning human "conversion" in his book on the atom bomb is incomprehensible apart from his earlier epistemological foundations, i.e., his philosophy of "the Encompassing" (Das Umgreifende)/1/ or "basic philosophical knowledge" (philosophische Grundewissen)./2/

The aim of this chapter, therefore, is to analyze that foundational thinking or "open horizon" within which Jaspers both approached the nuclear problem and illuminated the needed "conversion" in science, morality and politics, and religion during the decade of the Cold War. The role of "conversion" within each domain remains obscure and dark unless first grounded within the overall movement of his philosophizing. Because he himself has pointed out that all of his philosophical work, and not only his seminal Philosophie and Von der Wahrheit, reflects an attempt to think systematically upon the basic questions of the human situation,/3/ the present analysis cannot be confined exclusively to these writings./4/

The attempt to formally illuminate Jaspers's foundational thinking, however, faces from the outset a challenge related to stylistic and methodological difficulties./5/ Fr. Xavier Tilliette speaks metaphorically of Jaspers's philosophizing as tantamount to a journey down a complex winding river which bends back upon itself and gains force from the tributaries of thought which feed it, but which never itself ends./6/ We prefer to think of his method as an extended philosophical koan, since his language takes back the very assertions he posits, while various antinomies shake one from a dogmatic slumber into a "new" mode of thinking and doing. The effect of his style leaves one with a sense of relativity or of being "suspended" (<u>schwebend</u>) in thought./7/ In the <u>Philosophie</u>, dialectic takes on an elaborate form in the philosopher's campaign against positivist, philosophical, and theological forms of <u>Verfestigung</u>, i.e., "fixation, stabilization, consolidation."/8/ Thus it is not surprising that Jaspers has expressed a qualified regret that even respected interpreters and critics like Mikel Dufrenne and Paul Ricoeur have unwittingly turned his philosophizing into an ossified, philosophical doctrine./9/

The <u>koan</u> like nature of his philosophizing is evident when he speaks of bringing philosophical contents to mind only "to melt down the objectivities and make them vanish;" or when he states that "the formal precision of any philosophically substantial communication is the clarity of an object that dissolves again. We are indeed building by tearing down what we have built."/10/ If there is a redeeming factor in this paradoxical method, it is that he attempts to set forth his thinking on a methodical course. But while his philosophizing seeks to provide a systematic and encompassing framework for contemporary reflection on the human situation and a basis for universal communication, he categorically rejects the possibility of ontology. Since Kant, he feels there can be no "system" of ontology./11/ In contrast, his philosophical work is a systematically connected but open structure, an "<u>offenhaltende</u> <u>Systematik</u>."/12/

We have spoken of Jaspers's "philosophizing" rather than philosophy in order to convey the primacy of openness and movement for his foundational thinking. The real challenge, however, is to <u>enter</u> <u>into</u> <u>this</u> <u>movement</u> in order to understand its meaning./13/ For the freedom of philosophizing lies for Jaspers in thought itself as a form of self-conscious "inner action."/14/ To use his striking metaphor, philosophical flight only succeeds if the objective "wing" of philosophical content beats along with the subjective "wing" of existential appropriation. "Fulfilled meaning" is grounded from philosophical flight without the beating of both "wings."/15/

We can offer no adequate analysis of either the form or content of his foundational thinking, then, because as a movement of thought it can never be reduced to a set of doctrines or sterile concepts. We can only hope to set forth an example by touching upon its various "horizons"/16/ and structural principle of "transcending" in a broad fashion. For while there are basic ideas, concepts, and thought structures that are necessary for philosophizing, its real "point of reference lies not in the doctrine itself, but in the possible goal of the motion."/17/ This goal is communicated indirectly, through various systematizations of <u>Grundgedanken</u>. While he speaks variously of this goal as redirecting or "converting" us to a realization of universal communication, truth, freedom, philosophical faith, and ultimately Transcendence, he defines it in the <u>Philosophy</u> as being "to recognize, to train, to buttress an inner posture that will shape our judgment <u>in</u> <u>concrete</u> <u>situations</u>-- not in any calculable fashion, but as the proof of possible Existenz that has become sure of itself."/18/

Because Jaspers views his foundational thinking as a movement of striving to clarify a whole which is obscure and which is initiated by the "basic questions" we raise, we will begin by looking at the questions he appropriated from Kant and transformed into the basis for his own thinking in the present age (3.1). In turn, we will follow the point of departure of his foundational thinking from within the "fundamental situation" of human consciousness (3.2). It is out of this fundamental cognitive situation within the subject-object dichotomy that Jaspers raises the question of the Encompassing (3.3), explicates its various modes (3.4), and illuminates the role of philosophical faith as a barrier against any dogmatic reification of truth (3.5).

3.1 THE <u>KANTIAN</u> BACKGROUND OF <u>JASPERS'S</u> <u>BASIC</u> QUESTIONS

Jaspers acknowledges that "the basic questions" were formulated by Kant with "moving simplicity: What can I know? What shall I do? What may I hope? What is man?"/19/ These questions bespeak the scope of Kant's questioning and reflect the searching of reason in its entirety through the critical analysis of its employment in the experience of objective valid knowledge, the self, morality and religion. Jaspers stands directly with Kant insofar as Kant understood the method of philosophical questioning as allowing one to differentiate and think through the successive parts of a whole which is already contained, as an idea, in that which thinking initially searches after and in turn builds upon. As for Jaspers, more essential than the object of thought is the direction in which thinking moves. For Kant this was an anthropocentric move. The question, "What is man?", encompassed his other three questions, since it is homo-- and not God or world-- who mediates the search for meaning and truth. For Kant, "man is the area in which all the rest become reality for us," Jaspers writes, adding that "Being remains the essential [question], but man can approach and apprehend it only through his existence as a man."/20/

Jaspers's transformation of Kant's basic questions is wrought by what he perceives as the kind of life the present situation has produced: (1) a life where science and its consequences in technology now determine the fate of the world (hence the question, "What can we know in the sciences?"); (2) where human masses are linked by a technologically functioning organization, but not by their own "historicity" (hence the question, "How shall we realize the most profound communication?"); and (3), a life where the limits of scientific knowledge and the de facto failures in human communication have raised anew the question of truth's accessibility and meaning (hence the question, "How can truth become accessible to us?")./21/ His philosophizing subsumes Kants's four basic questions within these three, only to elaborate them in turn.

It would be wrong to suggest that the present situation is the sole determinant of Jaspers's transformation of the Kantian basic questions. For he critiques Kant's philosophy on the basis of three essentially epistemological grounds.

> (1) Kant's philosophy lays claim to the character of a science possessing the same universal validity as mathematics and physics. (2) It claims to provide fundamental a priori insights in regard to the material of the natural sciences and compelling insights in regard to the content of the ethical law (Metaphysics of Nature and Metaphysics of Morals) [...] (3) Kant's philosophy lays claim to systematic completeness; it is permeated with a multiplicity of systematizations./22/

While Jaspers's critique of Kant is beyond the scope of our present concern, a few comments are in order here./23/ First, Jaspers questions Kant's claim that philosophy had entered the "sure path of science." Kant confused the proper domains of science and philosophy by claiming for his philosophy what he attributed to be the essence of science, i.e., apodictic certainty. He lived in an age where thinking was regarded as science as long as it was methodical. To be sure, Kant's transcendental philosophizing is methodical, but "it is not a science like other sciences, because it has no object and because the method itself cannot be clearly defined."/24/ What is compelling, if not scientifically cogent, in Kant's philosophizing is the way his transcendental method leads the understanding to a "compelling failure." Occasioned by Kant's intricate methods of approaches and modes of representation, this failure delivers one from the phenomenality of existence, and forms the basis of an awareness of being experienced as "intellectual illumination."

Secondly, Jaspers objects to Kant's claim of having had universal a priori insight into the natural sciences (The Metaphysics of Nature) and ethics (The Metaphysics of Morals). These writings were indeed "doctrine" in the Kantian sense of an "elaboration of concrete and definite a priori knowledge of nature and morality" in contrast to his earlier Critiques./25/ Jaspers opposes Kant's doctrinal endeavour insofar as Kant appeals to the "I think" of transcendental apperception as an adequate source for the clarification of the relations between a priori and a posteriori judgments. While Kant's "doctrine" did correctly admit that "a priori forms are not possible without a posteriori factors and vice versa," Jaspers believes Kant's approach becomes questionable when he tries to gloss over the dividing line between these judgments.

> If Kant looks upon the "I think" of transcendental apperception as the condition of the possibility of all objects, it means that for him the a priori is, in all knowledge, distinct from the a posteriori. But when he goes on to derive from the "I think," first the categories, then the principles of knowledge of nature, two fundamentally different trains of thought become intertwined: first, the

elucidation (in the Transcendental
Deduction) of the phenomenon of
objectivity through the objective
representations which serve as guiding
threads and the operations which serve
as means of clarification; and second,
the supposedly unequivocal and
universally valid derivation of
definite principles governing our
knowledge of nature./26/

Jaspers acknowledges that "as an elucidation of
the fundamental situation of consciousness as such and
of its modes of objectivity" the transcendental method
indeed carries philosophical "conviction." But Kant's
thesis that all objectivity is conditioned by
subjective forms of the "I think" provides no grounding
for the derivation and systematization of the modes of
experience. "Kant himself says:", and here Jaspers
cites Kant without quotation as he is wont to do, "We
discern the a priori forms not in experience, but on
the occasion of experience." Commenting on this
proposition Jaspers adds that "we may infer, as Kant
did not, that future experience may provide the
occasion on which new a priori forms will become known.
Where the occasion of experience has not yet occurred,
the a priori can in fact not yet be known."/27/

Kant's transcendental method becomes uncritical
when it loses sight of the reciprocal relation between
a priori and a posteriori: "Just as there is an a
priori in every empirical concept, so, in the first
category of 'I think' there is also an a posteriori.
The first steps from the 'I think' to the concrete and
particular are not known solely through the
self-elucidation of reason, but are occasioned by
experience and then elaborated as pure a priori
forms."/28/ By interpreting the relation of a priori
forms and a posteriori factors in this fashion, Jaspers
makes room for a continuous growth of knowledge, one
not limited to the Newtonian physics of Kant's day.

Thirdly, Jaspers critiques Kant for claiming that
the scientific character of his philosophy represented
a "system." To be sure, there are systematizations and
arrangements that serve as methods of exposition in
Kant's thought, but "'the system'" is never to be
found, even if "Kant himself did not recognize" this.
He argues Kant went wrong in assuming that his "system
of reason" had obtained a complete whole. But none of
his explicit systematizations captures reason. Jaspers
admits that "the Idea of system, around which Kant
seems to circle," remains a legitimate, albeit endless

62

task. "Even in the transcendental elucidation of reason as a whole, the Idea, in every one of its forms, leads only to a provisional schema. It hovers, it circles, it guides us aloft and into the depths. But it cannot be fixated in any perfect form."/29/ There could not be a more perfect description of Jaspers's own method as an "open horizon."

In sum, then, Kants's question "What can I know?" has become both more concrete and more inexorable for Jaspers. And Kant's query, "What shall I do?', in an age characterized by "mass existence" can no longer be answered by an appeal to the categorical imperative alone. It must be complemented, Jaspers believes, by the grounding of every ethical act in communication: "The truth of generally valid laws for my actions is conditioned by the communication in which I act."/30/

The limits of our ability to know the world and ourselves in totality, as well as the limits of communication ("something is lacking even when it succeeds") also raises the question of truth's accessibility. Too often the failure of absolute knowledge of world and self causes, in Jaspers's words, "a confusion in which Being and truth vanish;" in turn and in vain, "a way out is sought either in obedience to rules and regulations or in thoughtlessness."/31/ Taking truth to be more than mere correctness in the sciences, Jaspers seeks the way to the grasp of truth via the Encompassing, within which various forms of truth can be differentiated without ever reifying it as absolute.

It is the basic impulses for knowledge, communication, and truth which provide the impetus for Jaspers's method. But these fundamental drives are not all. Through them we reach only "the path of searching" and not the primary aims of this searching itself, which is ultimately "man and Transcendence," the soul and Deity./32/ Thus Jaspers pushes Kant's last question "What is Man?" forward, now taking precedence over the question "What may I hope?" The changed order is not arbitrary. It would seem to reflect his radical transcendental humanism, especially when he writes, echoing Kant, "in the world, man alone is the reality which is accessible [...] the place at which and through which everything that is real exists for us at all."/33/

If Jaspers situates Kant's question "What is man?" before the question "What may I hope?", he also extends the question of humanity to ask directly "whether and what Transcendence (Deity) [Gottheit] is." For "if the Deity is, then all hope is possible."/34/ Although he repeatedly warns against any total objectification of God or Transcendence, he argues that the proposition, "Transcendence alone is the real Being", is a meaningful one insofar as it arises at the limits of our knowledge of world and self, and from the idea of hope itself. Our approach to the Deity is always mediated in the world concretely or incarnationally. It is wrong to separate the question about man from the question about Transcendence.

> Although in the world only man is reality for us, that does not preclude that precisely the quest for man leads to Transcendence. That the Deity alone is truly reality does not preclude that his reality is accessible to us only in the world; as it were, as an image in the mirror of man, because something of the Deity must be in him for him to be able to respond to the Deity. Thus the theme of philosophy is oriented, in polar alternation, in two directions: deum et animam scire cupio [I desire knowledge of God and the soul]."/35/

Jaspers has thus transformed Kant's famous four questions into the question of the meaning of science, communication, truth, humanity, and Transcendence. These are the areas with which his foundational thinking is ultimately concerned. As was the case for Kant, the question of being is still the essential one for Jaspers, but it can now only be approached through the fundamental situation of human existence.

3.2 "PHILOSOPHIZING STARTS WITH OUR SITUATION"

Jaspers tells us at the outset of his Philosophy that we do not begin at the beginning when, in the search for that which lies at the base of all that exists, we begin with the questions, "'What is Being?' or 'Why is anything at all? Why not nothing?' or 'Who am I?' or 'What do I really want?'" These questions arise first and foremost from the fundamental situation in which we find ourselves: "philosophizing starts with our situation."/36/ To be sure, he is interested in the formal question of being, but he retraces his steps to show us how he arrived at the question in the first place. The question of being is basic to philosophy but it is not our first question because philosophizing is not our first activity. We do not start out as metaphysicians. We move, rather, through a series of changes in our consciousness from basic human existence to that being which we can come to grasp as an awareness of Transcendence.

Insofar as he begins his philosophizing from within his perception of the fundamental situation of human existence, he bears methodological similarity to contemporary theologians of liberation for whom, generally, every formulation of a problem is made possible by previous human experience. In their case, however, they begin with the experience of massive poverty, oppression, and human suffering, while Jaspers begins with the cognitive situation of human consciousness within the subject-object dichotomy./37/

Jaspers asserts that answers to the question, "What is Being?," have most frequently reduced being to some form of objectivity, i.e., either as "objective being" (<u>Objektsein</u>), "subjective being" (<u>Ichsein</u>), or "being-in-itself" (<u>Ansichsein</u>)./38/ We go astray when we identify these formal concepts with absolute Being. The division does not give us three kinds of being that exist side-by-side, but rather "three inseparable poles of the being I find myself in."/39/ These poles are merely "modes" of being which must be differentiated from each other, which complement each other, but are not the source of being. Whatever "I" experience as being, this being is the appearance of being and not being-in-itself. The importance of the first person singular in the philosophizing process is a premise for Jaspers that cannot be overstated. As Oswald Schrag has pointed out, no one has truly begun to philosophize unless he or she philosophizes about him or herself. Philosophizing is only fully alive when it is personal./40/

As noted briefly in the Introduction, the questions we raise about existence grow fundamentally out of that situation in which we find ourselves. Inevitably, every interpretation is given orientation by some existential or social interest. The important thing is to make one's interest or valuation as conscious as possible. If not, we tend to fall back into ideological positions that absolutize images and interpretations deriving from a given cultural framework. The images and interpretations will be petrified and put forth as valid for all places and ages. Hence the limit of our own present situation.

Awakened within our situation by the possibility of human self-destruction and the immoral costs of militarism when so many suffer poverty and disease, we are challenged to search anew for being with all our powers. We perceive the nuclear arms race as a situation and motion that keeps transforming us along with itself. We concern ourselves with things and doubt if they matter. Children and adolescents tell us of their fears of nuclear war, and of not having a world in which to grow-up./41/ For others, young and old alike, the situation of our lives has become characterized by what Dr. Robert J. Lifton has called the "double life."/42/ Our lives move between two poles: from periods of "psychic numbing" in which we numb ourselves to the possibility of self-annihilation and the effects of global militarism upon the poor and oppressed, to seeking avenues of empowerment and action, channels through which the nuclear boundary might be known, acted upon, and overcome.

We attempt to find generally valid answers as to why we are in this situation and not another. We seek objective knowledge of the nuclear dilemma by orienting ourselves in a world of objective historical, political, scientific, economic, philosophical, ethical, or religious data. We are either tempted to reduce our knowledge of the nuclear situation to one of these aspects alone, or our "world orientation" advances endlessly in the direction of being manifested in the various complexities of the problem. Though we think we have grasped the situation, there is always more to it than that which meets our "objective" eye. But assuming for a moment that our inquiry into the problematical nature of the situation helps us find the answer we seek, what is actually taking place? What do we tend to do with the response?

Jaspers would say that when we become preoccupied with plans and "solutions" to problems in a given situation we tend to forget ourselves by turning ourselves into an object amidst the many objects that present themselves to our consciousness. The turn toward the objective is deceptive because we lose sight of our own possible freedom and subjectivity. But once we start questioning the objectivity we had taken hold of, we begin to see ourselves in the same situation all over again, but now changed through time. He writes of this form of existential conscientization: "I remain between beginning and end, fearful of nonexistence, unless I take hold, decide, and thus dare to be myself. For in awakening to myself I have a twofold experience:

in my situation 'the other'-- all that is not I, all
that is given and happens without me-- is as real and
resistant as I myself, in choosing and taking hold, am
real and free."/43/ Formally, it is only when we fail
in our search for "intrinsic being" within our
situation that we truly begin to philosophize. But now
the search for being becomes philosophizing on the
ground of "possible Existenz," and its method is
"transcending."/44/

To philosophize on the ground of possible Existenz
within the nuclear situation is first to get behind its
mere objectivity as a historical, socio-political, and
military reality. As we shall see more clearly in the
next chapter, Jaspers understands the historical
situation in terms of the the twin possibilities of
annihilation and totalitarianism. Formally, however,
he approaches humanity's "fundamental human situation"
in terms of human consciousness. Even the nuclear
problem is real only insofar as it appears in its
phenomenality; to analyze the problem foundationally,
therefore, we must first analyze human consciousness in
terms of the subject-object dichotomy./45/

3.3 THE SUBJECT-OBJECT DICHOTOMY
AND THE QUESTION OF THE ENCOMPASSING

Following Kant, Jaspers defines the basic
condition of our conscious existence as the
subject-object "split" (Spaltung) or dichotomy, whose
concept and reality is central to his foundational
thinking:

> The thing that we think, of which
> we speak, is always something other
> than ourselves, it is the object toward
> which we as subject are oriented. If
> we make ourselves into the object of
> our thinking, we ourselves become as it
> were the Other, and yet at the same
> time we remain a thinking I, which
> thinks about itself but cannot aptly be
> thought as an object because it
> determines the objectness of all
> objects. We call this basic condition
> of our thinking the subject-object
> dichotomy [....]

> I either construe the one and only
> being as being-in-itself, without
> noticing that I am making it an object

for myself in the process-- or I
construe it as this object of mine,
forgetting in this phenomenal
transformation [Verwandlung] of all
being that in objectiveness there must
be something which appears, and
something it appears to-- or I construe
it as subjective being, with myself as
ultimate reality, without realizing
that I can never be otherwise than in a
situation, conscious of objects and
searching for being-in-itself./46/

It takes "the basic philosophical operation" to
release us from the shackels of the subject-object
dichotomy. He gives us both a name for the operation
by which we come to an awareness of the idea of the
Encompassing, as well as a preliminary "definition" of
that Encompassing which defies definition when he
states:
The fundamental philosophical
operation at all times is, more or less
consciously, to transcend towards that
out of which the objective as well as
the thinking of the subject intending
the objective arises. What is neither
object nor act of thinking (subject),
but contains both within itself, I have
called the Encompassing./47/

While Jaspers understands the Encompassing as
neither subject nor object, he sees it as present
through subject and object as an inexhaustible depth
which repeatedly transcends both in the cognitive
"conversion" initiated through the basic philosophical
operation. This operation ascertains the Encompassing
by repeatedly transcending the object, yet always
within an object-thinking that remains inevitable.
Standing within the subject-object split, in which we
aim at objects and are tied to them, this operation
works a "turn about" [Umwendung] into an encompassing
that is neither subject nor object, but which comprises
both. And when our thinking inevitably turns the
Encompassing into an object, "philosophical sense"
instantly compels it to turn back to
non-objectiveness./48/

The question of the Encompassing follows from our
fundamental situation within the subject-object
dichotomy, from the fact that we always live and think
within an encompassing horizon that is essentially
surrounded by another horizon.

68

We always live and think within a
horizon. But the very fact that it is
a horizon indicates something further
which again surrounds the given
horizon. From this situation arises
the question about the Encompassing.
The Encompassing is not a horizon
within which every determinate mode of
Being and truth emerges for us, but
rather that within which every
particular horizon is enclosed as in
something absolutely comprehensive
which is no longer visible as a horizon
at all./49/

To be sure, Jaspers philosophizes about
"being-in-itself" (Ansichsein), but this is said to be
appropriated only through the indirect communication of
the philosophical task as a whole./50/ As a philosophy
of the Encompassing, his foundational thinking is a
receptive and non-objective illumination of the whole
of being in its various modes and relations. But it is
not an objective articulation of being in a finished or
stable form. Thus he speaks of his philosophy as
"periechontology" rather than ontology./51/ Commenting
on the fundamental difference between the two, Gerhard
Knauss notes that while ontology asserts directly what
being is, Jaspers's "periechontology" suggests only
"how Being could be for us."/52/

The difficulty with formulating the Encompassing,
of course, is that the moment we attempt to articulate
the dichotomous nature in which we find ourselves and
which we cannot see out of, we inevitably make it into
an object. And yet the Encompassing never becomes an
object or a given horizon of knowledge at a given
moment. As he says, it merely "announces itself" as
the "source" from which all new horizons emerge. Its
manifestation is always tied to the dichotomy of I and
object./53/ It always remains a boundlessly
illuminating background. Thus, in order to speak of
the relation that obtains in the subject-object
dichotomy he admits the idea of the Encompassing
becomes merely "an image by which to express what is
not visible and can itself never become object."/54/

Because of the paradoxical nature of the
Encompassing, Jaspers's philosophizing stands in
opposition to tendencies that absolutize either subject
or object-being. This balance is maintained through a
recognition of a "schematic antithetic" that obtains in

an equilibrium between "the polemic will towards the object" (i.e., positivism), and "the polemic will against the object" (i.e., idealism)./55/ As the absolutizing of the object, positivism can take various forms. The so-called "realist" who points to the empirically real as the nature of all of reality and truth that can be apodictically known, errs because he fails to recognize the creative and freeing role of thought on reality. The strict realist absolutizes immanence over and against transcendence, which Jaspers characterizes as "anti-philosophy" in the form of unbelief. Philosophical unbelief takes many forms, including demonology, the deification of man, and nihilism./56/ Similarly, the moralist who insists upon the validity of laws, norms, and ideals that are known unequivocally and always applicable, also misses the mark by falling prey to a legalism that does not recognize the "unconditionality of Existenz" in moral action. The aestheticist blunders by willing the objectivity of "form" over and against the infinite and fluctuating relationships of things. The ontologist fails by resting satisfied with some ostensibly complete conceptualization of being./57/

It is when the objective becomes absolutized in these ways that a "breakthrough to subjectivity" occurs as in Kierkegaard's revolt against Hegel. Subjectivity has an extremely important place in Jaspers's polemic against these various forms of bondage to object-being. Subjectivity, however, may also fail if it loses all relationship to the objective and becomes absolute. Common sense legitimately tells us that we must have reality against illusion, meaningful law against total relativity, form as against the nebulousness of endless movement, and the stability of conceptualized being against the dissolution of transitory being. Jaspers thus sees truth in both the opposition of the will toward the object and the subject-- an opposition which reflects the "suspended" character of his thinking. "Polemically both are right in their opposition to the obliqueness of the opposing side, but both are wrong in denying its peculiar kernel of truth."/58/ The tension between objective and subjective being is tentatively resolved in the movement out of both sides in the Encompassing, discussed in terms of its various "modes."

3.4 THE MODES OF ENCOMPASSING

Now consciousness is always awareness of something, and, conversely, "to analyze existence is to analyze consciousness."/59/ For Jaspers, each act of awareness is analyzed on the model in which a subject is related to an object, whether this be through sensory awareness, conceptual thought, feeling, emotion, or action. Since this intentional relation of subject to object is the horizon of all awareness, his analysis of the modes of the Encompassing essentially becomes an elucidation of the predominate ways in which a subject is related to an object. The primary modes of the Encompassing are thus twofold in accordance with the subject-object dichotomy, "the Encompassing which we ourselves are" [Das Umgreifende-das-wir-sind] and in which every mode of Being appears to us, and "the Encompassing that is Being itself" [Das Umgreifende, das das Sein selbst ist]./60/

3.4.1 The Encompassing of Subjectivity

By approaching being through an analysis of subjectivity, Jaspers seeks to work through the various modes of the subject-object dichotomy in order to acknowledge the limits that prevent us from grasping being as a totality. He defines "the Encompassing that we are" in terms of three "immanent" modes: "existence" (Dasein), "consciousness-as-such" (Bewusstsein über-haupt), and "spirit" (Geist)./61/

When Jaspers speaks of the fundamental situation of human "existence" he is speaking of Dasein as that being which appears as a definite something in space and time. As Dasein, "I exist" in my environment among temporal and spacial forces that limit me. This is the psychological "self," the self aware of one's self and others. It is the ego which is always objectified the minute we say "I am this body, this individual, with an indefinite self-consciousness."/62/ "We find existence as the unreflecting experience of life," it is "immediate and unquestioning;" everything must enter existence to be real for us, "just as to be thought, everything must enter into [consciousness-as-such]."/63/

It is the existential moment of "awakening" from positivity which brings for "existence" the awareness of situatedness and transciency. Jaspers emphasizes that to exist "means to be in situations" which we can "never get out of without entering into another."

Though we can transform situations, ultimately the "consequences of whatever I do will confront me as a new situation which I have helped to bring about, and which is now given."/64/ The situatedness of "existence" means that we live out of the obscurity of a never totally recoverable past, an ambiguous future, and certain death. It means "advantage or detriment, opportunity or obstacle," even as existence is inevitably confrontational, if not necessarily violent./65/ When "existence" is transformed into "possible Existenz" through a sense of historicity, one is led to an awareness of death and suffering as boundaries that exist for us without any action on our part, while struggle and guilt are boundary situations we inevitably help to create. When we "awaken" from the situation of Dasein into a conscious subjectivity in the form of "consciousness-as-such" (Bewusstsein überhaupt), only then do we search for being, for something that would give purpose or goal to "existence."

Our knowledge of Dasein is mediated through our awareness as "consciousness-as-such," i.e., what Jaspers refers to as the consciousness common to all in the midst of an individually varied consciousness of experience and reality. It is the Kantian "intellect" (Verstand) in both its indomitable cogency and inevitable limitation. In the consciousness we have as existents in the narrowness of individualization, we ourselves are an encompassing only with respect to consciousness of this particular existence. In contrast to the consciousness of Dasein as an inward and undifferentiated experience, consciousness-as-such refers to that dimension of consciousness in which we have universally valid knowlèdge of tangible objects. Most importantly, the move from consciousness of Dasein to consciousness-as-such requires "a leap between the multiplicity of subjective consciousnesses and the universal validity of that true consciousness which can only be one."/66/

Because our consciousness as living beings is split into the multiplicity of endless particular realities and imprisoned in the narrowness of the individual, it is not an encompassing per se. As consciousness-as-such we participate in universally valid truth; as such, we are an infinite Encompassing. If consciousness-as-such is not without existence, it nonetheless develops independently of existence. It does not require the motives or influences of existence in its thinking, though Jaspers is certainly aware of the effects of the body upon the mind.

Truth has a different meaning for existence and consciousness-as-such. Truth for existence is relative to the individual and what is suitable for his or her own self-preservation, "pragmatic endurance," or subjectivity. Truth for consciousness-as-such is universally valid. We are essentially one with others insofar as we participate in the impersonal and universal valid truth which consciousness-as-such yields as cogent evidence. Here truth appears as timeless, with our temporal activity being a more or less actualization of this timeless permanence. Because we all share in a universal consciousness, it follows for him that we also participate to a certain extent, if not in the same cogent way, in "a universally recognized, formal lawfulness in willing, action, and feeling."/67/

Spirit designates the third mode of the Encompassing that we are. It represents a totality which is not a closed object for knowledge, but one which remains a regulative Idea. Although it is oriented toward both the truth of consciousness-as-such and to the actuality of its "other," nature, the spirit is moved by ideas which connect and elucidate all of reality. It is the encompasssing in which we draft images and realize their forms in meaningful works of art, poetry, in the professions, in the constitution of the state, and in science. Spirit must employ the media of that which can be "objectively known, sensorily perceived, or purposefully done" in order to convey the contents of its creativity./68/

Insofar as it is bound up with a particular personal existence, the truth of spirit is not universally valid. As existential truth par excellence, it is bound to human praxis in the manifestation of convictions and deeds. It is of a totality that remains in constant movement. That which we think, act, and feel is not true in and of itself, but it is true to the extent that our every thought, act, and feeling stands within a larger totality.

If Jaspers believes we live and move and have our being as existence, consciousness-as-such, and spirit, he nonetheless maintains that we take our life from a primal source that lies beyond each of these "immanent" modes.

The cause of self-being, the hiding
from which I come to myself, my freedom
to make myself as my own free gift--
all this disappears in those three
modes of encompassing, unless they
amount to more. But this cause, this
freedom, this faculty of being myself,
of coming to myself in communication
with other selves-- this is what we
call possible Existenz./69/

Existenz is the "transcendent" mode of the
Encompassing of subjectivity. "Existenz is the
self-being that relates to itself and thereby also to
transcendence from which it knows that it has been
given to itself and upon which it is grounded."/70/
"The test of the possibility of my Existenz is the
knowledge that it rests upon transcendence;" as Jaspers
puts the matter repeated, "Existenz is only in relation
to transcendence or not at all."/71/ He prefers to
speak of "possible Existenz" since Existenz cannot be
glibly described, but only pointed or appealed to.
Indeed, any attempt to illuminate Existenz seems to be
self-defeating since the more authentic Existenz is,
the more silent it is./72/ It has no tangible object
side of its own like existence, thought, or the spirit,
although the elucidation of Existenz depends
essentially upon these three immanent modes of the
Encompassing which we are for its appearance./73/
Existenz breaks through the objectivity of these modes
as the presence of Transcendence in myth, theological
ideas, and speculative metaphysics. Only as possible
Existenz are we related to Transcendence, and even this
relationship is mediated by various symbols or
"ciphers" (Chiffern) which are always ambiguous and
open to infinite interpretation./74/

Existence, consciousness-as-such, and spirit
appear by themselves as something that we are in a
meaningful, albeit incomplete form. For they do not
say what is most significant about the human subject.
Only Existenz, "carries the meaning of every mode of
the Encompassing."/75/ "What I really am is the
encompassing of self-being. Self-being is
Existenz."/76/ As Existenz we are our true selves in
communication, historicity, freedom, and the
unconditional in situation, consciousness, and action.
These represent the existential categories of Existenz
for Jaspers. They are to be regarded as mere signals
or "signs" and not as objective universals,/77/ and in
each we participate in Transcendence. While we need

not "convert" to realize existence, consciousness-as-such, and spirit, the realization of possible Existenz is most definitely "part of a phenomenon of change, of having become different;" for while we realize each mode of the Encompassing as something we are, Existenz is only realized as "something we can be."/78/ Given the unobjectifiable nature of Existenz, Jaspers illuminates it in light of the modes of the Encompassing which we are.

First, Existenz is not the actual "I am" of Dasein, the subject of the psychological self. It is rather the source out of which we are capable of becoming different than what we are in the present. Existenz is thus more potentiality than the actuality of existence as shaped by genetics and cultural conditioning. For Existenz, the present is loaded with possibilities to be realized in action. Thus our possible Existenz is dependent upon decision: "To be means to decide about being" in time./79/ Time, however, is not a continuous passing for Existenz as it is for Dasein. Time is the very "phenomenality of Existenz" itself./80/ While Existenz is only realized in time and in a concrete existence, it is more than time and knows no death as does existence. Both time and freedom are conditional on the level of existence.

Secondly, if consciousness-as-such is that universal and impersonal subject that is substituted between different human beings, then Existenz is radically different in its unique historicity and relatedness to Transcendence.

The Encompassing which we are exists only in relation to something other than itself. Thus, as I am conscious only insofar as I have something else as an objective being before me by which I then am determined and with which I am concerned, so also I am Existenz only as I know Transcendence as the power through which I genuinely am myself. The Other is either the being which is in the world for consciousness as such, or it is Transcendence for Existenz. This twofold Other first becomes clear through the inwardness of Existenz. Without Existenz the meaning of Transcendence is lost./81/

75

In other words, without Existenz the three modes of the Encompassing that we are would be empty and meaningless. Existenz is the source from which all of the modes receive their "animation and ground," just as the meaning of Transcendence is lost without it: "There is no Existenz without Transcendence."/82/ It is in the recognition of our incompleteness as consciousness-as-such that we encounter potential Existenz, and it is in the hidden ground of Existenz that being is made manifest as Transcendence. Transcendence is not an abstract zero-point, limit-concept, or void to be treated with indifference. It is that reality of being only in relation to Whom as God (for the theologian) or Transcendence (for the philosopher) we are genuinely our true selves.

Thirdly, what one is as possible Existenz is especially illuminated in _existential_ _communication_. Indeed, _Existenzerhellung_ "starts with the experience of shortcoming in communication."/83/ Communication taken strictly on the level of "naive existence" is that communication taken in terms of motives and consequences that are understandable by psychology and sociology. With the leap to communication on the level of consciousness-as-such, communication is tied to clear, cogent, generally valid logical thinking. Here, however, the subject as the "intellectual self" is still limited and veiled. Even communication between two spirits as determined by artistic or creative ideas has not yet realized existential communication. For as Jaspers insists, while "communication in the idea, and in its realization by Existenz, will move a man closer to his fellow man than will the intellect, or a purpose, or primitive community," we still have not realized existential communication until we relate to each other in freedom./84/

Freedom in communication unfolds in the dialectic between solitude and union. If we lose ourselves in others, we lose healthy independence. Conversely, if we isolate ourselves communication grows empty. Solitude is the preparatory and anticipatory consciousness for manifesting communication as possible Existenz, and this is a continuous, arduous process. It is a "loving struggle" in which we must abandon mere self-preservation and self-concern as existence, and bounce back from angers and injured pride./85/

Love is also dubious without existential communication, since love is the "substantial source of communicative self-being."/86/ It remains a process, a movement which never completely fulfills itself in time, but keeps faith until the end. As existence, genuine love is questionable since we are given to vacillation between trust and distrust, the lure of the erotic, possessiveness, and legalism. When love stands in authentic relation to Transcendence, however, its beauty and wonder is essentially incomprehensible, a manifestation of an eternal presence or the I-Thou in time./87/

Seen as a whole, then, the encompassing of subjectivity constitutes for Jaspers a series of levels or stages proceeding from (1) an animalian existence, (2) through the stages of scientific understanding with its universal concepts and principles, and spirit with its creative insights, (3) to the consummatory stage of possible Existenz. Within this hierarchy of modes, the lower level is to be limited so as to be conditioned by the higher in such as way that communication on the level of existence must be under the condition that cogent truth remains valid and informed by the ideas of the spirit. By the same token, the higher level cannot be actualized in isolation, but only under the conditions of the lower. Thus, knowledge must not forget its actual purposes within and for the human community, and the spirit must not forget its dependence upon bodily existence./88/

3.4.2 The Encompassing of Objectivity

The Encompassing which we are is not the whole of being. The world and **Transcendence** constitute the Encompassing of objectivity. The world represents the "immanent" mode of the Encompassing of being itself. It shows "an immeasurable number of appearances to inquiry, but it itself always recedes and only manifests itself indirectly as that determinate empirical existence we encounter in the progress of our experiences and in the regularity of processes in all their particularity."/89/ As determined in the last chapter, the world is unfathomable and forever incomplete to scientific cognition. Neither totally comprehensible nor adequately conceived, it is more a regulative idea which challenges our research than an object for our knowledge./90/

Transcendence (**Transcendenz**) represents the "transcendent" mode of the Encompassing of objectivity or object-being. We never fully explore this reality, but, instead, "are touched by it, metaphorically speaking, and we touch it in turn-- as the Other, the

Encompassing of all encompassing."/91/ Jaspers distinguishes the Transcendence of "being-in-itself" from the transcendence which I am as Existenz./92/ The transcendence of Existenz should not be equated with that encompassing Transcendence which includes the transcendence of Existenz because Transcendence, through which Existenz gains or receives its certainty, is more unconditional than the transcending life of possible Existenz. This is why Jaspers illuminates Existenz as possibility and freedom in communication, on the one hand, and asserts that we are not able to predicate possibility and freedom to Transcendence, on the other. Transcendence stands by itself as the absolutely Other.

> [T]ranscendence is not Existenz. There is no Existenz unless there is communication, but [T]ranscendence is the being that needs nothing else to be itself. We cannot identify [T]ranscendence with Existenz because Existenz knows it is facing the deity; it does precisely not know itself as the deity./93/

To complete Jaspers's visualization of the Encompassing, reason is the "bond" between the various modes of Encompassing. Reason is isomorphic with Existenz since "Existenz only becomes clear through reason" and "reason only has content through Existenz."/94/ Reason must not be reduced to any one of the modes of the Encompassing that we are. If we take reason to be clear, objective thinking, then it is nothing more than the Encompassing of consciousness-as-such. If reason means the way to totalities or the life of the Idea, then it is the Encompassing of spirit. But reason is actually the "pre-eminence of thought in all modes of the Encompassing," and far more than just thinking. Jaspers articulated the role of reason in his 1935 Groningen lectures.

> [Reason is] what goes beyond all limits, the omnipresent demand of thought, that not only grasps what is universally valid and is an ens rationis in the sense of being a law or principle of order of some process, but also brings to light the Other, stands before the absolutely counter-rational, touching it and bringing it, too, into

being. Reason [...] can bring all the
modes of the Encompassing to light by
continually transcending limits,
without itself being an Encompassing
like them./95/

It is not surprising, therefore, that Jaspers
would later insist that a speculative "prognosis" for
the future of humanity confronted by the possibilities
of physical and political shipwreck must be thought
from within that "common room" where "reason's way of
thinking" is the medium for a loving struggle between
competing scientific world-views, political ideologies,
and religious faiths./96/

3.5 PHILOSOPHICAL FAITH: LIFE OUT OF THE ENCOMPASSING AND BARRIER AGAINST THE FALSE HYPOSTATIZATION OF TRUTH

The attempt to schematize Jaspers's foundations is
incomplete without drawing attention to the importance
of philosophical faith, a faith closely allied to both
reason and truth. For Jaspers, the schematization of
the Encompassing does not lead to "substantial truth,"
but only to the forms and directions in which truth
appears for us. And yet, it is precisely the
unreserved will or orientation toward the Encompassing
that harbours a germ of faith, just as Kant's honesty
about practical reason forced him to limit scientific
knowledge in order to make room for faith. This will
of philosophical faith constitutes a "readiness to keep
an infinitely open mind" in the approach to objects or
objective thinking, whether this be the objectivity of
the world or the objectification of our own subjective
being./97/

More precisely, and we shall have more to say
about this in Chapter Seven, philosophical faith means
the "presence" (Gegenwärtigsein) of being in the
various polarities that obtain within the
subject-object dichotomy. "This presence can in no
event be obtained by the understanding; it always comes
from a source of its own, which I cannot will, but
through which I will, am and know."/98/ In relation to
the modes of being which we are, faith, on the level of
existence, is akin to instinct; on the level of
consciousness, cogency; and on the level of mind or
spirit, conviction./99/ In short, faith is "the act of
Existenz by which Transcendence becomes conscious in
its actuality."/100/ It is life lived "out of the

Encompassing, it is guidance and fulfilment though the Encompassing."/101/

Philosophical faith acts as a barrier against the false hypostatization of truth insofar as it keeps an infinitely open mind and critiques any pretense to absolute philosophical truth in science, morality and politics, and religion. To be sure, the statement that there is only one truth does apply to the thinking of the intellect or consciousness-as-such, to the idea of one truth in reason, and to the truth of Existenz insofar as Existenz is by definition an individual truth according to Jaspers. But the One truth in philosophy is missed if it claims to be found in a single form, whether this be scientific positivism, political "realism," moral "idealism," or theological dogmatisms pretending to possess exclusively revealed truth. Only in the never reachable totality of all the modes could truth be truly one and perfect. Jaspers charts the various fields in which the detachment of truth in one mode of the Encompassing arises in absolutized form:

> Existence is made absolute in so-called pragmatism, biologism, psychologism, and sociologism; [consciousness-as-such] in rationalism; the mind in 'erudition'; Existenz in existentialism (which becomes nihilism); the world in materialism, naturalism, idealism, and pantheism; Transcendence in a-cosmism./102/

* * *

Jaspers's foundational thinking provides the epistemological framework for his approach to the problem of the atom bomb and the future of humanity. His philosophizing depends upon three transcending moments in world orientation, existential elucidation, and metaphysics. Generally stated, there is first the step from the idea of the Encompassing to its two-fold division into the Encompassing that we are and the Encompassing that being itself is. This division is grasped by consciousness-as-such and demands a repeated cognitive "conversion" within the subject-object split as affected by the basic philosophical operation; secondly, the step from the Encompassing that we are to its division into what we are as existence, consciousness-as-such, and spirit; and thirdly, the step from immanence to Transcendence, from the world to

Deity or ciphers of Transcendence, and then back to the realization of possible Existenz within the world./103/ That the modes of Encompassing are all rooted in the regulating idea of the one Transcendence, "the Encompassing of all encompassing," is a presupposition of Jaspers's philosophical faith./104/ For humanity confronted by the twin threats of nuclear annihilation and totalitarianism, this faith believes in the urgent necessity of a "conversion" away from claims to absolute truth, i.e., from the putative truth of one mode of encompassing in the form of another.

1. Das <u>Umgreifende</u> has been translated into English primarily as "the Encompassing." Ralph Manheim renders the term as "the Comprehensive" in his various translations, while Sebastian Samay uses "the Enveloping" throughout his <u>Reason Revisited</u>. For the sake of consistency, we use the term "Encompassing" throughout. Cf., Gerhard Knauss, "The Concept of the 'Encompassing' in Jaspers' Philosophy," in Schilpp, p.146.

2. Cf., VW, p.44 and PFR, p.61.

3. In his first autobiographical reflection of 1941, Jaspers acknowledged that he had attempted systematic outlines of his foundational thinking in his <u>General Psychopathology</u>, 1913 (a "systematization of methods"), <u>Psychology of Weltanschauungen</u>, 1919 (a systematization of "the sum total of the human possibilities of faith, world views, and attitudes"), and the <u>Philosophy</u> (systematization on the basis of his three methods of transcending). OMP, pp.182-3.

4. In this chapter we draw directly upon PHT I, pp.1-95, VW, pp.47-211, TS (=VW pp.1022-54), PSP, pp.1-23, PE, pp.3-29, WW, pp.28-38, and especially RE, pp.51-76 and PFR, pp.61-92.

5. Karl Jaspers, "Epilogue 1955 to the Third German Edition," PHT I, p.32.

6. Cf., Xavier Tilliette, <u>Théorie de la Vérité; Métaphysique des Chiffres' Foi Philosophique</u> (Paris: Aubier, 1960), p.7: "Chemin faisant, en effet, nous avons subi ou redouté la contagion de Jaspers, de son style de pensée, qui épouse à plaisir de longs méandres et grossit comme un fleuve de l'apport de divers affluents."

7. E.B. Ashton, "Translator's Note," PHT I, p.xiv.

8. PHT I, p.xiv.

9. In his "Preface" to the classic work by Mikel Dufrenne and Paul Ricoeur, <u>Karl Jaspers et la philosophie de l'existence</u> (Paris: Editions du Seuil, 1947), pp.7-8, Jaspers addresses what he sees as the inevitable hermeneutical problem interpretors confront in authentic philosophizing: "Aucun exposé d'une philosophie ne peut montrer cette philosophie dans son essence, ce fait est inévitable. Tout exposé interprète et aide le lecteur de l'original, en mettant en lumière les concepts et les rapports, en posant des questions, en faisant des textes une présence vivante. Mais l'exposé ne peut jamais rendre ce qui, pour le philosophie, était

peut'être le principal: ce mouvement particulier d'une pensée qui n'a pas seulement un caractère logique et qui ne peut apparaître que confusément lorsqu'on le présente dans un ordre systématique, mais qui crée un certain climat philosophique et permet d'accomplir quelque chose qui est à la fois le sens et le but de toute pensée, ces bonds intérieurs qui se produisent brusquement, ce devenir de celui qui pense, ces résolutions que s'éclairent par le truchement de la pensée et apparaissent comme ce qui porte authentiquement la vie [...] Il est impossible de reproduire un tel mouvement. Et c'est pourquoi il serait absurde de reprocher à un exposé de ne pas l'avoir suivi."

10. PHT I, pp.34.
11. PFR, p.75. Cf., GPT I, p.278. PHT I, p.34, 283-4. VW, pp.911-12. OMP, pp.174-5.
12. Kurt Hoffman, "The Basic Concepts of Jaspers' Philosophy," in Schilpp, p.95.
13. Cf., PHT I, p.34.
14. PHT I, p.18.
15. PHT I, pp.16-17. From a theological viewpoint this is the same problem as that of approaching Scripture non-dialectically; i.e., without a delicate balance between the "letter" and "spirit" of the text.
16. We must speak of the "horizons" (pl.) of the Encompassing since, "The Encompassing is not a horizon within which every determinate mode of Being and truth emerges for us, but rather that within which every particular horizon is enclosed as in something absolutely comprehensive which is no longer visible as a horizon at all." RE, p.52. Cf., PE, pp.17-18.
17. PHT II, p.281.
18. PHT I, p.34.
19. OMP, p.166. In this section we are following Jaspers's treatment and his criticism of Kant in GPT I, pp.318-21, 362-77, and his autobiographical overview of how he transformed Kant's questions in OMP, pp.158-85.
20. GPT I, p.320.
21. OMP, p.168.
22. GPT I, pp.362-3.
23. On Jaspers's relation to Kant, see Oswald O. Schrag Existence, Existenz, and Transcendence, pp.25-33 and Alan M. Olso, Transcendence and Hermeneutics, pp.72-90. Cf. also the articles by Knauss, Thyssen, and Kaufmann in the Schilpp anthology, and Jaspers's "Reply" thereto in Schilpp, p.856ff.

24. GPT I, p.364-65.
25. GPT I, p.366.
26. GPT I, pp.367-8.
27. GPT I, p.368.
28. GPT I, p.368. See also, Schrag, Existence, Existenz, and Transcendence, p.31.
29. GPT I, pp.371-2.
30. OMP, p.167.
31. OMP, p.167.
32. OMP, p.168.
33. OMP, p.168.
34. OMP, p.169. Cf., RA, p.406.
35. OMP, p.169.
36. Cf., PHT I, pp.43-5; PH I, pp.1-4.
37. The two now classic statements of this are Gustavo Gutierrez, A Theology of Liberation: History, Politics, and Salvation, trans. and ed. by Sister Caridad Inda and John Eagleson (Maryknoll, Ne York: Orbis, 1973), pp.6-15, and Juan Luis Segundo, Liberation of Theology, trans. by John Drury (Maryknoll, New York: Orbis, 1976), pp.7-25.
38. PHT I, p.47ff; PHI, p.4ff. Here we are following E.B. Ashton's translation of Jaspers's terms. We use interchangeably the terms "object-being" and "subject-being" with "objective being" and "subjective being" throughout the text.
39. PHT I, p.48.
40. Oswald Schrag, Existence, Existenz, and Transcendence, pp.9-10.
41. See Dr. William Beardslee and Dr. John Mack, "The Impact on Children and Adolescents of Nuclear Developments," American Psychiatric Association Task Force Report No.20, Psychosocial Aspects of Nuclear Developments (Washington D.C., 1982), pp.64-96; John Mack, "Psychosocial Trauma," in R. Adams and S. Cullen, eds., The Final Epidemic: Physicians and Scientists on Nuclear War (Chicago: University of Chicago Press, 1981), pp.21-34; Milton Schwebel, "Effects of the Nuclear War Threat on Children and Teenagers: Implications for Professionals," American Journal of Orthopsychiatry 52, No.4 (October 1982), pp.608-17; Gregory J. Walters, "The Psycho-Spiritual Impact of the Threat of Nuclear War on Children and Adolescents in the United States: 1960-1982," in Science, Knowledge, and Power: Selected Material from the Second National Conference of Canadian Student Pugwash, ed. by Mary Thornton and Jane Willms (Ottawa: CSP, 1984), pp.135-144; and recently, Thinking

about the Threat of Nuclear War: A Survey of Metro Toronto Students, prepared by Susan Goldberg for The Children's Mental Health Research Group (Unpublished Manuscript, Toronto, 1984).

42. Robert J. Lifton and Richard Falk, Indefensible Weapons, p.52ff. On the origins of Lifton's notion of "psychic numbing" in response to actual nuclear war by Hiroshima Hibakusha and to the threat of nuclear war, see his Death in Life: Survivors of Hiroshima (New York: Basic Books, 1967), pp.500-16.

43. PHT I, p.44.

44. PHT I, p.45.

45. PHT I, p.49.

46. WW, pp.29-30 and PHT I, p.48, PH I, pp.5-6.

47. Karl Jaspers, "Philosophical Autobiography," in Schilpp, p.73.

48. PFR, p.77. PGO, pp.131-2. Cf., PSP, p.22. That Jaspers's philosophizing in general and the "basic philosophical operation," in particular, function as forms of a cognitive "conversion" process has been noted by various commentators and critics. Alan Olson, Hermeneutics and Transcendence, pp.3-4, comments that for Jaspers true philosophizing "presupposes transcending; that is, it involves a movement beyond an undifferentiated natural standpoint through what one might call a series of conversions from constrictive to more encompasssing horizons of consciousness and thinking." (emphasis mine) In a critical context, F.H. Heinemann, Existentialism and the Modern Predicament (New York: Harper and Row, 1958), pp.68-70, speaks of Jaspers's philosophizing as a philosophy of "evanescence" and "elusiveness," a potential but not actual mysticism. Jaspers's thought, he writes, "liberates us from the particularity of objects and 'from the fetters of determinate thinking, not by relinquishing it but by carrying it to the extreme. Reversing our direction it forces us back from the impasse of solidification (Verfestigung). By freeing us from the bondage of finite existence it exercises a quasi-religious function of conversion." (emphasis added)

49. RE, pp.51-52.

50. Cf., PHT I, p.32.

51. PFR, p.75. Cf. VW, pp.160-61, where Jaspers lists eleven contrasts between ontology and periechontology. In classical Greek, the verb periechein has the root meaning of to hold

around, encompass, embrace, and surround. Jaspers distinguishes between an ontological and a periechontological basic knowledge or world-view. The similarity, if not identity, between Jaspers's concept of the Encompassing and periechontology has been conclusively argued by Gerhard Knauss, "The Concept of the 'Encompassing' in Jaspers' Philosophy," in Schilpp, pp.141-6. Knauss shows that Jaspers's understanding of philosophizing, as thinking out of totality, may be linked historically to the thinking of Anaximander, Plato, and especially Kant and Kierkegaard.

52. Gerhard Knauss, "The Concept of the 'Encompassing' in Jaspers' Philosophy," in Schilpp, p.167.
53. PE, pp.17-18.
54. WW, pp.,31-32.
55. Jaspers discusses both of these polemical attitudes in VW, pp.1022-29=TS, pp.25-31. Cf., PHT I, pp.226ff.
56. Cf., PSP, pp.114-149.
57. Cf., TS, 25-30.
58. TS, pp.31-2.
59. PHT I, 49.
60. VW, p.50. Diagrams of the various horizons of the Encompassing are set forth in VW, pp.48, 50, and 142. CF., RE, p.52, PE, p.20, and PFR, p.62.
61. RE, p.54. While it would certainly be erroneous to equate Jaspers's modes of the Encompassing to Hegel's philosophical system, one is struck by the similarity between Jaspers's "immanent" modes of subjectivity and Hegel's categories of consciousness, self-consciousness, reason, and spirit. Cf., G.W.F. Hegel, Phenomenology of Spirit, Trans. by A. V. Miller and with Analysis and Foreword by J.N. Findlay (Oxford: Clarendon Press, 1977), pp.58-383.
62. PHT I, p.54.
63. PFR, p.63.
64. PHT II, p.177.
65. PHT II, p.178.
66. RE, p.56.
67. RE, p.57.
68. PFR, p.64.
69. PFR, p.65.
70. PE, p.21. Cf., PHT I, p.56.
71. PHT III, p.7. Cf., PE, pp.25-6.
72. Cf., PHT II, p.127; PH II, p.145.
73. Cf., PHT I, p.54ff.
74. The primary sources for Jaspers's notion of "ciphers" are PHT III, pp.113-208, VW pp.1022-54

(=TS), and PFR, 92-285. On Jaspers theory of ciphers, see also Chapter Seven below.

75. RE, p.61. That this is the case is concisely expressed in the description of Existenz by Mikel Dufrenne and Paul Ricoeur:" [...] l'existence [Existenz] c'est l'individu au sens le plus élevé du mot: non pas l'individu biologique défini par le souci vital, mais l'individu libre défini par le souci de l'être; non pas l'homme pensant universellement et défini par un faisceau de règles intellectuelles, intemporelles et incorruptibles, [...] mais l'homme qui joue son destin dans le temps, devant la mort, dans l'Etat et avec ses amis, l'homme qui, par sa décision, peut se perdre ou se gagner, ou, comme dit Jaspers, 'venir à soi' ou 'se manquer.' Ce pouvoir d'être ou de ne pas être, lié à une décision que nul ne peut prendre pour lui, ne peut qu'ébranler profondément l'individu qui soudain le découvre, par-delà l'habitude de vivre, par-delà toutes les garanties sociales et même ecclésiastiques [...]" <u>Karl Jaspers</u>, p.22.

76. "Was ich eigentlich bin, ist das Umgreifende des Selbstseins. Selbstsein heisst Existenz." VW, p.76.

77. These "signs" or existential categories structure vol. II of the <u>Philosophy</u>; Cf., PHT I, p.56ff. and PFR, pp.66-8, where in the latter Jaspers circumscribes seven aspects of Existenz: (1) it is potential being, (2) freedom, (3) the ever-individual self, irreplaceable and never interchangeable, (4) historic, (5) it requires communication, (6) it cannot be known, and (7), it remains hidden as gift.

78. PFR, p.66. (emphasis added)
79. PHT, I, p.56. Cf., PHT III, p.57.
80. PHT I, p.57.
81. RE, pp.61-2.
82. PFR, p.66.
83. PHT II, p.51.
84. PHT II, pp.50, 54.
85. Cf., PFR, p.68. PHT II, pp.59-61.
86. PHT II, p.64, 66.
87. Cf., PHT II, p.65.
88. Cf., RE, p.59. That knowledge must not forget its actual purposes within and for the community, and that the spirit must not forget its dependence upon bodily existence apply well to both academic theology and the sexual ethics of the church. Historical knowledge of theology for its own sake comes up against limits when not

integrated into the personal life of the theologian. Church teachings on issues of sexuality go astray when divorced from empirical data.

89. RE, p.60.
90. Cf., PFR, p.69.
91. PFR, p.69; PGO, p.122.
92. This is a distinction which English translations of Jaspers do not always make clear. As Alan M. Olson points out, the problem for English readers is that Jaspers uses the verbal-noun Transcendenz with two referents. First, to refer to the subjective, experiential character of our being as possible Existenz through transcending-thinking. And secondly, as the "object" to which our transcendent acts, as possible Existenz, refer. Like Olson, we have tried in the second instance to use an upper-case "T" for Transcendence in order to indicate that it is "not merely a descriptive term, but one which bears within it something of the force of das Absolute or das Unbedingte." Alan M. Olson, Transcendence and Hermeneutics, pp.xviii-xx .
93. PHT III, p.58. Cf., PFR, p.82.
94. RE, p.67. PFR, p.73. In 1950 Jaspers announced his preference for describing his work as Philosophie der Vernunft rather than as Existenzphilosophie, RAT, pp.63-64; VWZ, p.50.
95. RE, p.65.
96. Cf., Karl Jaspers, "Wahrheit, Freiheit und Friede," in HS, pp.176-7.
97. PFR, p.82.
98. PG, p.19: "Glaube im weitesten Sinne heisst nun das Gegenwärtigsein in diesen Polaritäten. Denn diese Gegenwärtigkeit ist in keinem Falle durch den Verstand zu erzwingen, sondern ist immer aus einem eigenen Ursprung, den ich nicht wollen kann, sondern aus dem ich will, bin und weiss."
99. Cf., PSP, pp.20-22.
100. PG, p.20: "Eigentlicher Glaube aber is der Akt der Existenz, in der Transcendenz in ihrer Wirklichkeit bewusst wird." Cf., PSP, p.21-22.
101. PSP, p.22; PG, p.20: "Glaube is das Leben aus dem Umgreifenden, ist die Führung und die Erfüllung durch das Umgreifende."
102. PFR, p.83.
103. Cf., PE, p.21.
104. PSP, pp.31-2; PG, p.29.

CHAPTER FOUR

THE NUCLEAR PROBLEM AND ITS "SOLUTION"

4.0 INTRODUCTION

The movement of our thinking has thus far ranged from Jaspers's turn to historico-political thinking at the end of the Second World War and the dawn of the nuclear age in 1945 (Chapter One), to the historical and epistemological foundations (Chapters Two and Three) within which his analysis of the nuclear problem must be situated. Jaspers was nearly seventy years old when he started thinking seriously about the problem, and his approach grew out of the context of both his philosophy of history and foundational thinking. During the immediate post-war period he was concerned with the perils of total rule, total planning, and the possibility of absolute destruction on the road to a new world order founded upon law./1/ However, the year 1950 and the essay, "Das Gewissen vor der Bedrohung durch die Atombombe," signalled the real beginning of his concentrated analysis of the moral, political, and existential problems raised by the invention of the atom bomb. The ideas of this essay were further expanded in the Autumn of 1956 when he delivered his German radio lecture, "Die Atombombe und die Zukunft des Menschen." This address in turn provided the basis for his 1958 political **magnum** **opus** with the same title./2/ His acceptance speech, "Wahrheit, Freiheit und Friede," upon the conferral of the German peace prize for the book gave him the opportunity to speak about the three prerequisites of peace:

> First, no outer peace is maintainable without the inner peace of humanity. Secondly, peace exists only through freedom. Thirdly, freedom exists only through truth./3/

The deadly enemy of truth is totalitarianism, the fight against which he had earlier spoken in 1954 in the essay, "Im Kampf mit dem Totalitarismus."/4/

With these sources in view we must ask now: What is Jaspers's understanding of and "solution" to the nuclear problem? There is, of course, no lasting "solution" to the problem; indeed, the idea that we might "solve" the problem is based on the false premise of the "intellect" that all problems are soluble and those that are not are so only because we are asking the wrong questions./5/ This is why Jaspers never offered a definitive answer to the question "What shall I do?" in the nuclear situation. His treatment of the problem served only for orientation and illumination. "For thought alone," he writes, "there is no solution that might be worked out according to instructions [...] action, not thought, will bring the solution of the mystery-- the innumerable actions of innumerable people who have prepared themselves for this by thinking it through."/6/

The goal of this chapter is not to exhaust the content of the problem and its "solution," which is impossible given the scope of the chapter, but rather to portray in broad strokes the prominent lines of Jaspers's analysis during the original Cold War period. The attempt to reconstruct his major diagnostic and prognostic elements is imperative if we are to remain faithful to his encompassing method, and to analyze further the needed "conversions" in science, morality and politics, and religion within the context of his philosophizing as a whole.

Structurally, we will limit our approach to a summary exposition of the main lines of Jaspers's diagnostic analysis as set forth in terms of the twin possibilities of annihilation and totalitarianism (4.1). In turn, we take up the philosopher's concern for the "suprapolitical" guidance of a "new politics" (4.1.1), and highlight his personal stance on the question of the use of the atom bomb in defense of Western freedom (4.1.2). Moving to Jaspers's prognosis, we briefly illuminate the threefold role of "conversion" in science, morality and politics, and religion, focusing upon the role of "conversion" from kirchliche Religion to philosophical faith in the nuclear age (4.2).

4.1 THE TWIN POSSIBILITIES: ANNIHILATION AND TOTALITARIANISM

Jaspers portrays the nuclear problem in terms of the possible, though by no means certain, alternatives between human annihilation and totalitarianism./7/ In the first instance, the bomb represents both an essentially "new step" in the meaning and consequences of war, and a "new fact" insofar as humanity now possesses the capability for human annihilation. Three specific dangers related to the bomb's development include (1) the dangers inherent in the use of nuclear energy and hydrogen bomb tests; (2) dangers of unprecedented destruction should the use of nuclear weapons be used again in another world war; and (3) the danger of possible extinction of humanity itself as a result of nuclear war deaths and the cumulative effects of radioactive fallout in war. While all three dangers are real, the "new fact" of possible extinction has not been adequately confronted by the majority of people. Instead, we get side-tracked by related grave issues that work as a numbing factor against the great danger of extinction. The refusal to acknowledge the dangers, of course, contributes to the possible disaster and keeps us from the necessary "revolution" in our way of thinking and doing.

It has not merely become possible for human annihilation to happen, but as the scientists warn it is highly <u>probable</u> that it will. And yet, Jaspers considers this opinion to be a negative "judgement of the intellect" (<u>Urteil des Verstandes</u>),/8/ a prognosis which is by no means certain. A prediction of atomic doom, while even highly probable, is not certain knowledge in the same way as scientific knowledge. For history is not determined so much by inexorable laws of nature as it is by the acts of human beings in their freedom. The attempt to determine history in advance is scientifically false and destructive to authentic philosophizing. Predictions of atomic destruction are destructive to philosophy because they deny human freedom and responsibility.

And yet it is only by keeping the very real threat of annihilation ever before us that the probable destruction of the species might become improbable. This is what Dr. Robert J. Lifton has more recently called "imagining the real," borrowing the expression from Martin Buber./9/ Existential anxiety over the potential annihilation of humanity is a positive factor, according to Jaspers, since the threat itself provides an opportunity that humanity will work out the problem./10/ The first step, therefore, is to increase this fear so that citizens of nuclear power states might transform the ethos of society and thus bring forth rational politicians. They would in turn act upon the principle that rational communication and peace is possible for the world. And yet if fear is a natural and positive response to the threat of annihilation, a "perpetual peace" cannot be grounded upon that fear which is presupposed in the atomic balance of terror.

Now the problem of annihilation is equalled only by the threat of <u>totalitarianism</u>. Jaspers never equates this simply with dictatorship, Marxism, or racial theory.

> Totalitarianism is neither Communism nor fascism nor National Socialism, but it has appeared in all of these forms. It is the universal, terrible threat of the future of mankind in a mass order. It is a phenomenon of our age, detached from all the politics governed by principles of a historic national existence of constitutional legality [...] To speak in mythical terms, it seems like a soulless, daemonic something which seizes everybody-- those who drift into it blindly as well as those who half-knowingly bring it about. Totalitarianism is like a specter which drinks the blood of the living and so achieves reality, while the victims go on existing as a mass of living corpses./11/

The sources of Jaspers's conception of totalitarianism grow naturally from the soil of his experience under National Socialism, and from the definitive analysis of the origins of totalitarianism by Hannah Arendt./12/ From a sociological viewpoint, totalitarianism thrives wherever rapid historical change or dislocation has occurred as a result of the technological transformation of existence. Total rule exploits this severance of ties to any substantial historical contents in order to offer its own program as a means of salvation. In turn, conflicts of loyalty ensue along three lines: loyalty to country, the governing principle of the state, and self and Transcendence.

In the first case, all totalitarians claim to stand for the "fatherland," and view their opponents as unpatriotic. This happened in Germany with the free vote plebiscite of January, 1935 at a time when National Socialism could have been defeated. Instead, ninety-one per cent voted to "'come home to the Reich,'" which testified to a lack of substantial ties. On Jaspers view, that vote was "a mere dodge to cite a loyalty that would equate fatherland with its political regime even if this regime uproots the very basis of the ethics of the fatherland."/13/

Secondly, Jaspers warns against that totalitarianism which obliterates both freedom and human dignity by disrupting loyalty to the governing principle of the state. Totalitarianism and democratic freedom are at odds, in principle, because total rule allows no parties or legal opposition to exist within the state. Total rule undermines both the letter and spirit of the constitution which secures liberty by right and law. This also happened in Germany in 1933. Hitler succeeded in coming to power as a result of two fraudulent and illegal acts because the German Nationalists "dreamed of being able to use National Socialism, which they held in contempt, as a means for their own power-political ends while retaining control of it." First the Reichstag illegally expelled the Communists; in turn, it passed the "enabling act" which was tantamount to a repeal of the constitution by legal means. At the time it was not understood that this one irreversible act would constitute "the suicide of political freedom" in Germany./14/

Total rule eradicates, moreover, the freedom of assembly which is at the heart of trade unions, as well as opposition parties. Political pluralism is turned into one single party which claims to be identical with the workers and peasants. In the process workers lose the right to strike because, in theory, as owners of the industry through the state, they would be striking against themselves. Private property is replaced by state control of the means and modes of production in the form of small ruling power elites who actually become exploiters. "The differences in income, living standards, and luxuries are greater, in fact, than in 'capitalist' countries. The workers and peasants have lost their freedom in the name of co-ownership of all property which fails to affect their actual state of helpless exploitation."/15/ In the end everyone becomes "functionalized." And in order to maintain its rule of terror, total rule requires constant purges and persecution within the party machine, army, police, industrial management, and even the peasantry.

Thirdly, totalitarianism eradicates loyalty to self and Transcendence. To grow, totalitarianism must have individuals who do not want to be themselves, but who instead prefer obedience and the pleasure of "functioning" to truth. If modern total rule has only been made possible because of technology, Jaspers insists that technology as such does not bring it about. It is the principle of the lie, rather, which gives it its particularly abhorrent nature. By means of the lie and falsehood, a totalitarian leadership is able to monopolize truth completely. As in George Orwell's now classic Nineteen Eighty-Four, words lose all their meaning and are manipulated for ideological justification. "To the sophistical use of paralogisms," Jaspers writes, "Communism adds the sophistical use of turn-about dialectics. It justifies whatever happens to be wanted and commanded at the time, turning black into white, and A into Z."/16/ (The contemporary "nukespeak" that "more nuclear arms equal less arms" has a parallel here.) With so-called truth in the hands of the state leadership, the supremacy of power becomes an ostensible supremacy in justice as well. Legal controls become superfluous, and any act of criticism against the party leadership is seen as an act of war or criminality. Lost to falsehood and connivery is the freedom of political action, assembly, and partisan activity. In contrast to this poisoned atmosphere of lying, falsehood, and fear, only a common room of freedom and truth can unite individuals. Truth is the only "meeting ground for man as such," Jaspers writes, "even for enemies locked in a life-or-death struggle."/17/

Jaspers repeatedly warns that a life lived in freedom can paradoxically nurture the growth of attitudes and lifestyles that might imperceptibly lead to new forms of totalitarianism. This is why the fight against totalitarianism must be waged on both external and internal fronts. Internationally, freedom must be protected from the totalitarian designs for conquest by meeting force with force where necessary. Domestically, free individuals "must apprehend the danger in their own totalitarian trends and constantly perform a true purification [Reinigung], by means of freedom itself."/18/ Jaspers speaks of this internal fight for freedom as being a battle for "cultural freedom," and he chides those anti-Communists who would fight Communism with totalitarian methods./19/ In short, the fight against totalitarianism must be understood as a fight for both political and moral freedom.

> The enemy is neither Communism in itself nor Russia in herself, although today [1954] both are embodiments of totalitarianism and, as such, absolute enemies. The fight is a struggle for freedom within the free countries. It would become senseless if we were to lose at home what we are trying to

defend from outside attack. The inner struggle for the self-preservation of freedom and its possibilities [...] comes to be a showdown with ourselves [...] It is in this task that our forces meet or split or grow confused on the plain basic issue of our spiritual fate, and of its consequences in political reality./20/

The twin possibilities of annihilation and totalitarianism, then, constitute Jaspers's understanding of the nuclear problem. As he put it at the outset of his book, "by one, we lose life; by the other a life that is worth living. Both extreme possibilities bring us today to an awareness of what we want, how we would wish to live, what we must be prepared for."/21/ Both possibilities have transformed the present situation into a "boundary" for humanity as a whole.

4.1.1 The "Suprapolitical" Guidance of a "New Politics"

What are we to do in the face of these possibilities? Moral indignation against the use of the atom bomb will not improve the situation. Throughout history people have been indignant over the developments and sophistication of weaponry, but it has done nothing to stem the tide of technological inventions which result from research and development. Moreover, a "ban" against the bomb would be effective only if mutual, international arms controls were instituted. Even so, international arms controls would only provide a relative certainty that the atom bomb would not be used. He is led to the logical conclusion that the bomb can be abolished and a lasting world peace established only if war as such is abolished. For "as long as we have not eliminated war as an instrument of policy, the H-bomb still has a chance of triumphing sooner or later."/22/

A movement toward world peace, however, could be achieved only by a "new politics" based on the premises of free will and a rational assessment of the reality of the world military-political situation. While free will maintains that right and justice are to rule instead of force, human reality at the same time acknowledges that societies in the world will never be perfectly just. The human condition is such that law and order-- which needs a minimum of force to maintain itself-- exist side by side with, and inevitably includes, some injustice./23/ Nonetheless, five principles of world peace <u>ought</u> to be followed given the condition of <u>homo</u> <u>politicus</u>.

(1) Treaties are to be acknowledged as legally binding, and should be enforced by an international peace force.
(2) International law requires the renunciation of absolute sovereignty.
(3) The conclusion of peace internationally requires unrestricted communication, publicity, and no censorship.
(4) Nations should also be concerned with each other's internal affairs.
(5) The way for peaceful revision of all relationships, unjust political divisions and treaties must be left open./24/

Such principles are in fact repudiated by modern political states. The "old" Machiavellian politics continues as before, and the situation is exacerbated by the fact that the non-Western nations are appropriating European technology-- often without corresponding democratic political systems-- thereby adding fuel to the fires of contention raging between Russia, America, and the Western Alliance. The situation remains paradoxical. Since every invention in technology eventually becomes common knowledge, peace is preserved only at the price of an arms race and <u>pax</u> <u>atomica</u>. Jaspers is convinced that this peace of a sort will eventually lead to nuclear holocaust if not transformed into the basis for a lasting peace.

> To consider the balance of terror as a solution is only an easy-- and extremely dangerous-- way out. It is a handy way for men to go on living as they have in the past without being forced to face up to the terrible problem of atomic destruction./25/

The idea of eliminating war from the course of human history appears unreal, of course, to the so-called political "realist," just as the moralist's idea that there might be a change of humanity strikes the "realist" as naive and unrealistic in its demands. To be sure, all too frequently moral idealism merely condemns events in the name of its objective demands. And yet Jaspers is critical of the "realist" who points to both the long history of wars and conquests and the sordid nature of human existence as justification for his "realism." Guided by a pessimistic view of history and the future, the "realist" plans policies only for the moment. He is concerned only with not upsetting the political status quo. He does not ask whether human motives are true or right, but only about their political effect. When political "realism" turns absolute it becomes a ruthless political doctrine, as in the Hindu theory of Kautilya or an unqualified Machiavellianism. But even for Machiavelli there are two limits one cannot see beyond: the virtu of the great statesman who goes his successful way in conflict, leagued with fortuna. Both are "suprapolitical" forces that help make up the substance of political reality. As Thucydides and De Tocqueville recognized, "great statesmen" always want more than mere "realism" or reality to ground the norms of political action./26/ In short, "political realism" is insufficient and becomes unreasonable when it is made absolute in the form of a Realpolitik which wills power for its own sake. Left to its own devices, Realpolitik will lead to nihilism and eventually to total doom.

The continuation of the "old politics" and the balance of terror will eventually fail. Even if humanity were to achieve a politics based on general legal principles-- such as the idea of nuclear test bans and international arms controls-- these would be insufficient given the normal, unscrupulous course of force in political action. What is needed instead is a "new politics" which would be guided by a "suprapolitical" (überpolitische) ideal adequate for the nuclear age. In Jaspers's words, we may call this "ethics, self-sacrifice, reason-- yet each of these three is dependent upon the others, or at one with them. Distinction is only a way to make them communicable."/27/

The foundations for a "new politics" requires a deeper reflection on the meaning of force (Gewalt). If one looks upon peace as the natural condition of humanity, then war is the continuation of politics by other means (Clausewitz). If violence seems natural, however, then it would be more appropriate to reverse Clausewitz's famous dictum and say that "politics is the continuation of war by other means."/28/ Ideally, the goal of politics is not to muster the greatest force in order to hold everyone and every other state in check based on fear. It is, rather, to subordinate force to a law that is morally based and guided by "suprapolitical" ideals. To be effective, of course, the law must be backed by force. The problem of balancing this delicate relationship of law and force is particularly difficult at the international level, where force rarely operates from a common institution similar to a police force within the state.

> Law is effective only if the decisions of the legal authority must be enforced over all possible resistance. True, the idea of an objective, universally valid law is persuasive, but it can be realized only if opposing parties, convinced of being in the right and unable to agree, submit to superior authority because--in international as in domestic affairs--the loser admits that legality is better than force even in case of a miscarriage of justice. If the parties do not recognize the authority and think--between states--that they have adequate power, the result is war. It does not help to differentiate between aggressive and defensive wars, or to speak of just wars or holy wars. These judgments are not pronounced by superior authority; they are partisan judgments even if the parties are not identical with states but cut across them./29/

Moreover, in a world where the "fate of the earth" (Schell) is linked to the fate of every individual, the "rights of man" have also become authoritative for a "new politics." This is so for Jaspers because human rights "antedate the rationality which puts them into words but does not invent them;" their significance can only be grasped if they are experienced from the "origin of human existence."/30/ As with the principles of world peace, the problem is that human rights go unheeded; and Realpolitik, in its will to power, continues to utilize any methods it can for the sake of self-preservation.

Can the pacifist renunciation of force show us a way out of the nuclear conundrum? Jaspers has respect for the political principle of "nonviolence" (Gewaltlosigkeit) as embodied in Gandhi, but a politics based on sacrificial nonviolence is finally not sufficient. It was only because of British liberal democracy, with its recognition of freedom of speech and a refined legal system, that Gandhi's witness to truth was possible. Under a totalitarian regime, he

would have been quickly silenced. For "the extremity
of present world-wide realities, Gandhi gives us no
answers."/31/ The significance of Gandhi, however,
lies not so much in the inadequacy of his nonviolent
politics, as it does in his individual historicity and
commitment to truth and sacrifice. Gandhi incarnated
the "suprapolitical" basis of politics by his
consistent principle of nonviolence or truth principle
(satyagraha). Because his life was deeply rooted in
the principles of truth and being that transcend
politics, he lived both courageously and sacrificially.
Gandhi's life stands as an inspiring reminder that
sacrifice, as one element of the "suprapolitical"
ideal, is essential to true humanity./32/

If the "suprapolitical" ideal is to guide a "new
politics," then Jaspers believes it must be able to
motivate constructive political action commensurate
with the demands of the situation. A "new politics"
must be based on facts and empirical data pertinent to
the military and political situation./33/

How does he characterize this situation during the
mid-1950s? In the first place, America and the West
are seen as far inferior militarily in conventional
arms to Russia. While Russia is catching up with
America in nuclear arms, Russia is superior in missiles
to deliver nuclear warheads. Russia's statements to
the effect that she would not be the first to use the
bomb are mostly "propaganda," and the Americans'
attempt to distinguish between tactical and strategic
nuclear weapons is "self-deceptive." On his view-- and
this is an issue that moral theologians, philosophers,
and strategists continue to debate today-- the use of
any nuclear weapons, even tactical ones, would
certainly escalate to total war. To disavow this is
simply self-deceptive.

Secondly, the world situation is characterized
politically by the complete division of the earth, the
end of European colonial expansion, and the liberation
of peoples from European rule. The conflict between
the West and its former colonies cuts across the
conflict between Russia and Europe with America,
between totalitarianism and freedom. In the struggle
between the Russians and the Western Alliance,
"hegemony," "subjection," and "spheres of influence"
keep a peace of sorts, but provide no foundation for a
new "world order." With Kant, Jaspers envisions such a
world order in terms of the freedom of confederation
rather than as a world government. Russian politics,

in stark contrast, wants only one kind of world order: "world conquest with the goal of total rule as the universal solution."/34/

If "Western solidarity" is to be real, therefore, it must have an accurate understanding of the nature and function of totalitarianism, and Western political "neutrality" must be the exclusive privilege of small states. Holland and Switzerland are Jaspers's exemplary nations in this respect. They have served as a beacon of humanity during the checkered course of European political history. But neutrality is not "neutralism." And in a world in which incredible forms of totalitarianism have appeared, a "neutralism" which would not want to be drawn into the political antitheses of freedom and totalitarianism is simply impossible.

Thirdly, the problem of atomic doom has received little resolution from the United Nations and its attempts to achieve world peace. The UN's weaknesses center around its Charter and its failure as a legal institution. Jaspers identifies six shortcomings on the basis of the UN's ten years of existence:

(1) Executive power depends, not on the UN, but solely on the policies of the sovereign powers.
(2) Resolutions of the UN are not carried out.
(3) States that disagree with the aims of the UN use it in behalf of their own policies.
(4) The atmosphere is one of propaganda, not of law.
(5) The UN is thwarted by injustice.
(6) The authority of the UN serves as a means of evading responsibility./35/

What is needed is a Charter revision which would abolish the right of veto, expel offending nations that would violate international law, and establish a UN military force capable of mediating between conflicts, with force, where necessary.

Finally, reiterating themes from his earlier historico-political thinking, he sees in the present world situation the continuing "crisis" of decline confronting traditional ways of life, belief, and thinking brought about by technological developments. The impact of technology upon life and belief has effected both Westerners and non-Westerners alike, and has resulted in a technologically based unity of communication. The important question is whether or not this unity will grow into a "world communion of the human spirit," or whether it will provide a basis for mutual rejection, hatred, and totalitarian manipulation./36/

One thing is certain: the present situation will change militarily, politically, economically, and demographically in the future. With the increase of horizontal nuclear proliferation and the spread of fissionable material to the smaller nations, the world will truly know what it is to live "on a volcano." Technological changes will affect working methods and socio-economic patterns in such a way that great sacrifices will need to be made. Economics, like politics, will have to be based on a "suprapolitical" ideal, even as it utilizes scientific analysis in its assessment of economic problems, lest it fall prey to a materialist reductionism. And with the world closed to emigration, the problem of overpopulation will have to be met by a moral-political demand for birth control, lest demographic situations lead, as in the past, to territorial wars./37/

Given this analysis of the world situation, then, Jaspers argues a "new politics" must have two primary objectives: "liberation and self-preservation" (Freilassen und Selbstbehauptung). The former requires truth in dealing honestly with former colonial areas. The latter demands the protection of Western freedoms while working toward a new world order based upon a future "communication of reason."/38/

4.1.2 Jaspers's Stance on the Question of the Bomb's Use

Because the principles of world peace are repudiated and the "old politics" continues, however, Jaspers must answer the question of how far the objective of "self-preservation" might extend. He must confront the most difficult question of all: Ought the atom bomb be used for the sake of self-preservation against the forces of total rule if a decision should have to be made in the extreme moment?

Jaspers warns that the question of the use of the bomb must not be isolated from existing military and political reality. True, nuclear deterrence provides some possibility that it will never be used; even Hitler did not use poison gas because he feared that it would be used against his forces in retaliation. But this is no guarantee that the bomb will not be used in the future by someone with the will and power to do so, perhaps even someone compelled by a bizarre, "suicidal impulse"./39/ Thus as long as the bomb's use by the Russians (sic) is possible, he sees the absolute renunciation of its use as violating the principle of "self-preservation." As early as 1950 he had argued that the threat of totalitarianism must neither be ignored nor muted by the horrors of atomic destruction.

> In the extreme moment-- where the issue is being or non-being in the struggle of unlimited force, where the issue is freedom or slavery-- to be ready to unleash all power, but to renounce on the use of the atom bomb or an even worse weapon yet to be invented, would be a course of action which no person would advise at a point at which humanity would have already been abandoned./40/

Jaspers reiterated his affirmative stance on the question of the bomb's use in defense of western freedom again in 1958. But his formulation of the question is now more nuanced. On the one hand, he considers those who renounce the bomb's use in a "roundabout" or "forthright" fashion, and, on the other, those who hold open the necessity of its possible use given the possibility of another war./41/ He maintains that the "roundabout" renunciation of the bomb holds itself open to manipulation and eventually blackmail. Hitler practiced both prior to the invention of the atom bomb. By the same token, the "forthright" thesis that atom bombs must not be used under any circumstances is backed by the impressive argument that if all life is to be destroyed by atomic war, then war itself has become meaningless since total war would violate the very life it is meant to protect. To oppose this view ("survival at any price") seems anti-human and against the preservation of the human species.

In contrast, there are those who oppose renunciation of the bomb's use. They insist upon the equally lethal effects of totalitarianism. On this view, a world turned into a concentration camp is one scarcely comparable to even animal existence. Both positions, Jaspers argues, are dealing with uncertainties.

In all these arguments for and against the final risk, it must not be forgotten that both parties reckon with certainties that do not exist: with the total extinction of mankind by the superbombs or with the total corruption of humanity under total rule. Neither decision is <u>sure</u> to destroy either human life or a life that is worth living. [...] we see as yet no technical possibility of destroying all life [...] no one can be certain that totalitarianism would finally annihilate man's essence along with his freedom. Totalitarianism might change and disintegrate from within. Human existence might take a new grip on freedom and thus on its potential./42/

By turning the debate back into a "loving struggle" in which the factor of uncertainty provides a common ground between competing viewpoints, Jaspers attempts to overcome the choice between annihilation or totalitarianism. Rational communication, he believes, refuses to cling to either horn of the dilemma. He concludes that unlike animals, humanity is free to take risks for freedom. In the absence of apodictic certainty about whether or not the bomb's use would in fact lead to total annihilation, the value of freedom allows for extremely high risks. The ultimate risk of atomic war would not be a risk taken in order to die, but a risk for freedom. In his words:

Should the ultimate yardstick now, as ever before, be not a respect for life as such, but respect for a life worth living insofar as human freedom can make it so?
This phrasing must not be misunderstood: the risk of life in a struggle with all-violating force differs radically from any act against life in eugenic folly, racist mania, or medical error. Respect for the potential and the value of each single human life bars tampering with any supposedly unworthy individual lives.
Man is born to be free, and the free life that he tries to save by all possible means is more than mere life. Hence, life in the sense of existence

[Dasein]-- individual life as well as all life-- can be staked and sacrificed for the sake of the life that is worth living./43/

4.2 JASPERS'S "SOLUTION:" HUMAN "CONVERSION" IN SCIENCE, MORALITY AND POLITICS, AND RELIGION

Those who go on living just as they lived before have not grasped the danger. Merely to conceive it intellectually does not mean that it has been absorbed into the reality of one's life. Without a change of heart the life of mankind is lost forever. To survive, man must change [...] the question, What are we to do? can no longer be answered by directions as to how it is to be done: the question can only be answered by an appeal to slumbering possibilities. Conversion is not enforceable. All we can do is point to realities and make articulate the voices that for centuries have been calling for a change of heart./44/

As noted by Xavier Tilliette, among others, the theme of "conversion" is the leit-motif of Jaspers's book on the atom bomb in 1958./45/ The centrality of human change manifest in each and every individual's conduct of life is also paramount in Jaspers's earliest treatment of the problem in 1950:

Only with the change of the human world, which is one with the conversion [Verwandlung] of man, is an elimination of the atom bomb possible [...] Each individual stands confronted by the choice of which way he will live and work [...] wherever one's personal being does not let itself become pure, faithful, and reliable through constantly renewed resolution [Entschluss], one aggravates the illness and encourages destruction by means of the atom bomb, which is only a symptom of that illness./46/

Now if the physical and political salvation of humanity hangs upon the "conversion" of humanity, with our being and doing in the world, we must ask further about the content of this change. What does the

104

Verwandlung of humanity entail?   What areas   of existence are involved in this "change" (<u>Umkehr</u>)?

In the first instance, Jaspers's call for "conversion" bespeaks a <u>turn from abstract,</u> <u>intellectual</u> thinking <u>to</u> <u>an</u> encompassing <u>reason within</u> <u>the</u> <u>domain</u> <u>of</u> <u>science</u>. He maintains the scientists' hope for salvation, as movingly epitomized by Einstein, is erroneously placed in the very science that brought weapons of atomic destruction into existence.   There is profound truth in the scientists' belief that the spirit of science should be one of truth and reason, but it applies "only to a source of science, not to science itself, and not to modern scientific activity-- which, though still advancing in fact, is detached from the source."/47/ It is the spirit of philosophy which actually gives meaning to science and illuminates the sources of human existence.

The "conversion" from "the accustomed, self-sufficient intellectual way of thinking" to an encompassing reason upon which humanity's future rests is not a one-way street, however, but actually involves two steps./48/ The first is from merely "intellectual" (<u>Verstand</u>) thinking, i.e., from planning and from a definite knowledge of what can happen, to an encompassing, rational (<u>Vernunft</u>) thinking which opens up new possibilities.   The second step is then back again to rational thinking <u>in</u> the world of knowledge and planning.   Both steps are necessary since "reason presupposes intellect, and an intellect trying to be self-sufficient would remain empty."/49/   This encompassing reason includes the "practical insight" (<u>praktische</u> <u>Einsicht</u>) which transcends, by means of metaphor and "cipher," that intellectual thinking which works with finite objects.   Both practical insight and transcendent thinking lie within the encompassing domain of reason./50/

Now the root cause of humanity's failure to embody the "new" mode of thinking results from the confusion of the objective world of "cognoscible manifestations" (<u>erkennbaren</u> <u>Erscheinungen</u>) with "being as such" (<u>Sein</u> <u>an</u> <u>sich</u>)./51/ This is the failure to bring to awareness the dichotomy between subjective existence and objective reality which, as we saw in the last chapter, is foundational for Jaspers's thinking as a whole. The reality of the subject-object dichotomy grounds Jaspers approach to both the problem of nuclear deterrence or "the atomic balance of terror," and the question of the future. For when we look at the nuclear problem from a merely "objective," intellectual point of view we are forced to admit that we are headed on a course towards catastrophe. The scientific facts compel us to accept the annihilation of humanity or its manipulation under total rule as probable outcomes of present history. Perceiving reality through the eyes of the intellect, the so-called political "realist's" pessimism is indeed warranted. From the perspective of an encompassing reason, however, the prognosis for the future of humanity is more hopeful. Because reason does not operate on the principle of necessity like the intellect, it perceives that no historical knowledge is final or absolute.

Secondly, then, reason appeals to the existential and political freedom of human beings. We are not merely "objects" capable of scientific observation like rocks, tables, and chairs. There is more to humanity than that which is capable of quantification. And if, as Jaspers suggests, "we are certain of our freedom without understanding freedom" completely, this is because "there is something decisive about that which we ourselves decide."/52/ Freedom is never an object of knowledge which can be proved because it lies essentially in our humanity as such. Grounded in the mystery of the human person, freedom ultimately expresses itself in one's moral convictions and actions. And it is "action, not thought," which will bring about a "solution" to the nuclear problem: "the innumerable actions of innumerable people who have prepared themselves for this by thinking it through."/53/ Whereas the proof of the intellect lies in rigorous scientific method which yields conclusive results, freedom's "proof" lies in action. This "proof" is not through a "knowing" or any single action, but only through our daily actions and "the Existenz of individuals, which is attained primarily with others in an authentic, free community."/54/ To be certain of the source of freedom, however, a "conversion" of our thinking "from thinking which is lost in the objective, to thinking out of the Encompassing" is necessary./55/ "Where it is a question of freedom," Jaspers wrote in 1950 on the dangers and possibilities of freedom, "we step into a different dimension of both doing and thinking." For when we take a stand within the domain of freedom, "we are one with an Unconditional out of which we will."/56/

Confronted by the twin possibilities of annihilation and totalitarianism, we are faced with the question of how we will base our conduct and action, whether on the intellect and its planning or on an encompassing reason and its positive implications for moral and political freedom.

> The basis of our conduct lies either in a structuring or planning under the guidance of our knowledge thus far acquired, or it lies in that inner action [Handeln] in which we become our selves, in which we are free, and in which we prove this freedom by our conduct, and not by our knowledge of freedom. Whatever we become through this inner action qua rational being [Vernunftwesen], it is this being which will bring the guidance for that structuring and planning./57/

Because our "knowledge" of the future poses a limit to thought, and because our own freedom plays an equally significant role in imagining and creating the future, the question "What are we to do?" cannot be answered with practical instructions. Absolute directions in response to the question will not suffice. The question can only be answered by an appeal to unrealized human possibilities, to "inner action," and to the moral demands we make upon ourselves. If we have truly changed our lives and are now living out of an encompassing reason, Jaspers believes this change will preclude any actions that might contribute to humanity's march toward the abyss./58/

The needed human "conversion" demands a turn about from the selfish preoccupation with Dasein and the escape from freedom and sacrifice to the truthful realization of existential and political freedom. Jaspers justifies the use of the atom bomb and even the risk of all life for the sake of life with dignity by appeal to a higher moral evaluation of existential and political freedom over Dasein. Because physical conflict is inevitably marked by the risk and sacrifice (das Opfer) of life, he believes humanity has two basic choices in the nuclear age: "either the sacrifice-- unwanted by the overwhelming majority, accomplished by the daring minority-- is the existence of mankind itself, doomed because man cannot be free; or mankind sacrifices the means of force in gaining its ends in a struggle. But that would mean a change in man."/59/

107

If humanity is truly to relinquish brute force for achieving political ends, then this will necessarily include the sacrifice of "human existential interests" (menschlicher Daseinsinteressen) in order that humanity grow truly human and free. The sacrifice of the means of force would have to be repeatedly won through a "conversion" to individual and political freedom grounded in justice and truth. This is only possible with a radical change of humanity.

> If we must do everything to eliminate the atom bomb, the condition is that it not be done at the cost of eliminating a truly human life. The sacrifice of mankind's existence is avoidable only by a sacrifice of corresponding magnitude: by the surrender of existential entanglements that is required if men are to be changed. This sacrifice alone would be the firm foundation of a life worth living./60/

Because nobody can remain neutral with respect to the twin possibilities of nuclear annihilation and political totalitarianism, Jaspers believes that the total essence of humanity must be summoned in order to cope with the nuclear problem. No single way of thinking can bring about its lasting "solution." Even the "suprapolitical" guidance of a "new politics" as grounded upon morality, sacrifice, and reason is insufficient unless viewed as a whole, and knit together by an encompassing reason. In the following we find the moral-political analogue to Jaspers's foundational understanding of the "modes of the Encompassing which we are" as existence, consciousness-as-such, and spirit.

> The truth of this higher level of reason rests upon the reality of the preceding levels. No level can be confined to itself, none can be skipped. The thoughts of Realpolitik, confined to themselves, lead to nihilism and eventually to total doom. The moral precept, as self-sufficient moralism, leads to abstract logical conclusions and to the rigidity of judging actions by laws. Self-sacrifice becomes the blind sacrifice in which man, while rising

108

above himself, gives up being himself.
And reason, in turn, grows empty if it
is not embodied in realism, in morals,
and in sacrifice./61/

The truth of morality and sacrifice in the
"suprapolitical" guidance of a "new politics" rests,
therefore, upon their absorption in an encompassing
reason rather than a purposive, intellectual thinking.
In short, a "solution" to the nuclear problem requires
an ethical, sacrificial, and rational response that
might allow humanity to avoid the uncertain Scylla of
annihilation (loss of _Dasein_) and the Charybdis of
totalitarianism (loss of possible Existenz). Both are
possible consequences of the shipwreck of individual
and political freedom. Both can be avoided, but this
presupposes a radical and repeated moral-political
"conversion" of humanity.

At a third level, Jaspers's call for human
"conversion" in the nuclear age includes a redirection
from "formal religion" (_kirchliche Religion_) to
"philosophical faith" (_philosophische Glaube_). An
encompassing reason must neither be substituted for
so-called "political realism" or "common sense," nor
confused with "formal religion."/62/ Reason is present
in all three only so long as they do not become
absolute as _Realpolitik_, self-sufficiency, and a
dogmatic absolutization of God's will. In his
treatment of "the faith of the future" in 1949, Jaspers
had already avowed that "the decision on the future of
our Western humanity lies in the relation of our faith
to the Biblical religion."/63/ In his discussion of
the role of _kirchliche Religion_ and theology in his
book on the atom bomb he is concerned with the
possibility of "formal religion" to influence
spiritually, if not guide through planning, a "new
politics" suitable for the twin challenges of the age.
Four themes characterize his analysis./64/

First, Jaspers's analysis of "formal religion"--
like his treatment of Marxism and the question of
whether or not there is a basic process of history
apart from human freedom-- has the "philosophical
faith" of reason as its foundational supposition. This
should comes as no surprise since, as noted in the
previous chapter, Jaspers understands philosophical
faith as a concrete life lived out of the Encompassing
and barrier against the false hypostatization of truth.
This faith is distinct from the "revelational" faith of
believers in Jesus the Christ. Because philosophical

109

faith is essentially an activity by which we believe,
it knows itself only as "historic motion, trusting in
the source that tells it to hear and to heed what
reason perceives."/65/ It views all absolute creeds of
history-- whether Hegelian, Marxist, or Christian-- as
relative historical symbols or "ciphers" with which it
must be concerned, and against which it must struggle
when they become intolerant.

Because the future of humanity cannot be "known"
like scientific objects, the encompassing reason in
philosophical faith sees all creedal or ideological
predictions about the bomb as futile. This faith
believes that the process of history ultimately lies in
human freedom, and has only one limit: "it must be
intolerant of intolerance. Wherever creeds try to
prevail in the world by force, it must meet force with
force." Given his modified political "realism," or
better said, political rationalism, Jaspers can
summarize the political implications of philosophical
faith as a "liberation of whatever does not claim
totality by force."/66/

Philosophical faith also believes that "God's
will" is as ambiguous as religious symbolism itself; as
such, religions can neither justify the nuclear arms
race in the name of original sin, nor issue an
unconditional "No" to the question of the possible use
of the bomb. The search for "God's will" in the Bible
inevitably leads to contradictions and polarities, the
most striking pair being "world affirmation" and "world
denial." When theological world affirmation becomes an
affirmation of existence at the possible cost of
surrendering to total rule-- as in the case of those
who declare an unconditional "No" to the use of the
bomb-- then theologians actually place themselves above
Providence. Similarly, when "world denial" justifies
itself by appeals to faith, the last judgement, or
eternal salvation, and thus leads believers to become
inactive or indifferent toward the nuclear problem,
"Biblical religion" can again present a counter symbol.

In the case of the theologian's renunciation of the
bomb's use, Jaspers rebuts that one could say in
"symbolic language" [Chiffernsprache] with equal weight
that God may want the bombs to fall. God "may want man
to change freely-- to live if he does, to die if he
does not-- because in his present dissolute state he is
unworthy of life." Conversely, in response to
theological world denial, he states that "God may want
men to live and survive in the world, but not

unconditionally [...] God has not told man to destroy
himself but has given him a choice in time: survival,
on condition of changing into a better man, or doom."
These statements clearly do not represent philosophical
cynicism sneering at theological symbolization.
Jaspers's point is that the "redemption from atomic
death cannot succeed if everything else about man
remains as before."/67/ He is adamant in insisting
that nobody knows "God's will" with respect to the
question of the use of the atom bomb. To speak of
"God's will" contravenes the very idea of God. From
the perspective of philosophical faith an absolute
knowledge of God denies both the God of the Bible and
the "Transcendence" of philosophy.

Secondly, Jaspers maintains that the churches and
the traditional symbols of "formal religion" represent
both dangers and possibilities in the nuclear age. He
reminds us that the Churches cannot be neutral in
socio-political matters. If the churches frequently
spread a false calm, engage indirectly in the "old
politics", and shrink from "radical reason" by
objectifying faith in dogmatic phraseology,/68/ they
are nonetheless important and effective organizations
whose import for the course of human affairs cannot be
underestimated.

> In today's extremity, the best
> chance may lie in the churches, insofar
> as their members still believe. It
> cannot be their task anymore to justify
> wars and exhort men to keep arming,
> or-- in line with modern pacifism-- to
> outlaw war and forbid the faithful to
> take part in arming [...]
> This seems to be the great decision
> facing the churches. Will they, unlike
> their predecessors in history, be moved
> by the unprecedented challenge to
> commit themselves and their power in
> the world-- to hazard their own
> existence in the name of the God they
> talk about?/69/

Jaspers never diminished his conviction that "what
will become of the churches may decide the Western
fate,"/70/ nor his insistence that a change in the
appearance of "Biblical religion" requires a change in
the form of dogmatic beliefs. This includes the
incarnation of God in Jesus Christ, the doctrine of the
Trinity, obsolete obligations, and the belief in an

absolute Christian revelation as essentially different
from Hindu and Chinese revelation./71/ Most
importantly, the change in "formal religion" requires a
"rebirth of man," and he saw the best chances for this
as residing in the "Protestant principle": "no
mediator; direct contact with God; universal
priesthood-- and a corresponding institutional
dismemberment of the Church into many creeds and
independent congregations."/72/ Jaspers's
"ecclesiology", if we may speak of such, views
religious organizational unity with indifference. What
matters is that the one _existential_ _truth_ of
revelational faith be realized in the historicity of
Existenzen throughout various communities with diverse
forms. His view holds out a radical Christian
sectarianism which corresponds to a much needed radical
reason in revelational faith, which might, but need
not, turn into philosophical faith itself.

Thirdly, the future of humanity does not lie with
a change in the appearance of "Biblical religion"
within the churches alone. Also needed with this
change and the life of the believer is that
philosophizing which is accessible to all and not bound
to a particular revealed religion. It is a vital
concern of philosophizing both to clarify itself
vis-a-vis revelational faith and to call forth within
revealed religion human capacities for faith which
actualize truth through rational communication. In
short, philosophical faith has a vital role to play in
the pulpit in the nuclear age.

Finally, Jaspers affirms that "the real truth in
reason and religion is one and the same."/73/ Diverse
religious ciphers of Transcendence are of secondary
importance to the fact that humanity seeks and wants
the same with respect to the ultimate questions of
life. Instead of asking directly what makes life worth
living at the nuclear boundary, religion merely asks
symbolically about the "will of God," and demands that
humanity turn toward God. But it is the task of reason
to make sure that the truth of this admonition is not
falsified so as to relieve us of the burden of freedom.

Three final questions must be posed in order to
conclude our analytic reconstruction. First, is
Jaspers's call for a threefold "conversion" of humanity
within the domains of science, morality and politics,
and religion asking too much of humanity? His answer
is a resolute "no" as long as our understanding of what
it is to be human is not guided merely by objective

appearance and the intellect; if we do not forget our human freedom and its possibilities within the socio-political realm; and if we do not absolutize religious faith into dogmatic assertions which, at the same time, mask a particular political ideology.

Secondly, can an encompassing reason really be trusted? Yes. Reason not only can, but must be trusted if we are to have faith in our fellow human beings and not succumb to despair. All _false_ _hopes_ must be avoided, however, if we are to have confidence and hope in reason. These include the idea of a technological panacea such as an escape into outer space which merely reflects "the _hubris_ of technological omnipotence;" faith in an antidote to defend against radioactivity or some kind of "Noah's Ark" wherein human living conditions are artificially constructed; and faith in an eternally stable nuclear "balance of terror." The idea (common in our day in the slogan "peace through strength") that _fear_ of nuclear destruction and superior strength of nuclear weapons will prevent a nuclear Holocaust has a most plausible ring for Jaspers. And yet given his dependence upon Kant's understanding of the positive relationship between fear and morality in history, he declares that fear alone cannot bring peace. To be sure, the position for long-lasting deterrence has a certain common sense reasoning about it. Advocates of nuclear deterrence argue "from the immutability of human nature" and "simple causal determinants in the infinite complexity of surface events." But he resists the idea since "nothing is impossible if the captains-- against common sense, against reason, against the moral qualms that inhibit even criminals-- decide to drag everyone down with them."/74/ Here we must remember that Hitler stepped up the extermination of the Jews when he saw that the Reich's war effort was doomed. Finally, the idea of a divine revelation in some new prophet or a nuclear Apocalypse is equally false. Living under false illusions, we will only miss possibilities that might truly be realized.

What if reason fails humanity today? Jaspers's philosophical faith leads him to believe that we might have confidence nonetheless. For while reason is the final reality "in the world," it is not absolute reality. There is consolation in knowing that humanity _should_ follow the dictates of reason./75/ Ultimately, however, nothing but "transcendent reality" can give us final confidence. The idea of God is Jaspers's final

113

horizon, even in the face of the possible terminal situation of all humanity.

> If mankind destroys itself and nothing remains of that which is dear to us and makes life worth living, then we must submit ourselves like Job in ignorance. Despite this, as long as he lives, man, who becomes rationally conscious, remains free to pursue a life without fear in the direction in which the hidden Godhead appears to point the way./76/

Confronted by the possible shipwreck of all being humanity can nonetheless proclaim with the prophet Jeremiah: "that God is, is enough" (cf. Jer. 45:4-5)./77/ It is this same hidden Godhead or Transcendence who enlivens our sense of immortality. This comes to us both as a gift of reason and by responsible, loving actions. Ultimately, reason acknowledges that love alone is the foundation of hope.

> In our love for one another we become aware of our origin and of eternity. Here is the ground and assurance of our hope, which will enable us to live in our world by reason in the broadest sense of the word, and to direct our thoughts, impulses, efforts, beginning with our own everyday life, toward averting the final disaster that threatens./78/

* * *

As the foregoing analysis has revealed, Jaspers understands the nuclear problem essentially in terms of the twin possibilities of nuclear annihilation and political totalitarianism. His prognosis is grounded upon repeated "conversions" on the part of humanity within the domains of science, morality and politics, and religion. This includes a "conversion" from intellectual thinking to an encompassing rational thinking, from "internal" totalitarianism and Realpolitik to existential and political freedom, and from "formal religion" to philosophical faith and the reappropriation of "Biblical religion." It is to the more specific role of "conversion" within each of these domains, therefore, that we must now turn.

1. OGH, pp.204-210.

2. <u>Die</u> <u>Atombombe</u> <u>und</u> <u>die</u> <u>Zukunft</u> <u>des</u> <u>Menschen</u> brings
together much of what had gone before in his
earlier politico-philosophical thinking.
Structurally, his <u>diagnosis</u> of the problem
constitutes Parts One and Two of the work, "How
General Discussions Lead to Limits: Politics,
Ethics, Sacrifice" and "The Present Political
World Situation from the Western Standpoint,"
while his <u>prognostic</u> analysis is set forth in
Part Three, "Illumination of the Human Situation
in the Encompassing." These major divisions are
missing from E.B. Ashton's English translation.
In accordance with his philosophical method of
continually transcending the content of thought,
Jaspers wants the theoretical (Part One) and
concrete diagnostic (Part Two) sections to
contribute to his prognosis (Part Three), even as
this last section, and especially his final
chapter dealing with hope and the threat of total
annihilation, informs the particulars of the
diagnosis. This is why any reconstruction of his
understanding of the problem must consider both
his diagnosis and prognosis.

3. Karl Jaspers, "Wahrheit, Freiheit und Friede," in
HS, p.174: "Erstens: Kein ausserer Friede ist
ohne den inneren Frieden der Menschen zu halten.
Zweitens: Friede ist allein durch Freiheit.
Drittens: Freiheit ist allein durch Wahrheit."

4. In PW, pp.76-96. English translation, "The Fight
Against Totalitarianism," in PWT, pp.68-87.

5. Cf., FM, p.12; AB, p.32.

6. FM, pp.11,12; AB, pp.31-32.

7. Cf., FM, p.vii; AB, p.5.

8. FM, p.3; AB, p.21. While Jaspers considers all
judgments about nuclear doom and destruction to
be uncertain, this should not mislead one to
diminish his sober perception of potential
nuclear destruction. His understanding of the
possibility of destruction-- which undoubtedly
mirrors the physical development from the atomic
to the hydrogen bomb-- underwent clear
development between 1950 and 1958 as a comparison
of the following statements suggests:
    [1950]: "Infolge eines neuen Krieges können
weite Länderstrecken für lange unbewohnbar
werden, kann die Menschheit hingemordet werden,
dass nur ein Drittel oder weniger übrig bleibt
[...] Aber der Rest wird leben, der Erdball

weiter kraft des Sonnenlichtes gedeihen. Irgendwelche Überlieferungen, Werke, Bücher, Werkzeuge und Maschinen werden gerettet sein." Karl Jaspers, "Über Gefahren und Chancen der Freiheit," in RA, p.351.

[1958]: "One may be right in doubting that the day has come when all life on earth can be annihilated. But in ten years or less the day will come. This slight difference in time does not diminish the urgent need for reflection." FM, p.1.

9. Robert J. Lifton and Richard Falk, _Indefensible Weapons_, pp.111-25.
10. GBA, p.371: "Eine chance aber ist auch die gefahr selbst."
11. Karl Jaspers, "The Fight Against Totalitarianism," PWT, p.69.
12. Cf., _Ibid._, pp.69-74. See also, FM, pp.104-117; AB, pp.158-173. See also, Hannah Arendt, _The Origins of Totalitarianism_, new edition with added prefaces (New York: Harcourt Brace Jovanovich, 1973), Part Three, "Totalitarianism," pp.305-479.
13. Karl Jaspers, "The Fight Against Totalitarianism," PWT, p. p.76.
14. _Ibid._, p.70.
15. FM, p.104-105; AB, p.158.
16. Karl Jaspers, "The Fight Against Totalitarianism," PWT, p.77.
17. FM, p.106; AB, p.160.
18. Karl Jaspers, "The Fight Against Totalitarianism," PWT, p.81-82; PW, p.90.
19. _Ibid._, PWT, p.87: "With a speed that is sometimes uncanny, this necessary fight against all of the enemy's tangible powers has led anti-Communists to adopt totalitarian methods. We have seen how this happens in the creation of fear and mutual distrust, in inquisitorial and denunciatory procedures. Yet these are only a start. It is as though the battle against Communism had the devil in it; in the course of this fight, the fighter himself seems to be turning into the type of adversary. If I combat totalitarianism with totalitarian means, I unwittingly transform my own cause. In fighting the dragon I become a dragon myself. Thus my very victory would have set up the dragon's rule."
20. _Ibid._
21. FM, p.4; AB, p.22.
22. Karl Jaspers, "The Balance of Terror Won't Protect Us from the Bomb," _Realities_, No.181 (December 1965), p.27. Cf., also, ABR, p.41. FM, p.16, AB, p.39, and GBA, pp.372-3.

23. Cf., FM, p.17 and AB, p.40.
24. Cf., ABR, p.41-2. FM, pp.17-20; AB, pp.40-44.
25. Karl Jaspers, "The Balance of Terror Won't Protect Us from the Bomb," p.27. Cf., GBA, p.371.
26. FM, pp.249-251; AB, pp.343-346. Cf., ABR, p.50-51.
27. FM, p.13; AB, p.32.
28. FM, p.32; AB, p.58.
29. FM, pp.32-3 (emphasis added); AB, pp.59-60.
30. FM, p.35; AB, p.63.
31. FM, p.39.
32. Just before his death in 1969 Jaspers paid a special tribute to Gandhi, "One of Karl Jaspers' Last Commentaries: Gandhiji," The Courier (October 1969), pp.26-27. He wrote appreciatively: "By his spirit of self-sacrifice he showed that a 'supra-political" idea could be converted into a force for political action. Here lies the greatness of Gandhi in our times. For him, politics was not only inseparable from ethics and religion but was constantly and totally nurtured by them [...] Today we face the question: how can we escape from physical violence and war, and avoid the holocaust of nuclear weapons? Gandhi, through his action and words, has given us the true answer: only political values that transcend politics itself can provide the force that will save us" (p.27).
33. As Xavier Tilliette has noted, Jaspers's treatment of the actual historical situation in Die Atombombe is more exhortative than absolute in style: "[...] il est vrai qu'on aurait tort de forcer ce reproche, et d'incriminer le style assertorique de la conviction, qui se confond formellement avec celui de l'évidence apodictique. La forme apodictique, ici comme dans la lettre à Bultmann, est exhortative, non pas absolue. Il reste que des opinions particulières et discutables se couvrent du pavillon de la raison." "Jaspersiana," Archives de Philosophie 22 (1959), p.283.
34. FM, p.133.
35. Cf., FM, pp.144-48, and Karl Jaspers, "The UN Is Undependable," The New Republic (18 May, 1959), pp.12-13.
36. Cf., FM, pp.59-159; AB, pp.95-217.
37. Cf., FM, pp.174-183; AB, pp.236-246.
38. FM, p.75; AB, p.122.
39. GBA, p.372: "[...] die bösesten Möglichkeiten finden irgendwann einmal den Menschen, der die

Macht und den Willen hat, sie zu verwirklichen,
und sei es in einem wilden Selbstmorddrang, in
den er die Welt mit hineinziehen will."

40. GBA, p.372: "Im äussersten Augenblick, wo es um
Sein oder Nichtsein im Kampf uneingeschränkter
Gewalt geht, wo es sich um Freiheit oder
Knechtschaft handelt, alle Gewalt zuzulassen,
aber auf die Atombombe oder etwa noch zu
erfindende noch schlimmere Waffen zu verzichten,
dazu wird keine Humanität dann mehr raten, wenn
die Humanität schon längst verlassen ist."

41. Cf., FM, p.165 and AB, p.226. The latter
position was the official stance of the Roman
Catholic Church throughout the decade of the Cold
War. On the basis of Pius XII's teachings, e.g.,
John Courtney Murray S.J., argued that since
nuclear war might still be a necessity for the
defense of Western freedom against the Soviets,
then morally the possibility of nuclear war "must
be created." See Murray's "Remarks on the Moral
Problem of War," Theological Studies 20 (1959),
p.58.
Murray's point was that it is a moral
imperative to create the possibility of "limited"
nuclear war rather than succumb to the
determinism of total war between the superpowers.
Today, nearly thirty years later, the US Catholic
Conference of Bishops have expressed their
stongest doubt about the morality of a "limited"
nuclear war: "we [...] express our view that the
first imperative is to prevent any use of nuclear
weapons and our hope that leaders will resist the
notion that nuclear conflict can be limited,
contained or won in any traditional sense." The
United States Catholic Conference of Bishops,
"The Challenge of Peace: God's Promise and Our
response," Origins 13 (1983), p.16.

42. FM, p.167; AB, p.229. Cf., ABR, pp.52-54.

43. FM, p.169; AB, p.231.

44. ABR, p.48, 50. Cf., GBA, p.373.

45. Xavier Tilliette, "Jaspersiana," p.281: "Du
suprapolitique on attendra non une amélioration,
un "dégel," mais la conversion, le changement
(Wandlung) de l'homme, un nouvel éthos, un autre
être-humain, qui par contagion s'étendra aux
Etats. Le thème de l'Umkehr est le leit-motiv du
livre. C'est l'exigence impérieuse de ce temps.
La parole est aux individus, aux libertés."

46. GBA, pp.373 and 375: "nur mit der Veränderung
der menschlichen Welt, die eins ist mit der

Verwandlung des Menschen, ist eine Ausschaltung der Atombombe möglich [...]

Jeder Einzelne steht vor der Wahl, welchen Weg er gehen und für welchen er wirken will [...] Wer sein persönliches Dasein nicht in ständig wiederholtem Entschluss rein, treu, verlässlich werden lässt, verschlimmert die Krankheit und fördert die Zerstörung durch Atombomben, die nur ein Symptom jener Krankheit ist."

47. FM, p.199; AB, p.277.
48. Cf., FM, p.217; AB, p.298.
49. FM, p.205; AB, p.283.
50. Cf., FM, p.217; AB, p.298.
51. FM, p.214; AB, p.295.
52. GBA, p.374: "Wir sind unserer Freiheit gewiss, ohne Freiheit zu begreifen. Irgend etwas Entscheidendes liegt an dem, wozu wir uns entschliessen."
53. FM, p.12; AB, p.32.
54. Karl Jaspers, "Über Gefahren und Chancen der Freiheit" (1950), in RA, p.356: " [...] die Existenz des einselnen Menschen, der dadurch erst mit dem anderen in eine echte, freie Gemeinschaft gelangt."
55. Ibid., pp.356-57. "aus dem in Gegenständlichen verloren Denken in das Denken aus dem Umgreifenden."
56. Ibid.: "[...] Wir beschreiten, wo es sich um Freiheit handelt, eine andere Dimension im Tun und Denken zugleich [...] sind wir eins mit einem Unbedingten, aus dem wir wollen."
57. GBA, p.374: "Der Ansatz unseres Tuns liegt entweder in einem Machen, Planen unter Leitung unseres bis dahin erworbenen Wissens, oder er liegt in jenem inneren Handeln, in dem wir wir selbst werden, frei sind und diese Freiheit beweisen durch unser Tun, nicht durch ein Wissen davon. Was wir mit diesem inneren Handeln als Vernunftwesen werden, das bringt erst die Führung für jenes Machen und Planen."
58. Cf., FM, p.11, 326.
59. FM, pp.171-2; AB, p.234.
60. FM, pp.173; AB, p.235.
61. FM, p.188; AB, p.253-254.
62. FM, p.247; AB, p.340.
63. OGH, p.226.
64. FM, pp.251-261; AB, pp.347-364. Four theses dominate the analysis which corresponds to the four subdivisions in the German original: (1) arguments which appeal to "God's will", (2) the dangers and chances of the churches, (3) to

preach and to philosophize, (4) and the truth in formal religion.

65. FM, p.263; AB, p.366.
66. FM, p.264-265; AB, p.367-368.
67. FM, p.255; AB, p.353.
68. Jaspers most developed treatment of the "intellectual" methods of the churches may be found in PFR, pp.41-48. While much of his critique of "ecclesiastical religion" is no doubt centered upon the Roman Catholic church, it would be wrong to reduce his critique of churchdom and "formal religion" to this institution alone. Examples of "ecclesiasticism" which deserve "utmost distrust" and demonstrate that any "church" can become a power organization and a potential tool of fanaticism and superstition include: "the Inquisition; the Crusades; the religious wars; the actions taken by the papal Church against the Albigenses and Giordano Bruno [...] Luther's inflammatory squibs against the peasants and his counsels against the Jews, which Hitler followed to the letter [...] Calvin's ecclesiastic régime, his treatment of Servetus in particular [...] Spinoza's excommunication and denunciation by the Jewish synagogue." PFR, p.46.
69. FM, p.258; AB, pp.358ff.
70. PFR, p.321. Cf., OGH pp.224ff.
71. FM, p.257-58; AB, p.356.
72. FM, p.259; AB, p.360. Jaspers's cites the term "Protestant principle" in FM/AB and PFR/PGO without reference to Paul Tillich who had developed the theme in 1948 in The Protestant Era, abridged edition, trans. by James Luther Adams (Chicago: University of Chicago Press, 1957), esp., pp.vii-xxvi, 161ff.
73. FM, p.261; AB, p.364.
74. Cf., FM, p.321-324; AB, p.462-468. Cf., ABR, p.54-55.
75. Cf., FM, p.337 and AB, p.491.
76. GBA, p.377: "[...] wenn die Menscheit sich doch selber zerstört und nichts bleibt von dem, was uns lieb ist und das Leben lebenswert macht, dann beugen wir uns wie Hiob im Nichtwissen. Aber solange er lebt, bleibt dem Menschen, der sich vernünftig bewusst wird, offen, trotzdem und unerschüttert dorthin zu leben, wohin die verborgene Gottheit ihm den Weg zu zeigen scheint."
77. ABR, p.57.
78. ABR, p.57.

CHAPTER FIVE
"CONVERSION" TO REASON

5.0 INTRODUCTION

Jaspers's major criticism of the early atomic scientists who brought the bomb into existence and then, in turn, called for a "new way of thinking," was that they did not take their own call far enough. To be sure it was the scientists-- and not the generals or even politicians-- who were the first to bring the "new fact" about human annihilation to the public's attention, and for this we should be grateful. People who blame the scientists for the discovery of atomic energy or who see some kind of evil historical and technological process at work in the advent of nuclear technology fail to understand both the dire circumstances that brought the bomb into being, and the fact that technology lends itself to human possibility as much as it does to destruction.

Because the scientific and technological process is a progressive, one-way street, the important question is always one of what we want to do with technology: "Everything man produces in the course of technological progress is a new realization of his existential potentialities [...] technical creation keeps confronting him with new situations, each of which raises the question of what he will make of it, what he will do in it, in what sense he will master it or succumb to it."/1/ Because scientists are human they always face the question of what the consequences of their actions could and should be, given their own proper freedom. But as scientists they hold no special insights into the nature of reason's "new" way of thinking. They are neither more nor less capable of an encompassing rational thinking than other human beings.

According to Jaspers, the atomic scientists' initial hope for salvation placed too much hope in the very science that brought the nuclear menace into existence. Einstein called passionately for a "new mode of thinking" which would ground science in a spirit of truthfulness, reason, and humanity. In this call there was a profound truth. But Jaspers saw most of the early atomic scientists' thinking as turned "only to a source of science, not to science itself, and not to modern scientific activity-- which, though still advancing in fact, is detached from the source."/2/ For him it is the spirit of philosophy,

121

i.e., rational thinking, which gives meaning and goals to science and intellectual thought. It is a more detailed analysis of the "conversion" from intellectual to rational thinking, and thus the distinction and alliance between science and philosophizing, which constitutes the aim of this chapter.

Structurally, we will begin with the question of the nature of reason all the while bearing in mind that reason can be circumscribed but not defined (5.1). In turn, we will look at Jaspers's foundational differentiation between objective scientific knowledge and the awareness of philosophizing as a type of "non-knowledge" (5.2). This leads on to Jaspers's critique of other philosophers' views on the science/philosophy relationship (5.3), and his understanding of both the distinction and alliance between science and philosophy (5.4). We will conclude by pointing to the "conversion" to reason in science as essentially a "will to truth" (5.5).

5.1 WHAT IS REASON?

Jaspers has elucidated the meaning of reason in various of his works./3/ Reason's most basic characteristic is the <u>will</u> <u>to</u> <u>unity</u> within the Encompassing. This is not to be confused with the partial unities and truth obtained by "intellectual cognition" (<u>Verstandeserkennen</u>). For as Jaspers repeats time and again, if we confine ourselves to this path of truth, we lose the very truth by which we live. Instead, the impulse of reason seeks a deeper unity to which the unity of the intellect is merely a means. Reason presses constantly on to the place where totalities are broken through in order that it may grasp the truth that becomes apparent in the breakthrough: "By breaking up every attractive semblance of unity (whose insufficiency is thereby proved) it attempts to ward off the metaphysical breach and rending of Being itself, the real Unity."/4/

In its approach to this deeper unity, reason performs a unifying role in all situations. Because it is constantly on the move, reason "leads to self-knowledge and knowledge of limits, and therefore to humility-- and it is opposed to intellectual arrogance."/5/ By virtue of its humility, reason's lifestyle calls forth an awareness of the intersubjective nature of reality. "From the decay of mutual alienation," Jaspers writes, "reason desires to bring everything back into relation with everything

122

else."/6/ This unifying power of reason manifests itself in the sciences as "the drive to cross over every limit of any one science, as the seeking out of contradiction, relations, complementations, as the idea of the unity of all science."/7/

Reason is also one with the boundless will to communication, and this opens up possibilities for humanity even if confronted by the boundary of nuclear annihilation and the terrors of totalitarianism. To be sure, on the level of existence we exercise "political intercourse" in those inescapable situations in which we are either potential adversaries in the fight for living space, or potential partners in the joint realization of tangible ends./8/ Frequently a rupture of communication occurs as a result of the use of force on this level of being. But this is never final nor even fundamentally necessary according to Jaspers. For, "with imperturbable confidence in the boundless possibilites of the whole of Being, Reason demands that the risk of communication should be taken again and again. To deny communication is tantamount to denying Reason itself."/9/

For reason in temporal existence, truth is bound up with communication: "to be genuinely true, truth must be communicable."/10/ Reason reminds us, in other words, that we are not for ourselves alone, but that we need others without whom we cannot become ourselves or know truth. The truth which binds itself to communication, however, is never consummated in time because "existential communication" is never consummated in time. And yet Jaspers believes that the incompleteness of communication and thus of truth disappears in the presence of Transcendence. As he states mystically, "the continuous horizontal line of time in which we live is intersected by the vertical line of the unknown One which bestows meaning and fulfilment on the truth we receive in communication."/11/ Reason is simply the road of this philosophical truth in communication, and the university is the primary place where reason struggles for truth./12/

Reason also allows and indeed calls one to become a world citizen./13/ This was beautifully expressed by Jaspers after his turn to political philosophizing after the war:

If a man, looking at what may be coming, has to admit that he has been rejected by his political fatherland, then he will not be accepted by another native land that does not exist, but by the fatherland of human history. With his thinking he helps to prepare the coming of world citizenship. He looks for confirmation of his being at home in humanity as such. From the disaster that has overtaken his own historical origin, from what was noble in the past of his own native land, from the heritage of his great ancestors, always supported by the historical origins of his love, he now finds his way to the source of humanity, of concrete historical humanity. As a human being he will be related to all human beings as if they were all one great family. This is not a natural process but only becomes possible when a man is reborn [Wiedergeburt] through Reason./14/

The enemy of reason is the unphilosophical spirit which knows nothing and wants to know nothing of truth. The parting of the ways between reason and unreason occurs with the betrayal of those simple truths that the honest person takes for granted in daily life. Once a betrayal of truth has occurred, the only way out of its grip is by means of a radical "conversion" that leads to the decision to become our true selves through reason. The shapes of anti-reason which arise from this betrayal of truth and selfhood are subtle, however. Our resistance to the transforming "new way of thinking" is essentially a resistance to individual responsibility: "We do not want it to be true that it is up to every individual himself what will be and what will become of mankind."/15/ And like the Devil who quotes Scripture, "anti-reason uses the language of reason" just as "all non-philosophy uses that of philosophy."/16/

The role of myth is an example of the close link between reason and anti-reason, and it is particularly relevant to the nuclear problem today. For while Jaspers sees myth as containing reason and as being "the indispensable language of transcendent truth," myth must nonetheless submit itself to the control of reason. If the reason in myth is perverted, for example, there grows an urge in humanity "to be disengaged from the reality for which one is personally responsible and, by yielding to the enticing spectre of the irrational, to transfer it to a mysterious reality outside oneself."/17/

124

In our present situation, those who mentally equate nuclear Holocaust with the Christian Apocalypse represent an example of anti-reason. Through the perversion of the Christian myth, the symbolism of the bomb or the "nuclear image" (Lifton)-- i.e., the image of massive nuclear death and destruction-- is rendered meaningful. In this equation, the Christian myth of cataclysmic Apocalypse-- which does indeed convey a truth about human hope and responsibility-- merely serves functionally to grant eschatological immunity from the potentially devastating effects of nuclear holocaust./18/

Of supreme importance for Jaspers in the light of inevitable anti-reason in the world is the belief that reason exists only by <u>unconditional decision</u>, and not by nature. This decision for reason is a decision for freedom, truth, and responsibility. Unconditional decision stands over and against nature, against mere occurrence and necessity. If "freedom is the guidance out of the unconditional," then this guidance is clarified by reason, by philosophizing./19/

Reason also refuses to accept a <u>worst case prognosis of historical decline</u>. It always considers the forecast of ultimate catastrophe as uncertain. It never overlooks the range of possibilities in what may appear to be the most hopeless situation. The task of reason in the face of the nuclear menace, then, is to avoid wavering between a destructive fear which paralyzes all activity, and a self-forgetful business for its own sake./20/ A destructive fear is below human dignity, and work solely for its own sake is an intellectual life no longer directed by <u>Eros</u>, but one characterized instead by the forgetfulness of being. Even in view of the possible, indeed, "intellectually probable" end of all that we love, our task is to endure and to hope./21/

As Jaspers reiterates time and again, reason is not the intellect, rational thinking is not abstract thinking. In fact, reason must continually overthrow what has been acquired by the intellect./22/ Whereas abstraction is a clarifying instrument of the intellect, it becomes untrue when taken for an absolute truth. In contrast to abstract thinking, however, rational thinking "absorbs the abstractions, transcends them, and returns with them to reality."/23/

Applied to the nuclear problem, Jaspers pits reason against that abstract thinking of the intellect

125

which turns philosophical arguments, political opinions, proposals, and demands, and technological "solutions" into fallacies. While, to our knowledge, he never directly mentions "games theory" analysis of nuclear deterrence in his book on the atom bomb, the tone of the work clearly suggests a negative evaluation of such approaches to the nuclear problem. This verdict is rendered all the more conclusive if one argues the point from his evaluation of logic in general./24/ Jaspers's would have undoubtely agreed with Anatol Rapaport and Philip Green who, just a decade after his own treatment of the problem, convincingly argued that the use of games theory in planning nuclear strategy is pseudo-scientific and dangerous./25/

Political and technological fallacies of the intellect include "departmental thinking," in which we defer our thinking from the depth of the nuclear problem in its entirety to the authority of expert knowledge, military professionals, or officials in high places. Departmentalized thinking leads even governments and institutions to view their limited activity as absolute, and to carry it out regardless of the whole.

In this respect, and in the light of the history of nuclear deterrence strategy over the past forty years, one cannot but believe that nuclear deterrence, itself, has been turned into a form of "departmentalization" by both the East and West. To be sure, Jaspers acknowledged the necessity of atomic deterrence in the absence of internationally binding law. But he saw it as illusory as a long-term "solution" to a problem which requires nothing less than the crucial "conversion" of humanity to individual and political freedom, and a corresponding sacrificial renunciation of the means of force for obtaining political ends. At what point, then, does nuclear deterrence no longer accord with a vision of its only meaningful goal as the prevention of any use of nuclear weapons? Has not nuclear deterrence become "departmentalized" when it moves from "basic deterrence" to "extended deterrence," and when detailed plans for "prevailing" in nuclear war become the norm as has been the case in recent years?/26/

Now another fallacy of an abstract thinking which shuns reason is that it gives birth to political and technological "panaceas" which are put forward as total solutions to difficult problems, and to national policies which are detached from the interest of the whole international community. Political self-preservation "isolates itself," Jaspers writes, "when it views the self-preservation of all others as an obstacle rather than as a justified interest on their part. Thus American policy, which concretely represents the entire free world, becomes abstract when it considers the rest not as partners but as a glacis in the battle with Russia."/27/ Moreover, the idea that we can remedy the nuclear problem by some technological system, "total planning," or an escape into outer space reflects the arrogance of abstract thinking's technological overconfidence (Cf., "Star Wars"). All of these false abstractions of the intellect are merely the recourse of individuals who shun the concrete because they do not want to change. Eventually, however, they can only end in a void or in various forms of fanaticism.

In sum, then, reason creates the mental space or common room within which truth's full communication can take place, and not simply that of the intellect which frequently leads to abstract thinking. Reason reminds us that "there is no peace without freedom, but no freedom without truth."/28/

5.2 THE RELATIONSHIP OF SCIENCE AND PHILOSOPHY: A PRELIMINARY DISTINCTION

> In our present reality, the academic philosophy that boasts of its scientific character is helpless. What we need is not mere specialized knowledge, as in all the sciences, but a change in man, the kind he has become conscious of since Socrates and Plato. Philosophizing does not provide man with new, precise knowledge; it does not add a new science to the rest. It offers no suggestions, plans, or programs. But it can arouse the inner disposition from which these tangibles derive their guiding sense./29/

As suggested here, we will be hard-pressed to find specific "suggestions, plans, or programs" for life in the nuclear age as a result of a "conversion" to an encompassing philosophical reason. The new possibilities reason may open at our present boundary cannot be calculated or known in advance like the objects of scientific knowledge. For reason is the movement of philosophizing itself. Throughout all of Jaspers's original works, the relationship of science and philosophy/reason surfaces again and again. Indeed, it was precisely to demonstrate the philosophy-science relation that he set out to write both his Philosophie and his philosophical logic, Von der Wahrheit./30/

Jaspers has identified the two principle presuppositions of his philosophical endeavours in his autobiography. Recalling Max Weber, his first premise states that scientific knowledge is an "indispensible factor" in all philosophizing. The second declares that there is a different type of thinking which is not compelling nor universally valid, and which "yields no results that as such could claim validity as forms of knowability [Wissbarkeit]." This is philosophical thinking, whose "consequences arise out of the inner activity of its own procedures," and which not only leads one to their very self, but also, and just as importantly, awakens those sources which give science its very meaning. These two premises betray the fundamental distinction between scientific knowledge, or scientific reason as the organ of the intellect (Verstand), and philosophical reason (Vernunft) in Jaspers's thinking. And yet just as there are not "two worlds side by side," one which science explores and another with which philosophy is concerned, but "only one world;" so too, reason is one with philosophy and science./31/

As alluded to earlier, however, scientific knowledge is the only truly cogent type of "knowledge" (Wissen, Erkenntnis) that exists for Jaspers. This is not to say that philosophical thinking or reason yields no meaning or even truth. But it is to say that there is only one type of objective knowledge for him, and that this knowledge is discovered and known by scientific reason. As Sebastian Samay has noted, for Jaspers "knowledge is either objective, or it is no knowledge at all," but it cannot be applied to "any and every kind of mental act."/32/ And if science alone is knowledge, then it follows that philosophy is some sort of "non-knowledge" (Nichtwissen).

James Collins has clarified the philosophical meaning of scientific knowledge and that which is "knowable" for Jaspers./33/ First, in contrast to Nietzsche Jaspers does not equate the will to knowledge with the will to power. Instead, the impulse for knowledge is authentic and original to human nature.

This speculative quest for knowledge presupposes that the world is knowable. But this proposition can be understood to mean either (1) that all objects in the world are knowable, or that (2) the world as a "whole of being" is knowable. It is the general confusion between these two ways of interpreting the knowability of the world-- and, in particular, science's claim to the knowability of the world as a whole-- that gives birth to the substitution of science for philosophy. The logic of this perversion is understandable. For if all objects in the world are knowable only through scientific method, then we will see all truth about the world and reality as available only to scientific understanding. And from here it is only a short step to the further assertion, as Collins suggests, "that the real is coextensive with the totality of objects in the world."/34/ In the end, the only philosophical truth open to humanity is that type of truth mediated by the scientific method.

Jaspers construes the proposition that (1) objects in the world are knowable in a strictly Kantian fashion./35/ Science, in other words, is concerned only with determinate knowledge. "'Knowledge'", for Jaspers, "is not an indeterminate general term, covering every relation between the mind and things. Instead, it connotes one definite sort of thought: that in which a polar relation is set up between the subject and the phenomenal object."/36/ As for Kant, the content of objective knowledge of the world is always some particular, empirical mode or appearance of being, a phenomenon. And knowledge embraces the subject only insofar as the mind or spirit becomes an objective appearance which we hold, as it were, at arms length from ourselves.

Secondly, Collins reminds us that Jaspers denies the proposition that (2) science can furnish an image or system of the world as a whole. Tantamount to Kant's "regulative idea," the world can never become an object of scientific knowledge. As such, it falls outside the region of the knowable and thus lies beyond scientific inquiry. As we showed above in Chapter Two, this is precisely where scientific world orientation ends and "philosophical world orientation" begins. Because science can never know the total being of the world as such, but only determinate objects and laws about the world, then it follows for Jaspers that the unity of science cannot be realized through a single method and body of doctrine as the positivists would like./37/ Although the sciences fail to constitute a

<u>system</u> of world knowledge, they do represent a cogent, unified <u>systematic</u> of knowledge. In Jaspers's words, "scientific knowledge can only go as far as reality is grasped by our methods and enclosed within our categories," but "it is only when using the methodologically clarified sciences that I know what I know and what I do not know."/38/

Jaspers's critique of science suggests that neither the sciences nor philosophy can grasp all of being. To know determinate objects is not the same as coming to an awareness of the ground of being; we cannot <u>know</u> "being as such." Nonetheless, we may be able to use reason to apprehend being in some "non-objective" and "non-knowing" way. But as Collins rightly notes, Jaspers is left with the problem of coming up with some evidence for the contention that "being is wider than object-being," and that truth is something more than scientific knowledge alone./39/ Jaspers's "evidence," of course, is more in the nature of an appeal to an awareness of being as grasped by possible Existenz and an awareness of the various meanings of truth as grasped by philosophical reason. And science is an indispensible constituent of this reason./40/

From the foregoing differentiation between scientific knowledge and philosophy as a type of "non-knowledge" we can better understand Jaspers's own critique of other philosphers' views on the science-philosophy relationship (5.3), as well as his specific understanding of the distinction and alliance between science and philosophy (5.4). Both dimensions bear directly upon the spiritual "crisis" of the present age from which the nuclear problem has arisen. But modern science can offer no help whatsoever; "it cannot show us the way out of doom."/41/

5.3 <u>VIEWS</u> <u>REJECTED</u> <u>BY</u> <u>JASPERS</u>: <u>POSITIVISM</u>, <u>ANTI-SCIENCE</u>, <u>AND</u> <u>MARXISM</u>

Jaspers concisely posed the question of the relationship between science and philosophy in his inaugural lecture at the University of Basel in 1948 when he asked: "could any philosophy legitimately claim to be scientific?"/42/ If philosophy had from its beginning looked upon itself as science <u>par</u> <u>excellence</u>, the prodigious developments in modern science, especially in the nineteenth century, had changed this. These developments took place "largely outside philosophy, often in opposition to philosophy, and finally in an atmosphere of indifference to it."/43/ The result was that philosophy after that time was expected to be a science in the same sense as modern science. If not, it was argued, it would deal in mere abstractions and empty ideas.

Jaspers identifies two reactions to the view that philosophy had been rendered obsolete as a science by methodical, cogent, and universally valid knowledge, i.e., by truly modern science. The first view sees science's attack against philosophy as justified. On this view, philosophy has been superseded by true science and relegated to a knowledge of its history; that is, (a) as a knowledge of the history of science itself; (b) as a knowledge of the history of philosophical thought, insights and errors; and (c) as the knowledge of philosophical texts, whose data are to be preserved even if only for their aesthetic value.

Others espousing this first view reject all previous philosophy in an attempt to ground contemporary philosophy on an exact scientific foundation. They regard philosophy's task as establishing in theory the validity of scientific knowledge by means of epistemology, phenomenology, and especially philosophical logic as a mathesis universalis. Philosophy is thus regarded as a science among other sciences, carried on by specialists./44/

In contrast to the first view, a second view rejects philosophy's claim to scientific knowledge, but bases it instead on feeling, intuition, imagination and genius. If the first view falls prey to positivism, this second posture is markedly anti-scientific. Jaspers understands the latter as a reaction to the consequences of technology on contemporary life./45/ In effect, however, this deprecation of scientific inquiry merely mistakes the errors of science for science itself. Both the submission to science in the form of positivism and the rejection of science as cogent, methodical, and universally valid knowledge spell the end of philosophy according to Jaspers./46/

Now at the heart of the problem of philosophy's relation to science lay three different conceptions of scientific knowledge in the western tradition. The first, is patterned on the precise methods of modern science. The second is derived from the idea of a total philosophical system as found in Descartes, Hegel, and to a certain extent even in Kant, as was evident from Jaspers's critique and transformation of

Kant's basic questions above in (3.1)./47/ The third conception of scientific knowledge may be traced back to Plato's parable of the cave in Book VII of the Republic./48/ This conception is most akin to Jaspers's own notion of faith in the meaning of existential communication, and thus "truth," given their inextricable relationship, and it stands in sharp contrast to the knowledge of truth yielded by the intellect. Corresponding to these three conceptions of knowledge are three imperative philosophical tasks Jaspers identified in his post-war situation: first, to expose the false idea that total philosophical knowledge is scientific; secondly, to purify the sciences themselves; and thirdly, to purify philosophy itself from within the new conditions created by the modern sciences./49/

These three different conceptions of scientific knowledge bring us directly to Jaspers's critique of Marxism, since he sees all three as operative therein./50/ He admits that through its theoretical insights and investigations in the economic field, Marxism has had an important influence on the present epoch, both positively and negatively. But the scientific and economic influence of Marx has not been nearly as significant as his philosophical and political influence. As a philosophical thesis, Marxism regards the dialectical course of history as a "total process" which it purports to understand scientifically by means of the dialectical method. Jaspers sees an abberant type of philosophical faith operative here. Politically, Marxism presents itself as an "absolute truth that fulfills man's will and aspirations." Jaspers understands this as analogous to the Platonic idea of truth, but of an entirely different cast, especially when its political "faith" understands itself as "the true consciousness of the classless man."/51/ Let us briefly turn to the philosophical and political forms of this "faith."

Jaspers admits that Marx has made contributions to theoretical economics. Nonetheless, he argues that Marx is essentially a philosopher because even in his "purely scientific work" his insights tend to confirm a doctrinal belief in the whole process of history./52/ This "total insight" is nothing more than a part of Marx's own philosophical faith which views all previous history as ideological. Marx's own philosophy is then taken to be the one and only true science that has integrated theory and praxis (cf., Marx's Eleventh thesis on Feuerbach) through the acceptance of the dialectical truth of historical evolution. Marx's "philosophical faith," Jaspers writes,

> believes in the One; not in the one God, however, but in the one united science which includes the unity of science and action, science and philosophy. This 'unified' science may be roughly described thus: history is a part of natural history, of the evolution of nature into man. Natural science therefore, in all its fields, already refers to man and is essentially a human science. But the science of man includes natural science as an ever-changing product of the human mind. Hence there will be only one science and that is the science of history./53/

In sharp contrast to this unifying science of Marxism stands authentic modern science which is particular and accepts no single, universal method such as a dialectics of history. It is one thing to speak of economic knowledge gained by an inductive scientific method which is subject to repeated modification. But it is another matter altogether to identify this with a dialectical knowledge of the total process, which is merely an appearance of definitive knowledge. "Marx's absolute, exclusive claim," Jaspers concludes, "originates in a conception of philosophy as total, systematic knowledge; but at the same time, his doctrine is presented as a _result_ of modern science, from which it does not follow at all."/54/

Most importantly, Jaspers understands the scientific and philosophical Marx as inseparable from the political Marx./55/ Given Marx's critique of religious faith as an ideology born from the womb of individual and social alienation, it is ironic that he judges Marx's political influence as functioning like the influence of a religious faith in society. Echoing Max Weber, he asserted in 1950 that "Marx and the Marxists are warriors of the faith" with whom one cannot reason./56/ While this view was tempered and qualified through the last few decades of his life, he always felt strongly that Marx and Marxism harbor no illusions about the realities of force and power. They not only give a central place to the role of praxis in history, but the dictatorship of the proletariat demands the use of violence in the exercise of this praxis as well. Believing that he had the true faith, Marx's "political creed" justified any means to reach the end of the classless society in which non-violence and egalitarianism would reign supreme. But this creed erroneously believes it can do what no previous political system in history has been able to do: to make and carry-out "total planning" successfully./57/

Finally, although Jaspers agrees with Marx in seeing science, faith, and politics as a sort of philosophical unity, Marx's great "intellectual tragedy" was to destroy science in the name of science itself. Marx did this, he feels, by absolutizing the process of dialectic. This had two results. First, by turning everything in history into dialectic, dialectic itself became causality for Marx. And this causality is meant to be scientific and "conscious" in such a way that freedom and necessity can coincide. Secondly, Marxism turned dialectic into a form of sophistry. Truth and reason no longer have an eternal grounding, however, when all of reality is reduced to the movement of history. Dialectic thus becomes the sole cause of all historical events. These events are then taken to be radical transformations which, while destructive of capitalism, its ideologies, ethics, and "so-called rights of man," are nevertheless "creative" when viewed within the total movement of history. The idea is that if one brings about "nothingness," some form of "new being" will result. However, such a pseudo-science merely befuddles the faithful who remain subservient to the leadership, the party vanguard. The party line then becomes identical with the course of history, and as such, deviations from the party line are understood to be revolts against the course of history. In the end, history becomes a "deity" from which no appeal can be made./58/

It should be emphasized at this point that the Marxist view of history is just as irrational as that religious view of history which would equate nuclear Holocaust with the Christian Apocalypse as the preordained "will" of God. Both go wrong, he would argue, in assuming some kind of "total" knowledge of history, and by losing touch with the legitimate reason in myth. In so doing, both usurp the positive role of reason in our historico-political knowledge of the world./59/

In fairness to Marx, however, Jaspers does admit that Marx could never have imagined that the dictatorship of the proletariat would have been replaced by a tyrant or "Apparat." Nor that Marxism would have arisen in Russia and in various Third World countries, rather than in the West as a result of the industrial revolution as he expected. And Marx certainly could never have imagined the far-reaching implications of Lenin's slogan, "Socialism [...] is Communism plus electrification,"/60/ which marked the ultimate deterioration of Marxism into Marxist-Leninism. It was with this development and its concomitant evolution into a structure of "total planning," that Jaspers believes Marxist thought grew farther than ever from reason. We must also note Jaspers's insistence, contrary to many of the critics of his atom bomb book, that Weber's proposition, "you can't reason with warriors for the faith," cannot be the last word in dealing with the Communist world. For if humanity is to survive, and if we are to believe in reason, then reason demands a patient searching for rational communication by means of a purity of motive and an ethos of unconditional Existenz. We must keep talking, "jaw, jaw, jaw," as Winston Churchill said, even if talks between the free and totalitarian worlds occur under mutual preparations for violence, and with each side blaming the other for the perpetuation of the arms race. In such a situation Jaspers sees the very first step of reason as a step towards conflict resolution, and the "mutual acknowledgement that our opponent cannot give up the force that we retain."/61/

In sum, Jaspers's critique of Marx and Marxism opposes their making a supposed total knowledge of history the basis of "total planning." Such a claim is simply another form of philosophical "faith," albeit an aberrant one. In the East, this total planning is under the control of a single totalitarian organization, and thus stifles human freedom. In the West, various institutions and organizations engage in forms of planning which, to be sure, limit human freedom, but they do not destroy it altogether. At least the West, he avows, is still free enough to struggle politically for the direction in which it wishes its science and technology to move; and we are not to forget that the fight against totalitarianism is as much an internal struggle as an external one.

Such is the broad portrait of Marx and Marxism painted by Jaspers after the war and throughout the decade of the original Cold War. It must be noted that Jaspers saw "total planning" and false abstractions of the intellect based on psychological, economic, political and technological research, as great dangers for which both the East _and_ the West must be weary. The West is particularly susceptible to the thinking of the intellect, skewed as it is toward a type of total planning which expresses itself in aberrant forms. Economically, the West risks the subordination of all values to that "great leveler," money, which alienates humanity. Politically, total planning can lead to a wrongly organized power structure which induces the state to act against the will of the majority. Psychologically, the "old way of thinking" of the intellect expresses itself through the will to power, rapaciousness, and the lust of feeling superior to life by throwing it away in fits of fanaticism. Technologically, total planning dangerously expresses itself in the abstract faith that technology alone can guide us out of the nuclear dilemma. Faith in "intelligent invention," Jaspers warns, "produces instruments of production and of destruction simultaneously, to the point where both unlimited production and total destruction are possible."/62/

In other words, Jaspers sees "faith" in the ability to plan ostensibly total, technological "solutions" to the nuclear dilemma as merely representing a new form of _positivism_ specific to the nuclear age. And in this respect, Dr. Robert J. Lifton and Professor Richard Falk have more recently defined "faith" in the form of psychological, political, and military dependence upon nuclear weapons and nuclear technologies as "nuclearism."/63/ The parallel between Jaspers's critique of technological "panaceas" and Lifton and Falk's notion of "nuclearism" is striking. Whether Jaspers would have accepted their precise definition of "nuclearism" may perhaps be a moot question. But there can be no doubt that he foresaw and warned against the dangers of "faith" in totalistic nuclear technologies, and so-called "emergency" military contingency plans in a time of relative peace between the East and West./64/

For Jaspers, of course, the root cause of this new technological "faith" is a confusion between the intellect's role in scientific research and planning, and reason's guidance in the politico-historical sphere. Faith in technological "solutions" repeatedly runs the risk of matching the erroneous Marxist claim to an ostensible total knowledge of history based on dialectic as this claim is manifested socially, politically, and militarily in total planning. But if in the East "total planning transforms all human existence into a structure of mass organization-- a planning always confined to the finite horizons of the human intellect,"/65/ and in the process voids human dignity, then in the West this same total planning "entangles our existence in needless and pointless necessities" which become equally unbearable. By not limiting itself to what really can and must be planned, this form of total planning also abolishes freedom. As Jaspers puts it in a form which anticipates the key element of the "conversion" to existential and political freedom,

> The intellect that is behind all planning claims too much if it tries to direct the decisions of freedom, which are acts of reason. The trouble starts when overplanning puts a supposedly scientific guidance in place of change to rational freedom. Man can only change as an individual and then, perhaps, arouse the freedom of others, but the slightest touch of coercion would destroy what counts. The state of the world is changed by the achievement of reason within its circle, of the individual within his sphere./66/

5.4 THE DISTINCTION AND ALLIANCE BETWEEN SCIENCE AND PHILOSOPHY

With the distinction between scientific "knowledge" and philosophical "non-knowledge" and those views on the science/philosophy relationship which Jaspers rejected in mind, let us now turn to a more precise treatment of the dialectical relationship that obtains between science and philosophy. For Jaspers rarely speaks of the distinction between science and philosophy without at the same time speaking of their alliance. He can even say that philosophy "is 'science,' but science of such a sort that in the sense of modern scientific inquiry it is both less and more than science."/67/ While it is futile to proffer a "definition" of philosophy over and against science, we can take our approach to their distinction from the ways in which Jaspers sees philosophy as both less and more than science.

Philosophy is less than science insofar as it is not a cogent science. Science is cogent knowledge of the intellect because it proceeds from the impersonal intentionality of consciousness-as-such. It treats object-being according to controllable, plannable, and universally acknowledged methods. The same cannot be said for philosophy: "If we call science that which is cogently knowable for every understanding, and which for that very reason has actually gained universal recognition, then <u>neither philosophy nor theology</u> can be called sciences."/68/ Taking the meaning of science in a necessarily strict fashion, Jaspers repeatedly emphasizes that philosophy (and theology) do "not gain any tangible results, nor any intellectually binding insight."/69/

The reason this is so for philosophy is because it is not so much the mental act of the disinterested intellect or "consciousness as such" as it is a concrete act of Existenz in freedom. It is not determined by causal laws and so-called "value-free" (<u>wertfrei</u>) methods,/70/ but by the necessity of conviction lived and acted upon out of philosophical faith.

Being identical throughout the world, scientific cognition appears to be much more than philosophy, which has never gained universal acceptance in any shape or form. But diversity is merely the way in which philosophical truth <u>communicates</u> itself, while scientific truth is universal: "Scientific truth is one and the same for all,-- philosophical truth wears multiple material cloaks; each of these is the manifestation of a unique reality, each has its own justification, but they are not identically transferable."/71/

Philosophy is also <u>more than science</u>, then, precisely because it represents an existentially valid source of truth that is "inaccessible" to scientific knowledge. This truth rests primarily on an "inner awareness" (<u>Innewerden</u>) of the being of humanity and the being of the world as a whole. The sciences cannot encompass all of truth, but only the exact knowledge that is binding to the intellect and particular to each scientific method. Truth has a much greater scope, and "part of it can reveal itself only to philosophical reason." It is this "more" than science, i.e., this peculiar truth grasped through inner awareness by philosophical reason, which is usually meant by such "definitions" of philosophy as the way of learning how to die, as the knowledge of all being, as the way to the good life, or as the thinking of a faith in humanity. What all of these "definitions" amount to is that "philosophical thought is inward action; it appeals to freedom; it is a summons to [T]ranscendence."/72/

If Jaspers sees philosophy as both less and more than science, he also sees their methods as being essentially different. Whereas any specific object is the object of a particular science, the methods of philosophy have no object: "the methods of philosophy are methods of transcending the object. To philosophize is to transcend."/73/ To be sure, all thinking is inseparable from objects according to Jaspers. And in this sense the history of philosophy is merely an account of how human thought has succeeded or failed in transcending the objects of philosophy. But these objects, which he equates with the great creations of philosophy, function merely as "roadsigns" or "ciphers" which indicate the direction of philosophical transcending.

Now philosophy's lack of an "object" does not make it meaningless. It merely suggests, as we saw above, that philosophy is not objective knowledge, that it is not science. It seeks a grasp of being which is more than science. The inner awareness upon which philosophy rests is a form of non-objective and "non-knowing" thought which is not subject to the split between objective and subjective factors in knowledge. Instead, it desires to synthesize both objective and subjective elements within the idea of the whole, which scientific thought can never do since it is objective and finite.

As concerns the alliance between science and philosophy, Jaspers maintains that philosophy needs science just as much as science needs philosophy: "reason presupposes intellect, and an intellect trying to be self-sufficient would remain empty."/74/ And both science and philosophy must be made "pure" if we are to truly exercise the "new mode of thinking" to which Jaspers calls us in the nuclear age.

Philosophy needs science because today there can be no tenable philosophy outside the sciences. Indeed, philosophy proceeds from a "will-to-know" that finds its first realization in science. This is why Jaspers insists that anyone who wishes to philosophize must keep abreast of science and its developments, and must be skilled in scientific methods./75/ Philosophy also needs science because it is the only way to attain to a genuine "non-knowledge:" "It is as though the most magnificent insights could be achieved only through man's quest for the limit at which cognition runs aground, not seemingly and temporarily, but genuinely and definitively, not with a sense of loss and despair,

but with a sense of genuine internal evidence."/76/ In
other words, science assists philosophy by helping to
precipitate that inner awareness of non-knowledge.
This non-knowledge grows in scope and depth in
proportion to science's pursuit of empirical being or
data. Finally, philosophy needs science because
science prevents philosophy from mistaking itself for
science. Science recalls philosophy to its proper
vocation to follow the momentum of Existenz.
Ultimately, philosophy needs science because without
the truth of science, there can be no truth in
philosophy./77/

Conversely, science needs philosophy precisely in
order to keep science, itself, pure. For "the concrete
work of the scientist is guided by his conscious or
unconscious philosophy, and this philosophy cannot be
the object of scientific method."/78/ Philosophy helps
assist science in its search for goals and its own
meaning. It seeks, if not directly to imbue science
with value, at least to challenge science's
commitments, and to repeatedly raise the question of
value as the starting point of human interests.

Most important for our concern with the nuclear
problem, science needs philosophy's fight on behalf of
science against political and social forces that would
dictate from on high what the truth of science may or
may not be. This role for philosophy is no doubt one
that impressed itself upon Jaspers during the war
years, and seems just as relevant to the political use
of technologies in the present nuclear situation.
Whether acting in the form of public opinion or
governmental power, political forces "would like to
decide, and to assure by means of subservient
authority, what is to be true and how much of it can be
called scientific." In the fight against such "forces
of faith" that would take science into their aberrant
service, however, "philosophy is an ally of genuine
science and of any faith that presupposes freedom of
inquiry and research as its own premise."/79/

In sum, then, philosophy is different from science
as both more and less than science, but not as opposed
to it. Both are allies which need each other to keep
themselves pure. Their relationship is dialectical and
their dialogue must continually meet in that common
room of human thought where reason allows them to
complement each other. The distinction and alliance
between science and reason is tantamount to the
relation between Verstand and Vernunft. The intellect

is the indispensable medium through which reason must work, reason's organ or tool, but it is not identical with reason. For reason transcends the intellect, and calls it beyond its specific particularities, calculations and plannings, towards the ideal of an encompassing unity of thought and reality which never reduces truth to any one mode of being./80/

5.5 THE "CONVERSION" TO REASON IN SCIENCE
     AS THE "WILL TO TRUTH"

Let us conclude by first recalling one of Jaspers's basic suppositions that it is reason which reminds us that there can be "no peace without freedom, but no freedom without truth."/81/ It is ultimately truth, therefore, that must ground the quest for peace and freedom in the nuclear age. Truth has become the sine qua non for the future of humanity. In saying this, we must also say that this is the only exception to Jaspers's rule that worse-case prognoses of the future cannot be known apodictically. For without truth, humanity is sure to perish or fall prey to various forms of totalitarianism.

Secondly, it is reason which creates the "common room" within which truth's full existential communication can take place. "Philosophical truth is a function of communication with the other and with myself; it is the truth I live by and do not merely think about." Truth is essentially bound up with communication and action, then, since "a thought is philosophically true" only to the extent that "its thinking promotes communication."/82/

Thirdly, it is the will to truth that unites the dialectical relationship that obtains between the truth that is obtained by the methods of science, and the truth grasped by the methods of philosophy. This relation of truth is well expressed in one of Jaspers's last university addresses in 1960, Wahrheit und Wissenschaft ("Truth and Science")./83/ It is indicative of the centrality of truth for Jaspers that he should have chosen this title for a treatment of the meaning of the university confronted by the threat of a global nuclear catastrophe.

Jaspers appeals to the university as the important locus in which the unity between truth in science (as universally valid exactitude) and the truth in philosophy (as an encompassing truth that has the limits of science as its condition of possibility) ought to be maintained. This unity comes to light through a communicative struggle, and in an atmosphere of freedom and openness where the will leads the way towards a common understanding and reason. Reiterating the sobering anti-rational possibilities of human extinction and totalitarianism as set forth in his book on the atom bomb, on the one hand, and the non-deterministic possibilities of love and reason on the other, he affirms that reason is indeed present in the world as that force by which humanity can and ought to live. Democracy, itself, is grounded upon this reason and not upon scientific knowledge. If democracy is the only way for freedom, truth, and peace to be, then its success depends upon reason's way of thinking and the symbols which make this accessible to all humanity. And it is precisely the task of the university "to secure through knowledge, in the purity of its communicative struggle, the greatest luminosity for this reason."/84/ The university can fulfill this task only if professors and students alike daily practice the art of rational thinking. This needs the intellect at every turn, but it is more than cognition, and springs from an "inner conversion" (inneren Umkehr).

Jaspers concludes his address with reference to the role of "conversion" in science and philosophy. While he sees the familiarity with scientific problems as a "conversion" through self-criticism, this nonetheless remains only a "conversion" of the intellectual point of view. In marked contrast, the proper "conversion" through reason is already the primary "conversion" of the "will-to-truth" (Wahrheitswillen). As it was for Plato, the will-to-truth is the essence of "conversion" (Umwendung): "With conversion to a repeated will-to-truth," he writes, "men will always be grounded anew." But there can be "no truth without conversion."/85/

To be sure, "conversion" belongs to the very core of humanity as attested by the great religious traditions. But in the nuclear age the pressing question is whether or not "conversion" in the light of truth and reason is possible amongst so many different individuals, and under completely different conditions around the planet. For a global community confronted by the possibility of extinction and totalitarianism, the will to truth as "knowledge through science and conversion through reason" ("Erkenntnis durch Wissenschaft und Umkehr durch Vernunft") has become the

142

ultimate condition of the possibility for the future of
humanity:

It is as if we today have reached
fate's portal. It still stands open.
Either it will be finally closed
through the death of mankind, or we
step through in that we reach the path
of freedom through truth in the
constant inner conversion of individual
men. Doubt before this alternative can
crush us. Our mere understanding
[Verstand] thinks it sees the door
beginning to close.
Still, as long as there is time, we
must hope in virtue of our activity, of
the tiny but irreplaceable activity of
each individual. For it [the future]
rests with us, but not only with us.
If we think and live and make our
plans, and act in the earnestness of
rational faith [Vernunftglaubens], then
and only then can Transcendence perhaps
come to the aid of our conversion,
without our knowing how, without our
being able to count on it, without our
even being able to form a conception of
it-- except in terms of soaring
ciphers./86/

NOTES

1. FM, Chapter 12, "The Scientists and the 'New Way of Thinking,'" pp.187-208, at p.192; AB, Erstes Kapitel, "Was Denken die Forscher?," pp.256-288, at p.259.
2. FM, p.199; AB, p.277.
3. See, e.g., VW, pp.113-21. RE, pp.107-126. PE, pp.54-61. RAT. FM, pp.209-235; AB, pp. 289-339. PFR, pp.58-60, 72-74. Also, PHT I, pp.235ff., where Jaspers discusses the thinking of reason in idealism, and thereby suggests that we must consider his own philosophy as a rational idealism: "There is another kind of thinking which the idealist performs and calls rational thinking, the thinking of reason. He employs the intellect as a tool to grasp what lies beyond all intellect: the idea, as the being of the mind in the entirety of subject and object. This thinking is dialectical. No solid objectivity will be allowed to stand; instead, all there is will be taken up and resolved in a genetical analysis that moves in circles and has nothing to do with causal comprehension. It is a thinking in which I conceive myself both as subjective being and as the essence of all being, and this being, as opposed to positivism, is the freedom I have, in thought, to partake of the idea. Freedom and the mind are one and the same. Where being is dialectically understood as self-related subjective being-- in other words, as my own-- I am free; where I confront all else as merely alien, I am unfree." PHT I, p.235.
4. RAT, p.40.
5. RAT, p.39.
6. PE, p.55.
7. PE, pp. 55-56.
8. Cf., PHT I, p.90ff.
9. RAT, pp.42-43.
10. RE, p.77.
11. RAT, p.44. Cf., PE, p.60, ~where Jaspers speaks of reason as "mysticism for the understanding." This is not to suggest, however, that reason, which opens onto the truth of philosophical faith, equates philosophical faith with mysticism. On the contrary, for Jaspers philosophical faith and mysticism are incompatible. On this point, see Leonard H. Ehrlich, "Philosophical Faith and Mysticism," Bucknell Review 17, No.1 (March 1969), pp.1-21.

12. Cf., Karl Jaspers, The Idea of the University, ed. by Karl Deutsch and trans. by H.A.T. Reiche and H.F. Vanderschmidt (London: Peter Owen, 1965), pp.44-45; German original, Die Idee der Universität (Berlin: Springer, 1946).

13. RAT, p.62ff. Cf., Hannah Arendt, "Karl Jaspers: Citizen of the World," in Schilpp, pp.539-49.

14. RAT, p.62; VWZ, p.49.

15. FM, p.206.

16. RAT, p.70.

17. RAT, p.71.

18. There is ample research which reveals that underlying the religious right's political influence on U.S. nuclear policy is precisely the kind of equation of Christian Apocalypse with nuclear war that we believe Jaspers would find so dangerously irrational. See further, Gabriel Fackre, The Religious Right and Christian Faith (Grand Rapids, Mi.: W.B. Eerdmans, 1982), esp., Chap. 10, "Consummation," pp.87-97.

19. Karl Jaspers, Über Gefahren und Chancen der Freiheit," in RA, p.357: "Freiheit ist die Führung aus dem Unbedingten. Diese Führung wird sich im Philosophieren klar, in jenem Philosophieren, das zum Menschen als Menschen gehört."

20. GBA, p.377.

21. Cf., RAT, p.91.

22. Cf., PE, p.59.

23. FM, p.210.

24. Jaspers's negative evaluation of symbolic logic is evident in his book on Descartes's philosophy. In his treatment of the idea of a mathesis universalis, Jaspers writes, "Symbolic logic is perhaps the undertaking that came closest to Descartes. No one denies that the logisticians have made correct statements. The question is: what do these correct statements mean in relation to the whole of human experience; that is, are they important, or are they merely correct, but without consequences? In the latter case, they would be empty, serving only as a game to be played by people who happen to like it and are prepared to accept its rules," LDW, p.178; DP, pp.98-99.

25. Anatol Rapaport, Strategy and Conscience (New York: Harper and Row, 1964) and Philip Green, Deadly Logic: The Theory of Nuclear Deterrence (Columbus, OH: Ohio State University Press, 1966).

26. The literature on America's counterforce and countervailing strategy is immense. For one of its most vocal proponents, however, see Colin S. Gray, "War-Fighting for Deterrence," _Journal for Strategic Studies_ 7 (March 1984), pp.5-29; and Colin Gray and Keith Payne, "Victory is Possible," _Foreign Policy_ 39 (1980), pp.14-27.
    Steven Lee, on both consequentialist and nonconsequentialist grounds, has recently made a convincing moral argument against U.S. extended and "counterforce" deterrence policy in his "The Morality of Nuclear Deterrence: Hostage Holding and Consequences," in _Nuclear Deterrence: Ethics and Strategy_, ed. by Russell Hardin, John J. Mearsheimer, Gerald Dworkin, and Robert E. Goodin (Chicago and London: The University of Chicago Press, 1985), pp.173-190, at p.184ff.
27. FM, pp.211-12.
28. Karl Jaspers, "Wahrheit, Freiheit und Friede," in HS, p.176: "Kein Friede ohne Freiheit, aber keine Freiheit ohne Wahrheit."
29. FM, p.209.
30. Karl Jaspers, 1955 Epilogue to PHT I, pp.5-6. VW, pp.9-11.
31. PAT, pp.37-38 and PHT II, p.18.
32. Sebastian Samay, _Reason Revisited_, p.107. Samay notes, pp.21-35, that for Jaspers objectivity involves both the problem of the correlation between consciousness and its object, and that of the problem of objective knowledge in general. As for the first problem, an object must display "opposition, unity, and generality" in order to be a correlate of consciousness. As for the second problem, a fully objective act of knowledge must exhibit "validity, stability, and universality."
33. James Collins, "Jaspers on Science and Philosophy," in Schilpp, pp.115-140.
34. Ibid., p.125.
35. See, e.g., PHT I, pp.136-38.
36. Collins, "Jaspers on Science and Philosophy," Schilpp, p.125. It is worth noting Jaspers's contrast between Kant and Thomism with respect to the distinction between particular and total knowledge. In Kantian thought, he writes, "there is a radical difference between appearance and the thing-in-itself. In the Thomistic position particular and total knowledge are differentiated, _but both are recognized as knowledge;_ in the Kantian [position] all knowledge is particular and belongs to the world

of appearance; total knowledge is impossible; its place is taken by philosophizing in its soaring to totality as a kind of truth which differs in principles." Karl Jaspers, "Reply to My Critics," in Schilpp, p.800 (emphasis added). For a more detailed Thomistic analysis and criticism of Jaspers's thought, see James Collins, The Existentialists: A Critical Study (Chicago: Henry Regnery Co., 1952, pp.88-123, esp. pp.115ff.

37. Collins, "Jaspers on Science and Philosophy," Schilpp, pp.126-30.
38. RAT, pp.29-30.
39. Collins, "Jaspers on Science and Philosophy," Schilpp, p.130. "One of the major epistemological questions raised by Jaspers' philosophy," Collins notes, "concerns the way in which 'thought' and 'reason' can serve as common foundations for both scientific knowledge and 'existential' awareness." p.131, n.19.
40. RAT, p.8.
41. FM, p.201.
42. Karl Jaspers, "Philosophy and Science," trans. by Ralph Manheim, Partisan Review XVI (1949), pp.871-884, at 871 (Hereafter cited as PS). This text also appears as Appendix I in WW, pp.147-167. This work is an English translation of Jaspers's inaugural lecture at the University of Basel in 1948, "Philosophie und Wissenschaft," Die Wandlung 3, No.8 (1948), pp.721-33.
43. PS, p.871.
44. Cf., Sebastian Samay, Reason Revisited, pp.76-86, who has further identified two groups or schools of philosophers within this first view identified by Jaspers. The first is the "Progressivism" school. This can be traced back to Auguste Comte and his famous "three stages" thesis of human progress which develops from the "theological" to the "metaphysical," and finally to the "positivistic" stage, and in which positive science represents the highest achievement of human thought. The second is the "strenge Wissenschaft" school, which has Descartes and Husserl as its principle proponents.

Commenting on this second school, in which formal logic falls, Samay writes critically of Jaspers: "The currents that embody this attitude are not difficult to identify. Logical positivism and phenomenology are mentioned by name, and the references to method and mathesis universalis make us think of Cartesianism. Jaspers' view on the value of logic is short,

147

severe, and in many respects intolerably unjust. He admits its exactitude, but dismisses its importance. He considers it an empty and inconsequential game of manipulating formal relationships whose philosophical worth is slight (p.79.)."

45. In this regard, see Jaspers's general response to philosophical attacks against modern science and technology in his article, "Is Science Evil?", trans. by Irving Kristol, Commentary 9, No.3 (1950), pp.229-233. German original: "Vom Charakter der Modernen Wissenschaft," Der Monat, 1, No.12 (1949), pp.12-17.

46. PS, pp.871-73.

47. On Jaspers's critique of Descartes, see LDW, pp.170-85; DP, pp.93-104. Cf., Samay, Reason Revisited, pp.79-84. For Jaspers's attitude towards Hegelian phenomenology with its idea of a total philosophical system, see his critique of idealism in PHT I, pp.235-250.

48. Cf., GPT I, p.142ff.

49. PS, p.878. The task of purifying the sciences, philosophy and theology under the new conditions of modern science was the life project of Bernard J.F. Lonergan, S.J., Insight: A Study of Human Understanding, rev. ed. (New York: Philosophical Library, 1958 and London: Darton and Todd, 1958) and his Method in Theology (New York: Seabury Press, 1972). A comparison of Lonergan and Jaspers and the centrality of human change or "conversion" for both thinkers ought to be pursued in another context. On Lonergan's response to the challenge of modern science, see Kenneth R. Melchin, History, Ethics and Emergent Probability: Ethics, Society and History in the Work of Bernard Lonergan (Lanham, Md.: University Press of America, 1987), esp., Chapters Three and Four, "Probability" and "Emergent Probability," pp.59-113.

50. It is not surprising, therefore, that Jaspers undertook a critique of Marxism and psychoanalysis as two "texts" which point to the need for authentic science as the condition of all true philosophy. See the first of his three lectures entitled, "The Challenge of the Scientific Method," delivered at the University of Heidelberg in 1950. In RAT, pp.7-37.

It can hardly be doubted that Jaspers's philosophical concern with Marx and Freud (and Nietzsche) had an influence upon his disciple and critic, Paul Ricoeur, and Ricoeur's concern with these three "masters of suspicion." Cf. e.g.,

Paul Ricoeur, <u>Hermeneutics</u> <u>and</u> <u>the</u> <u>Human</u>
<u>Sciences</u>, pp.222-273, and John W. Van Den Hengel,
S.C.J., <u>The</u> <u>Home</u> <u>of</u> <u>Meaning:</u> <u>The</u> <u>Hermeneutics</u> <u>of</u>
<u>the</u> <u>Subject</u> <u>of</u> <u>Paul</u> <u>Ricoeur</u> (Washington D.C.:
University Press of America, 1982), pp.ix-xxi.

51. PS, pp.876-77: "This quasi-religious postulate
is the source of a new kind of fanaticism which
invokes not faith, [which it is], but modern
science, which charges its opponents with
stupidity, malice, or inability to overcome class
prejudice, and contrasts these with its own
universal human truth that is free from class
bondage and hence absolute." Cf., FM,
pp.227-282.

52. RAT, p.13. Cf., FM, p.278.

53. RAT, p.14.

54. PS, pp.876-7 (emphasis added).

55. RAT, p.16.

56. RAT, p.17.

57. Cf., FM, p.277, where Jaspers writes: "Marx [...]
took the step from mere historico-philosophical
contemplation of entirety, like Hegel's, to
political activity based on a supposed total
knowledge. To him, the historic-philosophical,
designedly contemplative insight became supposed
cognition and an instrument for making history--
as the engineer employs natural science to build
his machines. Because he thought he had total
knowledge of the process of history, Marx could
see a point in total planning, in which the
all-embracing activity of man coincides with the
supposedly grasped historic necessity."

58. FM, p.277. Cf., RAT, pp.18-19.

59. FM, Chapter 16, "Reason and Irrationality in Our
Historic-Political Knowledge of the World,"
pp.262-90; AB, pp.365-417.

60. FM, p.278.

61. FM, p.267 (emphasis added). Jaspers continues:
"Politics still continues as this constant
reference to possible force, as bargaining and
treaty-making contingent on a status quo, as
trickery and cunning. This fact, too, should be
acknowledged in any talks, for the time being--
for the point of rational communication is not to
abuse it for deception in the conflict of force,
but to create among men a vinculum that would
eventually make this form of conflict impossible.
If reason is not unconditional but lets itself be
degraded to a means of totalitarian deception or
free inertia, it is no longer reason." Cf., AB,
p.371.

For a recent, popular expression of the role of reason in rational communication, see Roger Fisher and William Ury, with Bruce Patton ed., Getting to YES: Negotiating Agreement Without Giving In (New York: Penguin, 1982), esp. pp.59-96.

62. FM, p.214.

63. Lifton and Falk, Indefensible Weapons, pp.ix, 190ff.

64. See, e.g., FG, pp.110ff., on "The World Situation." Cf., FM, p.281 and AB, p.388. Despite Jaspers's stringent posture toward the "Russians" in the 1950s, we have little doubt that he would take a negative view of the Reagan Administration's SDI proposal (Star Wars) to render nuclear weapons "impotent and obsolete." Is this not simply another fallacy of abstract, intellectual thinking? Precisely to the point is John Tirman's (ed.), The Fallacy of Star Wars. Based on studies conducted by the Union of Concerned Scientists (New York: Vintage, 1983). On the fallacy and dangers of SDI, also see Richard Garwin and John Pike, "Space Weapons: History and Current Debate," and Yevgeny P. Velikov, "Effect on Strategic Stability," Bulletin of the Atomic Scientists Supplement (May 1984), pp.2S-15S, and Hans Bethe, et al., "Space-based Ballistic-Missile Defense," Scientific American 251 (October 1984), pp.39-49.
    Supporters of SDI have not, of course, argued the positions for strategic defense without appealing to moral principles and argumentation. See, e.g., Joseph P. Martino, "Star Wars"--Technology's New Challenge to Moralists," This World 9 (Fall 1984), pp.15-29, and Colin Gray, "Strategic Defense, Deterrence, and the Prospects for Peace," in Hardin et al., Nuclear Deterrence: Ethics and Strategy, pp.285-298.

65. FM, p.282; AB, p.389.

66. FM, p.281 (emphasis added); AB, p.388.

67. PS, p.879. Cf., PHT I, pp.316-26, where Jaspers discusses the philosophy/science relation along similar lines: "philosophy is not science. We clarify it in distinction from science, rather, for it is both more and less than science. Second, philosophy itself is an original will to know, with scientific knowledge one of the directions in which we satisfy it. And third, it is engaged in a struggle for knowledge on behalf of science, against sham knowledge" (p.316).

68. MC, pp.105-6 (emphasis added).

69. PS, p.881.
70. Cf. Collins, "Jaspers on Science and Philosophy," Schilpp, p.133. To be sure, for Jaspers, science is value-free in the sense that it cannot set ultimate goals for the moral life and moral obligations, but it is certainly not _wertlos_ or without valuational factors. The very questions we bring to scientific endeavour and the objects we choose to investigate imply a priori valuation. Jaspers treats the question of whether science is both _wertlos_ and _wertfrei_ in VW, pp.322-3.

    However, as Ernst Moritz Manasse points out, the lines between Jaspers and Weber on the question of value-freedom cannot be easily drawn: "As Jaspers sees it, Max Weber pointed out the limits of empirical science in order to protect the '_existential_' freedom of the individual from the encroachments of the cogent. Weber's negations, as do Socrates', have a positive aim. Instead of stopping the flight of the spirit they are to stimulate it. Weber's determined separation of the scientifically knowable from what belongs to the realm of personal evaluation aims at more than the contrast between the rational and the irrational which leaves the latter without light and responsibility. On the contrary, Weber's whole energies were directed at narrowing the sphere of the irrational. In a gigantic effort he attempted to gather all the light which reason provides and to focus it on the secret sources of our choices and decisions. Thus he pointed to the true freedom while engaging his whole strength in the service of the un-ending rational analysis." "Jaspers' Relation to Max Weber," in Schilpp, pp.369-391, at p.371.
71. PS, p.881. Cf., PHT I, p.317, where Jaspers writes: "The crucial difference between philosophy and science lies in the kind of communication. Scientific results and methods are communicated from person to person as interchangeable [consciousness-as-such]. In philosophizing this becomes a mere medium in which not everybody will communicate at random but _one individual_ _with_ _another individual_, in a communication that involves commitment because it is historic. Philosophy as a linguistic structure is a means of communication with the unknown possible individual."
72. PS, p.882, 881.
73. PS, p.880. Cf., PHT I, p.317.

74. FM, p.205.
75. Cf., PS, p.879: "Any philosopher who is not trained in a scientific discipline and who fails to keep his scientific interests constantly alive, will inevitably bungle and stumble, and mistake uncritical rough drafts for definitive knowledge. Unless an idea is submitted to the coldly dispassionate test of scientific inquiry, it is rapidly consumed in the fire of emotions and passions, or else it withers into a dry and narrow fanaticism."
76. PS, pp.879-80.
77. Cf., PHT I, p.317: "philosophy means the pursuit of unconditional truth, and in this respect it is more than science. Philosophizing is the thought whereby, in possession of cogent insight, I ascertain the insight that is not cogent, the insight that is an explication of faith. But without the untouchable fundament of scientific insight, the other kind cannot attain its own truth." (emphasis added)
78. PS, p.878.
79. PHT I, p.326. In contrast, cf. Martin Heidegger, for whom technology is, positively, a mode of revealing, and not a challenging (Herausfordern): "Technology comes to presence in the realm where revealing and unconcealment take place, where alethia, truth, happens." "The Question Concerning Technology," in Martin Heidegger: Basic Writings, ed. David Krell (New York: Harper and Row, 1977), pp.295-296.
80. Mikel Dufrenne and Paul Ricoeur, Karl Jaspers, p.108, have concisely summarized the important dialectical relationship between science and philosophy for Jaspers in this way: "Ainsi la science tient sa dignité de ce qu'elle complémentaire autant qu'opposée à la philosophie. D'une part, elle trouve son impulsion dans la philosophie, d'autre part la philosophie précède d'une volonté de savoir qui trouve une premiere fois à se réaliser dans la science, et elle n'en peut méconnaître les résultats ni négliger les instruments. Moins qu'une lutte hostile de l'une contre l'autre, il y a une lutte fraternelle des deux pour une vraie science et une vraie philosophie. La science sert la philosophie en lui interdisant de se prendre pour une science et en la rappelant par là à sa vocation propre qui est de suivre l'essor de l'existence [Existenz]. La philosophie sert la science en lui révélant ses limites, en la

préservant du dogmatisme, en la maintenant au
contact de l'objet."

81. HS, p.176.
82. PHT II, p.100 (emphasis added) and PHT II, p.97.
83. Karl Jaspers, "Truth and Science," trans. by Robert E. Wood, <u>Philosophy Today</u> 6, No.3/4 (Fall 1962), pp.200-11. German text, <u>Wahrheit und Wissenschaft</u> and Adolph Portmann, <u>Naturwissenschaft und Humanismus: Zwei Reden</u> (Munchen: R. Piper and Co., 1960), pp.7-25.
84. <u>Ibid.</u>, p.210; <u>Wahrheit und Wissenschaft</u>, p.22: "Aufgabe der Universität ist es, dieser Vernunft durch Wissenschaft, in der Reinheit ihrer kommunikativen Kampfe, die grösste Helligkeit zu verschaffen."
85. <u>Ibid.</u>, p.211; <u>Wahrheit und Wissenschaft</u>, p.24: "Mit der Umkehr wird immer von neuem der Mensch gegründet. Keine Wahrheit ohne Umkehr."
86. <u>Ibid.</u>, p.211; <u>Wahrheit und Wissenschaft</u>, pp.24-5.

153

> Politically, it has become clear that only world peace can remove the threat of the atom bomb. To imagine that it will eventually be possible to wage wars without recourse to the atom bomb, to use it merely as a deterrent, is a delusion.
> However, since a state of world peace can scarcely be realized by political means alone, this idea inevitably arose: Man seems doomed unless he experiences an <u>inner change through his freedom</u>. But such a <u>conversion</u> cannot be the object of a new politics: it can only be the prerequisite of a new politics./1/

6.0 INTRODUCTION

Jaspers's hope for a "new politics" rests upon humanity's "conversion" to existential and political freedom. Grounded upon human freedom, the "new politics" will act on the principle that "ethos, reason, and self-sacrifice can awaken and find both the valor of self-preservation and the turn to a true will to peace."/2/ Devoid of "suprapolitical" guidance, political discussions of "realists" and "moralists" can only lead to dead ends in the nuclear age. We must look "beyond realistic politics and idealistic morality to the other thing, to the ground of all thinking."/3/ In short, both humanity's salvation and damnation proceed from human freedom. We are not to shift the possibilities of freedom to events, institutions, or technological panaceas, to causal relations and actions that might be analyzed sociologically. For "all freedom lies in the individual."/4/

The call for a moral-political "conversion" of humanity raises the question of the proper relationship between morality and politics in Jaspers's thinking. The aim of this chapter, therefore, is to elucidate the important role of existential and political freedom within the broader context of his philosophical foundations. Methodologically, we must limit ourselves primarily to his relevant politico-philosophical sources prior to and inclusive of his work on the atom bomb and the future of mankind./5/

Jaspers's distinction between the intellect and an encompassing reason is as important to his political thinking as it is to his understanding of the relationship between science and philosophy.

> Intellectual thought is the inventor and maker. Its precepts can be carried out and can multiply the making by infinite repetition. The result is a world in which a few minds devise the mechanics, creating, as it were, a second world in which the masses then assume the operative function. Rational thought, on the other hand, does not provide for the carrying-out of mass directives but requires each individual to do his own thinking, original thinking. Here, truth is not found by a machine reproducible at will, but by decision, resolve, and action whose self-willed performance, by each on his own, is what creates a common spirit./6/

If the intellect dominates the political realm and is untempered by the "suprapolitical" element of reason, then humanity assumes merely an operative function in the state and society. Here the form of the will becomes conditioned primarily by means-end relationships, instead of an unconditional volition and action grounded in "possible Existenz."/7/ In extreme situations, such as Germany in 1931,/8/ humanity then runs the risk of falling prey to totalitarianism or a blind political will, and of accepting a substitute for true political authority.

> Rational thinking, in contrast, ties both existential and political freedom to ethics, the unconditionality of action, sacrifice, and the leading of the Geist. Although reason must work within a given empirical situation assessed by the tools of the intellect, a historico-political prognosis of the future cannot be grounded solely upon intellectual prediction. "The intellect always predicts the negative" and knows only "what is doomed." But "man adds something new to the world, something not adequately comprehensible in terms of what went before, not even in retrospect. Nobody can foresee what men are capable of."/9/ Any truly realistic prognosis or "active forecast" of the future must therefore consider the illumination of possibilities in which human

156

freedom meets natural necessity in such a way that political freedom and new possibilities are never foreclosed beforehand./10/

Because Jaspers's foundational presupposition is that all "freedom exists as volition,"/11/ we must begin this chapter by elucidating existential freedom and Jaspers's understanding of the importance of the "grand will" before the nuclear boundary (6.1). This leads on to the role of unconditional action as the necessary basis for a "new politics" (6.2). In turn, we survey Jaspers's elucidation of political freedom (6.3) which entails the primacy of rational communication and community, and a "conversion" from a violent to a "loving struggle" in politics (6.3.1). We will close with an analysis of his appropriation of Weber's "ethic of responsibility" (6.3.2) and Kant's idea of "perpetual peace" (6.3.3).

6.1 ELUCIDATING EXISTENTIAL FREEDOM IN THE LIGHT OF THE WILL

Jaspers begins his elucidation of "self-being as freedom" in the _Philosophie_ with a phenomenological treatment of the will. He challenges both the denial of free will, and those assertions that affirm free will. Affirmations of free will tend merely to "objectify" that reality of freedom which remains epistemologically embedded in the twin antinomies of nature/freedom and being as such/appearance. The human will is not just a "forward-driving activity; its freedom is that at the same time it wills itself." Will is not volition proper until consciousness grasps the very end it pursues. Jaspers speaks of the will that is psycho-physically driven by motives, purposes, and goals as the "formal will." This is the will that wills something in particular. It can be empirically described and analyzed, albeit incompletely, as a psychological phenomenon. In contrast, there is the will that wills itself, the "grand will," which "is the active assurance of being which my volition of something derives from the ground of freedom."/12/

> The will originates in _Existenz_ [i.e., as the gift of freedom from Transcendence], gets the grandeur of its content from the _idea_, is mobile in the service of _passion_ and of vital _ends_, and machine-like as the final form of a long-standing discipline [i.e., as formal will]./13/

157

Formal will, or will at the level of existence, is inextricably tied to "reflex movements" and to "instinctive and impulsive actions." The case for free will cannot be established on this level since here the will is bound to the multiplicity of one's basic drives and needs. As Oswald Schrag has observed, the problem for Jaspers "is not so much the 'freedom of will' as it is the problem of 'freedom and will.'"/14/ To build a case for free will on the level of existence is bound to fail: "freedom is not in existence, and since the supposedly generally valid and demonstrable statements to affirm or deny it would nonetheless objectify its being, they cannot but pervert its meaning."/15/

Theses positing that the will is free or unfree have been marked by the debates over determinism and indeterminism within the western philosophical and theological traditions. Jaspers analyzes the indeterminist assertions of free will along three lines. The first appeals to acausality or indeterminacy and the proof of the so-called liberum arbitrium indifferentiae: in case of two strong possibilities, one or the other must be realized by choice rather than necessity as in the case of Buridan's ass. Standing equidistant between two bales of hay and drawn towards each, the ass would starve if it did not have the free will to decide. This argument, however, proves nothing about freedom proper in Jaspers's view, but only about coincidence and license. This is a freedom of "indifference."

A second assertion of freedom is a psychological concept of free will as "freedom of action without disturbance from outside." But can a sharp distinction be drawn between being compelled and not being compelled psychologically to act? Is a person really free if they choose death to confession, even at the cost of torture? To be sure, one has a psychological choice to act and choose, but on this view freedom becomes banal. For the freedom of action and choice always remains within limiting-- and therefore determining-- parameters such as force, fatigue, and the pressures of time. Psychological concepts of freedom never question whether one is in fact free to choose the standards by which one's choices are made. Freedom defined psychologically lacks substance with respect to the real point of freedom: "where I am myself in the original sense of being no longer objectifiable."/16/ In short, the psychological level of freedom is negative, and more of the nature of "caprice" (Willkur).

The third assertion of freedom which does not really amount to existential freedom concerns power relationships in society and in the state. Jaspers distinguishes personal, civil, and political freedom. By personal freedom he means that freedom of private life that may require only the possession of economic means to be free. This can exist even in a situation where civil and political liberty are lacking (e.g., Czarist Russia). Civil freedom may unfold even in a state of political unfreedom if the law grants equal protection (e.g., Imperial Germany). Political freedom allows every citizen to participate in the election of leaders (e.g., the United States).

While these three "objective" sociological freedoms cannot be doubted, they tell us nothing about the existential freedom of "possible Existenz" itself. The freedom of Existenz may be in doubt despite those other freedoms just as, conversely, existential freedom is possible-- however difficult-- for an individual even if these three objective freedoms are non-existent. We must want these "objective" freedoms to be real, since they are conditions of the appearance of freedom in existence. Political freedom gives weight to that "original freedom," as possible Existenz, which "lends substance to the objective ones; deprived of this fulfillment, they become delusive."/17/ Jaspers always maintained the foundational priority of existential freedom over political freedom, even if political freedom held the spotlight in his thinking after the war.

Related to the above three objective freedoms are two types of false "freedoms" rooted in the delusion of human independence. Psychological pseudo-independence manifests itself when we erroneously take it to mean the goal of the will to be free and secure in the world without others. In this case freedom is turned "into the defiance of a formal self as [consciousness-as-such], or into the stubborn self-reliance of an empirical individual." In the case of sociological psuedo-independence one sets out to secure and expand existence by "calculation, foresight, and prudence." Attempts to grasp at sociological security, however, give way to the negative will to power and domination. Obsessed by thoughts of security, Jaspers writes, "I entangle myself in the outward freedom of possession, of having persons and things depend on me. I silence my fears of existence by making sure of my power to dispose; I satisfy my pride in existence by feeling the effects of my power."/18/ In either case we remain dependent and in need of communication with others.

The **political** implications of these forms of pseudo-independence have given birth to three responses to the problem of "security" in the nuclear age./19/ The first position states that I am simply going to keep myself pure, that the problem of nuclear destruction and the effects of the arms race upon the poor does not concern me. But this position of "worldlessness" merely helps to bring about the probable calamity. Not to know the facts and act is an escape from responsibility. The second approach is one of "complicity" based on the will to power. It states that I want to be in on the military-political process which is one with a world-historical process. The third response is that of "defiant interdependence." Here one is morally outraged by the stupidity and malice of technological panaceas and the nuclear status quo, and thus seeks a different world through negation and defiance. Even so, one cannot escape metaphysical guilt, not to mention cynicism and eventual nihilism./20/ Worldlessness, complicity, and defiance all work against existential freedom and a resolution to the nuclear problem.

Now if the "conversion" to existential freedom is tied to the realization of "self-being" through volition (grand will), Jaspers admits that arguments both affirming free will (as acausal, psychological, or sociological) and arguments denying free will (based on natural necessity or statistical law) cannot settle the problem. Denials of free will are as wrong as its affirmation because "if I say the will is unfree, I am objectifying and refuting something other than what in my certainty of freedom constitutes its essence."/21/ Both determinists and indeterminists have fought the battle over necessity and freedom on the level of phenomenal objectivity, taking it for all of being. As such, they have often lost sight of that true existential freedom which can be neither demonstrated nor refuted by the intellect. Jaspers does not attempt to "prove" freedom, but only to elucidate its antinomical structure along the lines of Kant's paradoxical theory of two causalities./22/ What makes freedom possible is that the very question of freedom originates in the self who wills its existence. We can be aware of freedom only because, potentially at least, we are already free in asking about it. Without this possibility of being free, we could not even ask about freedom./23/

Though we can never say directly what freedom is, there are nonetheless "signs" by which Existenz can hope to recognize the presence of freedom./24/ First, knowledge is not identical with freedom, but it is indispensable to it. In the absence of knowledge there is little or no choice, and freedom is restricted. Knowing opens up possibilities; hence, the necessity to approach the nuclear problem on the basis of concrete empirical data. Secondly, freedom involves arbitrary acts. There is always an ingredient of spontaneity which renders choice unpredictable. The psychological freedom or "caprice" of which we spoke before is thus tied to, but not identical with, freedom.

Thirdly, at the moral level, there is no freedom without laws and moral norms which we recognize as binding. One is free here in the sense of bowing to an imperative we find binding within conscience. Jaspers speaks of moral "freedom" as "transcendental freedom in which I freely find myself by obeying valid norms;" it is "active as opposed to mere passive knowledge, and it is borne by a necessity as against the random relativity of arbitrary acts."/25/

Moral freedom qua transcendental freedom means appropriating those norms which issue from within a historical situation that is constantly changing. It demands reason's guidance to deal with ethical problems. Jaspers's position on the meaning and limits of moral norms stands close to what contemporary Catholic revisionist theologians would call a "mixed consequentialism."/26/ On this view, "proportionate reason" guides the moral agent through a wide range of complex and morally problematic human situations with a respect for the social, personal, and thus sexual factors,/27/ that necessarily tie moral judgment to human experience. Jaspers's moral historicity thus critically suggests that Kant's ethical "formalism" was not always clear./28/

Fourthly, freedom has as a sign that infinite whole represented by the becoming of an idea. This is related to the fact that without knowledge there is no freedom; but the call is continually to broaden one's world-orientation "by limitlessly visualizing premises and possibilities of action," and by allowing all motives to speak to and work within one. Freedom as idea is to "move in a medium of infinite objective relations and in infinite reflection within myself, so as there to integrate them in a present freedom."/29/

Fifthly, since knowledge is never adequate and since reflection on the idea can go on endlessly, freedom is tied to resolution manifest in concrete choice. As human beings, we are forced by the passage of time and events to choose and decide out of an unfinished totality. While choice at first might appear as a conflict of motives, eventually one comes to experience the very meaning of the "unconditional imperative" qua choice. "The unconditional attitude implies a decision, lucidly taken, out of an unfathomable depth, a decision with which I myself am identical."/30/ Resolution as gift of freedom and choice as rational will, however, must be differentiated.

> It is this choice [Wahl], in fact, that makes me aware of my original freedom, because only there do I know myself as my true self [...] In this choice I resolve to be myself in existence. Resolution [Entschluss] as such is not yet the rational will that makes me take some finite action "resolutely," despite everything. Nor does it lie in a heedlessly, blindly courageous existence. Resolution is what comes to my will as the gift [sic] that in willing I can really be--it is what I can will out of, without being able to will it. In resolution I plunge into freedom, hoping at the bottom of it to meet myself, because I can will. But what manifests my resolution is my concrete choice./31/

What must be kept in mind in the elucidation of the "signs" of freedom is that freedom inevitably unfolds either in opposition to or union with necessity. There is no such thing as a freedom that has overcome all opposition: "In existential freedom I see myself between two necessities--between the natural law, the irremovable resistance of reality, and the moral law, the rigid form of a rule."/32/ Or, as Jaspers states the same in his metaphysics, existential freedom is a "cipher" in which the "free man [...] can be a cipher to himself, as distinct from the empirically existing man whose cipher is his natural being [existence] or his [consciousness-as-such], not his being human."/33/

Moreover, it is the presence of an ethical "ought" which reveals that freedom exists. Reason reveals the necessity of the ethical law or categorical imperative whose "ought" implies a "can." Freedom is never "known" but it can be grasped nonconceptually by reason in the certainty of self-being through action. Freedom is not intelligible to the intellect because, as in Kant's view, freedom "lies only in the caprice that can decide rightly or wrongly, not in the intelligible freedom of the will, for which there is no choice, because it belongs eternally to the necessary laws of duty."/34/ Obligation (as ethical duty) and law (as natural necessity) are inseparable for Jaspers. With Kant he emphasizes the categorical imperative's unconditional demand, which "is not demonstrated by experience; but on the occasion of experience, it emerges in its inexorable, unerring power, which I can elude only by self-deception," by the evil will./35/

Evil is the conscious will to negate the self-being of existential freedom as possible Existenz. Good and evil are insubstantial; there are not good and bad works, and neither is untruth the same thing as evil. Because there is existential freedom there is evil, but only the will can be evil./36/ The evil will animates action within the socio-political sphere along various lines: the lying of totalitarian regimes, the blocking of diversity and the squelching of individual initiative, censorship-- and what today we call "disinformation"-- the curtailing of freedom of speech and assembly, the spurning of human rights, and, most dangerously, the possible evil impulse to bring the world to ruin through nuclear holocaust. If the "grand" will is determined by "a condition which is itself unconditional, discernible through pure reason, independent of all material aims in the world, a law that presupposes only itself,"/37/ then the evil will has another unconditionality which is against being. The evil will turns against itself "only by shrouding itself somewhere, by curbing its will to know, by breaking off communication."/38/

Finally, Jaspers's insists that existential freedom and Transcendence are inseparable. Existenz is in relation to Transcendence or not at all. The mystery of Existenz lies in its experience of freedom as a gift wedded to choice. "The more decisive our certainty of our freedom, the greater our certainty of the Transcendence we owe it to [...] Where I am authentically myself, I am certain that I am not through myself."/39/ The grand will is the way of this

163

gift of freedom insofar as possible Existenz is manifest in socio-political action. For in the final analysis, existential freedom is ultimately "proved" by action;/40/ and only action can provide a "solution" to the twin threats of annihilation and totalitarianism.

6.2 THE ROLE OF "UNCONDITIONAL" PRAXIS IN EXISTENZ AND POLITICS

For Jaspers, political theory, as one form of philosophical contemplation, is of one piece with political praxis. Philosophical contemplation is not passive reflection, but "ocular inspection, adoption, ascertainment, inner action."/41/ Though contemplation does involve introspection, this is related to the adoption of tradition and ultimately serves the realization of existential freedom: "As Existenz results from the real act of breaking through mundane existence, existential elucidation is the thinking ascertainment of that act."/42/ And as active contemplation, this inner action is a philosophizing whose ultimate point is "philosophical life-- what the individual does in the inner action that lets him be himself."/43/ In order to realize existential freedom in the nuclear age humanity must undergo a "conversion" at the level of life-praxis. From the perspective of Jaspers's foundations, this entails a turn from "conditional" to "unconditional" action./44/

Instinctive conditional action is without reflection proper. It is willed on the basis of Dasein, and thus devoid of Transcendence. It becomes purposive when we are aware of our underlying drives and when, by the intellect's calculation, we relate a given end to certain means. A purposive act is a mere means to an end. When our action is spurred by drives upon which we have reflected it becomes vital action grounded in those interests which motivate our conscious existence. Action founded upon the expansion of existence, the gratification of self, or pleasure, wealth, and power, are all essentially conditioned acts in existence. Conditional instinctive, purposive, and vital actions are tied to "situations" in the world, and they correspond, foundationally, to Jaspers's understanding of the modes of being that we are as existence, consciousness-as-such, and spirit.

In contrast, unconditional action is "an expression of self-conscious Existenz doing in phenomenal existence, with reference to its transcendence, what it considers essential for all

164

eternity." Whereas purposive action is always qualified by its end, unconditional action is willed as such; it has no final goal. When it serves a purpose in the world, this purpose is not a sufficient reason for the act. In contrast to vital action, unconditional action's "drive and reflection are illuminated by an assurance of being which does not lie either in the drive and its satisfaction or in the calculated end."/45/ Most frequently unconditional acts occur in the boundary situations of death, suffering, struggle, and guilt and are not visible to psychological research. To follow Jaspers's "unconditional imperative" demands that it not be subordinated to the requirements of mere existence. And this requires "a conversion from continuous selfbetrayal and impurity of motives to the seriousness of the unconditional."/46/

Action ceases to be unconditional where the grand will does the good only if it does not cost too much, and where the individual loses him or herself through mundane purposes. In this case action turns into empty praxis. When acts are tied to a mundane purpose, we tend to cling to existence at all costs, since purposes tend to lead to further purposes endlessly. Like Christ's call to lose our lives for His sake and "the other" in order to gain true life (cf., Mt.16:25 and par.; Jn.12:25), Jaspers would say that we ought to act unconditionally at the risk of losing existence (Dasein), if we are ever to gain the freedom of possible Existenz. Hence Jaspers's deep appreciation of Gandhi's life and emphasis upon the "suprapolitical" role of unconditional sacrifice, though Jaspers was less convinced of Gandhi's politics of nonviolent action in the nuclear age.

The "conversion" to existential and political freedom has the realization of "unconditional action" as one of its most important imperatives. If one is hard-pressed to give content to the form of the needed existential Umkehr, it is because there can be no adequate definition of an unconditional act. We are to conceive such an act "merely as an appeal, a sign that will not be comprehensible to me unless I translate it into my own being."/47/

It is in the light of this "appeal" to unconditional action that Jaspers's critique of various calls to political action must be understood. Concerning the question of equipping the German army with atomic arms in 1958, he called for "reason's way

of thinking" instead of that thinking which links truth
to absolute positions and thereby ruptures both truth
and communication. Slogan-like thinking such as
"Germany wake up, Jews perish" or "people take up your
arms," as expressed during the Second World War; or
"against nuclear death" and "peace at any price" as
echoed during the time of his writing of Die Atombombe
all represent untruth./48/ The content of slogan-like
thinking is virtually interchangeable insofar as it
short-circuits the possibilities of existential
communication, and thus, meaningful political action.

6.2.1 The Limits of "Purposive" Action

All political action is a type of "purposive"
conditional action along with technological and
educational action./49/ Political action is action
with reference to the will of other human beings. It
attempts to "arouse" and "shape" the will of those who
work with us, just as it works against political
opposition and resistance met in the form of human
will./50/ While political action is necessary for
shaping and arousing wills, it is nonetheless limited
by various factors. First, there is our inherent
inability to survey all of the factual conditions and
wills of those involved in shaping the political order.

Secondly, the goals and values of our
pre-understanding help establish and bring about
political and military events themselves. This point
is especially relevant to our present situation where
military strategists devise "Single Integrated
Operational Nuclear War-Fighting Plans" (SIOP); to
think and act upon the goal of fighting, "prevailing"
and "winning"/51/ in nuclear war is to help bring about
that reality of nuclear holocaust for which such
language is merely an illusion and the logic of
madness.

Thirdly, for Jaspers, the political world is
affected by "the unconditionality of Existenz, and by
ideas."/52/ What Jaspers calls "unconditional ideal
action" marks the true foundation of politics. Justice
is one such idea. It is different from the rules of
utilitarian purposive action and legal order, since it
can never be embodied perfectly in any form. But it
nonetheless provides an encompassing guide for action
within the political order./53/ Legally, "justice is
to become real through law on the basis of a guiding
ideal law, natural law."/54/ But this ideal law can
only take shape in the historical law of society. The

liberty of humanity begins with the validity of the written law in the State. Unconditional action and "suprapolitical" ideas such as justice are the very origin of legal and political philosophy./55/

While technological and educational action are closely related to political action, power, and freedom, these forms of action are not entirely appropriate for "solving" the nuclear problem. To be sure, technology radically influences the conditions under which political action takes place today. But if left to itself, technological action, with its strictly factual language and ideas, would destroy political action which needs "suprapolitical" ideas for its guidance. The intellectual guidance of technological action would, in the limiting case, merely turn the world into a man-made mechanism./56/ As the political theologian, Charles Davis, has similarly maintained, a "merely factual" technological language and action destroys both religious meaning and a genuine politics: "politics is not about facts but about possibilities."/57/

The political limit of _educational_ action lies in its very principle: "the aim and purpose of a cultivator or educator remain qualified by the originality of his object."/58/ The educator does indeed shape and arouse the will, preparing the individual for political action insofar as education transmits tradition which is a premise of freedom. Yet freedom can never be propagated as such, but only appropriated by the individual. "Handed down," Jaspers writes, political freedom "is not freedom any more [...] without a struggle, it is lost."/59/

Let us pursue further the idea of education in the nuclear age. Today we hear and speak of the vital task of conflict resolution and peace education. For Jaspers, peace education would mean that "non-purposive" education which is a requirement for the future of humanity, and which rests on four basic ideas: (1) the recognition of human rank coupled with the education of all; (2) teaching the nature of "total rule" along-side the sciences and humanities, i.e., classical and biblical traditions; (3) an appreciation of scientific knowledge apart from its technological utility; and (4) education for and visualization of a democratic civil ethos. "In the democratic idea," he writes, "politics itself is education." He believes his view of education to be in marked contrast to the so-called political "realist" for whom education is the competence of a few elite whose private lifestyle and morality is irrelevant to political action. The "realist" sees politics as a public affair unaffected by the private ethos, and thus an "appeal" to reason in every individual is utopian. But to Jaspers such "realism" is itself unrealistic. For the "foundation of politics is the hidden reality of all those whose nature emerges in political events [...] If the moral substance fails, Realpolitik will sweep all of them over the precipice."/60/

The tradition of political freedom in the West, then, which "is intended to make all other human freedoms possible",/61/ is not something that can be learned in the textbooks of political science, law, and history. There is no means-ends formula that might neatly be applied to obtain political freedom or realize the idea of democracy. Democracy is "historically manifold, and nowhere quite reliable," though Jaspers saw the incarnation of the idea in English, Dutch, Swiss, and American liberty, in the French Revolution, the Scandinavian states, and even in Bismarck's pseudo-constitutional Germany./62/ Ultimately, the idea of democracy rests in the possibilities of reason in humanity. The reason that moves in politics is for everyone to participate in through a unity of wills embodied in a legal state-order. Because reason is an authority in which all may or can share, the authority of teacher over student or technological expert over layperson has no bearing on the realization of political freedom. If the "old politics" is grounded on the educational principle of the struggle of all against all for existence, then education for a "new politics" will act on the principle that there can be honest, rational communication-- and thus peace-- between all people of good will./63/

6.3 ELUCIDATING POLITICAL FREEDOM
      IN THE LIGHT OF REASON

An encompassing rational thinking is essential to politics because it grounds the tasks of the "rational community" (Die Gemeinschaft der Vernünftigen) in the praxis of the state and its institutions./64/ This community is one of individuals who embody a hidden rational solidarity that is "suprapolitical," but which also takes the form of constructive and enduring political action. The rational community forms the authentic basis of human affairs. It is not a visible organization, and like the invisible church, its reality cannot be proved. The future of humanity depends upon reason's prevailing in all forms of human order-- in states, political parties, churches, schools, unions, and bureaucracies. No strategic think-tank, peace group, or government leadership can produce an encompassing reason and its conscience, but reason is the premise of the rational community and its "new politics."

The hallmark of the rational community and the basis of its authority is <u>boundless communication</u>, which stands in sharp contrast to the principles of the lie, secrecy, and terror that reign supreme in various forms of totalitarianism. Error and the possibility for correction are not only permitted by boundless communication, but they are required by it. Here there are no "final positions." Where one dares boundless comunication, the only reliable source is humanity itself, and not its pledges and contracts. The rational community rises and falls, then, in accordance with those "hidden existential forces that well and contract the loving communication itself."/65/

The indispensible condition for the expansion of the rational community is freedom for the public clash of minds unstifled by <u>censorship</u>. Jaspers rejects Plato's view that the ideal state should subject the power of poetry, music, and art to censorship because of their potential influence upon the ethos of each human being. And he rejects the censorship that is "recurrently sought by <u>ecclesiastical</u>" powers because "the spirit thrives only in freedom."/66/ He retains the call to responsibility of the Platonic precept, but chooses the path of peril that freedom brings to the destruction of creative potentialities by human censorship. In this way he sides with Kant who defended the freedom of the spirit as the premise of cultural creativity and political freedom.

Jaspers transforms the Platonic idea of philosopher-kings into the idea that philosophizing as the movement of reason, itself, can rule when materialized in societal institutions and nations as a whole. What Jaspers says of Kant is true of his own position: "The state of the world is shaped by a moral-intellectual process in the growth of nations, not by the insight of individuals."/67/ This is why even the most astute "stateman" will turn to others for political insight and understanding. The true statesperson will be persuaded by the rational community in which each citizen helps to control and correct the other, thereby enhancing reason. And yet, Jaspers's profound faith in the rational community stands over and against the ficticious idea of the sovereign will of the people.

> Democracy is not a fiction of the sovereign people as a personal ruler--an authority whose supreme wisdom is charged with the sole responsibility by all individuals, who then feel free of responsibility themselves. Democracy is every individual. Everyone himself is responsible for the way he lives, thinks, and works, for the actions he decides to take, and for the way he does all this in common with his neighbors. To feel free of this responsibility is the basic perversion of democracy./68/

Reason establishes the real meaning of the _idea_ of democracy and political freedom./69/ Because reason is a _way_ and not a final goal, the reason in democracy is never final, but continually changes shape and requires self-education, publicity of thought, an incessant common struggle for truth, and self-criticism. With Kant, Jaspers distinguishes between _forms_ of government (e.g., democracy, aristocracy, monarchy) and the "Republican constitution" or _manner_ of government whose only opposite is despotism. Both democratic and despotic rule may occur in all three forms of government as a merely "formal freedom," but the republican government is set up in keeping with the principle of the _freedom_ of the members of society, the _dependence_ of all on a common legislation, and thirdly, the law of _equality_./70/

Jaspers repeatedly warned that the great danger of the present historical situation is that merely formal democracy will give birth to facism, dictatorship, or Communist total rule within those countries in which the idea of democracy had been hastily established./71/ In this respect, he anticipated contemporary developments in Chile, Haiti, and the Phillipines, not to mention the totalitarian elements of Apartheid policy in South Africa. We must also ask if, in the age of the nuclear security state, a merely formal democracy is not the inevitable outcome of the absolute control and use of strategic nuclear technologies by an elite few?

Because Jaspers sees reason in democracy as aiming at equality insofar as this is possible, a government founded upon the concept of right requires laws that are subject to change and improvement. Here reason works by persuasion and not by arbitrary and illegal violence within the state, though he always upheld the right to revolt. This right took on special meaning in his understanding of the German political situation just before his death./72/ An encompassing reason believes that human rights take precedence over all unjust laws and institutions.

Reason also grasps the dialectical relationship that exists between existential and political freedom, between individual volition and the "state will." Whereas existential freedom is both prepolitical and "suprapolitical," political freedom is the actual condition of the way in which the state is governed, and it circumscribes existential freedom. Political freedom cannot exist without the will to existential freedom, but existential freedom is menaced in its realization if political unfreedom engulfs a people.

> Outer freedom of states and inner freedom through state government have permanence only through the existential freedom of individual human beings. This is why there is ambiguity in the word "freedom:" a despotic state can also have outer political freedom; a free democratic constitution can also have a nation of internally unfree men.
> Freedom begins as freedom of the individual, gains communal form in the Republican form of government, [and] maintains itself against oppression from alien states. In the entirety of these three elements is freedom real./73/

Political freedom, then, refers to that internal freedom of a people in which law prevails by means of a constitution. Political freedom is also bound to legitimacy or authority, since "freedom is empty unless it heeds authority, while authority is false unless it stimulates freedom [...] How the deity is conceived, how all things are shaped and pervaded by the present faith in it-- this establishes the strength of authority."/74/ Authority relates to both tradition and Transcendence as its historic source. Jaspers felt

both had become lost amidst humanity's preoccupation
with technological authority in the present./75/

Foundationally, freedom's relation to authority
can be defined sociologically, as Weber showed, in
terms of traditional (belief in the sanctity of past
traditions), rational (belief in the legality of
orders), and charismatic authority (belief in the
heroic power or exemplary character of a person)./76/
According to Weber, all forms of authority need faith
to be realized, and this is the central point for
Jaspers as well. "The crucial hallmark of free
conditions is faith in freedom."/77/ If in the
constitutional state faith and trust prevail, this is
because the state is grounded in a legitimate
authority. Where there is legitimacy, there is
internal political freedom because legitimate authority
puts force in fetters through the law. Jaspers opts
for a rational authority since, given the present
spiritual crisis and the rise of totalitarianism, he
saw the separation of politics and faith as an
important challenge to philosophizing. By this he is
not primarily referring to the traditional problem of
church and state, but to the need for a clarification
between faith and ideology. While he distinguishes
faith from ideology, he admits that "the separation of
politics and faith can itself be achieved only by
faith--by that relation to Transcendence which is
inherent in every historic religion and makes all of
them allies on the field of existence against random
nihilism."/78/

Jaspers's distinction between "negative" and
"positive" freedom establishes one of the basic
presuppositions of his political thinking.

> Legally, scope is left to the
> individual for the play of his
> arbitrary will (negative liberty),
> through which also he can shut himself
> off from others. Ethically, however,
> liberty consists precisely in the
> openness of life in being together that
> can unfold without compulsion, out of
> love and reason (positive liberty).
> Only when positive liberty has been
> realised on the basis of the legal
> safeguarding of negative liberty, does
> the proposition apply: Man is free in
> the measure in which he sees freedom

around him, i.e., in the measure in which all men are free./79/

In principle, political freedom recognizes that the individual has a dual claim to be both protected against force by the constitutional state, and to make his or her will felt through democracy. Max Weber had conceived "domination" in politics as "the possibility of imposing one's will upon the behavior of other persons."/80/ This, of course, is tantamount to Clausewitz's definition of war as the extension of politics by other means, and as we saw in Chapter Four, it is in line with Jaspers's Cold War advocacy. And yet, it is a fallacy of abstract thinking to believe that political power is solely power through force. Politics actually orients itself between <u>two</u> poles: "potential force and free association [...] Power politics and parliamentary politics are by nature opposed; how they join forces sums up the practice of politics until now and for an indefinite time to come."/81/

6.3.1 "Conversion" From Violence to the "Loving Struggle"

To be sure, politics is and has been throughout history primarily the wielding of force. But politics <u>ought</u> to be oriented toward free association as exercized through public discourse and debate. Our very attitude toward force is a "suprapolitical" element which helps motivate and shape political thinking. Physical force or violence is the most extreme form of that struggle or conflict which is an inevitable "boundary situation" of human existence. But conflict need not be violent. Through the guidance of the "suprapolitical" idea, struggle can also manifest "the meaning of the will to non-violence [...] sacrifice, political responsibility, soldierly virtue."/82/

> Peace is not the absence of struggle. But man can convert [<u>verwandeln</u>] the struggle from a violent one into a spiritual and loving struggle. The violent struggle dies in communication. Instead of superiority in victory, the result is communal truth. By means of such struggle each individual comes to him or herself. The loving struggle places all means of power, also the means of intellectual

173

forcefulness, which as a stronger rationality corresponds to physical strength, at the disposal of the partner in the same manner in which one makes use of them himself, and thereby cancels its fatal effects./83/

Reason guides the "loving struggle" in an attempt to limit force. Reason does not deny the reality of force in human existence, but it acknowledges that physical force or war between states can only be avoided if the concept of right prevails. Because law is morally based and real to the extent that it is enforcable both domestically and internationally, the challenge in the nuclear age must be to "convert" the violent struggle for existence into its other, the "loving struggle" for Existenz. The latter is realized only in that existential communication which presupposes the possibilities of reason in humanity and, ultimately, a solidarity concerning the possibility of Existenz between individuals./84/

6.3.2 Jaspers's Appropriation of Weber's "Verantwortungsethik"

Is existential communication and a "loving struggle" truly possible in politics? Jaspers's thinking in the Philosophie on the relation of existential communication and "political intercourse" reflects Max Weber's contrast between the "ethic of conviction" (Gesinnungsethik) and "ethic of responsibility" (Verantwortungsethik). A tension exists there between existential communication and "political intercourse." On the one hand, "political intercourse" is the form of state action since struggle is a boundary situation of human existence. Thus Jaspers writes, "I must, if I want to exist, accept the political realities and enter into their untruthful medium." On the other hand, the political medium of communication need not be untruthful. "Either both opponents grow untruthful, seeking nothing but power, or the one who seeks truth as well is rendered helpless before the other unless there can be power in truth itself." But if "political intercourse" alone should come to rule, it would destroy the chance of existential communication. "Existenz does not touch Existenz until that form is broken through, until men cease to deal with each other as enemies locked in a struggle for existence."/85/

Twenty-five years later in his book on the atom bomb, Jaspers again praises Weber's demand for an "ethics of responsibility" in political leadership./86/ Reiterating Weber's view on politics as a vocation, Jaspers argues that politics takes it cue from power and the possible use of violent force to maintain or obtain its ends. In this situation the practitioner of the "ethics of conviction" seeks to act rightly and leave the consequences to God. But he founders in the arena of political action because he must reject the means of force required to reach a given political end. Moreover, he is often inconsistent in carrying out the ethic. When intolerable violence occurs, the recourse is to violence with the plea that it be "final."

In contrast, the practitioner of the "ethics of responsibility" takes responsibility upon himself insofar as he can foresee the consequences of his political action. Enmeshed in the evil with which he must inevitably deal, the practitioner of the "ethics of responsibility" must therefore engage in "political intercourse" with its lies, trickery, and deception. As such, he must take any blame that comes as a result of his action. If he were to shift the blame, he would deny the very possibility that the act could be a political "exception."/87/ And yet, even Weber admitted that history has all too often shown that political action taken with a view to social responsibility has often ended up differently than expected./88/

Moreover, the Verantwortungsethiker wills power for a political end in contrast to the advocate of Realpolitik who wills power for its own sake. But if a political end is destroyed through the use of a particular means of force, then such political means would be senseless. In this case an "ethic of responsibility" would seem to require precluding means that, in themselves, would violate the given political end in question. Jaspers had noted this limit of the Verantwortungsethik in his early treatment of "Weber as a Politician."

> The ethics of responsibility includes belief in accountability for the consequences of one's actions, readiness for any kind of sacrifice though not for a sacrifice that would destroy the meaning of politics itself./89/

175

How does one determine if a given political act is responsible? With Weber, Jaspers ties his response to a _political_ _decision_ that is based neither on a calculable consequence of the "ethic of responsibility" nor on the unequivocal consequence of an absolute morality held by the "ethic of conviction." Instead, as we saw earlier, political decision is grounded upon unconditional praxis as possible Existenz. Unconditional action is capable of leaving its moral-political imprint upon the community precisely because it issues from a responsible and integral lebenspraxis. Thus the "political statesman" reaches a point where he understands the consequences of his action, but nonetheless says: "'I can do no other, here I stand.'"/90/ While the "ethic of responsibility" has the virtually impossible task of avoiding the extremes of moral absolutism and the will to power, it implies neither the endorsement of unprincipled political thinking and action, nor-- as the practitioner of Realpolitik is wont to secure-- the legitimation of an unlimited reason of state./91/

Jaspers differentiates, then, the practitioner of the "ethic of responsibility" from the apolitical practitioner of the "ethic of conviction" and the practitioner of Realpolitik who wills power as such. Whether or not he succeeded in avoiding the de facto position of Realpolitik-- given his legitimation of the use of the atom bomb at the risk of all life-- is a question to which we must return below. What he does add to Weber's Vorantwortungsethik, however, is the "suprapolitical" role of sacrifice. This is always historic and particular, and is the foundation of true humanity confronted by the twin threats of annihilation and total rule. Only sacrifice can make peace possible. "A lasting peace could only be achieved if the greatness, the strength, and the valor of the sacrifice hitherto shown in history by the soldier would now materialize in no lesser form."/92/

6.3.3 Is a "Perpetual Peace" Possible in the Nuclear Age?

Is a lasting peace grounded upon freedom and sacrifice really possible? Jaspers's understanding of the possibility of perpetual peace is so similar to the idea set forth by Kant in his 1795 essay that one is hard-pressed to find differences between them./93/ Neither thinker offers a final "solution" or political "program" for peace that might be implemented. That the question of the possibility of the passage from war to peace should be central to Jaspers's prognosis for the future of humanity is not surprising since it stands at the center of Kant's political philosophy as well./94/

First and foremost, the passage from the old to the "new politics," from war to peace, demands a passage from falsehood to truth.

> Only in the abandonment to truth is fulfilled freedom possible. There is no peace without freedom, but no freedom without truth. Herein lies the decisive point. Freedom is empty when truth, from which it springs and which it serves, is not intended [...]
> If we desire freedom and peace, then we must meet in a room of truth which has preeminence over all factions and standpoints, decisions and resolutions./95/

We become free and truthful only when we constantly turn back to that encompassing "common room" in which "reason's way of thinking" unites different political factions. In contrast, the so-called political "realist" (Kant's "political moralist") exploits the maxims of the old politics: _Fac_ _et_ _excusa_-- commit the war act and explain it later; _Si_ _fecisti,_ _nega_-- if you did it, deny that you are at fault by blaming others or human nature; _Divide_ _et_ _impera_-- set the leaders or the people against each other, and then conquer them all. These "sophistical maxims" are well known and do not fool anybody. The "realist" is not ashamed of them, of course, unless he fails in their execution. He believes the honor of politics lies in the aggrandizement of power./96/ The "new politics" of the "rational statesman" (Kant's "moral politician"), however, would make political leaders ashamed of following such maxims.

Jaspers also appropriates Kant's position on the _theoretical_ precedence of morality over politics. To be sure, the "radical evil"/97/ in humanity typically reverses the moral duty for the sake of the will to happiness. But the existence of evil does not refute the _theoretical_ precedence of morality, both "hypothesized" and "hoped" for by a practical, encompassing reason.

If Kant sharply divides politics from morality, real events from the

177

'ought,' he does so only to reunite them: "'Politics says, 'Be ye wise as serpents'; morality qualifies by adding, 'and guileless as doves.' Since both can exist in one precept, Kant sees no conflict between politics and morality; but the reason why there is no conflict is the precedence of morality, and this precedence lies in the certainty of its truth./98/

For Jaspers as for Kant, the theoretical certainty of the moral principle does not yield to the practical uncertainty of force. In Kant's words, "the tutelary divinity of morality yields not to Jupiter, for this tutelary divinity of force is subject to destiny."/99/ Or again, "'pure principles of right have objective reality, i.e., that they can be applied.' We are to act upon them, 'no matter what objections may be raised by empirical politics. Thus true politics can never take a step without rendering homage to morality.'"/100/ Jaspers would say political freedom cannot ultimately take a step without rendering homage to the moral freedom of possible Existenz. Theoretically, existential and political freedom go hand in hand. The moral "ought" of duty implies that humanity "can" act morally even in the political realm. For Jaspers, however, in a way that is perhaps much stronger than it is for Kant, this link between morality and politics implies a philosophical faith in the human ability to be both rational and moral.

And yet, as long as political "realists" continue to walk in the way of the old politics, then moral duty needs reason's political wisdom to guide the "rational stateman" through the uncertainty of force and bad actions in political life. This is why Jaspers nonetheless conjoins the "new politics" to an "ethic of responsibility," even if, as we saw in Chapter Four, this means using the atom bomb at the possible risk of all life.

For all their similarities on the relation between morality and politics, Jaspers differs slightly from Kant on the role of fear in its secret conspiracy with morality,/101/ and even more from the Kantian "progress" of history. Fear is ambivalent. It has both positive and negative possibilities in the nuclear age. It is positive insofar as it can bring people to an awareness of the seriousness of the human condition. Negatively, the fear of annihilation upon which deterrence has been based for the past forty years is merely a "false hope." It cannot provide a basis for a lasting peace. In response to Kant's optimism with respect to the "progress" of history, Jaspers writes,

> [Today] we have to add what did not apply in Kant's days--there is not much time. We have a breathing spell [...] If this interval is not utilized to prevent war as such, the doom of mankind seems inevitable [...] Nothing short of unprecedented fear could perhaps, as a natural factor, compel the assurance of peace; but as a mere institution this would have lasting success only if man were to permeate it with a new ethos, with a new spirit of sacrifice, with a new reason. Man will escape perdition only if he is changed in the Kantian concept of a 'revolution of the way of thinking.' Today he faces a great choice: the doom of mankind, or a transformation [Wandlung] of man./102/

That such a transformation of humanity is indeed possible is based upon his faith that a new unconditional ethic, spirit of sacrifice, and encompassing reason is indeed possible, and that Transcendence or the "hidden Godhead" will somehow point the way. It is to Jaspers's conception of philosophical faith, therefore, that we must now turn in order to complete the analysis.

NOTES

1. ABR, p.50 (emphasis added). Cf., HS, p.165.
2. FM, p.333; AB, p.480.
3. HS, p.166: "...über realistische Politik und idealistische Moral hinaus an das andere, den Grund von allem zu denken ist." Cf., ABR, p.52.
4. FM, p.233, 223; AB, p.324, 307.
5. This is not to suggest that Jaspers's last major political work, Wohin treibt die Bundesrepublik? (The Future of Germany), has little or no bearing upon his understanding of and "solution" to the nuclear problem. It is to admit rather that a systematic study of the points of convergence and divergence between this work and The Future of Mankind would take us far beyond the parameters of this thesis and require a separate chapter by itself. On the role of Jaspers as a critic of the Federal Republic, see Godfrey Carr, Karl Jaspers as an Intellectual Critic, pp.1-15.
6. FM, p.7; AB, p.25.
7. Cf., PHT II, pp.140-142.
8. Jaspers clearly saw the political failure of reason in Germany in 1931. Cf., MMA, pp.97-98.
9. FM, p.282; AB, p.389.
10. MMA, p.225ff. Jaspers discusses the meaning and limits of prognostic historical thinking in OGH, pp.141-52 and FM, pp.282ff.
11. PHT II, pp.133-153, at 133.
12. PHT II, p.133.
13. PHT II, p.142.
14. Oswald Schrag, Existence, Existenz, and Transcendence, p.151.
15. PHT II, p.145.
16. PHT II, p.146,147.
17. Cf., PHT II, p.147.
18. PHT II, p.148.
19. Here we are making a contrast between the delusion of independence as theoretically grounded in the Philosophy, and Jaspers's understanding of humanity's three basically false approaches to politics in FM, pp.329-332; Cf., AB, pp.476-480. On the delusion of the state's nuclear independence and the false quest for military "security" in nuclear weapons, see, Richard Falk's piece on "Nuclearizing Security," in Lifton and Falk, Indefensible Weapons, pp.144-169.
20. Cf., QGG, pp.71-73.
21. PHT II, p.150.

22. According to Jaspers, Kant tried to find a
    solution to natural science's inability to
    justify our consciousness of freedom in the
    phenomenal character of existence. For him, the
    antinomy of freedom and necessity rests on the
    fact that, on the one hand, everything is subject
    to causal necessity <u>ad</u> <u>infinitum</u>; and, on the
    other hand, on the fact that we see that a series
    of events begins with a first cause, suggesting
    thereby that there is freedom. Kant attempted to
    save freedom from phenomenal causality by his
    paradoxical theory of two causalities. The
    theory takes the nature/freedom alternative to be
    a false one. It states that not every effect in
    the world must arise either from nature or from
    freedom, but that <u>both</u> necessity and freedom can
    in fact be true of one and the same event or
    effect. With respect to an event's
    "intelligible" cause, an effect may be regarded
    as free. With respect to "appearances," it
    appears as necessitated by the course of nature.
    The problem, however, is that the "'intelligible
    character'"-- the thing in itself, the <u>noumenon</u>--
    which acts upon the phenomenal has a causal
    effect itself, namely, the causality or necessity
    of reason.
       Jaspers elucidates Kant's problematic in this
    way: "Freedom begins a chain of causality in the
    phenomenon, but in the sense that the phenomenon
    which results from former states through natural
    causality is produced from the intelligible by
    the causality of freedom. This effect of the
    atemporal on the temporal means that in the
    intelligible itself there is no freedom but the
    necessity of reason. Freedom first occurs in the
    relation of the timeless intelligible to the
    temporal phenomenon. 'Between nature and the
    intelligible a third term: freedom'" (p.301).
       While Kant's theory of two causalities offers
    "a rationally simple solution," it does so only
    "at the cost of involving a second objective
    world", that is, the objective causality of
    reason. And Jaspers admits that even for Kant,
    only the <u>intellectus</u> <u>archetypus</u>, the "intuitive
    divine understanding," could grasp the radical
    separation of intelligible freedom and phenomenal
    necessity as one. GPT I, pp.300-305.
23. Cf., Karl Jaspers, "Nature and Ethics," in <u>Moral
    Principles</u> <u>of</u> <u>Action</u>: <u>Man's</u> <u>Ethical</u> <u>Imperative</u>,
    ed. by R.N. Anshen, Science of Culture Series,

vol.VI (New York and London: Harper & Brothers, 1952), p.49. Also, PHT II, p.155.

24. Here we are following Jaspers's elucidation of existential freedom in PHT II, pp.154-174. We shall take up his foundational treatment of sign, symbol, and cipher in the next chapter.

25. PHT II, p.157.

26. For a summary of the mixed consequentialist position among contemporary Catholic theologians, see Richard M. Gula, S.S., What Are They Saying About Moral Norms? (New York/Ramsey: Paulist Press, 1982), pp.61-93.

27. For an example of a "new thinking" in contemporary sexual ethics see, André Guindon, o.m.i., The Sexual Creators: An Ethical Proposal for Concerned Christians (Lanham, Md.: University Press of America, 1986), Chapter Two, "A Theory of Sexual Ethics for Concerned Christians," esp., pp.34-37.

28. GPT I, p.298: "Where [Kant] himself propounds a system of definite ethical principles, he discloses the historical form of his thinking, and moves away from the source. His concrete prescriptions tend to veil the pure form of the unconditional. There is a cleft between Kant's categorical imperative and his concrete ethical demands. The categorical imperative marks an eternal source; the concrete prescriptions are in good part an expression of the excellent, but historically contingent, ethics of eighteenth century Germany."

29. PHT III, p.167.

30. WW, p.56.

31. PHT II, pp.158-9; PH II, p.180.

32. PHT II, p.169.

33. PHT III, p.157.

34. GPT I, p.300, 301.

35. GPT I, p.293.

36. PHT II, p.151.

37. GPT I, p.292.

38. PHT II, p.152.

39. PFR, p.95. Cf., WW, p.45.

40. PHT II, p.155.

41. PHT I, p.197.

42. PHT II, p.9.

43. PHT II, p.283

44. See, PHT II, pp.255-292.

45. PHT II, p.256. One will recognize in this distinction between conditional and unconditional-- or what Jaspers also calls the "unconditional imperative"-- action, Kant's

distinction between "hypothetical imperatives," which are technical and presuppose an end, and "categorical imperatives," which have their ground in themselves and lay claim to universal validity. Cf., WW, pp.52-62 and GPT I, pp.291-3.

46. WW, p.60. (emphasis added)
47. PHT II, p.257.
48. Cf., Karl Jaspers, "Wahrheit, Freiheit und Friede," in HS, p.177: "Es ist gewiss ein ungeheurer moralisher Unterschied, ob der Inhalt ist: "Deutschland erwache, Juda verrecke," "Volk ans Gewehr" (mit der Vorstellung von einem erst Europa und dann die Welt beherrschenden Deutschen Reich) oder ob er ist: "Gegen den Atomtod," "Friede um jeden Preis" (mit der Vorstellung von Rettung im Weltverhängnis durch eigene Gewaltlosigkeit). Wenn wir aber an Wahrheit und Freiheit als Voraussetzung des Friedens denken, erschreckt uns noch mehr als jeder Inhalt diese Denkungsart, die stärker ist als der Inhalt, sei dieser eine menschenfeindliche Lüge oder eine noch gutgemeinte Verschleierung der Wahrheit. Der Inhalt ist austauschbar." Die Unwahrheit der Denkungsart bleibt dieselbe."
49. See, PHT I, "Limits of Purposive Action," pp.145-156.
50. PHT I, p.148.
51. Colin Gray and Keith Payne, "Victory is Possible," Foreign Policy 39 (1980), pp.14-27.
52. PHT I, p.149.
53. PHT II, p.260. Along with unconditional ideal action, Jaspers identifies unconditional existential and transcendent action as directions (Richtungen) of unconditional action. Existential action is identical with ideal action, but can break through the idea, e.g., by calling justice into question, under certain circumstances. Transcendent action, on the other hand, refers to its "otherness:" "Any destructive or counterproductive act, any act that is irrelevant to the world because of the evanescence of its effects, can have this import which destroys the phenomenality of Existenz and idea." PHT II, p.261.
54. OGH, p.158.
55. Cf., PHT II, p.332.
56. FM, p.7. Cf., PHT I, "The World as Found, and as Made," pp.112-114.
57. Charles Davis, Theology and Political Society (Cambridge: Cambridge University Press, 1980), pp.156-7.

58. PHT I, p.148.
59. PHT III, p.26.
60. FM, p.315.
61. OGH, P.163.
62. FM, p.85.
63. Cf., FM, p.333; AB, p.480.
64. On the idea of the rational community and communication, see FM, pp.219-235; AB, pp.301-325.
65. FM, p.222; AB, p.305.
66. FM, p.225, 228 (emphasis added); AB, p.310, 314.
67. Karl Jaspers, "Kant's 'Perpetual Peace,'" in PWT, p.117.
68. FM, p.308; AB, p.439.
69. See, "Reason and Democracy," FM, pp.291-317; AB, 419-457.
70. Karl Jaspers, "Kant's 'Perpetual Peace,'" in PWT, p.91.
71. See e.g., Karl Jaspers, "Wahrheit, Freiheit und Friede," in HS, p.175-6.
72. We are referring here to Jaspers's critique of the proposed emergency laws, which included the construction of civilian nuclear bomb shelters. FG, p.39,41.
73. Karl Jaspers, "Wahrheit, Freiheit und Friede," in HS, p.175: "Äussere Freiheit eines Staates und innere Freiheit durch seine Regierungsart haben Bestand durch die existentielle Freiheit der einzelnen Menschen. Daher die Vieldeutigkeiten im Worte "Freiheit": Äussere politische Freiheit kann auch ein despotischer Staat haben. Eine freie demokratische Verfassung kann auch ein Volk innerlich unfreier Menschen haben.

    Freiheit beginnt als Freiheit des einzelnen, gewinnt gemeinschaftliche Gestalt in der republikanischen Regierungsart, behauptet sich gegen Unterdrückung durch fremde Staaten. Im Ganzen dieser drei Momente ist Freiheit wirklich." Cf., also, OGH, p.154; FM, p.216, AB, p.297.
74. Karl Jaspers, "Liberty and Authority," in PWT, p.37.
75. Cf., PFR, p.29.
76. OGH, p.159.
77. OGH, p.170. Cf., Karl Jaspers, "Liberty and Authority," in PWT, p.35.
78. Karl Jaspers, "Liberty and Authority, in PWT, p.51.
79. OGH, p.160.
80. Max Weber, Law in Economy and Society, in Max Rheinstein, ed., Max Weber on Law in Economy and

Society, trans. by Edward Shils and M. Rheinstein (New York: Simon and Schuster, 1954), p.323. Cf. also, Weber's "Basic Concepts of Sociology," section 8: "A social relationship will be called struggle in so far as the conduct of a party is oriented toward the intention of making his own will prevail against the resistance of the other party or parties" (p.9.).

81. KST, p.49.

82. FM, p.31; AB, p.57.

83. Karl Jaspers, "Wahrheit, Freiheit und Friede," in HS, p.174: "Friede ist nicht Kampflosigkeit. Aber der Mensch kann den Kampf verwandeln aus gewaltsamem Kampf in den geistigen und in den liebenden Kampf. Der gewaltsame Kampf erlischt in der Kommunikation. Statt Überlegenheit im Sieg ist das Ergebnis die gemeinschaftliche Wahrheit. Durch solchen Kampf miteinander kommt erst jeder zu sich selbst. Der liebende Kampf stellt alle Mittel der Gewalt, auch die Mittel der intellektuellen Gewaltsamkeit, die als stärkere Rationalität der stärkeren Muskelkraft entspricht, dem Partner in gleicher Weise wie sich selbst zur Verfügung und hebt damit ihre tödliche Wirkung auf."

84. Cf., PHT, II, pp.206-215.

85. PHT II, pp.90-91. The tension is never finally resolved by Jaspers. Elisabeth Young-Bruehl, makes this same point when she writes, "A central problem of Jaspers's political thinking is the relation of the rational community to the societal and political realms, or the relation of existential communication 'between man and man' and communication among men. Or, more generally phrased, the relation of the loving struggle of individuals to the struggle of arousing and shaping wills in the plural political realm. And this problem arises from two angles: first from the definition of political action as arousing and shaping of wills for mundane purposes, and second from the hiddenness of the rational brotherhood."Freedom and Karl Jaspers's Philosophy, p.66.

86. Jaspers's treatment of Weber's "politics as a vocation" in AB, pp.74-77 is untranslated in E.B. Ashton's translation of FM. The English translation of this section has recently been published by L. H. Ehrlich, E. Ehrlich, and G.B. Pepper, eds., Karl Jaspers, pp.416-421. Cf., also, Max Weber, "Politics as a Vocation," in Max Weber: Selections in Translation, ed. by W.G.

Runciman and trans. by E. Matthews (Cambridge: Cambridge University Press, 1978), pp.212-225.

87. We shall ground exception and authority within Jaspers's theory of truth in the next chapter. Suffice it to say here that, politically speaking, an exceptional act is one which is "unjustified and singular, an exception with which the actor identifies himself in time and eternity-- in time by answering personally for all the consequences, in eternity by taking the act upon himself." FM, p.44.

88. Quoting Weber, Jaspers notes: "'Grundtatsache aller Geschichte ist, dass das schliessliche Resultat politischen Handelns oft, nein: geradezu regelmässig, in völlig unadäquatem, oft geradezu paradoxem Verhältnis zu seinem ursprünglichen Sinn steht.'" AB, p.76. "'It is a fundamental fact of history that the eventual result of political action often, just about regularly, stands in a totally inadequate and often downright paradoxical relationship to its original meaning.'" L. H. Ehrlich, E. Ehrlich, and G.B. Pepper, eds., Karl Jaspers, p.419.

89. LDW, p.223.

90. AB, p.77.

91. Cf. AB, p.77: "The ethics of social responsibility is not identical with an absence of conviction. Rather, it turns out that: relative to the unequivocal ethics of moral conviction that does not take consequences into account and the Realpolitik of bare pragmatics of power which lacks conviction, the ethics of social responsibility is preeminent, i.e., the antithesis of the ethics of moral conviction and that of social responsibility becomes misleading." Translation by L. H. Ehrlich, E. Ehrlich, and G.B. Pepper, eds., Karl Jaspers, p.420.

92. FM, pp.55-56; AB, p.92.

93. Jaspers's indebtedness to Kant's essay is apparent throughout his book on the atom bomb (Cf., FM, pp.14-23, 334ff.) and especially in his article, "Kant's 'Perpetual Peace,'" in PWT, pp.88-124. Here we are also closely following Lewis White Beck's translation of Kant's Perpetual Peace: A Philosophical Sketch, in Immanuel Kant, Critique of Practical Reason: And Other Writings in Moral Philosophy (Chicago: University of Chicago Press, 1949), pp.306-345.

94. This thesis has been argued forcefully by Pierre Hassner, "Situation de la philosophie politique

chez Kant," in La Philosophie politique de Kant, par E. Weil et autres (Paris: Presses universitaires de France, 1962), p.78.: "on peut [...] interpréter toute la philosophie de Kant à la lumière du thème de la guerre et de la paix; on peut surtout, ce qui est moins gratuit, apercevoir au point d'arrivée de l'entreprise kantienne la nécessité d'une philosophie de la politique, et au centre de cette dernière le problème du passage de la guerre à la paix."

95. Karl Jaspers, "Wahrheit, Freiheit und Friede," in HS, p.176: "Erst in der Hingabe an Wahrheit ist erfüllte Freiheit möglich. Kein Friede ohne Freiheit, aber keine Freiheit ohne Wahrheit. Hier liegt der entscheidende Punkt. Freiheit ist leer, wenn nicht die Wahrheit gemeint ist, der sie entspringt und der sie dient [...]
Wollen wir Freiheit und Frieden, so müssen wir in einem Raum der Wahrheit uns begegnen, der vor allen Parteiungen und Standpunkten liegt, vor unseren Entscheidungen und Entschlüssen."

96. FM, p.334; AB, p.484. Cf., Karl Jaspers, "Kant's 'Perpetual Peace,'" pp.97-98 and Immanuel Kant, Perpetual Peace, pp.335-336.

97. Cf., Karl Jaspers, "Das radikal Böse bei Kant (1951)," in RA, pp.107-136. See also, Eduard Baumgarten, "Radical Evil: Pro and Con," in Schilpp, pp.337-367, and Jaspers's lengthy critique thereof in his "Reply to My Critics," in Schilpp, pp.863-869.

98. Cf., Karl Jaspers, "Kant's 'Perpetual Peace,'" in PWT, p.100.

99. Immanuel Kant, Perpetual Peace, p.331.

100. Karl Jaspers, "Kant's 'Perpetual Peace,'" in PWT, p.111. Cf., Immanuel Kant, Perpetual Peace, p.340. On the theoretical complicity between morality and politics in Kant, Pierre Hassner writes, "...en même temps qu'ils s'opposent, les deux mondes se reflètent et s'appellent. D'une part, les impératifs moraux doivent pouvoir être appliqués, l'action morale doit pouvoir s'inscrire dans le réel phénoménal; pour et par cela, elle doit pouvoir le modeler et s'y retrouver. D'autre part, la nature s'achève en histoire et l'histoire annonce la raison; la guerre des penchants naturels et des égoïsmes individual et collectifs tend à une paix qui, si elle n'est pas celle de la raison pratique, la préfigure du moins et lui ouvre la voie. L'écartèlement de la politique apparaît alors moins comme celui d'un dilemme que l'ambiguïté d'un schème ou d'un trait d'union. Il y a deux

politiques: la morale et l'immorale, celle du "politique moraliste" et celle du "moraliste politique;" mais l'immorale finit par servir a l'avènement ou du moins au progrès de la moralité." "Situation de la philosophie politique chez Kant," in La Philosophie politique de Kant, pp.82-83.

101. Professor Benoît Garceau, o.m.i., has set forth a brief critique of modern liberalism's optimism with respect to history and the ostensibly positive role of fear in bringing humanity to the realization of peace. He maintains that "La recherche de la paix par la voie du premier pas en vue du désarmament unilatéral progressiste et du partage avec les peuples défavorisés a besoin de présupposés anthropologiques différents de ceux qui ont inspiré la modernité" [especially Hobbes and Kant]. He then goes on to set forth two new presuppositions. "Première [...] ce ne doit plus être la peur de la violence et de la guerre qui nous pousse à écouter la voix de la raison, mais plutôt l'indignation devant le gâchis d'humanité que nous sommes en train de produire. Il n'est pas inutile de rappeler ici ce qu'Aristote disait de la colère: elle est une passion plus raisonnable que la peur. Puis, deuxième [...], ce que la raison doit prescrire, ce n'est plus simplement de renoncer, par calcul d'intérêts, à nos droits de nature et de consentir à ce que s'opère le passage de l'état de nature a l'état de societe civile, mais de renoncer d'abord au Léviathan que notre civilisation a accouché, puis nous résoudre à entreprendre le passage, qui ne dépend que de chacun de nous, de ce que nous sommes de fait, comme êtres biologiques rivés à nos déterminismes, à ce que nous pouvons devenir comme personnes libres capables d'accueillir autre que soi." "Anthropologie et Paix," Paper presented at the conference, "Quelle Paix pour Notre Temps/Quest for Peace in Our Day," May 16-18, 1986, Saint Paul University, Ottawa, Canada, p.6 (Mimeographed).

102. Karl Jaspers, "Kant's 'Perpetual Peace,'" in PWT, p.123; PW, p.134.

7.0 INTRODUCTION

As argued in the previous two chapters, humanity's "conversion" to both an encompassing reason in science and to existential-political freedom within society and the state is the condition of possibility of "perpetual peace" in the nuclear age. However necessary these first two "conversions" be, they are nonetheless insufficient. Writing in 1949, for example, Jaspers could state that the specific question of the future concerns "how and what man will believe." Without faith in humanity, new human possibilities, and, ultimately, Transcendence (or God), the positive realization of the tendencies toward socialism and world unity, and the possibility of a lasting peace, will miscarry.

> Faith is not a matter of the goals of volition, nor of the contents of reason that become purposes. For faith cannot be willed, it does not consist in propositions, between which one has to choose, it evades the programme. But it is the Comprehensive [das Umgreifende], by which socialism, political freedom, and world order must be borne along their path, because it is from faith alone that they receive their meaning [...]
> We cannot make our own transformation [Verwandlung] the goal of our wills; it must, rather, be bestowed upon us, if we live in such a fashion that we experience the gift./1/

Our treatment of Jaspers's analysis of the nuclear problem during the decade of the original Cold War (Chapter Four) highlighted the third element of his thesis: humanity's "conversion" to a "new" mode of thinking entails a turn towards philosophical faith. According to his evaluation, christian revelational faith and "formal religion" alone are inadequate for the demands of the new age. Thus, it is Jaspers's foundational understanding of the relationship between philosophical faith and revelational faith-- and the limits and possibilities of the latter at the nuclear boundary-- which determines the aim of this chapter.

A comprehensive treatment of the over-arching relationship between philosophical and revelational faith would obviously take us far beyond the focus and scope of this chapter, and require a separate work dealing at length with the diverse formulations of the question. These would include the meaning of Transcendence (the "hidden God" or Deity), the formal principles of transcending, existential relations to Transcendence,/2/ the relation between philosophy, theology, and mysticism, the question of religious pluralism, as well as specific problems arising from the confrontation and dialogue of Jaspers with the critics of his philosophy of religion: e.g., Barth (re. revelation), Buber (re. communication and prayer), Bultmann (re. demythologization of religion and Scripture), Gadamer (re. the primacy of language in hermeneutics), Fritz Buri (re. a personal relationship with God that avoids Christian exclusivity), and, most perhaps importantly, Ricoeur (re. Jaspers's method, faith's concretion, and the question of "guilt" versus human finitude, Christian sin, and the salvation of freedom)./3/ Although we cannot circumvent many of these diverse formulations, we must acknowledge from the outset the limits imposed by the question of the limits and possibilities of revelational faith in an age confronted henceforth by what Jaspers defines as the twin threats of annihilation and totalitarianism.

As argued in Chapter Three, philosophical faith is essential to Jaspers's "foundational thinking" or philosophizing as a whole./4/ While his early work, Psychologie der Weltanschauungen (1919), recognized that faith was not reducible to cognitive thought, and while he attributes to his wife a "mighty impulse" behind his own initial concern for faith,/5/ it was not until 1927/28 that he felt behooved to work out the relation between philosophical faith and revelational faith directly. At the end of a lecture course in metaphysics a Catholic priest expressed his gratitude to him and made the comment that he felt what he had learned was essentially theology. This took Jaspers aback: "I was discussing matters-- as a non-theologian-- which others considered to be theology; yet I was philosophizing. This had to be clarified."/6/

His Philosophie provided him with the first occasion for clarification. In philosophical world orientation (Vol. I) he identified the core of a world view or Weltanschauung as unobjectifiable faith and set forth a differentiation of philosophy and religion;/7/

in turn, he elucidated faith as a fundamental feature of "fulfilled absolute consciousness" of Existenz (Vol. II);/8/ and in his metaphysics he embarked upon a speculative illumination of the relations that obtain between the unconditionality of possible Existenz in relation to Transcendence/9/ as expressed in the language of "ciphers" (Vol. III)./10/ While the role of philosophical faith is again apparent in <u>Von der Wahrheit</u>, Jaspers's first direct clarification of the concept was published in 1947 as <u>Der philosophische Glaube</u> (<u>The Perennial Scope of Philosophy</u>). We have already made reference above to the importance of faith for the future in Jaspers's philosophy of history, <u>Vom Ursprung und Ziel der Geschichte</u> (<u>The Origin and Goal of History</u>)./11/ In 1954 his controversy with Bultmann over the question of the demythologizing of Scripture appeared as <u>Die Frage der Entmythologisierung</u> (<u>Myth and Christianity</u>). And his final elaboration of the relation between philosophical and revelational faith in 1962 was also his last major work in philosophy, <u>Der philosophische Glaube angesichts der Offenbarung</u> (<u>Philosophical Faith and Revelation</u>)./12/

With these sources in view, then, we begin this chapter with an analysis of the primacy of Jaspers's idea of philosophical faith (7.1) and its conflict with "formal religion" over both knowledge and authority (7.1.1). This leads on to the question of the existential verity of both philosophical and revelational faith (7.1.2); Jaspers's understanding of the radical antithesis of reason and catholicity (7.1.3); and the meaning and possibility of an historic, adoptive metaphysics (theory of ciphers) which might overcome the failure of communication between different and often competing faiths in the nuclear age (7.1.4). In turn, we shall take up Jaspers's characterization of the <u>limits</u> of revelational faith, and his understanding of the positive possibilities of a "conversion" from <u>kirchliche</u> to "Biblical religion" at the nuclear boundary (7.2).

7.1 THE PRIMACY OF JASPERS'S IDEA OF PHILOSOPHICAL FAITH

Jaspers's conception of philosophical faith is one with his "foundational thinking" and quest for the possibilities of authentic communication between <u>Existenzen</u> grounded in relation to Transcendence or God./13/ If existential freedom (possible Existenz) is never directly proved, it can be encountered in the act of existing, but only so long as the individual stands in relation to Transcendence or God. Transcendence is disclosed only insofar as we "leap" from, "turn about," or transcend the realm of immanence. Philosophical faith is an essential part of this dialectical process insofar as it affirms the leap as a form of transcending in thinking. This faith believes that all human beings can indeed meet with each other who, by the impulse of reason, sincerely will a movement toward the unity of truth out of the Encompassing. Jaspers admonishes that any attempt to characterize philosophical faith inevitably runs the risk of falsely objectifying it. Too often we erroneously take philosophical ideas for scientific knowledge, thereby evading what is paramount for the philosophical life, namely, "the rebirth of our nature in the act of transcending."/14/ This is why he can say that philosophical faith is ultimately expressed only in an "indirect communication of the total philosophical work."/15/

In philosophical world orientation he formally differentiates philosophy vis-a-vis religion, science, and art. Philosophy lies within each domain even if it can never become one with them. What they all have in common, however, is that "they bestow on man his proper sense of being-- religion by relating him to God, science by objective knowledge, art by symbolic visuality." While the tensions between philosophy and science and philosophy and art are conditional, the tension between philosophy and religion is an <u>absolute</u> one for the individual: "a genuinely religious person may become a theologian, but without an inner break he cannot become a philosopher, and the philosopher as such cannot without such a break become a religious person."/16/ And although the chasm between philosophy and religion is unbridgeable for the individual, it is precisely philosophy's relation to religion which gives philosophizing its reality and distinctiveness: "Religion remains for philosophy always a polar other, with which it is concerned, from which it receives stimuli, and to which it returns stimuli."/17/

Generally stated, the philosophy/religion relation is characterized by three foundational elements. First, philosophy <u>fights</u> against religion's claims to exclusivity and the materialization of Transcendence: "Xenophanes fought against the immortality of the mythical gods, Epicurus against fear of demons, Kant against superstition and priestcraft in established religion, Feuerbach against illusion, and Kierkegaard

against the church."/18/ It is religion's claim to
exclusivity that is the central phenomenon against
which Jaspers claims just cause in his battle against
religion. Secondly, philosophy not only respects the
core of religious faith as possible truth qua
existential truth,/19/ but it even takes the side of
religion in the struggle against "unbelief" and
"nihilism." It acknowledges the truth in religion's
rejection of these two forms of "anti-philosophy."/20/
Jaspers could not proclaim religious truth for himself
without a sense of falsely objectifying what he sees as
the historic and thus relative appearance of truth in
time. Thirdly, philosophizing rests upon a will to be
truthful that demands a readiness to continue searching
and the utmost clarity about the differences between
philosophy and religion. This means for Jaspers that
philosophy and religion are not two coordinated
possibilities from which to choose. "Religion," he
writes, "can be neither knowingly surveyed nor even
properly seen from the point of view of philosophy, nor
can philosophy from the point of view of religion. My
choice is made as I am or am not philosophizing, and as
I then take up resolutely what I am." Not only does
the Deity remain hidden, but "Transcendence even seems
to forbid a philosophizing human being to retreat into
religion."/21/

7.1.1 The Conflict with Religion
over Knowledge and Authority

The essential conflict between philosophy and
religion lay in claims upon knowledge and authority.
While Jaspers believes there need be no conflict
between faith and cogent knowledge, their struggle has
indeed been apparent in western history, as attested by
the Church's case against Galileo. From the
perspective of his foundations, the tension that
obtains between faith and knowledge lies in the
subject-object split itself. Faith is only real where
the "subjective" reality of faith is one with the
"objective" content of faith. This differentiation
between the "subjective" dimension of faith, i.e.,
"what believing is", and the "objective" dimension,
i.e., "what is believed in" is discussed in various of
his works./22/

> The faith through which I am
> convinced, and the content of faith,
> which I comprehend-- the act of faith,
> and the faith that I acquire by this
> act-- fides qua creditur and fides quae

193

creditur-- are inseparable. The
subjective and the objective side of
faith are a whole. If I take only the
subjective side, there remains a faith
that is merely a believing state of
mind, a faith without object, which in
a manner of speaking believes only
itself, a faith without inner content.
If I take only the objective side,
there remains a content of faith, as
object, as proposition, as dogma, as
inventory, as a dead something.
    Thus faith is always faith in
something. But neither can I say that
it is an objective truth that is not
determined by faith but determines it--
nor can I say that it is a subjective
truth that is not determined by the
object but determines it. Faith is one
in that which we separate as subject
and object, as faith by which and in
which we believe./23/

Because faith ultimately binds subject and object,
Jaspers sees the distinction between faith and
knowledge as a basic task of "Enlightenment."/24/ He
understands this in terms of a philosophical attitude
which is opposed to superstition and prejudice, and not
in terms of the historical movement itself, which is
often regarded among theologians as having given rise
to the lack of faith in the modern world. He takes it
to be a "false enlightenment" which would base
knowledge, will, and action solely on the intellect,
assert that the individual can know and act by him or
herself alone, or refute the importance of the
"exception" and "authority" for the right orientation
of life. Instead, he writes, "true enlightenment,
while it does not from outside, by intention and
coercion, impose a limit upon questioning, is aware of
the factual limit. For it not only elucidates
prejudices and common beliefs which were hitherto
unquestioned but also elucidates itself." Most
importantly, "it does not confound the methods of the
understanding [Verstand] with the contents of
humanity."/25/

    This confusion between the methods of the
intellect and what it is to be human is at the heart of
the conflict between philosophy and religion in dealing
with knowledge. As noted in detail in Chapters Three
and Five, Jaspers asserts that the modern empirical and
natural sciences have an exclusive claim to cogency and
universal validity by means of their evidential method

194

as truly "known" by the intellect. While there is no
single universal method, their truth rests on a
verification which can be universally repeated by
anyone who follows the appropriate method(s). In this
sense, knowledge is independent of the thinker's way of
being and worldview.

Faith, in contrast, cannot make such a claim.
While a tenet of faith will inevitably assume the form
of something we know objectively through the authority
of tradition, faith exists merely by virtue of one's
commitment. "What I can prove," Jaspers writes, "I
need not believe any more. If I seek objective
assurance about a tenet of faith, I have already lost
my faith."/26/ Though it is absurd to want an
intellectual proof of faith, it is not meaningless to
elucidate faith by transcending thinking. The real
problem results when faith is articulated in words,
thereby becoming unavoidably objectified in thought and
action. Since whatever appears within the objectivity
of thought is subject to its rules and criticism, it is
not surprising that a conflict of interpretation
occurs. And rightly so, since Jaspers maintains that
the use of thought on behalf of faith turns destructive
if it pretends to do anything more than assist in the
self-clarification of faith:

> In assertive judgments, faith is
> expressed as cogent knowledge. This
> knowledge can either be understood on
> the level of possible cogent
> knowability--in which case it comes
> into conflict with what can really be
> cogently known-- or else we know it as
> the explication of believing Existenz
> and **make** **no** **claim** **of** **cogency** **for** **it**
> **precisely** **because** **it** **is belief**. As
> such its aim is not to subjugate but to
> appeal [...] The conflict can be
> avoided only if the believer has become
> aware that for him the cogently
> knowable can never coincide with his
> intrinsic faith-- and can therefore not
> contradict it either./27/

It is as an "appeal" from faith to faith or,
better, from faith to "non-knowledge," that we are to
understand Jaspers's own elucidation of the "contents"
of philosophical faith. In his earliest treatment, he
identified three propositions of philosophical
faith./28/ In his philosophy of history, he spoke of

the "categories" of eternal faith in terms of "faith in God"-- as the certainty of Transcendence or God, "faith in man"-- as a possibility of his or her freedom, both individually and socio-politically, and "faith in possibilities in the world"-- as an openness that extends beyond the limits of finite cogency to the incalculability of the whole./29/ A few years later in a radio series, he set forth five propositions:/30/ "(1) God is; (2) there is an unconditional imperative; (3) man is finite and imperfectible [sic]; (4) man can live in God's guidance; (5) the world has evanescent reality between God and Existenz."/31/ These propositions, he feels, have their own source in a basic experience of human existence. By our very nature as human beings it is difficult to elude their truth. They are not to be glibly taken for a creed or dogma which is followed because of their institutional authority. Rather, they should be communicated in order that we might understand each other through them, even though they inevitably give rise both to false knowledge and to an unending dialogue with those who advocate their negation in unbelief.

In sum, then, the idea of philosophical faith "is not a knowledge I have, but a certainty that guides me." It is "the ground before any cognition," even though in faith, "cognition shines more brightly, but is never proved." To be sure, philosophical faith is allied with knowledge insofar as it "wants to know what is knowable, and to be conscious of its own premises." But it is forever immersed in dialectics which lead to insoluble antinomies at the boundary, "where being becomes faith, and faith becomes the apprehension of Being in the seemingly absurd." And while knowledge is also "subject to an infinite progression of critical doubt" which keeps it cogent, faith's form of compellingness "has to prove itself by existential vigor."/32/ It does so through the lifestyle and witness of the individual who wills to read the ciphers of Transcendence within the world.

Now if the conflict between faith and knowledge is reconcilable when one properly detaches cogent knowledge from the quasi "knowledge" of faith, the conflict between philosophy and religion with respect to authority would appear to be irreconcilable for Jaspers. The quasi "knowledge" in which faith understands itself always remains in an antinomy: "either authority will make the truth of this knowledge generally valid, or original independence will let us adopt or reject it at our peril."/33/ However, it must be emphasized that for him to speak of the knowledge of faith in terms of such an either/or is neither to deny the crucial role of authority for both philosophy and religion, nor, more importantly, is it to deny the transcendent ground of all genuine authority./34/

For, on the one hand, philosophical independence needs authoritative tradition precisely in order to develop its substance and come to itself, even though its deliberate submission to authority would be a loss of Existenz and thus faith. As Jaspers puts it, "philosophical faith venerates traditional philosophy but does not maintain an attitude of obedience to it. It does not look on history as an authority, but as one continuous spiritual struggle." On the other hand, religious authority would be illusory if it did not have an origin beyond the reach of the philosopher, or if it were a matter simply of obeying dogmatic rules. The social power of the churches and their import as a prod of philosophizing attest to religious authority's import. In this respect, it seems Jaspers would prefer that one err on the side of an objectified philosophical or religious tradition and authority, than on the side of a groundless, pseudo-originality and independence. But while he feels "the truth in the surrender of self-being to transcendence,"/35/ this truth appears to him as an authority in the world, and not as Transcendence itself.

Despite the fact that philosophy and religion are at odds with each other over authority, they nevertheless hold in common the existential truth, when manifest respectively, of unconditional action and active faith. Active faith is "the certainty of being [Seinsgewissheit] in which unconditional action originates; it is historicity." The historicity of faith ushers into unconditional action or it is not faith at all. The important question is "how historicity is originally with us: whether in dependence on objectivity, which is authoritative and thus not subject to proof, or in independent adoption." But whether manifest through philosophical independence or authority, "Existenz is original only when it is historic, and historic only when it is original."/36/

The centrality of the historicity of faith for Jaspers means that the truth of faith's "decision" is absolute and unconditional for the believer whether others believe as she or he does or not. Nothing objective guarantees the truth of one's faith, whether it be historical evidence, authority, or some type of religious revelation, even though one's action is telling of the nature of one's faith. The authority of tradition, philosophical or religious, may awaken one to his or her own historic truth and faith, and may, in turn, be adopted and testified to in word and deed. But if tradition becomes an alienating historicity, it can land one in a contradiction that would destroy a person's authentic freedom unless rejected. It is through a loving struggle with others that we clarify and ground our own sense of historic adoption or rejection, even if it is not possible to will or choose one's historic authority per se. As authentic authority, it is compelling for possible Existenz. Because one does not choose authority per se, all one can do is explain how the truth of authority in its various modes declines and loses its power./37/

7.1.2 Philosophical Faith and Truth

The conflict between philosophy and religion with respect to authority cannot be properly grasped without pursuing further Jaspers's foundational theory of the universal, transcendent unity of truth as One. On this theory, the "exception" (Ausnahme)-- best witnessed to by the philosophical independence of Kierkegaard and Nietzsche-- and "authority"-- as revealed in religious tradition-- authentically break through historic truth in multiple, but finite, human realizations in time./38/ Jaspers sees the plurality of truth residing in each of the modes of the Encompassing: in existence as preservation, in consciousness-as-such as cogency, in spirit as conviction, and as the truth of Existenz in faith. These modes are continually confronted by untruth-- especially in the form of absolutization and nihilism-- which leads dialectically through the movement of reason to another, deeper truth. For the one truth as authority to be present, it would have to permeate all of the modes of the Encompassing and join them in a present unity. This is not possible since, as subjects, we always remain in historic motion, and thus can never obtain to a fixed form of truth in time. Thus Jaspers affirms with Hegel that "truth is in league with actuality against consciousness."/39/

The historicity of possible Existenz always experiences truth in the polarities of exception or authority in relation to Transcendence. Although they are opposites in their historic manifestation, they nonetheless belong together as pointing to the ground of all truth. Both are configurations of the break through of the One truth as they appear in immanence.

Jaspers's hermeneutic of the Encompassing, as seen through the lens of philosophical faith, sees every break though of the one truth as a break through of a universal. "What is broken through," he writes,

> is always a constructed unity; it is every configuration that is closed off in itself, it is the unity of the state, of social institutions, of occupation and marriage, of every historic ordered unit [...] The forces that break through are either the specific Encompassing or another Encompassing or, if the unanimity among the Encompassings is lacking, a singular out of the depth of Being: the Encompassing of all Encompassing [das Umgreifende alles Umgreifenden]./40/

Stated differently, each mode of the Encompassing keeps breaking through the inevitable solidification of its own mode. For every interpretation of the break through of truth there is a counter-position which presents itself: law/arbitrariness, truth/falsehood, universal validity/particularity, and regularity/interruption. Ultimately, the difference between these counterposed sets of possibilities is that "all interpretation soon presupposes, unnoticed, some kind of order, whereas the expression of bottomlessness must exhaust itself in pure negations."/41/ Hence, the "irrational" is also understood to be a break through, but an empty one.

Given Jaspers's twofold conception of the nature of the continual break through of each mode of the Encompassing by forces within each mode, and of every encompassing by other encompassings, we can now better understand the import of the "basic philosophical operation" for his foundational thinking. Life out of the Encompassing is conceived either, negatively, as a decision for solidification or reduction of the modes of encompassing; or, positively, as a transcending, "turning about," leaping, or cognitive "conversion" that provides and safeguards the limited break through of the One truth of the Encompassing within time. His philosophical faith of communicative reason is thus ultimately a faith _in_ the Encompassing and the open-ended nature of truth as historically manifest through the modes of being which we are, the world, and Transcendence. And he readily acknowledges that his faith in das Umgreifende is merely one speculative heuristic, among others, that can and will be broken through by other encompassings.

It is in the light of this understanding of the exception and authority as configurations of the break through of truth in time, then, that one must evaluate the conflict between philosophy and religion. To be sure, an individual cannot fight the battle on both fronts. And yet it is a necessary conflict if the authentic and historic truth of the independent philosopher and the individual guided by the authority of revelational faith are to come to self-clarification through philosophical and theological thinking, respectively.

7.1.3 The Antithesis of Reason and "Catholicity"

Both philosophy and religion need each other for self-clarification on the way toward the unity of truth in time. But if the exception and authority are the main configurations of the historic break through of truth in time, then Jaspers's philosophical faith understands reason and catholicity to be the two main configurations of the directedness of humanity toward this truth in time. Unlike the polarities treated thus far, the relationship between reason and catholicity appears as the great and final antithesis within his theory of truth./42/

As noted in Chapters Three and Five, the basic characteristic of reason is its will to unity. As the "bond" between the various modes of the Encompassing, reason provides the impulse toward that unity of truth which is never fulfilled in time. Reason affirms the essential historicity of truth as manifest in the various horizons or modes of being which we are. Jaspers refers to any position or institution which claims the fulfillment of truth in time as that of "catholicity" (Katholizität), a concept which is more general than the catholicism of the Roman Catholic church, though certainly quite applicable to it./43/ Be it in culture (e.g., the "slogans" of mass existence), politics (e.g.,. totalitarianism, fascism, or imperialism), or religion (e.g., dogmatic exclusivity, whether Catholic or Protestant), catholicity is the great rival or antithesis of communicative reason. Clearly, faith in the nuclear age cannot be a "catholic" one, as Jaspers understands it, if humanity is to avoid the twin possibilities of annihilation and totalitarian mass movements, attain "suprapolitical" guidance for politics, and appropriate anew the spiritual insights of the "axial age."

Now reason and catholicity can and will function within <u>both</u> authority and the exception. But the difference lies in the precise <u>way</u> in which reason's impulse toward unity is concretely manifest in them: whether truth is conceived as bound to open communication, or as a truth valid for and binding upon all:

> Either the historic unity becomes unconditional not only for the historic human being living in it but becomes absolutely universally valid, i.e., the only true unity. For example, a revelation is exclusively the only true one, such as God incarnate who appeared only once.
> Or there remains the knowledge about the multiplicity, the consequence of which is the unconditionality not only of one's own historicity but also of the recognition of the historicity of the other person./44/

The recognition of the unconditionality of one's own historicity and that of the other can only be maintained in <u>original</u> historicity. This is threatened by forced historicity, on the one hand, and by the nihilism of historical relativity, on the other. At least catholicity and reason hold one thing in common: the rejection of an absolute historical relativity.

Jaspers's philosophical faith also sets "communicative methods" against "catholic methods." By catholic methods he means "those institutions, modes of behavior, practical rules which seek to bring about and to hold fast for an unlimited time to the universal oneness of human community based on a faith in catholic authority." Such methods, he asserts, occur in forms of thinking, as well as in practical and political behavior. For example, in the <u>thinking</u> of a "rational system" or a closed ontology, the contents are objectified and turned into a systematic unity which is taken to be universally valid (e.g., Thomas and Hegel). In <u>practical</u> behavior, one principle holds supreme, namely, that the center of catholic power and decision hold. Jaspers's analogy to the papacy seems explicit when he writes that in the case of conflict authority "rests solely with the earthly representative of the apex of this truth." As such, the "exception" is denied status, even as "the hierarchy of sociological possibilities does allow for perennially keeping one's distance, supra- and subordination, being-more or being-less."/45/ The _political_ behavior of the leaders of catholicity is marked by an "empirical realism" with respect to the preservation of the catholic system, power, and authority.

Communicative methods, in contrast, are marked by the impulse toward rational communication. Although catholicity and reason are both universal, Jaspers sees the former as a closed universality, the latter as open: "reason remains boundlessly open and moves out of the primal source of each historic Existenz, having achieved its certainty in its immediacy to transcendence." With communicative methods order and authority are never absolute. The attempt is continually made to reach out to others whose origin is different from one's own. Assistance with one's essence grows only through authentic communication. Only in this way does one find himself or herself through a loving struggle. Here no individual can help another with the aid of practical or technical acts in the realm of the intellect.

> All that is possible is the community of those who are themselves [...] Since, however, man is so often helpless in the absence of his self-being, he strives to go beyond the limit of what is possible to man and receive help from the other even in his innermost self. And there were men who believed they could render this help. They did not awaken the other maieutically, as did Socrates, but transmitted the truth directly to the other as did Christ. Christ first grants the grace which transforms man so that he becomes capable of receiving the faith in the perfect truth that did not reside in him before.
> But whoever philosophizes can neither give nor receive such truth. He can neither possess nor receive truth but can merely grow toward it in mutual communication./46/

The way one grows toward the one unity of truth in communication is through concrete life lived out of philosophical faith in search of being as world, self, and Transcendence. In formal terms, Jaspers's search for being occurs through the categories of transcending qua objectivity at large, reality, and freedom./47/ Formal transcending culminates in Jaspers's theory of ciphers, which Fr. Tilliette has referred to as the "masterpiece," the most original and precise contribution of his speculative metaphysics./48/ Indeed, in Jaspers's theory of ciphers we see the cornerstone of his philosophical faith.

7.1.4 Ciphers as the "Word" of Philosophical Faith

In the Philosophie Jaspers first set forth his understanding of the meaning and possibility of an historic, adoptive metaphysics as the "reading" of ciphers. In Von der Wahrheit, he considers the "cipher" or "symbol" as a form of the completion of truth in time./49/ In his book on the atom bomb he chides the churches and theologians for their use (political) of religious symbolism with respect to "God's will" and the question of the use or non-use of nuclear weapons and deterrence. What are the foundational aspects of his theory of ciphers which bear directly upon the question of the limits and possibilities of revelational faith in the nuclear age?

Jaspers's theory of ciphers comes as the culmination of his foundational thinking. The theory responds to previous philosophical attempts to resolve the subject-object dichotomy on the basis of either the subject (aberrant idealism or subjectivism) or the object (the reductionism of positivism) alone. He believes the dichotomy is only overcome in an encounter with the world of phenomena as the "cipherscript" of being at the limits of empirical knowledge. For at those boundaries where the world and self are no longer self-explanatory, where death, suffering, conflict, and guilt appear, the self grasps the finitude of the intellect and its own finiteness as a "being in foundering" (Sein im Scheitern)./50/ While, negatively, the foundering of cognitive thought presents a limit to thinking about the finite world, this experience of foundering positively opens onto the encounter with Transcendence./51/ Transcendence is revealed through experience insofar as it is heard by the individual in the historic actuality of possible Existenz. In Jaspers's words, "it is only in the absolute consciousness of Existenz that a direct language of transcendence is truly, substantially present."/52/ Jaspers speaks metaphorically of ciphers as the "language" of Transcendence; they have metaphysical objectivity only insofar as they are "heard" by the historicity of possible Existenz./53/

In order to grasp the meaning of the "metaphysical objectivity" of ciphers we must recall Jaspers's distinction between being as "object-being," "subject-being," and "being-in-itself." In thinking, being is never grasped in itself, but only as it appears for us in the subject-object dichotomy. Being in its appearance always takes a determinate form. Jaspers's foundational thinking takes knowledge to be "a state of being directed towards an opposite other." In its most cogent form, it requires "objectness [Gegenständlichkeit] (for without it no thought is, in fact, possible); secondly, perceptibility (for without it there is, in fact, no content, no stuff, no differentiation); thirdly, validity (for without it there is no certainty of conscious knowledge)."/54/ Objectivity, in its most cogent form, necessarily comprises these three moments.

There is, however, a _fuller_ "Objectivity" (Objektivität) of knowledge which surpasses that particular objectivity of knowledge which comes together in these three moments. In our encounter with the world of phenomena we sense that the objects of empirical experience are not the ultimate ends of knowledge. We feel or surmise-- even if only through a dark glass, to paraphrase St. Paul-- that objects bear a meaning that transcends their empirical dimensions, and that the self is grounded in something other than itself. Jaspers speaks of this other as the "presentness" (Gegenwärtigkeit) of being. We come to this "knowledge" of a fuller objectivity by the leading of reason; and, in turn, reason's continual movement of thought leads to the fulfillment of _love_ in the depths of this full objectivity:

> Reason in its unending movement finds a foothold through an Objectivity [Objektivität] in which love has its fulfillment. This Objectivity can no longer be any one of the objects [Objekt] which become objects [Gegenstand] of knowledge. For the completion of truth is not attained in an object as an end of knowledge, but in something objective, which transcends all empirical knowledge, something which is not really an

object, in something objective which we
call cypher or symbol or metaphor./55/

The fuller objectivity comprises not just
universally valid determinate objects in the sense of
"phenomena of reality" as "object-being," but it also
includes "signs [signa or Zeichen] of Existenz" as
"subject-being," and symbols or ciphers of
Transcendence. Ciphers are not "objects" of knowledge
in the same way that rocks, the calculus, and quasars
are; but they are in some sense meaningfully
"objective" revelations of Transcendence for possible
Existenz, but only in suspended and ambiguous form. To
be sure, signs of Existenz, such as expressions of
selfhood and freedom, can be taken as psychological
phenomena and merely regarded as cognitively
indifferent or as nonsense. Such a critique of the
validity of existential discourse, however, reduces or
negates the existential truth of such signa./56/

What we need to recall here is that, unlike
objectified phenomena of reality and signs of human
Existenz, ciphers of Transcendence lack specific
phenomenality for Jaspers. As metaphysical objects of
thought, ciphers do not have the same function as real
objects. Thus Jaspers speaks of ciphers as "the other"
in which being is present as a "vanishing object;"/57/
as vanishing metaphysical objects, the ciphers of
Transcendence are indeed experienced by possible
Existenz as the "presentness" of being. But they
cannot be cognized, only "listened" to./58/ Jaspers
wants to free Transcendence from all objective
determinations as symbol or cipher without abandoning
objectivity altogether. In order to elucidate this
paradox it is helpful to clarify the difference between
sign, symbol, and cipher, since he speaks of symbol
synonymously with both sign and cipher, depending upon
the type of symbolism involved, whether "conscious
symbolism" (bewusste Symbolik) or "unconscious
symbolism."

Conscious symbolism means "'having' things in the
world through their relationship, through the fact that
one relates to the other as something which is
otherwise as well, in the sense of signs, of metaphors,
comparisons, representations, models."/59/ As a
conscious symbol, a sign indicates the other, and has a
clear, univocal determination. In the sign there is no
necessary connection between the sign and that which it
represents as, for example, in the case of notations
used for understanding in mathematics and chemistry.

205

In unconscious symbolism, in contrast, the symbol and the symbolized are inseparable. It is in this sense of <u>unconscious</u> symbolism that Jaspers speaks of ciphers. He prefers to distinguish the cipher from the symbol because he feels we often mistake a conscious symbol for a sign. The symbol is frequently taken for a real, objective representation of an other as in the case of the incarnation of God in Christ. In contrast, the ciphers denote "language."

> [Ciphers are] the language of a reality that can be heard and addressed only thus and in no other way-- while a symbol stands for something else, even though this may not exist outside the symbol. What we mean by the symbol is the other thing, which thus becomes objective and comes to be present in the symbol. Yet symbols may turn into elements of the cipher language./60/

The signification of the cipher or unconscious symbol, then, cannot be separated from that which is signified in it, even though our thinking inevitably tends towards objectification of the cipher language. The "conversion" of objects into the cipher status depends upon that formal transcending in which ciphers ultimately remain "hidden in all objectivity."/61/ Transcendence or being is revealed only insofar as the cipher is "suspended" in the act of transcending toward the transparent, full "objectivity" of being. This overcoming of the subject-object split is the classical, and exceedingly rare, experience of the mystics. The signification of ciphers is not that something present signifies something absent; rather, signification lies in that "presentness" which is no longer translatable into knowledge of something. Jaspers's hermeneutics of ciphers believes that "being-a-cypher is a signification which signifies nothing else. Signification is itself only a metaphor for being-a-cypher. Language is a metaphor only when it is articulated by a cypher-status."/62/

The metaphysical experience of "presentness" is the reading of the <u>first language</u> of Transcendence. Experience is both the source of empirical knowledge and the assurance of Transcendence. But metaphysical experience of the transparency of Transcendence in ciphers requires that <u>all</u> forms of experience come together. This includes experience as "sense perception," life experience, "cognitive experience,"

"thinking," and "intuitive experience."   It is as the
experience of   the   first "language" of   Transcendence
that Jaspers perceives the existential reality of
revelational   or   religious   faith   for   the   believer,
including the faith of the prophets and the historical
Jesus./63/

The direct "hearing" of the language of ciphers
leads   to   the   universalization   of   the   language   of
Transcendence in   the   process   of   communication, and
takes   place   through   three   intuitable   metaphysical
content forms, namely, as "myth in a particular form,"
as the "revelation of a world beyond," and as "mythical
actuality."   In this second language of Transcendence,
he writes,   "the   language of   man   comes to join   the
language   of   Being."/64/   Given   the   necessity   of
overcoming dogma and the absolutization of faith in the
nuclear age, Jaspers maintains the theologian should
read the many ciphers of the God of the Bible, as well
as the   fulfilled ciphers of history,   authority,   and
tradition at the level of myth.   As is clear from his
debate with Karl Barth,/65/ he believes the theologian
fails   to   "read"   God's   revelation   as   a   suspended,
ambiguous cipher of Transcendence.

Speculative   metaphysics,   in   which   possible
Existenz reads the original cipher-script by writing a
new one   by means   of   analogy, constitutes   the   third
language of Transcendence.   The speculative language
has been spoken throughout history in many ways, e.g.,
by factual   world   orientation, by   the   self-contained
metaphysical system, through self-existence under   the
guise of "proofs" for God, and through "reminiscence"
and "foresight." But speculation never gets beyond the
cipher;   it   is   only   nearer   to   or   farther   from
Transcendence.   In contrast to prayerful communication
with the   living   God   of the   prophets   and   of   Jesus
Christ,   speculation   "is   a   kind   of   thinking   that
attempts a contemplative being with transcendence [...
a] thinking that drives us to think the unthinkable.
It is mysticism to the intellect that wants cognition,
but it is lucidity to a self-being that transcends in
it."/66/ In speculation, the philosophical faith of
possible Existenz must bear the fate that it will never
approach the "hidden God" directly.

If reading the three cipherscript languages of
Transcendence takes on various concrete forms such as
myth, art, religious doctrines, and speculative ideas,
then the nature of ciphers is endless.   The
cipherscript includes potentially all of reality.   To

the eyes of philosophical faith the cipherscript
includes ciphers of Transcendence as Deity (the one,
personal, and incarnated God); ciphers of immanence as
nature, history, rational being; and ciphers of the
existential situation such as physical and moral evil.
And yet absolute being remains nameless: "If we speak
of it, then we use an infinite number of names and
cancel them all again. That which has significance is
itself Being [...] The cypher is the metaphor which is
Being, or the Being which is metaphor." Thus there is
no definitive interpretation or exegesis of ciphers:
"to interpret, I would have to split what is only in
union. I would compare a cipher with transcendence,
but transcendence only appears to me in the cipher
script; it is not the cipher script."/67/
Interpretation becomes a metaphorical act, a game. To
be sure, this is an eternally significant game in which
we struggle restlessly for the reality of being,
Transcendence, or God within the cipherscript of all
being. But there is no definitive "key" with which to
unlock the cipherscript. Reading the language of
ciphers remains an ongoing task and a challenge to the
creativity of the human spirit. When ciphers turn
intolerant, destructive, rupture communication, spurn
reason and the good, or when they are imposed on others
by physical force and violence as in religious wars and
total rule, they must be met with resistance at every
level.

If all things may become ciphers, and if they have
reality and truth, must they not therefore be
verifiable in some meaningful way? On Jaspers's view
the being of ciphers is indeed verifiable in world
orientation "by making something perceptible or
logically compelling, by producing and achieving
something," and in existential elucidation "by my way
of dealing with myself and with another, of being
assured of myself by the unconditionality of my
actions."/68/ But the truth of ciphers is never
directly verifiable since it is game that does not
claim to be valid in the same way as scientific
cognition. When we read the various ciphers of
Transcendence, we are thrown back upon our own
responsibility in inner action. In turn, we verify
them through our life-praxis.

Insofar as the features of objective speech are
put into suspension in the cipher, it is doubtful
whether anything is said about the ciphers of
Transcendence by the "word" of philosophical faith.
The transcending leap beyond objectivity in the world

of ciphers, and ultimately in the uninterpretable cipher of "being in foundering," may best be seen as a leap into silence, though Jaspers speaks of this as a "silence that says everything."/69/ He insists that philosophical faith does not usher into mysticism as a flight from the world. For the will to realization in the world is, itself, the will to hear ciphers on the road toward liberation and freedom.

> Life in the world is linked with that ultimate origin only by a readiness for existential action in the world-- which is the reception and production of ciphers. Ciphers come to be real in language, and realities come to be ciphers [...] Instead of evaporating in the abstraction of the negative One, instead of emptying the world in mystical union, the fulfilled presence of Transcendence reconstitutes itself for Existenz, audible in the ciphers."/70/

The last liberation of humanity standing now at the end of the axial age, and after centuries of bloody struggles for freedom in the West, is the "ascent from God to the Godhead, form the ciphers to what makes them speak."/71/ The consequences of such a liberation would mean that "my" God is no longer God for all humanity; that we no longer legitimate our own existence and self-interests in the name of God; that we relinquish clothing our worldly struggles in the garb of a struggle of God against the evil empires of the world; and that we stop taking God for reason, which is always a limited, human reason.

In the final analysis, philosophical faith believes not in the final judgement of God's justice at the end of time, but in the uninterpretable cipher of "being in foundering" as the decisive cipher of Transcendence. The foundering or "shipwreck" of all existence and Existenz in space and time, of all documents and traces of human greatness, unconditionality and creativity, is the final cipher, the encompassing ground of all that ciphers are. The uninterpretable cipher of "being in foundering" does not let any one cipher become absolute, even the cipher of the personal God. But neither does it destroy the other ciphers nor the cipher of the one personal God. In view of the possible foundering of all existence before the twin possibilities of nuclear annihilation and totalitarianism, Jaspers appeals to the final "conversion" of faith in existence, namely, the "leap" from fear to serenity./72/

Philosophical faith believes the difficult road to peace lies solely in "long-suffering." If "passive suffering" is an empty, non-committal self-relinquishment, "active sufferance" allows one to experience the foundering of all existence and yet work for peace as long as one's strength remains. "In sufferance," Jaspers writes in concluding the final volume of the Philosophy, "lies the not-knowing of the kind of faith that makes men active in the world without any need to believe in the possibility of a good and definitive world order." Sufferance means one will cling to being, Transcendence, or God in spite of foundering. Assurance in this suffering only comes, however, from that possible Existenz which must be regained again and again. But that one can attain such an assurance is due to a reason beyond the Existenz of self-being, to transcendent being. That "there is being suffices," that God is, is enough./73/

7.2 THE LIMITS AND POSSIBILITIES OF REVELATIONAL FAITH

While religion is not completely ascertainable from the perspective of philosophical faith, it nonetheless reveals elements which the philosopher surveys, including the idea of God, ritual and community, prayer, and the faith in revelation or revelational faith (Offenbarungsglaube)./74/ While the idea of the one God in Greek philosophy is intellectually sublime-- the result of "individuals of a high human type and a free philosophy"--the idea is more powerful in the Old Testament, as witnessed by the "incomparable faith of the prophets," because the prophets' faith arises from a direct experience of God./75/

Philosophical faith views worship, prayer, and sacraments as "unconditional acts" which are irrelevant to possible purposes in the world. They acquire an ethical relevance, however, when translated into forms of action in the socio-political order, e.g., as "orgiastic destructiveness," "militant world conquest," or religious terrorism. The cult, by definition, is an act of the community linked by the "objective transcendence" that attends it. Cult liberates the individual "from his possible freedom" insofar as it "permits unconditional action without personal self-being." It is an "analogue" of philosophical reflection, in which "I step out of the world and come to myself in transcendence, taking new strength back with me into the day, and deriving dignity and substance from the process."/76/ The real difference between the two lies, in Jaspers's view, in the hazardous nature of philosophical reflection. Here there is no rule, it is in historic transformation, and it has no visible objectivity to hold on to in times of trouble, as has the believer.

Similarly, Jaspers sees prayer, the lifeblood of christian faith and praxis, as a form of unconditional action marked by a real relation to the living and personal God. But here again he draws a distinct line between ritual and prayer as "transcendent realities for the one who stands within them," as "the soul's intercourse with God," and active contemplation as that type of faith in which "Existenz concerns itself with the hidden God." When it is truly personal and primal prayer stands at the boundary of philosophy. But prayer becomes philosophy "in the moment when it is divested of any pragmatic relation to the godhead or desire to influence the godhead for practical ends." Now prayer, as active contemplation, marks a final break with "the concreteness of a personal relation to a personal God."/77/

It is primarily on the basis of a different understanding of revelation that Jaspers differentiates philosophical and revelational faith. As witnessed to by religious believers, revelation is "the immediate utterance of God localized in time and valid for all men, through word, commandment, action, event." For them, "God issues commandments, establishes a community, walks among men, founds a cult." And this happens by some sort of "objective invasion" from without. In his final work on the subject, Jaspers identified three historical forms of the faith in revelation witnessed to by prophets who proclaimed what God commanded them, by churches and priests who declare texts to be inspired and claim to interpret them correctly, and by the apostles who testified to the incarnation of God in Christ. And yet, all three forms require an additional authority to determine which prophets are genuine, which texts are inspired, and whose apostolic testimony counts. Hence Augustine's famous line, "Ego vero Evangelio non crederem nisi me catholicae Ecclesiae commoveret auctoritas [...] I would indeed not believe the Gospel if the authority of the Catholic church did not prompt me as well." In

211

contrast Jaspers, the believer in the Encompassing out of philosophical faith, does not void these three sources of testimony, but conceives of them as ciphers instead. They can only be true "as man's claim upon himself, not as the vindication of a claim on others."/78/

These three forms which witness to a unique, objectively revealed truth are not limited to Christianity alone, but are derivative from aspects of the "Biblical religion"/79/ itself, to which Jews, Greek Orthodox, Catholics, Protestants, and Muslims alike belong; negatively, it is their exclusive and absolute understanding of revelational faith which he defines as "orthodoxy." He sees this frequently manifested in the Jewish doctrine of law, in national or civil religion ("the Israelite cult of Yahweh, Calvin's nationalism or certain expressions of Islam"), and, especially, in the Christian faith that sees Christ as God. "The Christian does not say: this is my way, but, this is the way," while the Church declares "Extra ecclesiam nulla salus."/80/ These "orthodox" claims of an objective revelation (Offenbarung) as absolute and exclusive mark the limit of religious faith today.

In contrast, philosophical faith recognizes the generic revelation of the one truth (Offenbarwerden von wahrheit) within the Encompassing./81/ Here the revelation of truth comes not from Christ or Scripture, but as a series of awakenings in the process of transcending through the inner action of the mind. This faith recognizes the religious truth of the other, where authentic, and seeks to avoid gathering the truth of all religions into one composite truth. The one truth of Transcendence is historical and absolute only in the existential moment of the individual as possible Existenz. Because the generic idea of revelation is inextricably wed to Jaspers's notion of the experience of freedom in the historicity of possible Existenz as the "exception" or "authority," he must reject an objective redemptive history conceived as an absolute event or as a prerequisite for the salvation of all humanity. Hence, as noted in Chapter Two, the notion of a Christian Heilsgeschichte with Christ as the axis is seen as merely one myth among others. Like other ciphers of history, it must be tested for its existential strength and the truth it lends to daily living.

Jaspers aligns his generic view of revelation with the authentic "liberalism" of Lessing, Kant, and Goethe. With them he rejects absolute obedience to sacred texts and religious officials in the church, since reason and freedom are higher authorities. While not denying the absolute Transcendence of God, who always remains "hidden," he insists that all we can perceive are human action, words, and experience./82/ The Deity does not speak through the commands and revelations of others, but only through existential selfhood and freedom. Freedom and Transcendence are inseparable; Existenz is in relation to Transcendence or it is not at all. Freedom in relation to Transcendence or God is not for Jaspers, as the traditional critique of Pelagianism might suggest, strictly a matter of willing or "philosophical choice" alone./83/ His idea of freedom as gift seems to come close to, without ever actually touching, the Christian notion of grace:

> In my freedom I am not through myself, but am given to myself, for I can fail myself and cannot force my freedom. Where I am authentically myself, I am certain that I am not through myself [...]
> With the realization of this freedom, however, we realize too that it is not self-made but granted. The false assurance of being free by virtue of freedom alone, of a baseless, absolute freedom, is shattered by the experience that it may default. The more decisive our certainty of our freedom, the greater our certainty of the Transcendence we owe it to./84/

In sum, then, philosophical faith views orthodoxy's claim that an objective revelation of God is an actual, historical event which has taken place in the world, and which precedes faith, as a failure to clarify the Encompassing within the subject-object split. Transcendence, God, or the "Encompassing of all Encompassing" never become clear to us apart from our own subjectivity. The reality of being is present only in the suspended objectivity or metaphorical "language" of the cipher "heard" by Existenz. Speech about God's action or "word" is only a cipher by means of which the subject-- qua potential Existenz-- conceives, perceives, and questions that which is manifested to it as a reality. An answer to the question of whether we start with subjective revelation (as an inner awareness or awakening) or objective revelation (as the direct "Word of God") ultimately ends in a hermeneutical circle: "We say either that revelation is the process of becoming revealed to the subject, which conceives revelation in itself as something objective; or, that reason in the movement of reason subjects its revelation to the test of rationality." What is significant for Jaspers is not so much the circular nature of faith as is the different meanings of the circles in philosophy and theology. In philosophizing, the circles are to be continually breached, whereas he sees the circle of the faith in revelation as "self-satisfied" with itself, as one which "secludes itself in its salvation, on the ground of its reality."/85/

Given Jaspers's foundational understanding of the break through of existential truth in the "exception" and "authority," it is not surprising that he should see philosophy and theology as akin insofar as both elucidate their respective origins and faiths. As Xavier Tilliette points out, the theological origin both demands respect and always remains a challenge to the philosopher, just as philosophy must remain a challenge to the theologian. The philosophy/theology relation is essentially a "critical" one./86/ Jaspers admits that philosophy grows from religious soil, even as it struggles against its own roots in the form of a "secularized religion". Moreover, creative theology often adopts philosophical concepts. There is both creative philosophy (e.g., Bruno, Spinoza, Kant) and creative theology (e.g., Origen, Augustine, Nicholas of Cusa, Luther). But when theology loses touch with the practical elements of religious life such as prayer, ritual and cult, and community life, it is a cause of alarm for the philosopher who seeks utmost clarity about their distinction. The attempt to fit the substance of theology into philosophy-- and thus "eliminate authority, retain the theological historicity, and thus create a religion"/87/-- should be rejected both by genuine theology and a truthful philosophy.

The attempt to create a philosophical religion by eradicating myth from religion is no doubt the crux of Jaspers's at times vindictive critique of Bultmann's program of "demythologization."/88/ Although he acknowledges that Bultmann has made important contributions to our historical knowledge of the New Testament and the Bible as a whole, his evaluation of him as a __theologian__ is cast in a more critical light: Bultmann fails to read Biblical genres against each other in their loving struggle for truth-- a project for theological hermeneutics more recently brought to light by Paul Ricoeur;/89/ he is almost indifferent at times to the Old Testament; he reduces the New Testament's portrayal of Jesus primarily to St. Paul and St. John without adequately treating the Synoptics; and, he fails to be critical of St. John's mythical justification of early Christian anti-Semitism./90/

Most importantly, Jaspers rejects Bultmann's interpretation of the __skandalon__ of the Gospel in terms of God's summons to a decision for __Christ,__ overladen as it is with features of the Pauline-Lutheran doctrine of justification. He believes the real __skandalon__ of Christianity comes "wherever and whenever a man claims to speak in the name of God," and in the reality of the terrible injustice done to an innocent man in the suffering of Jesus on the Cross. It lies in the radicality of the idea of freedom in which every individual "achieves inner peace in a resolve grounded in his own historicity [...] through the freedom [Transcendence] has given me."/91/ Bultmann is thus neither a true liberal nor an "orthodox" authoritarian, but instead a "most peculiar mixture of false enlightenment and high-handed orthodoxy."/92/ Whether carried out by Bultmann or other theologians, the complete unification of theology and philosophy is damaging to the integrity of philosophy and inimical to the fate of the Biblical teachings.

7.2.1 "Conversion" from "kirchliche" to "Biblical Religion"

It is in a reappropriation of "Biblical religion" that Jaspers envisions the distinct __possibilities__ of revelational faith in the nuclear age: "the decision on the future of our Western humanity lies in the relation of our faith to the Biblical religion."/93/ This emphasis grew out of his boundary experience under Nazi rule, during which the Bible was the "'book which was our comfort for those twelve years.'"/94/ If philosophical faith fights against the claim to exclusivity that is inherent in Scripture it also recognizes that this claim is not __necessary__ to Biblical religion. Jaspers speaks positively of Biblical religion as "one of the wellsprings of our philosophy," in which "irreplaceable" truth is gathered./95/ The religious counterpart to philosophical transcending in speculative metaphysics is expressed in the demand of the Old Testament: do not make any image or likeness of God, for "I am that I am."/96/

The key to overcoming exclusivity in Biblical religion lies in the retrieval of "eternal truth" from reductionist fixations upon particular elements in Scripture. To do this it is necessary to re-establish the polar tensions in these elements and, in turn, elucidate their truth through philosophical faith. In addition to the polarities of "world denial" and "world affirmation" already mentioned in connection with his book on the atom bomb, Jaspers had earlier cited the tension between cultic and prophetic religion ("For I desired mercy, and not sacrifice; and the knowledge of God more than burnt offerings," Hosea.vi.6 and cf., Amos v.21), between law and spirit ("I will put their laws in their inward parts, and write it in their hearts," Jeremiah xxxi.33, vii.8), between the idea of the "chosen people" and the universal God ("Are ye not as children of the Ethiopians unto me, O children of Israel? says Yahweh," Amos ix.7), and between the man Jesus, proclaimed in faith as the Christ, and the hidden God ("Why callest thou me good? there is none good but one, that is, God," Mark x.18). Through the experience of the tensions, polarities, and dialectic of Scripture, elements of truth surface which constitute the philosophical faith of Biblical religion. These include:

> [...] the idea of the one God; the realization of the absolute nature of the decision between good and evil in finite man; love as the fundamental actualization of the eternal in man; the act-- both inward and external-- as the test of man; types of moral world order which are always historically absolute, although none of their manifestation is absolute or exclusive; the incompleteness of the created world, the fact that it does not stand by itself, the inapplicability of all types of order to borderline cases, the experience of the extreme; the idea that the ultimate and only refuge is with God./97/

Both in his early treatment and in the developments of his final work on the relation between philosophical and revelational faith, the main possibilities of transformation in revelational faith remain the same: claims to an objective religious revelation should give way to philosophical revelation or an "awakening" heard through the ciphers of Transcendence; dogmatic religious truth should cease to be exclusive and become intolerant only of intolerance; and, especially given the essential Jewishness of Jaspers's thought, Jesus should no longer be exclusively believed in as the God-Man, Christ, which is merely one cipher of the Deity among others. Rather, Jesus is an "exception," a "cipher of man" along with Socrates, Buddha, and Confucius./98/

The Incarnation of God in Christ, the myth of the "Godman," represents an example of fulfilled "catholicity," and must be understood in light of the radical antithesis between reason and catholicity./99/ For if the one God had actually revealed himself in the world in a single form in space and time, then the authority of this revelation would be valid for all. If such a revelation <u>were</u> true, in it would lie a unity of Transcendence and "world-being," a unity of all encompassings, of the one absolute truth. But Jaspers's subjunctive mood gives way to the indicative: "no man is God," and "Jesus is in truth not really the unity of all modes of the Encompassing."/100/ "The fact remains that a Godman in Jesus Christ has been believed in, and faith itself has spoken in such propositions; the thought and the reality in such proclamatory faith is a stumbling block to philosophizing."/101/

Against propositions of faith in the Godman an equal number of objections might be posed. First, assertions of faith should not be confused with assertions about the world, as is the case when believers speak of the miraculous suspension of natural laws. We err when we try to "prove" propositions of faith; they cannot be proved, but only testified to in deed. Secondly, catholicity's transformation of individual historicity into a universally true historicity confuses reason's approach to truth as a particular break through of the universal as the "exception" and "authority." Thirdly, that "God is a human being or that a human being is God is absurd." The idea itself is "in contradiction with the soaring thinking to Transcendence and with original consciousness for which the one God, as creator of the world, is reality."/102/

To be sure, while the absurd escapes proof by definition, it is nonetheless a form of the appearance of Transcendence for Jaspers's philosophical faith, which frequently draws upon Kierkegaard for inspiration. The question is not whether the absurd itself is to be accepted or rejected with a resolute yes or no, it is not that of "either-or," but only whether certain distinctions within the absurd are to be rejected. And to the eyes of philosophical faith, the idea that God is a human being is an absurdity which leads astray. It does not lead to an "upswing" of love towards Transcendence, but binds the philosopher in a dogma whose representation can be believed only through a certain violence of thought.

> The Christian doctrine in its _theological_ development formulates contradictions in paradoxes. The basic dogmas are incomprehensible, their absurdity is expression of their mystery. The solution to the contradictions by making them comprehensible is virtually heretical. It is in principle impossible to raise [_aufzuheben_] them. All possible solutions are set aside as a crown of heresies around the center of the insoluble mystery which reveals itself in the paradox. For the Christian the mystery of the absurd is the end and limit of comprehension. Here the comprehension of incomprehension in the definitive form of these dogmas will not allow itself to be crossed. Philosophizing, however, denies this boundary. It finds no repose in the absurd of the faith enclosed in dogma./103/

What the absurdity of the Cross reveals is that Christ, the "Godman," was really in the world in "_foundering_," which is the true image of his revelation. The truth of Christ is that "the oneness in action is not possible in time; that unity is grounded only on the rupture of existence; that every immanent unity in an image of a completion, beauty, spendour, even a vital completion, is impossible."/104/ Kierkegaard drew out the negative consequences: Christ is a martyr; the imitation of Christ and Gospel Christianity is a martyr's existence; the "negative decision" is for the "annihilation of the intellect in the absurd," the rejection of realization in the world./105/ The foundering on the Cross reveals the incompatibility of the exception and authority, and of the inaccessible unity of truth in time. Jesus, as a "cipher of man," reveals "that a man who lives and thinks as he did, a man who is true without any restriction, must die at the hands of men, because human reality is too untruthful to bear him." And "in truth," writes Jaspers elsewhere, "one cannot theologize Kierkegaard and affirm the Church."/106/ Having appropriated Kierkegaard's radical thesis of Gospel Christianity, Jaspers prefers to speak of "Biblical religion" rather than Judaism or Christianity. Thus it is not surprising that he should see the greatest chance for the "conversion" of kirchliche Religion in the Protestant principle.

Finally, Jaspers insists that the incomparable and mysterious efficacy of the absurd in Scripture comes from Biblical religion as a whole, and not only from the New Testament witness to the cipher of Incarnation, which is only one moment among others. Indeed, what marks the real primacy of "belongingness" to the Biblical religion-- from Judaism to Catholicism to Eastern Christianity-- is "a radical conversion, purification and deepening of this Biblical religion through men of originally powerful faith and honesty."/107/ Jaspers encourages making "the human Jesus and his faith prevail"/108/ because it is vital to the future of the Biblical faith confronted by the nuclear problem. This ultimately means preserving the cipher of the one God, the hidden God, unblurred: "That the one God is grounded only on a break of existence and is not reached in the world in action, is philosophically to preserve God unblurred. The mythification of the Godman-- which Jesus essentially did not endorse: 'why do you call me good, nobody is good except the one God'-- is, in contrast, the annihilation of revelation become truth."/109/ Standing in a boundary situation before the end of the world, Jesus also admonishes us today that the only alternative is "with God or against God; good or evil."/110/

1. OGH, p.214, 223; UZG, p.268, 278.
2. These three areas correspond to the chronological subject matter of Jaspers's metaphysics, PHT III, pp.3-112. We should recall here that possible Existenz is related to Transcendence originally in boundary situations. The relationship is never unequivocal, but lies in alternatives whose resolution in synthesis is always transitory. Jaspers counts among the alternatives of Existenz's relation to Transcendence, defiance and surrender, rising and falling, diurnal law and order and nocturnal passion, and the oneness of truth for the individual whose historical determination or concretion is always put into doubt by the diversity of existing possibilities. PHT III, pp.61-112.
3. On the debate between Jaspers and the critics of his philosophy of religion, see Paul Ricoeur, "The Relation of Jaspers' Philosophy to Religion," in Schilpp, pp.611-642; Xavier Tilliette, Karl Jaspers: théorie de la vérité, métaphysique des chiffres, foi philosophique (Paris: Aubier, 1960), pp.190-228; Leonard Ehrlich, Karl Jaspers: Philosophy as Faith, pp.65-97 and 172-176; Alan M. Olson, Transcendence and Hermeneutics, pp.146-182; Adolph Lichtigfeld, "The God-Concept in Jaspers' Philosophy," in Schilpp, pp.693-701; and John F. Kane, Pluralism and Truth in Religion, pp.105-133.
4. Professor Leonard H. Ehrlich writes in an apt metaphor that "the stream of Jaspers's thought can be regarded as the confluence of the conception of reason, which has its main source in Kant, and that of Existenz, which has its main source in Kierkegaard; it is fed by the experience of the different modes of Being, channelled by the rockbed of modern science, and issues into the open sea of philosophical faith." Karl Jaspers: Philosophy as Faith, p.117.
5. PAT, p.78.
6. PAT, p.77.
7. See, PHT I, pp. 255-262, 294-313.
8. See, PHT II, pp.243-246.
9. See, PHT I, pp.75-95 and PHT III, pp.3-32.
10. Jaspers's speaks concisely of the meaning of ciphers or cipher-script as a "transmutation of the world into a mediation between us and the

unique God." Translation of VW, p.1051, in Schilpp, p.xviii.

11. See the section on "Faith" in OGH, pp.213-231.
12. In addition to these major works, cf. also RE, pp.141ff., PE, pp.79-94, and WW, esp., p.67ff., 82ff., the latter in which Jaspers's stated principles of philosophical faith provide the structure for the work as a whole.
13. Jaspers declares in his autobiography: "Since my _Philosophie_ (1931) I have publicly advocated philosophic faith as the meaning of the philosophic doctrine." PAT, p.81. Cf., also, PSP, p.48.
14. PSP, p.22.
15. RE, p.141.
16. PHT I, p.297.
17. Karl Jaspers, "Reply to My Critics," in Schilpp, p.779.
18. PHT I, pp.300-301.
19. Cf., Xavier Tilliette, _Karl Jaspers_, p.110.
20. PSP, p.137.
21. PHT I, p.302. Despite philosophy's communicative recognition of the truth of religion for the religious person at the existential level, Jaspers insists philosophy must not confuse, as Hegel did, its proper truth with that of religion. On this point, see Tilliette, _Karl Jaspers_, p.109.
22. PHT II, pp.244-245. Cf., PSP, p.13ff. and PFR, p.18ff.
23. PSP, p.13.
24. WW, pp.85-95. Cf., PFR, p.9.
25. WW, p.89-90.
26. PHT I, p.304.
27. _Ibid_. Jaspers's discussion places the critique of the validity of religious discourse and the _truth_ of the discourse of faith on two different levels, the former pertaining to the intellect or consciousness-as-such, the latter to the spirit and the conviction of a believing Existenz. Much of the contemporary analytical critique of religion reflects (and rightly so) this real conflict between faith and knowledge. But a critique of the validity of religious discourse is not the final word: it cannot critique the _origin_ of religion at the same time. If it tries, it fails to differentiate these two modes of the encompassing that we are.
       This same point has been critically argued more recently by Professor Benoît Garceau, O.M.I. Professor Garceau sets forth a philosophical

explication of both the importance and limits of the critique of the validity of religious discourse. He shows why the critique of the origin of religion by the masters of suspicion (Marx, Freud, and Nietzsche) rests upon a value judgment against religion which is actually based upon a critique of the validity of the discourse of religious faith. For Garceau, as for Jaspers, the important issue of critique and hermeneutic in the philosophy of religion is not the question of the validity of the discourse, but its own proper truth: "La vérité du discours de la foi, comme celle de toute interprétation des signes, consiste dans la correspondance entre ce discours et ce qui est compris comme signifié par les signes et dans la correspondance entre cette compréhension et le signifié des signes. Puisque les signes par définition ne sont jamais évidents, la critique de leur interprétation est une tâche complexe, jamais définitivement achevée, impliquant a la fois l'évaluation du discours par rapport a la compréhension et l'évaluation de celle-ci par rapport au signifié. Il s'agit là bien sûr d'une critique effectuée d'abord par le croyant, immanente à la vie de la foi, pratiquée dans l'exercice même de la foi en vue de sa propre vérité. C'est un fait trop ignoré par beaucoup d'analystes de la religion que la première critique de la religion vient de la foi elle-même. S'il est vrai que la critique est toujours provoquée par une crise, il y a, intérieure a la vie de la foi, une double crise par laquelle elle passe nécessairement si elle est consciente d'elle-meme et qui la force à assumer à l'égard de ses sources et de son propre discours la fonction critique: la crise produite par la transcendence du signifié par les signes et celle produite par la particularité et la contingence de son discours, toujours menacé de ne pas pouvoir dire ce que le croyant croit être vrai pour tous les hommes." Garceau, "Critique et herméneutique en philosophie de la religion," in <u>Rationality</u> <u>to-day.</u> <u>La</u> <u>rationalité</u> <u>aujourd'hui</u>, par H.-G. Gadamer et autres, edité par Theordore F. Geraets (Ottawa: Editions de l'Université d'Ottawa, 1979), pp.373-380, at 379.

28. PSP, p.34.
29. OGH, p.219.
30. WW, p.85.
31. <u>Ibid</u>. With the last of these five propositions we are following the translation of "Die Welt hat ein verschwindendes Dasein zwischen Gott und

Existenz" rendered by Professor Leonard Ehrlich, <u>Karl</u> <u>Jaspers</u>: <u>Philosophy</u> as <u>Faith</u>, p.138.

32. PFR, p.18 (emphasis added) and PSP, p.12,13 and PHT II, p.245.
33. PHT I, p.307.
34. See, e.g., Karl Jaspers, "Liberty and Authority," in PWT, p.36.; VW, pp.781, 816-17. On the formal meaning of authority, see PE, p.47.
35. PSP, p.26 and PHT I, p.309.
36. PHT II, p.245; PH II, p.281. PHT I, p.309.
37. PE, p.51: "To what authority I own my maturing into selfhood, what authority I have seized upon and devoted myself to (though perhaps only to its remnants) is a matter of my transcendentally grounded destiny. But it is not possible to compare authorities consciously, to test them, and subsequently to choose which I think is true or best. By seeing authority as authority, I have already chosen it."
38. Jaspers's understanding of "exception" and "authority" is inextricably tied to his theory of the various modes of the meaning of the One truth of the Encompassing. He takes up the nature of these two configurations in the break through to truth in VW, pp.745-830, and in the second lecture on truth in <u>Existenzphilosophie</u>, translated by Richard F. Grabau in PE, pp.33-61, and by E. Ehrlich, L.H. Ehrlich, and G.B. Pepper, eds., <u>Karl</u> <u>Jaspers</u>, pp.240-255.
39. Karl Jaspers, quoted in Ehrlich, Ehrlich, and Pepper, eds. <u>Karl</u> <u>Jaspers</u>, p.246. Cf., PE, pp.43-44.
40. <u>Ibid</u>., p.275. Cf., VW, p.720.
41. <u>Ibid</u>., p.278. Cf., VW, p.723.
42. Jaspers's treatment of reason and catholicity appears in VW, 832-868. Substantial excerpts from this section have been translated for the first time in English by Ehrlich, Ehrlich, Pepper, eds., <u>Karl</u> <u>Jaspers</u>, pp.280-291.
43. Jaspers explains in a footnote what he means by the word "catholic:" "Das Wort katholisch is in diesem Kapitel also nicht ohne weiteres auf die katholische Kirche zu beziehen. Wovon die Rede ist, das ist überall in der Welt und auch in der katholischen Kirche sichtbar. Diese Kirche im Ganzen aber enthält viel mehr." VW, p.833, n.1. Ehrlich, Ehrlich, and Pepper, eds., <u>Karl</u> <u>Jaspers</u>, p. 281 translate this as: "In this chapter the word "catholic" should not automatically be applied to the Catholic Church. What we are talking about here can be seen everywhere in the

world and thus also in the Catholic Church.
However this church, taken as a whole, contains
much more than this."

Later in the same chapter Jaspers speaks
with qualification of the sublime, transcendent
truth of Roman Catholicity, and links catholicity
directly, and much more broadly, to an exclusive
view of revelation when he writes: "In the
Catholic Church catholicity is indeed
extraordinarily effective, but it is grounded in
sublime transcendental truth. Because of this
the Church carries contents that continually
break apart catholicity, even in the Church
itself. The truth of the heretic lives in the
Church. Catholicity can sometimes appear to the
observer as unessential, as a misfortune of
Christianity, which is linked with the
foundational thinking of an exclusive
revelation." This is our translation of: "In der
katholischen Kirche ist Katholizität zwar
ausserordentlich wirksam, aber sie ist in der
sublimen transzendenten Wahrheit gegründet.
Dadurch trägt sie Gehalte in sich, die die
Katholizität stets wieder sprengen, auch in der
Kirche selber. Es lebt die Wahrheit der Ketzer
in der Kirche. Die Katholizität kann manchmal
dem Betrachter wie ein Unwesentliches, als ein
Verhängnis des Christentums erscheien, das
verknüpft ist mit dem Grundgedanken der
ausschliessenden Offenbarung." VW, p.857.

Having pointed to Jaspers's foundational
understanding of "catholicity," we believe it is
nonetheless impossible to weaken the primarily
critical force of his view of the Roman Catholic
Church, cf., e.g, PGO, pp.45-92; PFR, pp.37-49.
As Professor Alan Olson points out, "There can be
little doubt that Jaspers' harangue against the
notion of "Catholicity" is in large measure
informed...justifiably, by what he perceived as
the perverse capitulation of the church and its
leadership as symbolized by the infamous
Concordat of Pius XII [sic] with Adolph Hitler."
Transcendence and Hermeneutics, p.141. One
suspects, furthermore, that Jaspers's treatment
of the characteristics of catholicity also
indirectly reflects his dialogue with, and
critique of, Heidegger; cf., e.g., Schilpp,
second and augmented edition, 1981, p.75/12.

44. Karl Jaspers, quoted in Ehrlich, Ehrlich, and
Pepper, eds, Karl Jaspers, p.281. Cf., VW,
p.833.

45. Ibid., p.285, 287. Cf., VW, p.843, 845.
46. Ibid., p.289. Cf., VW, p.847.
47. Cf., PHT III, p.39-56.
48. Tilliette, Karl Jaspers, p.63.
49. See, PHT III, pp.3-32, 113-208. VW, pp.1022-1045 (=TS). Cf., PFR, pp.92-285.
50. PHT III, p.192; PH III, p.219.
51. Jaspers's approach to Transcendence is a negative philosophizing, a metaphysical transcending which conjures being for Existenz only to relinquish it in turn: "Formally, the idea of transcendence is laid down in a strictly negative definition without any substance: Consciousness and the Existenz that appears to itself in consciousness are not everything." PHT I, pp.88-89.
52. PHT III, p.113. Cf., Ehrlich, Ehrlich, and Pepper, Karl Jaspers, p.115.
53. Cf., PHT III, pp.7-8: "Metaphysical objectivity has a special character prior to all temporary concretions. It is the function of a language that makes transcendence intelligible in the consciousness of Existenz. The language of this objectivity enables an Existenz to bring to mind what it cannot know as consciousness at large. It is not a general language, not a language of all Existenz as a community of rational beings; it is always a historic language. It will link some and be inaccessible to others. Diluted into a generality, it is entirely different only in the ways of its creation and original adoption. In existence the transcendent language is like another world of objects. Our word for the objects of this world is ciphers. While in world orientation each object is itself, identical for everyone and thus explorable with general validity, the objective language of this second world is audible to possible Existenz alone. Yet everything objective is a possible cipher if it is adopted in transcending, brought to mind in a way that will make transcendence appear in it."
54. TS, p.21.
55. TS, p.19.
56. PFR, p.94.
57. VW, p.256: "Im metaphysischen Gegenstand ist ein Anderes, das Sein an sich, gegenwärtig. Der Gegenstand is nicht als er selbst, sondern in ihm ist das Sein gemeint. Der metaphysische Gegenstand ist entweder Chiffer oder verschwindender Gegenstand."
58. TS, pp.21-22.

59. PHT III, p.124; PH III, p.141. Cf., VW, p.401 and L.H. Ehrlich, <u>Karl Jaspers: Philosophy as Faith</u>, p.159.
60. PFR, p.95, n.1.
61. TS, p.39.
62. TS, p.42.
63. PHT III, p.114. Cf., PFR, p.92.
64. Karl Jaspers, quoted in Ehrlich, Ehrlich, and Pepper, p.314. Cf. PHT III, p.115.
65. Cf., PFR, pp.108-112, 325-329. Though Barth can say that "'revelation of God's Word is divine sign language,'" Jaspers believes he confuses the nature of signs with that of the unconscious symbol or cipher. Barth erroneously takes God's Word as an unequivocal sign of a real divine act in space and time, and thereby interposes the idea of a revealed reality between the hidden God and human Existenz. What Jaspers denies is not the reality of the cipher of Transcendence revealed in the God of the Bible, but the theologian's claim that the Christian revelation of God's Word in Christ is unique among other signs of Transcendence because revealed in the testimony of apostles, disciples, the church, and sacraments. Most importantly, Jesus is not a cipher of God's own reality, but an "exception," an extraordinary witness to the "cipher of man" as a "being in foundering."
66. PHT III, pp.118-119 and cf., p.133.
67. TS, p.42-43.
68. PHT III, p.132.
69. PHT III, p.61.
70. PFR, p.284. (emphasis added)
71. PFR, p.284, 285.
72. PHT III, pp.204-208 and PFR, p.283.
73. PHT III, p.207.
74. See PHT I, pp.296-298. PSP, pp.78ff. PFR, pp.17-21.
75. PSP, p.80-81.
76. Cf., PHT II, pp.274, 275, 277.
77. PHT I, p.297; PHT II, p.274, 275. PSP, p.82. In his final treatment of cult, sacrament, and church, Jaspers could write that "the point always seemed to me to be whether a cult, in action, prayer, meditation, is approached as a cipher or looked upon as the reality of God's presence. Where worship was regarded as a cipher it seemed it could be solemn and serious in freedom, weighty in suspension, without loss of vigour. Where the experience was regarded as divine reality, however, it struck me as a case

of magic-- that is to say, as a causality without causality, a reality without reality." PFR, p.112.

78. PSP, p.83 and PFR, p.15-17, 37, 323.
79. PSP, p.88. By "Biblical religion," Jaspers does not mean some abstraction from each of these denominational or confessional forms, but rather the comprehensive scope out of which all of them arose. Cf., also, MC, pp.37-51.
80. PFR, p.342. Cf., PSP, p.88, 95, 102.
81. MC, p.41; FE, pp.41-42.
82. Cf., MC, p.42. Cf., PSP, p.84: "The word of man is not the word of God."
83. We emphasize this point in an attempt to be honest to Jaspers's thinking, especially since there are those who see in his philosophizing a thorough-going humanistic Pelagianism. This is the position of Soren Holm who maintains that in "Jaspers' work faith is the expression of an active attitude towards life. It is not something which is bestowed on man as a gift of grace, as Luther doubtless opined it to be, however obscurely he may have set forth this view. Whereas faith and revelation may be described by a line pointing 'downwards' from God to man, from supra-nature to nature, faith in Jaspers' view becomes a human achievement, which may be described by a line pointing 'upwards' from man to Transcendence, and without passing outside the domain of Jaspers' philosophy we may give to this Transcendence the name of God." Holm, "Jaspers' Philosophy of Religion," in Schilpp, p.669.

Admittedly, the thrust of Jaspers's understanding of philosophical faith as an active, historic motion which trusts "in the source that tells it to hear and to heed what reason perceives" (FM, p.263; AB, p.366) has its starting point "from below," if you will. But the question of the directionality of the relationship between possible Existenz/freedom and Transcendence in Jaspers is a foundational antinomy in his thinking, and is therefore not unequivocal. It would be unfair to say that for Jaspers the Existenz-Transcendence relationship moves in only one direction. This would be tantamount to reducing Jaspers's thinking to a strict subjectivism, that cuts off the subject-object dichotomy of existence. Jaspers certainly maintains that the freedom of possible Existenz rests upon an awareness of something other than itself. As he frequently repeats, "I

am not everything." This is clear when he writes
that "strict unconditionality makes me aware, not
only that my existence is not selfmade and is the
helpless prey of certain doom, but that I do not
have myself alone to thank for my freedom either.
In some way or other, the realization of
unconditionality will occur only in relation to
its transcendence." PHT III, pp.5-7.
84. WW, p.45 and PFR, p.95.
85. PFR, p.95, 116.
86. Xavier Tilliette, Karl Jaspers, p.211.
87. PHT I, p.313. Jaspers's understanding of the
separation between philosophy and theology is by
no means unequivocal. In the Philosophy the line
between them is clearly drawn. But later, in his
dialogue with Bultmann, he asserts that
"philosophy and theology [...] might ultimately
be united, as they were in Plato, in the Stoics,
in Origin, in St. Augustine, and in Nicholas of
Cusa. Should this come to pass, we must keep in
mind an important distinction: theology and
philosophy may become one, but not religion and
philosophy." MC, p.51. (emphasis added)
Moreover, he himself was a church member in
the later years of his life: "I consider myself
a Protestant, I am a church member, and as a
Protestant I enjoy the freedom to ascertain my
faith, the faith on the basis of which I like to
think I live, without mediators, in direct
relation to transcendence, guided by the Bible
and by Kant." MC, p.78. Professor Edith
Ehrlich, a student of the philosopher and a good
friend of Karl and Gertrude Jaspers, once
mentioned in a personal discussion that had the
Jaspers's had children, they would have been
raised in the Christian (Lutheran) faith.
88. MC, pp.4-11. Jaspers argues that Bultmann's
demand for the demythologization of religion is
based not only upon a false view of modern
science and the modern world, but also upon a
false conception of "scientific philosophy" which
bases itself exclusively and incorrectly on
Heidegger's Sein und Zeit. While he sees the
attempt to do away with a "superstitious"
reification of myth in religion as positive, he
believes it is justified only if it insists on
restoring the mytho-symbolic reality in the
cipher language of myth. The work does indeed
operate, he asserts, "with existential terms; in
fact, it derives from Kierkegaard, Luther, and
St. Augustine. But at the same time it operates
scientifically, phenomenologically, objectively.

The appeal to selfhood, to authenticity, and to actual being-- a sinking into the original, historical facticity (Sosein), in order to be appropriated-- the appeal to earnest questioning in a hopeless situation, is present as it is in the great philosophical tradition, though the ideas of that tradition tend to acquire a hollow sound. At the same time, Heidegger's thought is presented in objective terms, as a doctrine, and as a result it commits us no more than the traditional systems. What we have, then, is a noncommittal, phenomenological knowledge, and by the same token, a learnable, usable knowledge that is a perversion of philosophy [...] Bultmann can employ the Existentialia as an alleged discovery of scientific philosophy, useful for the exegesis and appropriation of Biblical texts. Such a use of the Existentialia was made easier by the fact that they themselves originate in a thinking rooted in the Bible."

Moreover, Jaspers rejects the distinction between existentialist analysis (existentialer Analyse) and existentialist thinking (existentiellem Denken), whether introduced by Heidegger or Bultmann, which he feels lead to the following consequences: "Existential analysis seeks to formulate with scientific objectivity that which can have meaning only in terms of existential thinking; what was meant by the Existentialia only as a sign, an indication, is turned into a thing; what has meaning only as a summons to awaken, or a stimulus to unrest, is treated as universally valid cognition. What can be achieved only through inward commitment becomes a matter of noncommittal knowledge; responsibility for things said is confined to scientifically rational responsibility, instead of extending to inner meaning and consequences; thinkers take the liberty of speaking in the name of 'abstract consciousness' [Bewusstein überhaupt] where they are entitled to speak seriously only for themselves; an illusion of knowledge is created in matters where everything depends on the ground that is never known and that, since Kierkegaard, has been called Existenz; conceptual definitions congeal what only a transcending thinking can achieve step by step, each meaningful only to the degree that it evokes an inner resonance [inneren Handeln] and becomes real in the actual life [Lebenspraxis] of the thinker." MC, pp.9-10; FE, pp.13-14.

For his part, Bultmann's response to Jaspers's notion of cipher, which he labels as

Jaspers's "magic word," points to the heart of the conflict between the hermeneutics of Christian liberalism and the hermeneutics of the Encompassing: "To define the myth as a cipher of transcendence merely describes the problem of interpretation; it scarcely solves it" (MC, p.161).

89. See, e.g., Paul Ricoeur, "Preface to Bultmann," pp.49-72, esp. at 57ff., and "Toward an Idea of the Hermeneutic of Revelation," pp.73-118, both in Essays on Biblical Interpretation, ed. by Lewis S. Mudge (Philadelphia: Fortress Press, 1980).

90. MC, pp.20-21. We agree with the criticism of Harold A. Durfee, "Karl Jaspers' Christology," Journal of Religion 44 (1964), p.145, who argues that Jaspers's distinction between the message of Paul and the message of the Synoptic Gospels appears as a continuation of an outdated liberalism in New Testament studies. Recent New Testament scholarship is much more conscious of the Jewishness of both Paul and the Gospel of St. John than Jaspers admits.

91. MC, pp.83,81.

92. MC, p.55. Cf., PSP, p.95 and PFR, pp.360-363. Despite Jaspers's and Bultmann's similar views regarding the human being's understanding of him or herself in the world, and the necessity of risk and commitment needed for humanity to understand itself in relation to transcendent being, in the final analysis, their often heated dialogue reveals a glaring hermeneutical boundary that separates Jaspers's philosophic faith from Bultmann's Christian faith. Further on this point, see Eugene Thomas Long, Jaspers and Bultmann: A Dialogue Between Philosophy and Theology in the Existentialist Tradition (Durham, North Carolina: Duke University Press, 1968), esp., p.151.

93. OGH, p.226. The primary sources for Jaspers's understanding of "Biblical religion" are PSP, pp.76-114 and PFR, pp.329-346.

94. Karl Jaspers, "Von der biblischen Religion," Die Wandlung, I (1946), p.407, quoted by Julius Izhak Loewenstein, "Judaism in Jaspers' Thought," in Schilpp, p.655.

95. PSP, p.88.

96. PHT III, p.60. Cf., VW, p.692.

97. PSP, pp.96-99 and 105-106.

98. Cf., PSP, pp.103-104. PFR, pp.330-337. VW, p.854.

99. See VW, pp.850-855, and section (7.1.3).

100. VW, p.854: "Jesus ist in Wahrheit gar nicht die Einheit aller Weisen des Umgreifenden."

101. VW, p.851: "Da aber der Tatbestand vorliegt, dass ein Gottmensch in Jesus Christus geglaubt worden ist, und dass ein Glaube sich in solchen Sätzen ausgesprochen hat, ist der Gedanke und ist die Wirklichkeit des in ihm sich aussprechenden Glaubens ein Anstoss des Philosophierens."

102. VW, p.852: "Dass Gott Mensch oder ein Mensch Gott sei, das ist absurd. Es widerspricht dem sich zur Transzendenz aufschwingenden Gedanken und auch dem ursprünglichen Bewusstsein, dem der Eine Gott als Schöpfer der Welt Wirklichkeit ist."

103. VW, pp.859-860: "Die christliche Lehre in theologischer Entwicklung gestaltet Widersprüche zu Paradoxien. Die Grunddogmen sind unbegreiflich, ihre Absurdität ist Ausdruck ihres Mysteriums. Die Lösung der Widersprüche im Begreiflichmachen ist gerade häretisch. Es ist grundsätzlich unmöglich, sie aufzuheben. Alle nur möglichen Lösungen lagern wie ein Kranz von Häresien um die Mitte der Unlösbarkeit des in der Paradoxie sich kundgebenden Mysteriums. Christlich ist das Ende und die Grenze des Begreifens das Mysterium des Absurden. Hier will das Begreifen des Nichtbegreifens in der bestimmten Form dieser Dogmen sich nicht überschreiten lassen. Das Philosophieren aber verwehrt diese Grenze. Es findet in dem Absurden des dogmatisch gefassten Glaubens keine Ruhe."

104. VW, p.854: "Das Scheitern des Menschen am Kreuze ist die Gestalt seiner Offenbarung. Darin liegt die Wahrheit, dass das Einssein in der Tat nicht möglich in der Zeit ist, dass die Einheit nur auf den Daseinsbruch zu gründen ist, dass jede immanente Einheit in Gestalt einer Vollendung, einer Schönheit, eines Glanzes auch vitaler Vollendung unmöglich ist." Cf., GPT I, p.89.

105. VW, p.855.

106. PFR, p.338, 349.

107. VW, pp.853-854, at p.854: "eine radikale Verwandlung, Reinigung und Vertiefung dieser biblischen Religion durch ursprünglich glaubenskräftige und redliche Menschen." (emphasis added)

108. PFR, p.338.

109. Cf., VW, p.855: "Dass das Eine nur auf den Daseinsbruch zu gründen und in der Welt in der Tat nicht zu erreichen ist, ist philosophisch unverschleiert zu bewahren. Die Mythisierung des

Gottmenschen-- von Jesus wahrscheinlich gar nicht vollzogen: 'Was nennst du mich gut, niemand ist gut ausser dem einen Gott' -- ist dagegen die Vernichtung der offenbar gewordenen Wahrheit."

110. GPT I, p.90.

CHAPTER EIGHT
ON THE POSSIBILITIES AND LIMITS OF "CONVERSION"
AS A "SOLUTION" TO THE NUCLEAR PROBLEM

8.0 INTRODUCTION

In the previous chapter we completed our analysis of Jaspers's understanding of the role of "conversion" in the nuclear age by elucidating his view of the relationship between philosophical and religious faith, and his foundational understanding of the limits and possibilities of revelational faith in the light of the nuclear problem. Here we pose one final question to Jaspers: What are the possibilities and limits of his understanding of "conversion" in the light of our present "situation" and as seen from the perspective of contemporary christian faith?/1/

It is of course impossible to set forth a comprehensive response to this question given the limited scope of the present chapter and the genre of the work as a whole. We can neither characterize the full parameters of the present nuclear debate, which have been frequently touched upon already, nor can we claim anything more than an inroad into the question of christian faith's view of "conversion" and philosophical faith in light of the nuclear problem.

While we believe Jaspers's thesis concerning the role of "conversion" within science, morality and politics, and religion is important and indeed necessary, we also believe it is insufficient in the light of the present situation as seen from the perspective of our own christian faith. In turning to the question of the limits of Jaspers's understanding of human "conversion," we must from the outset emphasize that to "critique" Jaspers actually means, as Leonard Ehrlich has noted, "to show what one believes, in Jaspers's sense of faith."/2/

With this supposition in mind, then, we will begin this final chapter by briefly noting what we believe to be a shortcoming of Jaspers's primary valuation of rational communication (8.1), followed by the limits of his construction of the nuclear problem in the light of our present situation and faith (8.2). Because this study has been conceived as a "dialogue" with the philosopher and as an "experiment" in christian social ethics and theology, focus must be given to the question of how our own christian faith views Jaspers's understanding of the "conversion" to philosophical faith in the nuclear age. In a "Concluding Theological Postscript" (8.3), therefore, five lines of "critical" analysis are set forth which take as their methodological point of departure Jaspers's understanding and critique of revelational faith and kirchliche Religion as set forth in his atom bomb book and in his final treatment of the relationship between philosophical and revelational faith (cf. 4.2). In this final section we draw upon previous criticism of Jaspers's view of christian faith (by S. Holm, P. Ricoeur, F. Buri, and A. Olson), and summarize recent theological formulations of the meaning of conversion along the mainlines of christian political and liberation theology in response to the rise of the social question during the past two decades. While we touch upon the christological implications of the meaning of the conversion to "the other," particular the enemy, and the possibilities of creative nonviolent action (a truly "loving struggle") for both interpersonal and international relations, their fuller development must wait for another context.

8.1 FROM THE INTELLECT/REASON DICHOTOMY
       TO THE PRIMACY OF THE OTHER

It is beyond the scope of this chapter and the work as a whole to attempt a "critique" of Jaspers's philosophy of science and his characterization of modern science's origins, boundaries, and domains, as well as his critique of positivism, anti-science, and scientific Marxism. Professor George B. Pepper has convincingly argued that Jaspers's preoccupation with the limits of the sciences is unduly restrictive and fails to recognize the positive contributions which the contents of the sciences can have for philosophy, particularly as exemplified in the thought of Pierce and Whitehead, and as developed in the dialogues of Habermas with Marxism, Ricoeur with Feudianism, and James Hillman with Jungianism./3/ Mindful of the limitations of Jaspers's view of the sciences, we have nonetheless identified many of the positive implications of Jaspers's "foundational thinking" and his call for an encompassing rational thinking commensurate with the demands of the nuclear age. We do not, therefore, intend to "critique" Jaspers's foundational thinking or his understanding of the subject-object dichotomy. Our concern here is more modest, and focuses instead on Jaspers's valuation of the primacy of rational communication between human beings-- a value which is necessary in the nuclear age

234

to be sure, but one which does not go far enough given the basic human needs of the present situation.

As we have seen time and again, central to Jaspers's illumination of what it is to be human is faith in the possibility of a universal, rational communication between human beings confronted by the twin threats of annihilation and totalitarian mass movements. But we must ask, as Professor Benoît Garceau has recently done,/4/ from where does Jaspers understand that it is primarily in the possibility of universal communication that humanity realizes its proper truth? Does not belief in this particular possibility inevitably work as a value judgment or criterion of selection among others?

Moving beyond the binary schema of the "intellect" and reason as established by Kant, reviewed and corrected by Hegel, and reappropriated and exploited by Hannah Arendt and Jaspers in this century, Professor Garceau proposes that there is a more basic experience of belief that Jaspers's foundational epistemological distinction between the scientific intellect and encompassing reason fails to illuminate. It pertains to that belief which is lived in unconditional friendship and designated by the expression "I believe in you" (je crois en toi). It no longer concerns faith in something-- even if this be the possibility of universal communication-- but rather faith in someone. Rejecting the belief that one can reserve "knowledge" (connaissance) only to the object knowledge (savoir objectif) of the scientific intellect,/5/ he proposes a third scheme: "that of the objective knowledge of things by the praxis of observation, explication, and theorization, the knowledge of self by reflection, [and] the knowledge of the other by the interpretation of signs."/6/

"Knowledge" of the other by the mediation of signs is lived in interpersonal relationship in an "engagement" that is different from that truth obtained by either the methodological postulates of science or the thinker's decision to progress faithfully and continually toward those demands and possibilities of his or her own being. Instead, the "knowledge" of the other is only possible in the measure to which "praxis engages itself unconditionally for the value of the person of the other."/7/ Secondly, this "knowledge" of the other is lived as the reception of a revelation. Precisely through the gestures and words of the other, through signs, the "presence" (cf. Jaspers's concentration on the Gegenwärtigkeit or "presentness" of being) of a possible way of being human manifests itself in its truth. To be sure, we only have access to this truth through our own proper interiorization and engagement, but it is always from the other that we first learn-- and not from self-reflection-- about that which is possible in the human being. Finally, and perhaps most importantly, this "knowledge" of the other is marked by "apophatisme". By this he means

> the certitude that the other in who
> I believe is never reducible to that
> which I perceive of him, nor that which
> I think of him; indeed, that he is not
> even reducible to that which he has
> made, nor that which he says of
> himself, not that which he thinks of
> himself. That which is possible in him
> cannot be reduced to that which is
> actually manifest by himself. He is
> always taken to be a being which
> transcends each of his manifestations--
> for a being, as Dostoïevski said, who
> has never said his last word. I have
> no need to recall that without this
> certitude forgiveness does not make
> sense./8/

This "third way" of the primacy of faith in "the other" points to a weakness of philosophical faith, even if Jaspers's notion of communication between possible Existenzen bears some similarity to it. To be sure, Jaspers maintains that "reason is potential Existenz which in its thinking is continually directed upon an other, upon the Being which we are not, upon the world, and upon Transcendence."/9/ And when he speaks of the "production and reception of ciphers" in speculative thought, the "cipher of man" is the primary cipher for him. Only in and through this cipher is the final cipher of Transcendence experienced. But does the reception of the "cipher of man" include the unconditional affirmation, "I believe in you?", as outlined above? We would like to see in Jaspers's thinking a much stronger expression of this unconditional belief in the other, in which the other is not circumscribed either by what we know of him or her, or by the other's deeds and self-knowledge. Where Jaspers does speak of the reality of the existential "certitude" of the person as opposed to some sham total knowledge, and unconditional faith in the other (even in the "masses") beyond the horizon of one's self, then religious and philosophical faith will no doubt find a common room for mutual clarification and dialogue.

Unconditional faith in the other has important implications for a much needed theology of the enemy in the nuclear age, since the "otherness" of the other person for the christian believer is inextricably tied to the otherness of Christ and God's unconditional love for all people, including the Soviet people./10/ In our present situation in which the Soviet Union has been defined as an "evil empire" and its people objectified as an absolute "enemy," unconditional belief in the other has become a condition of possibility for the future. All too often the "enemy" merely represents a mirror of the self, a projection of those things which we cannot tolerate, acknowledge, or accept within ourselves.

Existentially, the most direct access we have to the sinful and fallen aspects of ourselves comes by way of our treatment of "the other," those we dislike, the "enemy." Politically, the superpowers have such nuclear overkill potential today that both are at the mercy of the other not to launch a pre-emptive first strike. A de facto condition of "mutually assured destruction" (MAD) exists, and will continue to do so in the future, despite recent trends toward nuclear "counterforce" and "war-fighting" strategies, and the prospect of arms reductions at both the intermediate and strategic levels. Within an historical situation in which one nuclear Trident submarine could wreak havoc upon, if not annihilate over 200 Soviet cities and their inhabitants, the future of humanity is no longer bound simply to our own existential and political freedom, but to the very destiny of our "enemies" as well. We do well to recall here with Levinas that "war does not manifest exteriority and the other as other; it destroys the identity of the same."/11/

8.2 THE LIMITS AND POSSIBILITIES OF JASPERS'S CONSTRUCTION OF THE NUCLEAR PROBLEM TODAY

As noted in Chapter Four, the twin possibilities of nuclear annihilation and political totalitarianism are a constant element in Jaspers's exceedingly nuanced and dialectical construction of the nuclear problem. Although he saw total human annihilation as a technological uncertainty in 1958, he was convinced self-caused human extinction would be possible in time with the development of more powerful and numerous bombs. As suggested in 1950 in "Das Gewissen vor der Bedrohung durch die Atombombe," however, Jaspers would no doubt agree with those contemporary moral philosophers who argue that if war at low levels is wrong, war at high levels is also wrong. Showing this to be the case is a much stronger reason for the condemnation of nuclear war than a survivalist mentality which simply condemns extinction as such./12/

Today, in the light of both Jonathan Schell's controversial Fate of the Earth with its humanistic eschatology and supposition that the species is "biologically immortal,"/13/ and more recent "nuclear winter" research by R.P. Turco and P.R. Ehrlich,/14/ scientists, philosophers, and theologians continue to debate the possibility of human extinction and "omnicide."/15/ Ehrlich and others conclude, on the basis of worst case circumstances, that "the possibility of the extinction of Homo sapiens cannot be excluded," though the study admits that "it seems unlikely [...] Homo sapiens would be forced to extinction immediately [...]"/16/ No doubt there are some in the peace movement who have an interest in exaggerating the probable effects of nuclear holocaust for all life on earth, just as there are those in the military-industrial-academic complex who would minimize the research findings. The point is, however, that serious discussion about possible human extinction is taking place at this juncture in history. The way to folly, even if not certain extinction, is even more clear now than it was thirty years ago when Jaspers set forth his analysis of the problem.

A "critical" analysis of Jaspers's posture towards political totalitarianism and the Soviet Union in 1958 demands a nuanced evaluation. We should like to make clear from the outset that we disagree with those critics who see in Jaspers's construction of the nuclear problem a simple choice between only two "objective" alternatives, either annihilation or total rule. Despite Jaspers's very real Cold War advocacy, he never takes either alternative to be absolute in terms of human freedom, nor does he ever discount possibilities for change within the Soviet Union and Eastern Bloc countries. Concerning the debate over outfitting the German army with nuclear weapons in the late 1950s, for example, Jaspers clearly attempted to steer a middle course between the sloganistic positions of "better dead than red" or "better red than dead."/17/

Furthermore, it is one thing to suggest, as some of the earlier critics have, that Jaspers's construction of the nuclear problem articulates a thoroughgoing "better dead than red" philosophy, and another to say that he stood in principle for the priority of freedom, truth, and human dignity over mere physical existence (Dasein)./18/ To be sure, throughout the decade of the original Cold War Jaspers accepted the possible use of the atom bomb where the issue is one of "being or non-being," "freedom or slavery" in the struggle against unlimited force. And yet, if Jaspers had truly given heavy philosophical attire to the expression of "better dead than red" in Die Atombombe book, as some of his staunchest critics have putatively argued, this view would contradict his own forceful critique of so-called political "realism" and Realpolitik which wills unlimited power as such (cf. 6.3.2). Such an attribution would not square with his vision of a "new soldier" devoted to the cause of a new "world order;" a "new soldier" who-- on both sides of the ideological conflict-- might some day refuse to use nuclear weapons demanded by the politicians or generals./19/ Jaspers emphasizes that "no one can be certain that totalitarianism would finally annihilate man's essence along with his freedom."/20/

Much of the previous political criticism of Jaspers's Cold War posture has failed to emphasize his understanding of the Janus face of total rule. For while Jaspers fought against the threat of external totalitarianism, he was equally, if not more, concerned with the existential and domestic implications of total rule within the West. His fight against totalitarianism was as much if not more a "struggle for freedom within the free countries;" it is more a "showdown with ourselves," than an external fight against Soviet hegemony./21/ While even today it would be untrue to gloss over the very real differences between the competing political ideologies and practices of the East and West (the task of the christian as peacemaker in this situation, however, is another question), and misguided to equate the "national security" state with total rule, we nonetheless believe that Jaspers's critique of totalitarianism is, in principle, applicable to the contemporary race for space-launched nuclear weapons, space-based anti-ballistic missile systems, and anti-satellite weapons. When "nuclearism"-- i.e., psychological, political, and military dependence on, and faith in, nuclear weapons as a "solution" to the dilemma of "security")/22/-- takes on the form of an

239

absolute worldview, then nuclear weapons themselves, more than Soviet and other forms of national totalitarianism, are the far greater threat to humanity. When this happens nuclearism becomes a type of military and strategic "total planning" for ostensible "security." It represents the apotheosis of that technological and "intellectual" hubris which is yet another "false hope" to be shunned if reason is to aid us at the boundary. To be sure, technological research will continue. But the important question concerns the ethical guidance of "purposive," technological action. The technological program forgets that if war is to be defended against, then war and war-making as an institution must be abolished. To believe that nuclear weapons, particle beams, and chemical lasers in space will be used only for "moral" or "defensive" purposes-- not to mention the question of technological, ⌐conomic, and militarily feasibility-- evades the real issue: the needed change or "conversion" of humanity.

If we argue against those critics who see in Jaspers's political thinking a thoroughgoing "better dead than red" stance, then how are we to evaluate Jaspers's affirmative stance on the question of nuclear use (cf. 4.1.2), and his belief that the risk of the possible sacrifice of "all life" can be made for the sake of life worth living should a decision have to be made in the extreme situation?

In response to this question, it should be emphasized that Jaspers's twelve year experience under the thumb of National Socialism and Hitler's tyranny left an indelible mark on his political thinking. World War II remained the predominant model for his thinking about nuclear war during the original Cold War decade. In this respect the political limit of Jaspers's Cold War advocacy may be stated in the form of a proposition: Jaspers's construction of the nuclear problem in the 1950s negatively articulates the final boundary of the "old politics," even as it positively points the way toward the "suprapolitical" guidance of a "new politics."

Today, however, we see how the comparison of the Soviet Union with Nazi Germany is a model which is sorely inadequate. Scholars of Soviet strategy have suggested historical shifts in both Soviet strategic attitudes and war aims. According to David Holloway, who sits on the editorial board of The Bulletin of the Atomic Scientists, while it has been difficult for the

Soviet Party to accept that nuclear war could permanently reverse the course of history and lead to the defeat of socialism, the chief aim of their preparations has in recent years been nuclear war prevention./23/ Even the most staunchly skeptical would have to admit that the West has witnessed a "new" mode of thinking (glasnost) under Secretary-General Gorbachev, despite the brutal war in Afghanistan and human rights violations against political dissidents and Soviet Jewry. Gorbachev's January 1986 proposal to eliminate nuclear weapons by the year 2,000,/24/ and an apparently sincere desire to divert military resources to the Soviet economy serve as examples. In contrast, the Reagan Administration's recent failure to abide by the terms of the SALT II treaty, reciprocate the Soviet's unilateral test ban moratorium, and maintain the terms of the 1972 ABM treaty (the so-called "narrow" interpretation of the treaty) represent a breach of trust in the eyes of many. Jaspers's fight against a merely "formal democracy," and his belief that the inner struggle for the self-preservation of freedom is essentially a showdown with ourselves is a timely warning.

Prima facie, Jaspers's personal willingness to risk total annihilation does indeed fail to take the limit of Weber's Verantwortungsethik seriously, despite his differentiation between the Verantwortungsethiker and the advocate of Realpolitik. For if the "ethic of responsibility" includes belief in accountability for the consequences of one's action and the readiness for any kind of sacrifice, it does not accept, as Jaspers himself admitted in his earlier treatment of Weber,/25/ those political means, such as the use of nuclear weapons, which would most likely destroy the very meaning of politics itself. The absolute limit of the "ethic of responsibility" has been clearly reached when the use of nuclear weapons holds out the likely prospect of destroying the state along with those values the state is meant to protect, including worthy life, human dignity, and law.

Today there is a growing consensus among strategists that even a "limited" nuclear war would very likely lead to the crossing of the nuclear "firebreak," and thus to total war./26/ It is precisely this empirical assumption which led the U.S. Catholic Conference of Bishops, in their 1983 pastoral letter on war and peace, to a "highly skeptical" assessment of the real meaning of a so-called "limited" nuclear war and of the morality of nuclear weapons

241

use./27/ On the basis of utilitarian, deontological, and just war foundations alike, moral philosophers and theologians are increasingly arguing against any use of nuclear weapons, and to a lesser extent, the immorality of nuclear deterrence itself./28/ As Kai Nielsen has written regarding the question of the use of nuclear weapons in defense of western values, "the human devastation to 'victor' and 'vanquished' alike is just too great to make it a morally tolerable option. On moral grounds it is intolerable and on prudential grounds it is insane."/29/

At a foundational level, however, Jaspers's construction of the nuclear problem and his personal willingness to sacrifice "all life" for the sake of life with dignity turns back upon his understanding of "struggle" as a boundary situation, the unconditionality of moral action, his notion of historicity, the existential truth of "possible Existenz," and the witness of the "exception" in boundary situations. Jaspers clearly appropriates Max Weber's distinction between the "ethics of conviction" and the "ethics of responsibility," and the unconditionality of a "political decision" that is based neither on a calculable consequence of the Verantwortungsethik, nor on the unequivocal consequence of the absolute morality held by the Gesinnungsethik (cf. 6.3.2). But if both Weber and Jaspers recognize that these two ethical standpoints are often combined in the "rational statesman," Jaspers nonetheless goes beyond Weber by emphasizing the "suprapolitical" role of sacrifice in moral action, and by reiterating the dialectical interplay between the ethics of normal and extreme situations.

For Jaspers, the twin possibilities of human annihilation and political totalitarianism represent a Grenzsituation for humanity as such. Foundationally, the pivotal boundary situations of "death," "suffering," "struggle," and "guilt" transcend mundane reality, and create a space where human existence is potentially given its authentic meaning in freedom. "Death" and "suffering" are boundary situations that exist for us without any action on our part. "Struggle" and "guilt" are boundaries insofar as we help bring them about through our own doing. But they are boundary situations precisely because we cannot exist without bringing them about./30/ "Struggle" exists at the "unconscious" and "conscious" levels, as well as from "the idea and from Existenz." The first two concern the material conditions of existence, the third concerns a struggle for achievements of the human mind, for both rank and echo./31/ Jaspers's survey of the forms of "struggle" leaves us with two essentially different modes which, for all their differences, nonetheless rebound into the other.

> A struggle by force may be coercive, limiting, oppressive, and, conversely, space-making; in this struggle I may succumb and lose my existence.
> A loving struggle is nonviolent, jeopardizing without a will to win, solely with the will to manifestation. In this struggle I may hide, dodge, and fail as Existenz./32/

More importantly, he maintains that one cannot decide in advance how one will act in the boundary situation, nor can , one ever completely eliminate elements of freedom and uncertainty when it arises. As we have tried to show time and again, Jaspers always attempts to situate the debate over morality and politics within a common room of reason wherein the violent struggle for existence could be turned back into the loving struggle for Existenz. The challenge his construction of the nuclear problem poses is to prevent denial of the real possibilities of annihilation and total rule on the one hand, and to work for "rational communication" and moral-political freedom so that the extreme situation might never arise on the other. Dr. George B. Pepper well summarizes Jaspers's position on the annihilation/totalitarianism debate when he writes that Jaspers's position

> concerns a boundary situation for which there can be no universal norms. For Jaspers no criterion can provide a compelling prescription about what makes life worth living in situations which have life or death alternatives. For these situations each person must appeal to Transcendence and assume the responsibility for the worldly consequences. Jaspers in effect held very specific if not rigid moral norms about sexuality, law, and politics. In "boundary situations," however, everyone is called to be an "exception."/33/

When Jaspers's construction of the nuclear problem is seen in the light of his foundational notion of boundary situation, then, it is impossible to read a thoroughgoing "better dead than red" posture into his thinking. And for the record, we should not like to be misunderstood as advocating either absolute pacifism, or the "better red than dead" position as it is commonly understood. With Jaspers, we reject the alternatives-- dead/red or red/dead-- as false and polemical. The really basic question is whether or not it is better to submit to injustice than to commit it, or to be either dead or red than a murderer of innocent noncombatants, including women and children. Here we do well to recall the words of the contemporary German philosopher, Ernst Tugenhat:

> Consider how many countries are under the domination of the Soviet Union today. This is something we accept. Consider that terror and torture reign in many other countries connected with our own western system. This is something we tolerate and indirectly even support. Consider further that in large parts of the world millions of people die every year of hunger. This too is something we tolerate, though it need not be the case if it were not for our armaments. Why then should we choose to threaten not only our enemy and ourselves, but the whole of humanity with destruction, simply to avert the possibility that we might be threatened by a fate which would be no worse than those we tolerate for others?/34/

Given Jaspers's experience under Hitler's total rule, his understanding of Soviet military capabilities and foreign policy in 1958,/35/ and, most importantly, his ethics of Existenz linked to the boundary situations of human existence-- or what he calls "the antinomical structure of existence"/36/-- he was willing to risk the annihilation of all life for the sake of life with dignity from the perspective of his own historicity and faith. Given our understanding of the present nuclear situation and the risk of even limited uses of nuclear weapons crossing the nuclear "firebreak" to total war, Jaspers's construction of the nuclear problem represents a limit to our own faith. But we admit that he helps us clarify what is at stake in decision-making in the boundary situation. For wherever the extreme life or death situation arises, each of us has finally to account to God for our decision and action, which inevitably reflect a moral "stance" tied to one's faith and historicity.

8.3 CONCLUDING THEOLOGICAL POSTSCRIPT

Turning now to the question of how christian faith views the limits of philosophical faith in the nuclear age, we must say from the outset that it is neither possible nor useful to attempt a systematic "critique" of philosophical faith wherein theological argument is juxtaposed to Jaspers's survey of the idea of God, cult, religious community, prayer, and the "faith in revelation" as set forth in the previous chapter. While we indeed must take our stand on theological ground proper, such a method would be inappropriate given Jaspers's understanding of the external nature of religious faith vis-a-vis philosophical faith. A systematic juxtaposition of the principles of christian and philosophical faith, while perhaps useful for another context, would indubitably fail to capture the communicative import of faith for the nuclear problem. Instead, we will set forth five lines of critical analysis which take Jaspers's critique of revelational faith and kirchliche Religion in the nuclear age as their methodological point of departure. If the christian ethician may not entirely be able to live and move and have one's being within "the Encompassing," and this is not to reject the import of Jaspers's foundational thinking, one can at least raise questions in good will from the perspective of one's own faith and Lebenspraxis.

(1) In his book on the atom bomb, Jaspers asserts that "God's will" is not to be substituted for reason in an attempt to interpret the meaning of history in the light of possible human self-destruction, or to evaluate the legitimacy of the possible use of the bomb. Religious language is human language, and therefore inevitably ambiguous. It has not only metaphysical limits, but limits for the socio-political order as well. Foundationally, religious language is bound to the "first" and "second" languages of Transcendence as the experience and mythical articulation of Transcendence manifest in testimony and theology. And yet as religious language, theology never quite obtains, on his view, to the "third" language of speculative metaphysics in which "possible Existenz" reads the original cipher-script of being by

245

writing a new script. This is why Paul Ricoeur can note that Jaspers's philosophizing appropriates religion and theological language, even as it "raises to the rank of 'metaphysical speculation' that religious faith over which it has triumphed [...] Religion dissolves first into mythical figures. Then the mythical ciphers themselves subserve speculative ciphers. Prayer is definitely reduced into 'existential contemplation'."/37/

Now if the original primitive ciphers of Transcendence "speak" through the figures of art, myth, religion, and finally metaphysical systems, they are all mediated by human language-- including metaphysical "systems" or systematics such as his own philosophizing. Jaspers admits that being a cipher is a signification that signifies nothing else, and that signification is only a metaphor for being a cipher. He acknowledges that the philosophical cipher of Transcendence and the authentic (unconscious) religious symbol both reveal the "presentness" of being when the features of "objective" speech are put into suspension. But is anything really said, then, by either the unconscious symbolism of religious faith or the philosophical ciphers of Transcendence? Can one yet meaningfully speak of Transcendence, or must we remain silent? As Soren Holm asks, is Transcendence real, or is only the cipher real? Is God to be understood "ontologically" or only "axiologically?"/38/

Religion and theological language regain their meaning or existential truth for Jaspers not so much in opposition to the cipher as within the movement of the historical reading of ciphers. As such, religious interpretations or statements concerning the legitimacy or immorality of the use of the bomb, or the meaning of history in the light of possible annihilation, actually assume the same metaphysical status as the philosophical interpretation of ciphers. The truth of possible Existenz in its own historicity is truth whether that be as an "exception" or through "authority." Logically, then, we are led back to a conflict of interpretation over which unconscious religious symbols or philosophical ciphers carry more possibility, meaning, and historic truth in the nuclear age. Is there any final criteria by which to decide this question, save the absolute subjectivity of the individual in relation to his or her own truth?

Moreover, if both Jaspers and the religious believer can admit that "the will of God" is or can be a meaningful symbol or cipher, must the christian not appropriate the "content" of such a "will" personally, as a truth and "will" that summons me absolutely? Here at the level of existential truth, proper, there seems to be more in common between religious and philosophical faith than Jaspers would admit. This is why his survey of revelational faith appears at times as a caricature of christian faith. In the same vein, are religious authority and tradition, the christian community, and prayer such "objective," warm, and consoling realities as he suggests? Does the theologian not also know that God is "hidden?" And is the revelation (Offenbarung) of God in Torah and the Logos (Jn.1: 1-18) not a dynamic reality toward Whom the believer is continually moving or transcending in faith? In short, is not the "revelation" of religious faith also a "becoming" revelation, in Jaspers's sense of Offenbarwerden, rather than a static reality with which the believer rests self-assured? Is christian faith not a striving or wrestling with God, like Jacob at Peniel (Gen.32: 28-30)? Is it not a real battle against the "radical evil" incarnate in the socio-political injustices and oppression of the world, against those real spiritual powers that keep human beings from both existential and political freedom (Eph.6: 10-20)?

To be sure, Jaspers positively prods us to keep the reading of symbols and ciphers to a "loving struggle," and within an encompassing room of reason. At a time when the religious and political Right in North America is increasingly behooved to link nuclear Holocaust with a triumphant christian Apocalypse, philosophical faith has something extremely important to say: beware of the limits of worldview; what we believe contributes to the shaping of reality. And yet, if one is searching for the unity of humanity at this juncture of history, as Jaspers was on the basis of "rational communication," then whether the "cipher of history" is liberal progressive or Marxist, believers in both worldviews must be disconcerted by the possibility of nuclear war, and the burdens of global militarism upon the poorer nations of the South. There is an element of absurdity about the number of nuclear weapons and the outrageous costs of militiarism which transcends any theoretical or philosophical account of the meaning of history. Arms transfers to the Third World create present genocide for many countries; and nuclear war between the superpowers would not be some kind of event within history, it would be the very dissolution of human history. The

christian may believe with Jaspers "that God is is
enough" in the face of possible nuclear self-
destruction. But somehow his final "cipher" of
Transcendence as a "being in foundering" in the world
does not go nearly far enough in the face of the
present genocide and social injustice that exists in so
many parts of the world. In this situation the
believer's hope rests, as St. Paul tells us, in the
Cross of Christ as the ground and assurance of an
"unseen" hope (Rom.8: 18-25).

(2) Jaspers also maintains that without
philosophical faith, revelational faith (christian or
otherwise) is inadequate for the urgent demands of
freedom and liberation in the present age. But if
Jaspers critiqued Bultmann for trying to create a
philosophical religion by eradicating myth from
religion, what keeps his own philosophical faith from
the charge of having created a secularized or global
philosophical religion for humanity at the end of the
"axial age?" He himself once wrote that the renewal of
religious faith is to be interpreted "as a return to
the primal source, as a renewal of the philosophical
faith that is implicit in the religious, as a
transformation [Verwandlung] of religion into
philosophy (or philosophical religion)."/39/

What, then, is the precise relationship between
religious and philosophical faith? This question may
be clarified if we ask about the essential thrust of
Jaspers's basic questions. We agree with Ricoeur when
he writes that the basic question remains for Jaspers
one of "absolute reality, that is to say, the question
of Being qua Being and of the appearing of Being;" and
that consequently, "Religion becomes a philosophical
question when its own dialectic of deliverance is
transferred to the properly philosophical problem of
absolute reality."/40/ For Ricoeur, in other words,
Jaspers's contrast between the Biblical idea of the
unique revelation of God in history with the universal,
evanescent symbolism of ciphers reflects two different
problem areas: the former reflects a concern with the
freedom of salvation, while the latter's concern is
ultimately with metaphysical speculation on being or
absolute reality. Thus Ricoeur, the
philosopher-theologian of religious freedom in the
light of hope, critiques the philosopher of the
Encompassing for Jaspers's "annexation" of religion by
philosophy. Ricoeur believes Jaspers substitutes the
christian idea of sin for the boundary situation of
"inevitable guilt," and the mediation of sin through

248

forgiveness for the "I will" of philosophic choice at the price of a too radical voluntarism. And if Ricoeur rightly acknowledges the "culpability of theology" which the "pretension" of religious mediation and "catholicity" has attested, he rightly warns of its philosophical counterpart:

> The culpability of theology signifies also a contrary culpability of philosophy, a hybris of great philosophical systems, even (or especially) if these systems are systems of God. The philosophy of Existenz does not escape this charge either [...] 'Vanity' has extended to the Self as to everything else. There is no less of a pretension in the Ursprung of 'existential' philosophy than in the I think of Kantian philosophy or the Spirit of Hegelian philosophy. The admirable and redoubtable freedom of the Socratic doubt has always to be saved from its subtle bondage./41/

Furthermore, can philosophical faith escape the charge of a certain "objectification," though bent on transcending any particular "object?" Is it not something experiencially, metaphorically, and linguistically particular? Xavier Tilliette has creatively shown how philosophical faith possesses creedal elements insofar as it is an I who believes, even if it be within the endless domain of the Encompassing./42/ And what would the renewal of religious faith look like if it were truly transformed into philosophical faith? What would it look like in historic, communal mediation and practice? We have seen how Jaspers considered himself to be a "liberal" Protestant who advocated the "Protestant principle" and the "invisible" essence of the church in extremis. Would the Transcendence of philosophical faith gather the community to celebrate the gift of "possible Existenz," to "read" collectively its manifold world of ciphers, or to render thanksgiving for the bread of life which sustains the possibility of Dasein and Existenz in the modes of the Encompassing which we are? Would philosophical faith gather to remember the "great philosophers" of the "Axial Age", those "paradigmatic" individuals who have manifested the partial break through of truth in time as "exceptions" or "authorities?" Could philosophical faith believe that

249

Socrates, Buddha, Confucius, and Jesus all affect the promise and fulfillment of the future and the possibility for universal communication in the same way?

As these questions imply, one of the central limits of philosophical faith in relation to christian faith comes down to the problem of historicity, and the instantiation of faith in textual, dogmatic, and institutionalized forms. As Dorothee Sölle has asked,

> does not that philosophical faith which has been rendered autonomous and severed from the tradition and institution of the church, remain more under the spell of religion than he himself knew? [...] Is it not possible that we cannot afford to dispense with those congealed experiences of meaning present in scripture and tradition, when the presentation and conveyance of existential immediacy is at issue?"/43/

The problem of the instantiation of philosophical faith is the problem of an existentialist hermeneutics which tends, as Emmanuel Levinas notes, to reduce the "alterity" or otherness of Transcendence to the "sameness" of the horizon of the subject./44/ Where Jaspers's chides "orthodoxy" for its fixation upon mediating agencies, one can conversely charge his "liberalism" for trying, at times, to stand outside of these same mediating agencies./45/

(3) Jaspers maintains that the christian churches represent both dangers-- through "political" maneoverings-- and possibilities insofar as they might incorporate philosophical faith and reappropriate "Biblical religion" at the nuclear boundary. Here we cannot adequately treat the changes in christian ecclesiology and theology since Jaspers's comparison of philosophical and revelational faith in the early 1960s, nor the positive implications of "peace ecumenism" in the nuclear age./46/ Instead we must ask if Scripture or, indeed, "Biblical religion" does not also present us with a view that human history has a meaning and a pattern that leads to a unity of humankind based on a universal, loving communication. To be sure, the Bible itself is not this story of unity, and the christian community, as one manifestation of that religion, is certainly not the "Reign of God" on earth. Moreover, the christian believer can

and must welcome Jaspers's loving struggle against religious exclusivity and clerical authoritarianism which has been on the rise in recent years. Eschatology, that "encompassing" idea of Biblical faith, is the only cure for "catholicity." From a Biblical viewpoint, however, humanity is called to be one humanity, no matter how fragmented the human race may be. And from the christian perspective, which shares in "Biblical religion," humanity is able to create a new humanity through the following of Christ.

So shall at last we attain to the unity inherent in our faith and our knowledge of the Son of God-- to mature [adulthood], measured by nothing less that the full stature of Christ. (Eph.4:13, NEB)

When Jaspers speaks of the possibilities of "Biblical religion" one discovers the essential thrust of his religious philosophizing: the movement of his philosophizing towards the Biblical idea of an unpictured God. This is most aptly expressed in his appreciation of the second commandment: "Thou shalt not make unto thee an image or likeness" (cf., Ex.20:4). Unfortunately, he never draws out the full implications of the "objectification" of idols and false gods in the nuclear age. Faith is confronted today by the ideological deification and reverence of weapons of mass destruction as powerful bearers of the mysterium tremendum. Believers can no longer justify placing absolute trust in weapons of mass destruction and the dogma of nuclear deterrence: "Some boast of chariots, and some of horses; but we boast of the name of the Lord our God" (Ps.20:7).

Indeed, for the believer, not to make any image of God is to find, or be found by, the right God, and to reject and stuggle against the false gods of human thought and deed. The Decalogue of the Hebrew Bible begins by saying that we must not believe in nor serve false gods, the Lord God is a God who frees people from slavery and bondage (Ex.20:2-3). To be sure, the first commandment demands the undivided and unconditional worship of Yahweh. Whether this faith must be "intolerant," however, is another question. For the commandment also suggests that the only true God is the God of freedom, who will not allow us any of the comforts of religion (Ex.20:4). Living faith tears us away from the old traditional shrines and native places. It forbids us to make an image of God by which

251

we might wield numinous power, or invoke God's name in some kind of magical rite. Herbert McCabe has well appropriated the commandment for christian faith today: "You must deny the other gods and you must not treat Yahweh as a god, there are no gods, they are all delusions and slavery. You are not to try to comprehend God within the conventions and symbols of your time and place; you are to have no image of God because the only image of God is man."/47/

Here we must ask how far the philosopher has gone in truly appropriating the "Biblical religion" of which he speaks so highly? Is the Ursprung of his thinking in the final analysis Biblical or Greek? Whose Weltanschauung gains final ascendancy, that of Plotinus, Plato, Kant, and Kierkegaard, or Jeremiah, Jesus, Augustine and Luther? Can one appropriate all the "great philosophers" and still claim to be tied to the origin of "Biblical religion?" Moreover, if Jaspers admits that "possible Existenz" can be related, through the existential truth of authority, to a personal or incarnate God concerning whom we speak in the form of ciphers, how can he then demand that faith finally ground itself out beyond all ciphers, as Fritz Buri has asked?/48/

(4) We must also ask how far philosophical faith can boundlessly communicate with the cipher of Incarnation today? Can it communicate with the cipher of the passion, death, and resurrection of Jesus Christ, with the man Who through His "being in foundering" upon the Cross revealed the "presence" of Transcendence? This is a "presence" revealed by the giving of self to "the other," and to the complete "otherness" of God as revealed in the cry of dereliction (Mk.15:34; Mt.27:46; cf., Ps.22:1). We agree with Alan Olson who observes that Jaspers's negative reading of the cipher of Incarnation is both a philosophical and political one. Jaspers's rejection of the cipher is not due so much to its authentic mythical aspects, which as we have seen his theory of truth allows, as it is to the embodiment of the cipher in authoritarian church structures./49/ The Vatican's signing of the Concordat with Hitler, of course, left an indelible imprint on him.

Though the believer must acknowledge with Jaspers the importance of the struggle against kirchliche Religion, dogmatic "orthodoxy," and the need for a new Biblical hermeneutic, the christian must finally live and move and have his/her being out of the "fulness" (pleroma) of Christ, rather than the fulness of "the Encompassing," however necessary the latter might be from a foundational perspective. For it is through Christ that "all things hold together" and have their essential being (Col.1: 15-20). Christ remains the Alpha and Omega of history (Rev.1:8) for the believer who ought never to pass self-righteous judgement upon other faiths and religious traditions. It is with Christ that we are called beyond mere "existence" to live in that nonviolent mode of being which manifests the reconciliation of all things, including the love of the other, even the "enemy." It is in unconditional praxis and sacrifice for "the other," and the promise of the future Reign of God that we grasp the eschatological meaning of the possibility of "perpetual peace" as a gift of Shalom. Transcending even the One "encompassing of all encompassings," the trinitarian modes of God's being as Creator, Redeemer, and Sustainer move one to declare "that God is is enough," and, indeed, that the future finally belongs to God even in the face of possible annihilation.

Christians can certainly agree with Jaspers, against Schell's humanistic eschatology and quest for "biological immortality," that the human project goes far beyond merely physical Dasein. But what should bother American christians most about the possible use of nuclear weapons (again) and the risk of annihilation is not that we may all well be killed if a nuclear war occurs, but that we may be spiritually implicated in the murder of millions of Soviets who are loved by God unconditionally. Schell's humanistic survivalism is ironically the mirror image of those Christians who cannot resist speculating about the imminent end of the world, and thereby possibly contributing to its realization. Survivalists and christian triumphalist apocalypticists are theologically presumptuous since they fail to understand that the Christian expectation of the end can be hopeful only because we believe history to belong finally to God. If all that stands between us and despair is the prospect of the indefinite continuation of the human species, we indeed live in a hopeless world (cf. Eph.2:14-22). As Stanley Hauerwas reminds us, conscious of the imperative for christians to strain every muscle to work for peace with justice,

Christians are a people who believe that we have seen the end; that the world has for all time experienced its decisive crisis in the life and death

253

of Jesus of Nazareth. For in his death
we believe that the history of the
universe reached its turning point. At
that moment in history, when the
decisive conflict between God and the
powers took place, our end was resolved
in favor of God's lordship over this
existence. Through Jesus' cross and
resurrection the end has come; the
kingdom has been established. Indeed
it had to come in such a fashion for it
is a kingdom that only God could bring
about./50/

(5) Finally, Jaspers emphasizes in his atom bomb
book that "individual believers in revelation can be
close to individuals who philosophize. Their judgments
and their ways of life can coincide in fact." With
this statement the theologian must certainly concur.
He also maintains that the will of Existenz in the
world is inextricably linked to its origin only "by a
readiness for existential action in the world." Here
again one must agree. But when Jaspers goes on to
define this action essentially in terms of "the
reception and production of ciphers,"/51/ his emphasis
upon the historicity of Existenz appears to give way to
the primacy of speculative thinking.

The boundaries which confront humanity today--
global militarism, the population explosion, environmental deterioration, and catastrophic thermonuclear
war-- all demand a faith in action which is more than
the mere "reception and production of ciphers." To be
sure, philosophical transformation in the sense of a
"rebirth to a true life"/52/ in the Platonic sense is
indeed necessary in order to overcome the fragmentation
of the human condition today. But it is insufficient
from the perspective of christian faith. For at the
heart of "Biblical religion," there exists another
vision and summons to revolutionary thinking and doing
on behalf of the dispossessed. This is a vision
towards a future world of freedom that is not primarily
grounded upon the ideals of liberal bourgeois society,
nor upon the communicative media of domination and
competition so characteristic of our society. Rather,
the vision is grounded upon that summons of God to
"conversion," to a "turning back" to Yahweh and
neighbor, to human "repentance" (metanoia) from sin and
the evil will. Herein lies the Ursprung of the freedom
of "Biblical religion." "Conversion" for the christian
believer is grounded upon the authentic and repeated
turn-about to the "invisible God" (Col.1:15) revealed
in Christ, and to the "the other" to whom He calls us

254

to love (Jn.15:12). It is grounded upon a turn toward the participation in the "salvation of all flesh," where "flesh" as distinct from "body" (cf. _Dasein_) refers to interpersonal and social existence, to the group existence of humanity. This vision of freedom aims at universal peace and justice (II Pet.3:13), with a view toward the day in which there will be no more mourning and pain (Rev.21:4).

To speak of _religious_ "conversion" in the nuclear age is not primarily to speak of a theology of individual salvation in which the gospel has to do merely with "the soul" or one's autonomous existence or existential "decision" before God. It is not to imply that christian faith is only concerned with making people individually good, self-controlled, and loving in their immediate relationships. To be sure, this view of "conversion" is necessary but woefully insufficient for the socio-political exigencies of our time. For we know that far too frequently it tends merely to support the socio-political _status quo_ with its injustice and oppression under the guise of civil religion. The more traditional or "orthodox" view of conversion is faulty because "a good man is hard to find in an unjust society," and because "men whose good will has been cultivated exclusively in immediate personal relationships amongst their families, friends, and acquaintances are quite frequently blind to large and devastating social injustice and to the agony of people whom they do not meet socially."/53/

Today we have begun to enter upon a "post-individualistic" phase of history, as Karl Rahner has written in his theological reflection on the future of humanity's self-manipulation./54/ The conversion to and love of God has its medium and form in the love of neighbor, which is not simply ideology or the inclination of the affections. As the religion of the experience of "absolute future" in Jesus Christ, christian faith is and must be a reality which sends us into the world to act. Loving intercommunication must take on a new form as the servant of a new humanity. "Humanity" no longer exists merely as an idea, as an ideology, but must begin to exist as a concrete reality. Society is slowly and inevitably reconstructing itself along truly new lines, and it can be a partner in this task of loving one's fellows which is the form and medium of that love in hope and faith through which the absolute future "arrives."

255

Because self-manipulation cuts across all fields of human endeavour, planning and control have become a necessity for human continuity and survival. Similar to Jaspers's emphasis upon the existential grounding of socio-political freedom, Rahner reminds us that a christian transcendental anthropology "can never accept an absolute separation of the ethics of man's inner disposition from the ethics of his external actions and practical norms." But christian anthropology does acknowledge human freedom to act contrary to our nature in absurd and contradictory ways, and to reject self-determination and the creative transformation of our human nature as the call of the christian's vocation to salvation. The dogma of Original Sin stands as a sign of the limit of an irreversible self-manipulation, and warns us that any human action in history will remain a "one-way process" in the future. For history continues under the law incurred by its guilty beginning, involving death, futility, contradiction and suffering. No self-manipulation on the part of humanity can abolish this law, which indeed stands as a sobering warning for those who would risk the threat of nuclear war and environmental destruction./55/

To speak of the role of "conversion" today is indeed to acknowledge many of the intellectual, moral and political, and philosophical elements of Jaspers's call for human "conversion," for a "new" way of thinking and doing. From the perspective of christian faith, however, it also means realizing that encompassing "conversion" which has come to be articulated by the new movements in the mainstream of "political" and "liberation" theologies. These trends in theology have rightly spelled an end to the excessive individualism of existential theology and the metaphysic of subjectivity which it implies. For they are not primarily concerned with transcendental subjectivity, and the primacy of the existential locus of faith, values, and decision, but rather with the public, societal, and political dimensions of faith and hermeneutical narrativity.

The response of "political theology" to the question, "what are we to do at the nuclear boundary?", begins with a kulturkritik which takes our secularized "spiritual situation of the time" seriously. J.B. Metz understands this task as a critic of middle-class religion, as keeping the dangerous memory of the freedom in Jesus Christ alive, and as an appropriation of the future in the memory of suffering./56/ The post-Enlightenment rise of religious privatization, the crisis of tradition, authority, and metaphysical reason all point to the need for a "theological enlightenment of the Enlightenment" and its subject, the middle class citizen. With these tasks we would certainly concur.

Metz is on less solid ground, however, when he argues that Kant's definition of Enlightenment as a freedom of the individual to make public use of his or her reason in all things had primarily the value of a moral appeal, an ethics of autonomy if you will, and thus was not a call to create new social conditions of freedom. The subject to whom Kant referred, Metz argues, was the "propertied citizen who lacks the moral strength to make use of his own intellect and to become politically what he has already been both socially and economically for a long time,"/57/ i.e., a middle class elite. In the logic of this Kantian metaphysical reason, Metz continues, praxis developed not so much as a praxis of liberation, but as a "praxis of control," particularly of nature in the interest of the market. If Jaspers goes a long way toward correcting Kant's lack of emphasis upon "the social question," the term is used here as a conscientious anachronism, we would still like to see a greater concern in this direction, particularly given the demands of our present situation./58/

In our situation, christian theology and faith must set forth an eschatological understanding of christianity in response to the exchange nature of modern industrial society in which religion has no public place. "Conversion" from the old to the new mode of theological thinking means that theology may no longer fulfil the role which industrial society expects of it as "the cult of the new subjectivity," to use Jürgen Moltmann's expression./59/ Political theology fights against that theology which presents itself as a "doctrine of the faith." The nuclear problem demands a turn away from the philosophies and theologies of existence for which "existence" is the relation of the individual to him or herself as this emerges in reflection. Such theologies assign faith its home in a subjectivity and spontaneity which is non-object-ifiable, and which cannot be grasped in any social roles. It localizes faith in that ethical reality which is determined by one's "decision" and "encounter," but not by the pattern of social behaviour and the self-contained rational laws of the economic circumstances in which the individual lives. As such, the christian ethic is reduced to the "ethical demand" to accept one's self and to take responsibility for the world in general. But this ethic is no longer able to provide any normative ethical instructions for the ordering of socio-political life, even though based on the idea of christian love. As Moltmann has rightly noted, the self which emerges in this old theology "becomes the 'pure receiving' of the trans- cendent and divine [...] It sees 'God' not as a God of the world or of history or of society, but rather as the unconditioned [sic] in the conditional, the beyond in the things of this world, the transcendent in the present."/60/

Requiring a "conversion" to a theology of hope, the new theological thinking views reality in terms of the horizon of the expectation of the Reign of God. All proclamation of the Word of God stands within this eschatological tension. Even if we speak of this Word as a "cipher" of Transcendence for the sake of dialogue with the philosopher, the difference between the eschatological tension of the Word of God and the "word" of philosophical faith lies in the future orientation of the former's proclamation. As future, the Logos is not a final objectified revelation as Jaspers believes it to be, but a Word whose call is continually moving us toward God's future promise of hope-- a promise which demands the continual "con- version" toward "the other" through both hearing and doing of God's word./61/ Our Lord, come [Maranatha] (I Cor.16:22), stands as the believer's expression of hope as we work toward a lasting peace with justice, even as if salvation depended solely on us.

The inseparable unity of faith's theory and love's praxis implies a new way of thinking about sin and forgiveness as well./62/ Contemporary christian faith believes that we must depoliticize the Pauline understanding of sin which concerns only God and the individual soul, and thus endorses the socio-political status quo. Dorothee Sölle finds "conversion" or "turning about" (Umkehr) as a better word for the forgiveness of sins in our present situation because it promises a new beginning that is not grounded and secured in the privilege of having. She affirms with Jaspers that "liberation is possible only as the liberation of all."/63/ "Conversion" for this liberation cannot take place by oneself alone because it is destroyed whenever it appears as something solitary and private. "Conversion" is more than forgiveness because it includes the future and not merely a static past. Ultimately it means not buying into the pressure our society places upon us to achieve; it means struggling lovingly against built-in competition, loneliness, non-communication (especially with the elderly), and the insistence upon privileges.

What religious "conversion" entails today is a turn to that form of community and commitment which Dietrich Bonhoeffer spoke of as "the cost of discipleship,"/64/ and Matthew Lamb, going beyond the earlier political theologians, as "agapic praxis."/65/ The "conversion" to agapic praxis is a turn not so much to the "greats" of history as to the victims of history. Lamb holds out a vision of transformative communites grounded in agapic praxis and prophetically narrative theologies expressive of a disjunctive imminent expectation of redemption by the victims of history. Such agapic praxis is crucial for christian discipleship confronted by the social sins of racism, sexism, ecological destruction, politico-economic oppression, and a rampant militarism leading toward annihilation. Drawing upon Metz's twofold dialectic of suspicion and recovery of Karl Rahner's transcendental theology, and Bernard Lonergan's "generalized empirical method" and macroeconomics, Lamb reminds us that the question of the relationship between theory and praxis is crucial for a proper understanding of the role of conversion in the nuclear age. He calls for a praxis inextricably tied to a theory of social transformation which takes seriously the Enlightenment, critical theory, and earlier attempts by political theologians to reconstruct dogma as socially critical./66/

Finally, it seems certain that the turn to christian discipleship today must begin with that spirituality or Lebenspraxis of liberation which centers on "the other." As Gustavo Gutierrez writes, this is "a conversion to the neighbor, the oppressed person, the exploited class, the despised race, the dominated country." This encompassing conversion means "a radical transformation of ourselves; it means thinking, feeling, and living as Christ-- present in exploited and alienated man." Ultimately, it believes that we "can stand straight [...] only when our center of gravity is outside ourselves."/67/ Christian faith believes that the "new" thinking and doing commensurate with the demands of the present situation lies in this "evangelical conversion" and its communication-- a nonviolent being grounded in Christ's revolutionary love and solidarity. As Walter Wink puts it: "love of enemies has, for our time, become the litmus test of authentic Christian faith."/68/

259

What all of the foregoing authors have in common is a commitment to a biblical vision of humanity, shalom and justice which takes seriously the integration of theory and praxis, and the individual and socio-economic dimensions of christian faith. Conversion is not understood in terms of an assent to dogmatic beliefs, but rather an ongoing process of faithful transcending that continues throughout the life of christian discipleship and within the context of authentic community. Having emphasized the social, political and economic dimensions of conversion here, we do not wish to deny the importance of personal conversion in the nuclear age. For as the U.S. bishops reminds us in their pastoral letter on economic justice,

> The transformation of social structures begins with and is always accompanied by a conversion of the heart. As disciples of Christ each of us is called to a deep personal conversion and to 'action on behalf of justice and participation in the transformation of the world.'/69/

8.3.1 The Role of "Conversion" in the Nuclear Age: In Appreciation of Jaspers's Philosophical Faith

Our "critique" of the limits of Jaspers's understanding of the role of "conversion" in the nuclear age is tied to our own historical situation, christian faith, and an acknowledgement of the positive possibilities of his analysis of the nuclear problem, and thus of his philosophical faith. Karl Jaspers's thinking on the nuclear problem represents an articulation of the possibilities of his philosophical faith. By the very selection of data and ideas within that whole which constitutes Jaspers's philosophy of encompassing reason we have frequently acknowledged the positive and necessary significance of his thinking for our historical situation. The importance of human "conversion" within the domains of scientific and rational thinking, moral and political freedom, and religious and philosophical faith is especially urgent given the narrowly defined parameters of the present nuclear debate which are frequently detached from the question of what it is to be human.

Throughout this work we have attempted to listen carefully and openly to Jaspers's philosophizing, mindful that only an encompassing methodological

260

approach could do justice to his thought on the nuclear problem. It has been necessary to situate his clarion call for the "conversion" of humanity within the broader context of his philosophical thinking as a whole. In order to give his call to "conversion" in his atom bomb book more determinacy, it was necessary to ground it within the context of his own experience of total rule (Chapter One), his conception of past and present history (Chapter Two), "foundational thinking" (Chapter Three), construction of the nuclear problem during the original Cold War period (Chapter Four), and, in turn, within the specific scientific (Chapter Five), ethico-political (Chapter Six), and metaphysical (Chapter Seven) horizons which issue from, and flow into, the open sea of his philosophical faith. If we have been faithful to Jaspers's own method, our analysis should not have yielded any objective "results" per se, but simply a transformation in our awareness of the ways in which we think about, and actively respond to, the nuclear problem.

We have also shown why previous political criticism of Jaspers's thesis on "conversion," particularly the charge of "indeterminacy," is only a half truth. This criticism fails to acknowledge how and why the thesis of "conversion" in the atom bomb book is inextricably linked to, and consistent with, Jaspers's earlier historico- philosophical method as a whole.

By way of summary, we have argued that the role of "conversion" is crucial for the whole of Karl Jaspers's transcending thinking, and not simply his thesis in his book on Die Atombombe und die Zukunft des Menschen.

For the philosophy of history, "conversion" implies both the appropriation of and turn toward the insights of the "axial age" as the spiritual basis for universal communication in the present "crisis" situation, in which new foundations have been laid for humankind by modern science and technology.

Within the horizon of his foundational thinking, the needed transformation functions as a type of cognitional "conversion" realized through "the basic philosophical operation" which continually turns the subject-object split of human consciousness into "the Encompassing."

The "conversion" in science requires turning from the reductionism of the "intellect" (Verstand) and instrumental reason's preoccupation with technology and technological panaceas, to an encompassing reason that recognizes the "will to truth" as the cognitional condition of possibility for the human future.

In morality, the repeated "conversion" turns one from the preoccupation with Dasein to life as "possible Existenz," from the evil will to the "grand will," and from purposive, conditional action to unconditional praxis.

The "conversion" in politics turns the politician from the "old politics" based on the balance of nuclear terror to the "new politics" grounded upon a "suprapolitical" rational communication and sacrifice; from the violent struggle for existence to the "loving struggle" for Existenz; and from the nihilism of Realpolitik to an "ethic of responsibility" which believes in the possibility of "perpetual peace." The condition of the possibility of physical existence (Dasein) has been shown to be inextricably tied to the realization of existential (as "possible Existenz") and political freedom as legally grounded in the concept of right, democratic process, and rational communication.

Jaspers's political presuppositions, still applicable today in a world of nation states equipped with nuclear weapons, are tersely expressed in two beliefs: (1) the freedom of the individual depends upon the freedom of all; and (2) there can be no peace without freedom, but no freedom without truth. Jaspers never equates totalitarian rule simply with dictatorship, Marxism, or racial theory. To be sure, his fight against totalitarianism is waged at the level of both moral existence and political life, both domestically and internationally. But much of the previous criticism of Jaspers's Cold War posture has failed to emphasize his understanding of the Janus face of total rule. His struggle against totalitarianism was primarily a struggle for freedom within the free, democratic countries of the West, a showdown with ourselves.

Furthermore, developments in the world's military and political situation between his analysis in 1958 and his 1966 work, Wohin treibt die Bundesrepublik? (The Future of Germany) significantly influenced his thinking. Jaspers's opposition to the proposed emergency laws in the latter work, including the idea of building civilian bomb shelters which were justified in the name of the "Red menace," is a case in point. "This menace did exist once, after 1945," he could write, but "today the threat is a mirage."/70/ It would, of course, require a separate treatment to analyze further developments in Jaspers's global and German political thinking between 1958 and his death in 1969.

For revelational faith, theology, and the churches, Jaspers argues the needed "conversion" is from kirchliche religion to the reappropriation of "Biblical religion," from the dogmas and absolute truth claims of revelational faith and ecclesiastical authority to the reception and production of ciphers through philosophical faith. The quest for human liberation and freedom through the reception and production of ciphers is seen as urgent since competing "faiths" are now armed with nuclear weapons and methods of total rule. He reminds us that the churches must have a deeper influence on the faithful, and believers must be willing to hazard the church's institutional existence in the name of God's shalom and justice.

In a spirit of dialogue with Jaspers, and in an awareness of the limitations of our own christian worldview, however cursorily stated here, we have not sought to argue the superiority of christian faith and ethics over and against philosophical faith and the ethics of Existenz, nor to set forth a christian view of "conversion" over and against that of Jaspers's philosophical understanding thereof. We understand our critique in terms of a loving struggle between two faiths that need each other for self-clarification. In this respect, this work represents only a prolegomenon to the larger question of the relationship between philosophical and religious faith in the nuclear age.

While there are insufficiencies in Jaspers's understanding of the role of "conversion" from the regional perspective of christian faith and social ethics, his thinking nonetheless helps positively clarify some of the basic issues involved in science, morality and politics, and faith in the nuclear age, even the most central one of all for christian faith today: the importance of human metanoia, conversion toward the God of Jesus Christ and to the other, to the victims of history and injustice and even "the enemy." It is through the "conversion" to God (Transcendenz) and "the other" that both philosophical and religious faith can work together for rational communication, moral-political and economic freedom, and human liber-

ation and solidarity amidst the challenges of the
limits to growth and "nuclearism."/71/

Karl Jaspers's philosophical faith has taught us
much about the importance of the "conversion" to
reason, and about that which is possible in humanity as
such. And we are grateful for his reminder that love
alone is the fundamental horizon of hope for the future
of humanity standing before the nuclear boundary.

> In our love for one another we
> become aware of our origin and of
> eternity. Here is the ground and
> assurance of our hope, which will
> enable us to live in our world by
> reason in the broadest sense of the
> word, and to direct our thoughts,
> impulses, efforts, beginning with our
> everyday lives, toward averting the
> final disaster that threatens./72/

NOTES

1. We would like to thank Professor George B. Pepper for his comments on an earlier version of this chapter.
2. Leonard Ehrlich, <u>Karl Jaspers: Philosophy as Faith</u>, p.229.
3. George B. Pepper, "Karl Jaspers on the Sciences: In Retrospect" (Forthcoming). More positively, Pepper points out that, for Jaspers, conflicting philosophical positions ultimately concern those "forces" that are being served by a particular thinker. The real issue for Jaspers is one of authentic, communicative self-expression or magic. And Pepper reads the concept of "courageous humility" as a central virtue of Jaspers moral philosophy. Critically, Professor Peppers argues that Jaspers's critique of the "forces" operative in Marxianism, Freudianism, and Demonology fails to engage their theoretical fertility and misses the socio-historical contexts of the modern scientific enterprise. In this respect, Habermas, Ricoeur, and Jung stand as representatives who have rightly worked for a more positive reading of the "forces" operative in the three domains. In the final analysis, Jaspers's Kantian basis for science must give way to developments in our understanding of the scientific enterprise as identified by Polyani, Kuhn, and Dreyfus.
4. Benoît Garceau, o.m.i., "De la connaissance d'autrui par la médiation de signes," in <u>L'Altérité Vivre Ensemble Différents: Approches Pluridisciplinaires</u>, Recherches nouvelle série--7, ed. par Michel Gourgues et Gilles-D. Mailhiot (Montréal et Paris: Editions Bellarmin, du Cerf, 1986), pp.119-131.
5. <u>Ibid.</u>, p.123: "Pour rendre vraiment justice a l'expérience de la foi en quelqu'en, il semble qu'il faille élargir la cadre noétique dont on s'est le plus souvent servi, en commençant par admettre qu'on n'a aucune raison de réserver la connaissance au savoir objectif de l'entendement scientific."
6. <u>Ibid.</u>, p.123: "celui de la connaissance objective des <u>choses</u>, par la pratique de 'observation, de l'explication et de la théorisation, la connaissance de <u>soi</u> par la réflexion, la connaissance d'<u>autri</u> par l'interprétation de signes."
7. <u>Ibid.</u>, p.124.

8. <u>Ibid</u>: "la certitude que l'autre en qui je crois n'est jamais réductible a ce que je perçois de lui, ni à ce que je pense de lui, voire qu'il n'est meme pas réductible a ce qu'il a fait, ni à ce qu'il dit de lui-même, ni même a ce qu'il pense de lui-même. Ce qu'il y a de possible en lui ne peut être réduit à ce qu'il est de fait et manifeste de lui-même. Il est toujours tenu pour un être qui transcende chacune de ses manifestations, pour un être, disait Dostoïevski, qui n'a jamais dit son dernier mot. Je n'ai pas besoin de rappeler que sans cette certitude le pardon n'a pas de sens."

9. RE, p.92.

10. We would like to thank Dr. George B. Pepper for bringing this point to our attention within the present context.

11. Emmanuel Levinas, <u>Totality and Infinity: An Essay on Exteriority</u>, trans. by Alphonso Lingis (Pittsburgh: Duquesne University Press, 1969), p.21.

12. See, e.g., Richard Routley, "Metaphysical Fall-out from the Nuclear Predicament," <u>Philosophy and Social Criticism</u> 10, No.3/4 (Winter 1984), pp.19-34; and William C. Gay, "Nuclear War: Public and Governmental Misconceptions," in <u>Nuclear War: Philosophical Perspectives</u>, ed. by Michael A. Fox and Leo Groarke (New York, Berne, Frankfurt am Main: Peter Lang, 1985), pp.11-25, and earlier as "Myths About Nuclear War: Misconceptions in Public Beliefs and Governmental Plans," <u>Philosophy and Social Criticism</u> 9 (Summer 1982), pp.115-144. Routley and Gay are not critical of the call to eliminate nuclear weapons, but only the manner in which the argument is often made. Both believe that even on the "post-attack" assumptions of governments nuclear war and current nuclear policies are <u>immoral</u>.

13. Jonathan Schell, <u>The Fate of the Earth</u> (New York: Alfred A. Knopft, 1982), p.118.

14. K.P. Turco <u>et al</u>., "Nuclear Winter: Global Consequences of Multiple Nuclear Explosions," <u>Science</u> 222 (1983), pp.1283-92; and P.R. Ehrlich and others, "Long-term Biological Consequences of Nuclear War," <u>Science</u> 222 (1983), pp.1293-1300.

15. The term "omnicide" has been coined recently by the American philosophers John Somerville and Ronald Santoni to refer to the extinction of all forms of sentient life. See, John Somerville, "Nuclear 'War' Is Omnicide," in <u>Nuclear War:</u>

Philosophical Perspectives, ed. by Fox and Groarke, pp.3-9; and, Ronald E. Santoni, "Nuclear Insanity and Multiple Genocide," in I. Charny, ed., Toward the Understanding and Prevention of Genocide (Boulder: Westview Press, 1984), pp.147-153; and "The Arms Race, Genocidal Intent, and Individual Responsibility," Philosophy & Social Criticism 10, No.3/4 (Winter 1984), pp.9-18.

16. P.R. Ehrlich and others, "Long-term Biological Consequences of Nuclear War," p.1299.

17. Karl Jaspers, Wahrheit, Freiheit und Friede," in HS, p.177.

18. This is clear from Jaspers's struggle with the possibility of suicide under Hitler's tyranny. See his moving journal entries from 1939-1942; SchW, pp.143-62, and the English translations in L. Ehrlich, E. Ehrlich, and G.B. Pepper, Karl Jaspers, pp.535-543, esp. 541-3, where he writes: "[March 11, 1940] It cannot be God's will to have endured all, if this enduring is a slow tormenting annihilation in total helplessness and indignity. Man may put an end to himself if he cannot be effective anymore, if no one needs him, if he is abandoned, betrayed, shunned (he may do it together with someone if both are affected together in this manner)-- but he does not have to put an end to himself. It is not a law but his free will, his consent"....
[May 2, 1942] "If I cannot protect Gertrud against brute force, I, too, have to die-- this is simple human dignity.-- But that is not decisive and not enough" [...] To become one in death is the fulfillment of love-- it is like a kindly fate that permits us to die together, while mere nature, when it cause death, forces the survivor to go on living"....
[October 3, 1942] "The Christian demand, that one may not take one's life under any circumstances, is seductive. This is a thought that permits even the cowardice that wants to stay alive even if the beloved person is ruined by other persons. As if one could then continue, in good conscience, to be in the world and philosophize. God's demand, the prohibition of suicide, is played off against the genuine, historically concrete demand which is really felt to be God's demand and not an abstract law: not to deny oneself, to stand by the most beloved person without reservation."

19. Cf., FM, p.53. AB, p.84. FG, p.95-96.

20. FM, p.167; AB, p.229. ABR, p.52-54.

21. Karl Jaspers, "The Fight Against Totalitarianism," in PWT, p.87.
22. Lifton and Falk, Indefensible Weapons, p.ix.
23. David Holloway, The Soviet Union and the Arms Race, second ed. (New Haven and London: Yale University Press, 1984), esp., "Thinking about Nuclear War," pp.29-62.
24. The Gorbachev Proposal of January 1986 proposed: (Stage 1, 5-8 yrs) to ban on all intermediate missiles from Europe (i.e., the cruise, Pershings, and SS20s), a reduction of strategic weapons by 50% with a ceiling of 6,000 each, and, in a novel move, the Soviets suggested freezing French and British nuclear levels but not counting them; (Stage 2, 1990-1997) to induce all nuclear powers to ban tactical weapons and continue to reduce strategic levels; (Stage 3, 1995-2000) to eliminate all remaining nuclear weapons.
25. LDW, p.223. Cf. also above, 6.3.2.
26. For statements to this effect by McGeorge Bundy et al., General A.S. Collins, Jr., (former deputy commander in chief of U.S. Army in Europe), and Harold Brown see the Pastoral Letter on war and peace of the United States Catholic Conference, "The Challenge of Peace: God's Promise and Our Response," Origins 13, No.1 (May 19, 1983), p.14, n.61, 62.
27. Ibid., p.16. The bishops do not directly condemn any use of nuclear weapons. But they do reject it as an "unacceptable risk." Jaspers, of course, would still find "just war" approaches to the ethics of war and peace unacceptable, since they are based on ostensibly universal moral norms that are made into absolute proscriptions. For a recent discussion of the relative merits and applicability of the pacifist and, especially, the just-war approaches to the nuclear ethics debate, see Kenneth R. Melchin, "Just-War, Pacifism, and the Ethics of Nuclear Policy," Eglise et Théologie 17 (1986), pp.41-55 and his "Military and Deterrence Strategy and the 'Dialectic of Community,'" in P.B. RILEY and T. FALLON, eds., Religion and Culture: Essays in Honor of Bernard Lonergan, S.J. (Albany, N.Y.: SUNY Press, forthcoming 1986).
28. Russell Hardin et al., eds., Nuclear Deterrence: Ethics and Strategy (Chicago and London: University of Chicago Press, 1985); and the review article by, Gregory J. Walters, "'The Challenge of Peace': Philosophers and

Strategists on Nuclear Use and Deterrence," Eglise et Théologie 17 (1986), pp.355-386.

29. Kai Nielsen, "Commentary: Doing the Morally Unthinkable," in Nuclear War: Philosophical Perspectives, ed. by Michael A. Fox and Leo Groarke, p.59: "even if the most gulagish conception of Soviet world domination were accepted as plausible, that domination, that enslavement, could not last forever and would plainly be the lesser evil to the human destruction that would be unleashed by nuclear war."

30. PHT II, p.204: "There is no way in which I might hold back, since by merely existing I take part in their [i.e., struggle and guilt] constitution. In any attempt to avoid them I shall prove either to be constituting these two situations in another form or to be destroying myself. I deal with death and suffering existentially, in a boundary situation that I see; struggle and guilt I must inevitably help to create before, placed in them as boundary situations, I can become existentially aware of them and adopt them, no matter how."

31. PHT II, pp.205-206: "I fight, first, for the material basis of my life; I fight, second, for creation in the agon of minds; and I fight, third, to manifest Existenz in questioning love. But struggle is not just an interrelation of human beings; it goes on in the individual as well. Existenz is the process of self-becoming, which is a struggle with myself. I stunt possibilities that are inherent in me and coerce my impulse; I shape my given propensities, question what I have become, and am aware of being only when I do not recognize my being as something I own."

32. PHT II, p.206.

33. George B. Pepper, letter dated 13 April, 1987.

34. Ernst Tugenhat, Rationalität und Irrationalität der Friedensbewegung und ihrer Gegner (Berlin: Europaïsche Perspektiven GmbH, 1983), quoted in Anthony Kenny, The Logic of Deterrence (Chicago: University of Chicago Press, 1985), pp.33-34.

35. Jaspers's analysis of Russian global influence came at the height of their hegemony. According to the Washington based Center for Defense Information, 1958 was the highpoint of Soviet influence in the world. At that time, "Soviet-influenced countries had 31% of the world's population and 9% of the world's GNP, not

including the Soviet Union." In contrast, "in 1979 the Soviets were influencing only 6% of the world's population and 5% of the world's GNP, exclusive of the Soviet Union." Center for Defense Information, "Soviet Geopolitical Momentum: Myth or Menace?: Trends of Soviet Influence Around the World from 1945 to 1980," The Defense Monitor 9 (January 1980), pp.4-5.

36. PHT II, "The Boundary Situation of the Dubiousness and Historicity of All Existence," p.218: "In every boundary situation I have the ground pulled out from under my feet, so to speak. There is no solidly extant existence I might grasp as being. There is no perfection in the world if even loving communication must come to appear as a struggle. Whatever existence would pose as intrinsic being, it will fade before the question about the absolute. The fact that all existence is open to question means that we can find no rest in it as such. And the form in which the boundary situations everywhere show existence to be inherently dubious and brittle, this is what we call its antinomical structure."

37. Paul Ricoeur, "The Relation of Jaspers' Philosophy to Religion," in Schilpp, pp.611, 628.

38. Soren Holm, "Jaspers' Philosophy of Religion," in Schilpp, p.688. Also cf. Jaspers response, "Reply to My Critics," in Schilpp, p.781-782.

39. PSP, p.106.

40. Ricoeur, "The Relation of Jaspers' Philosophy to Religion," in Schilpp, p.631.

41. Ibid., p.641-642. To Ricoeur's charges of the vanity of subjectivity, philosophical and aesthetic gnosis, and the cancellation of the unconditional nature of the "existential" relation to Transcendence by the manifoldness and unending nature of ciphers, Jaspers replies with two remarks. First, that "no man in the final analysis knows about himself, even though he stands in the quietude of a faith, since in time this quietude can at any moment be overthrown." And secondly, that Ricoeur's critique "could be a misunderstanding due to the inescapable form of philosophizing for which I have striven hard. 'Existential' reality cannot be anticipated. In philosophizing which finds expression in writings the suspension of possibilities must remain, in order that the genuine character of original Existenz may not bind itself absolutely to the objectivity of the assertion of another. The tentative character of communication is the necessary form of unconditional seriousness. A

philosophy which does justice to its task must offer an appearance of adhering to the non-obligatory character of the manifold, which latter the author rejects absolutely both in his reader as well as in himself. But this rejection can be carried out, not by a declared confession, but always only by the historical acts of one's own Existenz which gives an account of itself to Transcendence." Jaspers, "Reply to My Critics," in Schilpp, p.781.

42. Xavier Tilliette, Karl Jaspers, p.122.

43. Dorothee Sölle, "'Thou Shalt Have No Other Jeans before Me,'" in J. Habermas, ed., Observations on 'The Spiritual Situation of the Age,'" p.159.

44. Emmanuel Levinas, Totality and Infinity, p.19ff.

45. Thus Ricoeur, "The Relation of Jaspers' Philosophy to Religion," pp.638-639, can ask: "Does not the philosopher run the risk of losing the 'narrowness' and the 'commitment' of Existenz when he embraces the totality of myths-- those of Greece, those of India, those of Christianity-- like a Don Juan courting all the gods?"

Leonard Ehrlich has, in defense of Jaspers, critiqued Ricoeur's linkage of freedom and vanity, guilt and forgiveness to what he sees as the latter's Christian orthodoxy. He sees Ricoeur's very conception of faith as tied to the specific orthodoxy of the Christian doctrine of salvation, which thus sets up the problem of historicity as an alternative: "either this faith based on the highest authority of revelation, or many faiths; and if many faiths, then a Don Juanism of faith." Ehrlich believes that the theologian finally "lacks the means of presupposing a diversity of faiths" and a "conception of freedom whereby the self, in such a confrontation [with other faiths], is no less responsible for the authority which it follows as is the authority for the truth of his faith." Ehrlich, Karl Jaspers: Philosophy as Faith, p.76-77.

46. Cf., Gregory J. Walters, "The World Council of Churches on Nuclear Deterrence: A Call to Peace Ecumenism," Mid-stream XXIV (1985), pp.29-43.

47. Herbert McCabe, Law, Love and Language (London and Sydney: Sheed and Ward, 1968), p.119.

48. Fritz Buri, "Concerning the Relation of Philosophical Faith and Christian Faith," trans. by Charley D. Hardwick, Journal of the American Academy of Religion XL/4 (Dec. 1972), p.455: Jaspers's faith "must throw the anchor of its trust into a form of being which is incapable of

becoming a cipher. This is an *amor* *fati* (Jaspers' own term) where all questions come to rest in a *unio* *mystica*, and this is precisely its problem because just here it threatens that personal being which is of such importance to Jaspers [...] With this Transcendence, the 'fundamental position' (Grundwissen) and the basic philosophical operation (philosophische Grundoperation) are no longer any use. There appears, thus, also to be a trojan horse for Jaspers's philosophy: the philosophical turn to God with the goal that lies behind all mysticism, 'the desire to become God.'"

49.   Alan Olson, Transcendence and Hermeneutics, p.141, notes that "because of the noetic-speculative character of transcending thinking, Jaspers is more concerned with the dynamics of heightening consciousness than he is with the givenness of the symbol or myth to be interpreted." Moreover, "since hermeneutics of transcending-thinking is always grounded in Existenz, the meaning of any interpretation is for Existenz and Existenz alone. Given the interrelatedness of these two factors, Jaspers's interpretations of the cipher of God inevitably lack what Ricoeur terms "the consistency of world" that can make them finally convincing." He concludes that "religious symbols and myths tend to be interpreted by Jaspers not as they are given and therefore mediated by the texts and institutes that are their embodiment, but as he believes they should be given in order to be consistent with what he terms 'philosophical faith.' Indeed, without closer attention to the processes of mediation, transcending-thinking itself dissolves either into solipsism or into the esoteric air of gnosticism." On Jaspers's "political" reading of the cipher of Incarnation, see also Chapter Seven, n.43.

50.   Stanley Hauerwas, Against the Nations: War and Survival in a Liberal Society (Minneapolis: Winston Press, 1985), p.165.

51.   PFR, p.284.

52.   Ibid., p.192.

53.   McCabe, Law, Love and Language, p.163.

54.   Karl Rahner, "The Experiment Man," in Theological Investigations, vol.9, trans. by Graham Harrison (London: Darton, Longman & Todd, 1972), pp.205-224.

55.   Ibid., p.214-215, 223.

56.   J.B. Metz, Faith in History and Society, trans. by David Smith (New York: Seabury, 1980), pp.32-46, 88-99, 100-118. For a more recent

appropriation of Metz's notion of "dangerous memory" as applied to U.S. culture and basic christian communities, see the work of Bernard J. Lee and Michael A. Cowan, Dangerous Memories: House Churches and Our American Story (Kansas City, Mo.: Sheed & Ward, 1986), esp., Chapter 6, "Mystical Politicism." Lee and Cowan remind us that christian discipleship involves an integration of theory and praxis, the mystical and the political: "There is not first the mystical and then the political; rather, how we should be in the world together, in all our social structures, is part of the reality of who God is for us, and is of an immediate piece with our experience of God. The political is of the substance of the mystical" (p.12).

57. Ibid., p.43.
58. We cannot here enter into the important debate between those who, on one side, see in Kant's ethics (and therefore, with qualification, Jaspers's) an autonomy isolated from human social and historical reality, and, on the other side, those who attempt to recover from Kant's account of autonomy a fundamental referent to a moral world that exhibits human mutuality and interdependence. For an elaboration of the former position, we have in mind Alasdair MacIntyre's After Virtue, second ed., (Notre Dame, Ind., University of Notre Dame Press, 1984); for the latter postion, see Philip Rossi, "The Foundation of the Philosophical Concept of Autonomy by Kant and its Historical Consequences," Concilium 172 (1984): 3-8.
59. Jürgen Moltmann, Theology of Hope, trans. by James W. Leitch (London: SCM, 1967), pp.304-334, esp., pp.311-316.
60. Ibid., p.314.
61. Ibid., p. 326: Proclamation of the word is "valid to the extent that it is made valid. It is true to the extent that it announces the future of the truth. It communicates this truth in such a way that we can have it only by confidently waiting for it and wholeheartedly seeking it. Thus the word has an inner transcendence in regard to its future. The word of God is itself an eschatological gift. In it the hidden future of God for the world is already present. But it is present in the form of promise and awakened hope. The word is not itself the eschatological salvation, but acquires its eschatological relevance from the coming salvation."

273

62. Dorothee Sölle, _Political_ _Theology,_ trans. by John Shelley (Philadelphia: Fortress Press, 1974), pp.83-107.

63. _Ibid._, p.102.

64. Dietrich Bonhoeffer, _Letters_ _and_ _Papers_ _From_ _Prison_ (London: Collins, 1971), p.17: "There remains an experience of incomparable value. We have for once learnt to see the great events of world history from below, from the perspective of the outcast, the suspect, the maltreated, the powerless, the oppressed, the reviled."

65. Matthew Lamb, _Solidarity_ _With_ _Victims:_ _Toward_ _a_ _Theology_ _of_ _Social_ _Transformation_ (New York: Crossroad, 1982), pp.13-14: "Agapic praxis entails a "conversion-- a _metanoia_ which literally means a 'change of mind (_nous_)'-- whereby the revelation of God's identification with victims begins to heal the irrationalities of the manifold biases which harden human hearts and darken human reason."

66. Lamb's (and thus Lonergan's) project for theology and Jaspers's for philosophy bear striking similarities insofar as both are concerned to over come the illusory opposites of sacralism and secularism, and to steer a course between idealism and positivism. Both are fighting to overcome the yokes of ecclesial and bureaucratic elitism in the quest for a transcendentally grounded freedom. But if Jaspers rightly rejects the ideological and dehumanizing dimensions of religious dogma or "orthodoxy," he often fails to acknowledge the positive value of dogma (e.g., creedal confessions) as expressive of a faith and call for _metanoia_ frequently at odds with the plausibility structures of the _Imperium_ _Romanum._ As Lamb notes, "Conversion is always a withdrawal from bias and sin; it is always a continuing transformation 'not yet' fully achieved. Religious solidarity with the victims of history is never an easy, comfortable, automatic or cheap grace. Conversion can shatter; religious symbols and language can become the property of a clerical elite who pay only lip service to the revelation of values. Religious authorities can too easily fall into patters of domination and control. When this occurs in the religious option, sacralism merges. Sacralism guarantees salvation for the cheap price of a lip service orthodoxy and a routine obedience to law. God becomes identified with the mighty and powerful of this anguished world." _Ibid._, p.10.

67. Gustavo Gutierrez, A Theology of Liberation, trans. and ed. by Sister Caridad Inda and John Eagleson (Maryknoll, N.Y.: Orbis, 1973), pp.204-205.

68. Walter Wink, "My Enemy, My Destiny: The Transforming Power of Nonviolence," Sojourners 16 (1987), p.30.

69. National Conference of Catholic Bishops, Economic Justice for All: Pastoral Letter on Catholic Social Teaching and the U.S. Economy (Washington D.C.: USCC, 1986), p.164.

70. FG, p.36. Here one might make a case for a historical parallel between Jaspers and another philosopher, Bertrand Russell, who later rejected (or in Jaspers's case, modified) his earlier views given historical developments in the arms race and military political situation. In his early essay, "The Future of Mankind" (1950), Russell accepted threatening war against the Soviet Union if it would not negotiate something similar to the Baruch proposal for the international control of nuclear weapons. But because of the growth of the Soviet stockpile of nuclear weapons and the development of the hydrogen bomb, Russell came to reject his earlier view in one of the appendices to his Common Sense and Nuclear Warfare (1959). We would like to thank Professor William C. Gay for bringing Russell's development to our attention in his, "The Nuclear Debate and American Philosophers: 1945 to 1985," paper presented on July 31, 1986 at Paderborn University in the German-American Conference on "Religion and Philosophy in the United States of America," Paderborn, West German (mimeographed).

According to Dr. G.B. Pepper, Russell's later position (i.e., "better red than dead") must have been in Jaspers's mind in his book on the atom bomb, as suggested by the English title, though it is never explicitly mentioned in either the English or German editions. Jaspers's point with his hidden interlocutor was that there could be no grounded moral basis for Russell's later position (Pepper maintains that Russell's former position was equally untenable). Speaking of Jaspers's position with respect to the academic debate with Russell, Pepper writes: "no one can prescribe for another what makes life worth living in situations whose alternatives are life or death. Each person must testify to what Transcendence offers and commands in such

275

situations. Therefore Jaspers defended the choice of death [but not the slogan "better dead than red"] rather than submission to totalitarian rule without prescribing it for all. But since no one can predict the future or predetermine the responses of freedom, even totalitarian regimes can be changed. This clearly implies that the choice of better red than dead could also be tenable. Jaspers didn't state this because the conditions of the debate required him to oppose the better red than dead position as a moral prescription." George B. Pepper, Personal correspondence, letter dated 13 April, 1987.

71. The christian social ethicist Gibson Winter has creatively articulated some of the foundational philosophical underpinnings of nuclearism. He reminds us that the threat of the technological mind (Jaspers's "intellectual thinking") to modernity does not derive from its strengths, but from the mind's failure to know itself as a secondary and useful mode of being in the world: "nuclearism [...] is the terminal stage on a path that has been more destructive than creative. To turn from this path now means a conversion in our whole way of life. It means a religious and moral shift from domination to participation, reestablishing our moral, political and spiritual connection." Gibson Winter, "Hope for the Earth: A Hermeneutic of Nuclearism," Religion and Intellectual Life, 3 (Spring 1984), p.24.

72. ABR, p.57.

BIBLIOGRAPHY OF WORKS CITED

N.B. Section IA below lists the original edition of Jaspers's selected German works cited either in the notes or text of this study, followed by the English translation if available in section IB. If an edition other than the German or English original is given, this is the text from which quotations have been taken. For a comprehensive bibliography of the writings of Karl Jaspers to 1973 (compiled by Kurt Rossmann to 1957 and revised and continued from 1958 to 1973 by Gisela Gefken), see Paul A. Schilpp, ed., The Philosophy of Karl Jaspers, The Library of Living Philosophers, vol.9, rev. 2nd ed. (Lasalle: Open Court, 1981), pp.871-904.

I. WORKS BY KARL JASPERS

A. In German

1.   **Allgemeine Psychopathologie.** Berlin: Springer Verlag, 1913.
2.   **Aneignung und Polemik: Gesammelte Reden und Aufsätze zur Geschichte der Philosophie.** Ed. by Hans Saner. Munich: R. Piper & Co., 1968.
3.   **Antwort: Zur Kritik meiner Schrift "Wohin treibt die Bundesrepublik?"** Munich: R. Piper & Co., 1967.
4.   **Die Atombombe und die Zukunft des Menschen: Politisches Bewusstsein unserer Zeit.** 4th ed. Munich: R. Piper, 1960 [1958].
5.   **Chiffren der Transcendenz.** Ed. by Hans Saner. Munich: R. Piper & Co., 1970.
6.   **Descartes und die Philosophie.** 3rd ed. Berlin Walter de Gruyter & Co., 1956 [1937].
7.   **Einführung in die Philosophie: Zwölf Radiovorträge.** Munich: R. Piper, 1953 [and Zurich: Artemis, 1950].
8.   **Existenzphilosophie: drei Vorlesungen gehalten am Freien Deutschen Hochstift in Frankfurt a.m., September 1937.** 3rd ed. Berlin W. de Gruyter, 1964 [1938].
9.   **Die Frage des Entmythologisierung von Karl Jaspers und Rudolf Bultmann.** Munich: R. Piper, 1954.
10.   **Freiheit und Wiedervereinigung.** Munich: R. Piper & Co., 1960.
11.   **Die geistige Situation der Zeit.** 5th partially rev. ed. Berlin: W. de Gruyter & Co., 1955 [1931].

12. Die grossen Philosophen: Erster Band, Die massgebender Menschen: Sokrates, Buddha, Konfuzius, Jesus; Die fortzeugenden Gründer des Philosophierne: Plato, Augustin, Kant; Aus dem Ursprung denkende Metaphysiker: Anaximander, Heraklit, Parmenides, Plotin, Anselm, Spinoza, Laotse, Nagarjuna. Munich: R. Piper & Co., 1957.

13. "Heimweh und Verbrechen." Gross' Archiv für krim. Anthropol. 35, no.1:1ff.

14. Hoffnung und Sorge: Schriften zur deutschen Politik, 1945-1965. Munich: R. Piper & Co., 1965.

15. Die Idee der Universität. Berlin, Heidelberg: Springer Verlag, 1946.

16. Kleine Schule des Philosophischen Denkens. Munich: R. Piper & Co., 1965.

17. Lionardo als Philosoph. Bern: A. Francke A.G., 1953.

18. Max Weber: Politiker, Forscher, Philosoph. 4th ed. Munich: R. Piper & Co., 1958 [Oldenburg: G. Stalling 1932].

19. Nietzsche: Einführung in das Verständnis seines Philosophierens. Berlin: W. de Gruyter & Co., 1936.

20. Nietzsche und das Christentum. Hameln: Bücherstube, 1946 and Munich: R. Piper & Co., 1952.

21. Nikolaus Cusanus. Munich: R. Piper & Co., 1964.

22. Philosophie. 3 vols. Vol.I, Philosophische Weltorientierung; Vol. II, Existenzerhellung; Vol. III, Metaphysik. 3rd ed. Berlin: Springer-Verlag, 1956 [1932].

23. Philosophie und Welt: Reden und Aufsätze. 2nd. ed. Munich: R. Piper & Co., 1963 [1958].

24. "Philosophische Autobiographie." In Karl Jaspers. Ed. by P.A. Schilpp. Stuttgart: Kohlhammer, 1957.

25. Der philosophische Glaube angesichts der Offenbarung. 2nd ed. Munich: R. Piper & Co., 1963 [1962].

26. Der philosophische Glaube: Gastvorlesungen. Zurich: Artemis, 1948.

27. Provokationen: Gespräche und Interviews. Ed. by Hans Saner. Munich R. Piper & Co., 1969.

28. Psychologie der Weltanschauungen. Berlin: Springer Verlag, 1919.

29. Rechenschaft und Ausblick: Reden und Aufsätze. 2nd ed. Munich: R. Piper & Co., 1958 [1951].

30. Schelling: Grösse und Verhängnis. Munich: R. Piper & Co., 1955.

31. **Schicksal und Wille:** Autobiographische **Schriften.** Ed. by Hans Saner. Munich: R. Piper & Co., 1967.
32. **Die Schuldfrage.** Heidelberg: L. Schneider, 1946.
33. **Strindberg und van Gogh: Versuch einer pathographischen Analyse unter vergleichender Heranziehung von Swedenborg und Hölderin.** Bern: Bincher, 1922.
34. **Vernunft und Existenz: Fünf Vorlesungen.** Gehalten vom 25 bis 29 Marz, 1935. Groningen: J.B. Wolters, 1935.
35. **Vernunft und Widervernunft in unserer Zeit: Drei Gastvorlesungen.** Munich: R. Piper & Co., 1950.
36. **Vom europäischen Geist.** Munich: R. Piper & Co., 1947. Appeared originally in French translation by Jeanne Hersch. **L'Esprit européen.** Paris: La presse française et étrangère, O. Zeluck, 1946.
37. **Vom Ursprung und Ziel der Geschichte.** 4th ed. Munich: R. Piper & Co., 1963 [1949].
38. **Von der Wahrheit: Philosophische Logik, Erster Band.** Munich: R. Piper & Co., 1947.
39. **Wohin treibt die Bundesrepublik? Tatsachen-Gefahren-Chancen.** 7th ed. Munich: R. Piper & Co., 1967 [1966].

B. In English Translation

40. **The European Spirit.** Trans. with an intro. by Ronald Gregor Smith. London: SCM Press, 1948. (Translation of item 36)
41. **Existentialism and Humanism.** Ed. by Hanns E. Fischer. Trans. by E.B. Ashton. New York: Russell F. Moore Co., 1952. (Translation of part of item 29)
42. **The Future of Germany.** Trans. by E.B. Ashton. Chicago: University of Chicago Press, 1967. (Translation of "Aspekte der Bundesrepublik," part three of item 40, **Wohin treibt die Bundesrepublik?** Chapter VI and the Postscript also contain material from **Antwort,** item 3)
43. **The Future of Mankind.** Trans. by E.B. Ashton. Chicago: University of Chicago Press, 1961. (Translation of item 4)
44. **General Psychopathology.** Trans. by J. Hoening and M. W. Hamilton. Chicago: University of Chicago Press, 1963. (Translation of item 1)
45. **The Great Philosophers: The Foundations, The Paradigmatic Individuals: Socrates, Buddha, Confucius, Jesus; The Seminal Founders of Philosophical Thought: Plato, Augustine, Kant.**

Ed. by Hannah Arendt. Trans. by Ralph Manheim. London: Rupert Hart-Davis, 1962. (Translation of part of item 12)

46. **The Idea of the University**. Ed. by Karl Deutsch and Trans. by H.A.T. Reiche and H.F. Vanderschmidt. London: Peter Owen, 1965. (Translation of item 15)

47. **Karl Jaspers, Basic Philosophical Writings: Selections**. Ed. Trans. with introductions by Edith Ehrlich, Leonard H. Ehrlich, and George B. Pepper. Series in Continental Thought, Vol.10. Athens, Ohio and London: Ohio University Press, 1986.

48. **Leonardo, Descartes, Max Weber: Three Essays**. Trans. by Ralph Manheim. London: Routledge & Kegan Paul, 1965. (Translation of items 17, 6, and 18)

49. **Man in the Modern Age**. Trans. by E. and C. Paul. 2nd ed. Garden City, New York: Doubleday and Co., 1951 [London: Routledge & Kegan Paul, 1933]. (Translation of item 11)

50. **Myth and Christianity. An Inquiry Into the Possibility of Religion Without Myth**. By Karl Jaspers and Rudolph Bultmann. Trans. by Norbert Guterman. New York: Noonday Press, 1958. (Translation of item 9)

51. **Nietzsche and Christianity**. Trans. by E.B. Ashton. Chicago: Henry Regnery Co., 1961. (Translation of item 20)

52. **Nietzsche: An Introduction to the Understanding of His Philosophical Activity**. Trans. by C.F. Wallraff and F.J. Schmitz. Tucson: University of Arizona Press, 1965. (Translation of item 19)

53. **The Origin and Goal of History**. Trans. by Michael Bullock. New Haven: Yale University Press, 1953. (Translation of item 37)

54. **The Perennial Scope of Philosophy**. Trans. by Ralph Manheim. London: Routledge & Kegan Paul, 1950 [and New York: Philosophical Library, 1949]. (Translation of item 26)

55. **"Philosophical Autobiography."** In The Philosophy of Karl Jaspers. The Library of Living Philosophers, vol.9, pp.1-94. Ed. by Paul A. Schilpp. Rev. 2nd ed. [including chapter: "Heidegger"]. Lasalle: Open Court, 1981. (Translation of item 24)

56. **Philosophical Faith and Revelation**. Trans. by E.B. Ashton. New York: Harper and Row, 1967. (Translation of item 25)

57. **Philosophy.** 3 vols. Trans. by E.B. Ashton. Chicago: University of Chicago Press, 1969-71. (Translation of item 22)

58. **Philosophy and the World: Selected Essays and Lectures.** Trans. by E.B. Ashton. Chicago: Regnery, 1963. (Translation of item 23)

59. **Philosophy Is for Everyman: A Short Course in Philosophical Thinking.** Trans. by R.F.C. Hull and G. Wels. New York: Harcourt, Brace and World, 1967. (Translation of item 16)

60. **Philosophy of Existence.** Trans. by Richard F. Grabau. Philadelphia: University of Pennsylvania Press, 1971. (Translation of item 8)

61. **The Question of German Guilt.** Trans. by E.B. Ashton. 2nd ed. New York: Capricorn Books, 1961 [New York: The Dial Press, 1947]. (Translation of item 32)

62. **Reason and Anti-Reason in Our Time.** Reprint ed. Hamden, Conn.: Archon Books, 1971 [London: SCM Press, 1952]. (Translation of item 35)

63. **Reason and Existenz: Five Lectures.** Trans. by William Earle. London: Routledge & Kegan Paul, 1956. (Translation of item 34)

64. **Strindberg and Van Gogh.** Trans. by O. Grunow and D. Woloshin. Tucson: University of Arizona Press, 1977. (Translation of item 33)

65. **Truth and Symbol From "Von der Wahrheit."** Trans. with an intro. by Jean T. Wilde, William Kluback and William Kimmel. New York: Twayne, and New Haven, Conn.: College and University Press, 1959. (Partial translation of item 38)

66. **Way to Wisdom: An Introduction to Philosophy.** Trans. by Ralph Manheim. 4th ed. New Haven: Yale University Press, 1960 [1951]. (Translation of item 7)

II. ARTICLES BY JASPERS

B. In German

67. **"Die Atombombe und die Zukunft des Menschen (1956)."** Radiovortrage. (In item 14): 153-172.

68. **"Erneuerung der Universität."** Die Wandlung 1, Nr.1, Heidelberg, L. Schneider. (Also in item 14): 66-74.

69. **"Das Gewissen vor der Bedrohung durch die Atombombe (1950)."** (In item 29): 370-377.

70. **"Kierkegaard (1951)."** (In item 29): 137-157.

71. **"Philosophie und Wissenschaft (1948)."** (In item 29): 240-259.

72. "Über Gefahren und Chancen der Freiheit (1950)." (In item 29): 349-369.
73. "Vom Charakter der Modernen Wissenschaft." Der Monat, Berlin, Vol. I (No.12): 12-17.
74. "Wahrheit, Freiheit und Friede (1958)." (In item 14): 173-185.
75. "Wahrheit und Wissenschaft." In Jaspers, Karl. Wahrheit und Wisssenschaft, pp.5-25. Portmann, Adolph. Naturwissenschaft und Humanismus. Munich: R. Piper, 1960.

B. In English Translation

76. "The Atom Bomb and the Future of Man." A radio address. Trans. by Norbert Guterman. Evergreen Review 2 (1958): 37-57. (Translation of item 67)
77. "The Axial Age of Human History." Commentary 6 (1948): 430-435.
78. "The Balance of Terror Won't Protect Us From the Bomb." Realities, New York, No.181 (1965): 27-29.
79. "The Fight Against Totalitarianism." (In Item 58): 68-87.
80. "The History of Mankind as Seen by the Philosopher." Universitas 6 (1964): 211-220.
81. "Is Europe's Culture Finished?" Trans. by E.B. Ashton. Commentary 4 (1947): 518-526.
82. "The Importance of Kierkegaard." Trans. by Erwin W. Geissman. Cross Currents 2 (1952): 5-16. (Translation of item 70)
83. "Is Science Evil?" Trans. by Irving Kristol. Commentary 9 (1950): 229-233. (Translation of item 73)
84. "Kant's 'Perpetual Peace." (In Item 58): 88-124.
85. "Liberty and Authority." (In Item 58): 33-56.
86. "Nature and Ethics." In Moral Principles of Action: Man's Ethical Imperative, pp.48-61. Science of Culture Series, vol.VI. Ed. by Ruth N. Anshen. New York and London: Harper and Brothers, 1952.
87. "Nietzsche and the Present." Trans. by Ralph Manheim. Partisan Review 19 (1952): 19-30.
88. "On My Philosophy." In Existentialism from Dostoevsky to Sartre, pp.158-185. Rev. and expanded ed. Ed., trans., and with an intro. by Walter Kaufmann. New York: New American Library, 1975.
89. "One of Karl Jaspers' Last Commentaries: Gandhiji." The Courier 22 (October 1969): 26-27.

90. "Philosophy and Science." Trans. by Ralph Manheim. Partisan Review 16 (1948): 871-884. (Translation of item 71)

91. "The Rededication of German Scholarship." Trans. by Marianne Zuckerkandl. The American Scholar 15 (Spring 1946): 180-188. (Translation of item 68)

92. "Reply to My Critics." In The Philosophy of Karl Jaspers, pp.747-869. Ed. by Paul Authur Schilpp. Lasalle: Open Court, 1981.

93. "Truth and Science." Trans. by Robert E. Wood. Philosophy Today 6 (1962): 5-25. (Translation of item 75)

94. "The UN Is Undependable." The New Republic (18 May, 1959): 12-13.

III. WRITINGS ABOUT JASPERS

95. Arendt, Hannah. "Jaspers As Citizen of the World." (In Item 124): 539-549.

96. Baumgarten, Eduard. "Radical Evil: Pro and Con." (In Item 124): 337-367.

97. Buri, Fritz. "Concerning the Relationship of Philosophical Faith and Christian Faith." Journal of the American Academy of Religion 40 (1972): 454-457.

98. Carr, Godfrey Robert. Karl Jaspers as an Intellectual Critic: The Political Dimension of his Thought, European University Studies, series XX, Philosophy Vol.125. Frankfurt am Main, Bern, New York: Peter Lang, 1983.

99. Collins, James. The Existentialists: A Critical Study. Chicago: Henry Regnery Co., 1952.

100. _____. "Jaspers On Science and Philosophy." (In Item 124): 115-40.

101. Dufrenne, Mikel and Ricoeur, Paul. Karl Jaspers et la philosophie de l'existence. Paris: Editions du Seuil, 1947.

102. Durfee, Harold A. "Karl Jaspers' Christology." Journal of Religion 44 (1964): 133-148.

103. Ehrlich, Leonard H. Karl Jaspers: Philosophy as Faith. Amherst: University of Massachusetts Press, 1975.

104. _____. "Philosophical Faith and Mysticism." Bucknell Review XVII (1969): 1-21.

105. Habermas, Jürgen. "Karl Jaspers: The Figures of Truth." In Philosophical-Political Profiles, pp.45-52. Trans. and with an intro. by Frederick G. Lawrence. Cambridge, Mass. and London, England: MIT Press, 1983.

106. **Heinemann, F.H.** Existentialism and the Modern Predicament. New York: Harper & Row, Harper Torchbook, 1958.

107. **Holm, Soren.** "Jaspers' Philosophy of Religion." (In Item 124): 667-692.

108. **Kane, John F.** Pluralism and Truth in Religion: Karl Jaspers on Existential Truth. American Academy of Religion Dissertation Series, No.33. Ed. by H. Ganse Little, Jr. Chico, Ca.: Scholars Press, 1981.

109. **Knauss, Gerhard.** "The Concept of the 'Encompassing' in Jaspers' Philosophy." (In Item 124): 141-175.

110. **Lefebre, Ludwig B.** "The Psychology of Karl Jaspers." (In Item 124): 467-497.

111. **Lichtigfeld, Adolph.** "The God-Concept in Jaspers' Philosophy." (In Item 124): 693-701.

112. **_____.** "Jaspers in English: A Failure Not of Communication But Rather of Interpretation." Philosophy and Phenomenological Research 41 (1980/81): 216-222.

113. **Loewenstein, Julius Izhak.** "Judaism in Jaspers' Thought." (In Item 124): 643-666.

114. **Long, Eugene T.** Jaspers and Bultmann: A Dialogue Between Philosophy and Theology in the Existentialist Tradition. Durham, North Carolina: Duke University Press, 1968.

115. **Manasse, Ernst Moritz.** "Jaspers' Relation to Max Weber." (In Item 124): 369-391.

116. **Olson, Alan M.** Transcendence and Hermeneutics: An Interpretation of the Philosophy of Karl Jaspers. Studies in Philosophy and Religion, vol.2. The Hague: Martinus Nijhoff, 1979.

117. **Pepper, George B.** "Karl Jaspers on the Sciences: In Retrospect." In Karl Jaspers Today: Philosophy at the Threshold of the Future. Ed. by Leonard H. Ehrlich and Richard Wisser. Forthcoming, Univ. Press of America, 1988.

118. **Piper, Klaus, ed.** Karl Jaspers: Werk und Wirkung, Zum 80. Geburtstag von Jaspers. Munich: R. Piper, 1963.

119. **Ricoeur, Paul.** "The Relation of Jaspers' Philosophy to Religion." (In Item 124): 611-642.

120. **Rigali, Norbert J.** "A New Axis: Karl Jaspers' Philosophy of History." International Philosophical Quarterly 10 (1970): 441-457.

121. **Samay, Sebastian, O.S.B.** Reason Revisited: The Philosophy of Karl Jaspers. South Bend: University of Notre Dame Press, 1971.

122. **Saner, Hans.** Karl Jaspers in Selbstzeugnissen und Bilddokumenten. Reinbeck: Rowohlt, 1970.

123. _____, ed. Karl Jaspers in der Diskussion. Munich: R. Piper, 1973.
124. **Schilpp, Paul A.**, ed. The Philosophy of Karl Jaspers. The Library of Living Philosophers, Vol.9. Revised 2nd edition [including chapter: "Heidegger"]. Lasalle: Open Court, 1981.
125. **Schneiders, Werner.** Karl Jaspers in der Kritik. Bonn: Bouvier, 1965.
126. **Schrag, Oswald.** Existence, Existenz, and Transcendence: An Introduction to the Philosophy of Karl Jaspers. Pittsburg: Duquesne University Press, 1971.
127. **Simon, Gabriel, SS.CC.** Die Achse der Weltgeschichte nach Karl Jaspers. Analecta Gregoriana 147, Series Facultatis Philosophicae: section B, n.13. Roma: Libreria Editrice dell'Universita Gregoriana, 1965.
128. **Sölle, Dorothee.** "'Thou Shalt Have No Other Jeans Before Me." In Observations on "The Spiritual Situation of the Age:" Contemporary German Perspectives, pp.157-168. Ed. by Jurgen Habermas. Trans. and with an intro. by Andrew Buchwalter. Cambridge, Massachusetts and London, England: MIT Press, 1984.
129. **Sternberger, Dolf.** "Jaspers und der Staat." (In Item 118): 133-141.
130. **Tilliette, Xavier.** "Jaspersiana." Archives de Philosophie 22/2 (1959): 280-292.
131. _____. Karl Jaspers: Théorie de la vérité, Métaphysique des chiffres, Foi philosophique. Paris: Coll. 'Théologie', vol. 44, Aubier, 1960.
132. **Wallraff, Charles.** "Jaspers in English: A Failure of Communication." Philosophy and Phenomenological Research 37 (1977): 537-548.
133. _____. Karl Jaspers: An Introduction to His Philosophy. Princeton, N.J.: Princeton University Press, 1970.
134. **Young-Bruehl, Elisabeth.** Freedom and Karl Jaspers's Philosophy. New Haven and London: Yale University Press, 1981.

IV. WRITINGS ON NUCLEAR WEAPONS, WAR, AND PEACE

Adams, Ruth, and Cullen, Susan, eds. The Final Epidemic: Physicians and Scientists on Nuclear War. Chicago: Educational Foundation for Nuclear Science, 1981.
Beardslee, William and Mack, John. "The Impact on Children and Adolescents of Nuclear Developments." In Psychosocial Aspects of Nuclear Developments, pp.64-96.

American Psychiatric Association Task Force Report No.20: Washington D.C., 1982.

Bethe, Hans A. et al. "Space-based Ballistic-Missile Defense." Scientific American 251 (1984): 39-49.

Center for Defense Information. "Soviet Geopolitical Momentum: Myth or Menace?: Trends of Soviet Influence Around the World from 1945 to 1980." The Defense Monitor 9 (January 1980): 1-24.

Ehrlich, P.R. and Others. "Long-term Biological Consequences of Nuclear War." Science 222 (1983): 1293-1300.

Fisher, Roger and Ury, William. Ed. by Bruce Patton. Getting to YES: Negotiating Agreement Without Giving In. New York: Penguin, 1982.

Fox, Michael A. and Groarke, Leo, eds. Nuclear War: Philosophical Perspectives. New York, Berne, Frankfurt am Main: Peter Lang, 1985.

Garceau, Benoît, O.M.I. "Anthropologie et Paix." Response paper presented at the conference, "Quelle Paix pour Notre Temps/Quest for Peace in Our Day," May 16-18, 1986, Saint Paul University, Ottawa, Canada. (Mimeographed)

Garwin, Richard and Pike, John. "Space Weapons: History and Current Debate." Bulletin of the Atomic Scientists Supplement (May 1984): 2S-9S.

Gay, William C. "Myths About Nuclear War: Misconceptions in Public Beliefs and Governmental Plans." Philosophy and Social Criticism 9 (Summer 1982): 115-144.

_____. "The Nuclear Debate and American Philosophers: 1945-1985." Paper presented on July 31, 1986 at Paderborn University in the German-American Conference on "Religion and Philosophy in the United States of America." (Mimeographed).

Goldberg, Susan. "Thinking About the Threat of Nuclear War: A Survey of Metro Toronto Students." Prepared for the Children's Mental Health Research Group. Toronto, 1984. (Mimeographed)

Gray, Colin. "War-Fighting for Deterrence." Journal for Strategic Studies 7 (March 1984): 5-29.

Gray, Colin and Payne, Keith. "Victory is Possible." Foreign Policy 39 (1980): 14-27.

Green, Philip. Deadly Logic: The Theory of Nuclear Deterrence. Columbus, OH: Ohio State University Press, 1966.

Ground Zero. Nuclear War: What's In It For You? New York: Pocket Books, 1982.

Hardin, Russell, Mearsheimer, John J., Dworkin, Gerald, and Goodin, Robert E. eds. Nuclear Deterrence: Ethics and Strategy. Chicago and London: The University of Chicago Press, 1985.

Holloway, David. The Soviet Union and the Arms Race. 2nd ed. New Haven: Yale University Press, 1984.

Kenny, Anthony. The Logic of Deterrence. Chicago: University of Chicago Press, 1985.

Lee, Steven. "The Morality of Nuclear Deterrence: Hostage Holding and Consequences." In Nuclear Deterrence: Ethics and Strategy, pp.173-190. Ed. by Russell Hardin, John J. Mearsheimer, Gerald Dworkin, and Robert E. Goodin. Chicago and London: The University of Chicago Press, 1985.

Lifton, Robert J. The Broken Connection: On Death and the Continuity of Life. New York: Simon and Schuster, 1979.

_____. Death in Life: Survivors of Hiroshima. New York: Basic Books, 1967.

Lifton, Robert J., and Falk, Richard. Indefensible Weapons: The Political and Psychological Case Against Nuclearism. Toronto: CBC Enterprises, 1982.

Mack, John. "Psychosocial Trauma." In The Final Epidemic: Physicians and Scientists on Nuclear War, pp.21-34. Ed. by R. Adams and S. Cullen. Chicago: University of Chicago Press, 1981.

Martino, Joseph P. "Star Wars"-- Technology's New Challenge to Moralists." This World 9 (1984): 15-29.

Melchin, Kenneth R. "Just-War, Pacifism, and the Ethics of Nuclear Policy." Eglise et Théologie 17 (1986): 41-55.

Murray, John C., S.J. "Remarks on the Moral Problem of War." Theological Studies 20 (1959): 40-61.

Nathan, Otto and Norden, Heinz, eds. Einstein on Peace. New York: Schocken, 1968.

Nielsen, Kai. "Commentary: Doing the Morally Unthinkable." In Nuclear War: Philosophical Perspectives, pp.57-61. Ed. by Michael A. Fox and Leo Groarke. New York, Berne, Frankfurt am Main: Peter Lang, 1985.

Nuclear Weapons Databook, Vol.I, U.S. Nuclear Forces and Capabilities. Ed. by Thomas B. Cochran, William M. Arkin, and Milton M. Hoenig. Cambridge, Ma.: Ballinger, 1984.

Popkin, Richard H. "The Triumphant and Catastrophic Apocalypse." In Nuclear Weapons and the Future of Humanity: The Fundamental Questions, pp.131-150. Ed. by Avner Cohen and Steven Lee. Totowa, N.J.: Rowman & Allan, 1986.

Rapaport, Anatol. Strategy and Conscience. New York: Harper and Row, 1964.

_____. "The Technological Imperative." Paper delivered at the University of Waterloo Conference on Philosophy and Nuclear Arms, September 28-30, 1984. (Mimeographed)

Regehr, Ernie. "Canada and the Arms Trade." The Ploughshares Monitor VII (1986): 13-16.

Routley, Richard. "Metaphysical Fall-out from the Nuclear Predicament." Philosophy and Social Criticism 10, No.3/4 (Winter 1984): 19-34.

Russell, Bertrand. Common Sense and Nuclear Warfare. London: Allen & Unwin, 1959.

_____. "The Future of Mankind." In Unpopular Essays. London: Allen & Unwin, 1950.

Santoni, Ronald E. "Nuclear Insanity and Multiple Genocide." In Toward the Understanding and Prevention of Genocide, pp.147-153. Ed. by I. Charny. Boulder: Westview Press, 1984.

_____. "The Arms Race, Genocidal Intent, and Individual Responsibility." Philosophy & Social Criticism 10, No.3/4 (Winter 1984): 9-18.

Schell, Jonathan. The Fate of the Earth. New York: Alfred A. Knopf, 1982.

Schwebel, Milton. "Effects of the Nuclear War Threat on Children and Teenagers: Implications for Professionals." American Journal of Orthopsychiatry 52 (1982): 608-17.

_____, ed. Behavioral Science and Human Survival. Palo Alto, Calif.: Science and Behavior Books, 1965.

Somerville, John. "Nuclear 'War' Is Omnicide." In Nuclear War: Philosophical Perspectives, pp.3-9. Ed. by Fox, Michael and Groarke, Leo. New York, Berne, Frankfurt am Main: Peter Lang, 1985.

Tirman, John, ed. The Fallacy of Star Wars. Based on Studies Conducted by the Union of Concerned Scientists. New York: Vintage, 1983.

Turco, K.P. et al. "Nuclear Winter: Global Consequences of Multiple Nuclear Explosions." Science 222 (1983): 1283-92.

United States Catholic Conference. "The Challenge of Peace: God's Promise and Our Response." Origins 13 (1983): 1-32.

Velikov, Yevgeny P. "Effect on Strategic Stability," Bulletin of the Atomic Scientists Supplement (May 1984): 12S-15S.

Walters, Gregory J. "The Challenge of Peace: Philosophers and Strategists on Nuclear Use and Deterrence." Eglise et Théologie 17 (octobre 1986): 355-386.

_____. "The Psycho-Spiritual Impact of the Threat of Nuclear War on Children and Adolescents in the United States: 1960-1982." In Science, Knowledge, and Power: Selected Material from the Second National Conference of Canadian Student Pugwash, pp.135-144. Ed. by Mary Thornton and Jane Willms. Ottawa: CSP, 1984.

_____. "The World Council of Churches On Nuclear
    Deterrence: A Call to Peace Ecumenism."
    Mid-Stream 24 (1985): 29-43.
Weisskopf, Victor F. "The Task for a New Peace
    Movement." Bulletin of the Atomic Scientists 43
    (January/February 1987): 26-32.
Wink, Walter. "My Enemy, My Destiny: The Transforming
    Power of Nonviolence." Sojourners 16 (1987):
    30-35.
Winter, Gibson. "Hope for the Earth: A Hermeneutic of
    Nuclearism." Religion and Intellectual Life, 3
    (Spring 1984): 5-29.

                V. OTHER WORKS CITED

Abbot, Walter M., S.J., ed. The Documents of Vatican
    II. Trans. by Msgr. Joseph Gallagher. New York:
    America Press, 1966.
Arendt, Hannah. The Life of the Mind. One volume
    edition. New York and London: Harcourt Brace
    Jovanovich, 1978.
_____. The Origins of Totalitarianism. New edition
    with added prefaces. New York: Harcourt Brace
    Jovanovich, 1973.
Bonhoeffer, Dietrich. Letters and Papers From Prison.
    London: Collins, 1971.
Davis, Charles. Theology and Political Society.
    Cambridge: Cambridge University Press, 1980.
Fackre, Gabriel. The Religious Right and Christian
    Faith. Grand Rapids, Mich.: W.B. Eerdmans,
    1982.
Garceau, Benoît, O.M.I. "Critique et herméneutique en
    philosophie de la religion." In Rationality
    to-day. La rationalité aujourd'hui, par H.-G.
    Gadamer et autres, pp.373-380. Edité par
    Theordore F. Geraets. Ottawa: Editions de
    l'Université d'Ottawa, 1979.
_____. "De la connaissance d'autrui par la
    médiation de signes." In L'Altérité Vivre
    Ensemble Différents: Approches
    Pluridisciplinaires, Recherches nouvelle série--
    7, pp.119-131. Ed. par Michel Gourgues et
    Gilles-D. Mailhiot. Montréal et Paris: Editions
    Bellarmin, du Cerf, 1986.
Gathered for Life: Official Report VI Assembly World
    Council of Churches. Ed. by David Gill. Geneva
    and Grand Rapids: WCC and Wm. B. Eerdmans, 1983.
Guindon, André, O.M.I. The Sexual Creators: An Ethical
    Proposal for Concerned Christians. Lanham, Md.:
    University Press of America, 1986.
Gula, Richard M., SS. What Are They Saying About Moral
    Norms? New York/Ramsey: Paulist Press, 1982.

Guttierez, Gustavo. A Theology of Liberation. Trans.
and ed. by Sister Caridad Inda and John Eagleson.
Maryknoll, N.Y.: Orbis, 1973.
Habermas, Jürgen, ed. Observations on "The Spiritual
Situation of the Age:" Contemporary German
Perspectives. Trans. and with an intro. by
Andrew Buchwalter. Cambridge, Massachusetts and
London, England: MIT Press, 1984.
Hassner, Pierre. "Situation de la philosophie
politique chez Kant." In La Philosophie
politique de Kant, pp.77-103. Par E. Weil et
autres. Paris: Presses universitaires de France,
1962.
Hauerwas, Stanley. Against the Nations: War and
Survival in a Liberal Society. Minneapolis:
Winston Press, 1985.
Hegel, G.W.F. Phenomenology of Spirit. Trans. by A. V.
Miller and with Analysis and Foreword by J.N.
Findlay. Oxford: Clarendon Press, 1977.
Heidegger, Martin. "The Question Concerning
Technology." in Martin Heidegger: Basic Writings,
pp.287-317. Ed. with intro. by David F. Krell.
New York: Harper and Row, 1977.
Kant, Immanuel. Perpetual Peace: A Philosophical
Sketch. In Kant, Immanuel. Critique of
Practical Reason: And Other Writings in Moral
Philosophy, pp.306-345. Trans. and ed. with an
intro. by Lewis White Beck. Chicago: University
of Chicago Press, 1949.
Kaufman, Gordon. Theology for a Nuclear Age.
Manchester and Philadelphia: Manchester
University Press and the Westminster Press, 1985.
Lamb, Matthew. Solidarity With Victims: Toward a
Theology of Social Transformation. New York:
Crossroad, 1982.
Lee, Bernard J., S.M. and Cowan, Michael A. Dangerous
Memories: House Churches and Our American Story.
Kansas City, Mo.: Sheed & Ward, 1986.
Levinas, Emmanuel. Totality and Infinity: An Essay on
Exteriority. Trans. by Alphonso Lingis.
Pittsburgh: Duquesne University Press, 1969.
Lonergan, Bernard J.F., S.J. Insight: A Study of Human
Understanding. Rev. ed. New York:
Philosophical Library, 1958 and London: Darton
and Todd, 1958.
_____. Method in Theology. New York: Seabury
Press, 1972.
Lukacs, Georg. "L'Esprit Européen devant le Marxisme."
La Nef 3 (November 1946): 39-41.
MacIntyre, Alasdair. After Virtue: A Study in Moral
Theory. Second edition. Notre Dame, Indiana:
University of Notre Dame Press, 1984.

McCabe, Herbert. Law, Love and Language. London and Sydney: Sheed and Ward, 1968.

Melchin, Kenneth R. History, Ethics and Emergent Probability: Ethics, Society and History in the Work of Bernard Lonergan. Lanham, Md.: University Press of America, 1987.

Metz, J.B. Faith in History and Society. Trans. by David Smith. New York: Seabury, 1980.

_____. "The Responsibility of Hope." Philosophy Today 10 (1966): 280-288.

National Conference of Catholic Bishops. Economic Justice for All: Pastoral Letter on Catholic Social Teaching and the U.S. Economy. Washington D.C.: USCC, 1986.

Moltmann, Jürgen. Theology of Hope: On the Ground and the Implications of a Christian Eschatology. Trans. by James W. Leitch. London: SCM, 1967.

Rahner, Karl. "The Experiment Man." In Theological Investigations, vol.9, pp.205-224. Trans. by Graham Harrison. London: Darton, Longman & Todd, 1972.

Ricoeur, Paul. Essays on Biblical Interpretation. Ed. by Lewis S. Mudge. Philadelphia: Fortress Press, 1980.

_____. Hermeneutics and the Human Sciences: Essays on Language, Action and Interpretation. Ed. and Trans. by John B. Thompson. Cambridge: Cambridge Univ. Press and Paris: Editions de la Maison des Sciences de l'Homme, 1981.

Rossi, Philip. "The Foundation of the Philosophical Concept of Autonomy by Kant and its Historical Consequences." Concilium 172 (1984): 3-8.

Sölle, Dorothee. Political Theology. Trans. by John Shelley. Philadelphia: Fortress Press, 1974.

Segundo, Juan Luis. Liberation of Theology. Trans. by John Drury. Maryknoll, New York: Orbis Press, 1976.

Spender, Stephen. "The Intellectuals and Europe's Future." Commentary III (1947): 7-12.

Tillich, Paul. The Protestant Era. Trans. by James Luther Adams. Abridged ed. Chicago: University of Chicago Press, 1957.

Van Den Hengel, John W., S.C.J. The Home of Meaning: The Hermeneutics of the Subject of Paul Ricoeur. Washington, D.C.: University Press of America, 1982.

Weber, Max. Law in Economy and Society. In Max Weber on Law in Economy and Society. Ed. and with an intro. by Max Rheinstein. Trans. by Edward Shils and M. Rheinstein. New York: Simon and Schuster, 1954.

_____. "Politics as a Vocation." In Max Weber: Selections in Translation, pp.212-225. Ed. by W.G. Runciman and trans. by E. Matthews. Cambridge: Cambridge University Press, 1978.

ABBREVIATIONS OF WORKS CITED

(N.B. In order to facilitate cross-referencing, the corresponding entry number to Jaspers's primary sources in the Bibliography of Works Cited is listed below)

AB	Die Atombombe und die Zukunft des Menschen #4
ABR	"The Atom Bomb and the Future of Man" #76
DP	Descartes und die Philosophie #6
EDP	Einführung in die Philosophie #7
EH	Existentialism and Humanism #41
EP	Existenzphilosophie #8
ES	The European Spirit #40
FE	Die Frage der Entmythologisierung #9
FG	The Future of Germany #42
FM	The Future of Mankind #43
GBA	"Das Gewissen vor der Bedrohung durch die Atombombe" #69
GPT I	The Great Philosophers: The Foundations #45
GSZ	Die geistige Situation der Zeit #11
HS	Hoffnung und Sorge #14
KST	Philosophy Is for Everyman #59
LDW	Leonardo, Descartes, Max Weber #48
MC	Myth and Christianity #50
MMA	Man in the Modern Age #49
NC	Nietzsche and Christianity #51
OMP	"On My Philosophy" #88
OGH	The Origin and Goal of History #53
P	Provokationen #27
PAT	"Philosophical Autobiography." In Schilpp, ed. Karl Jaspers #124
PE	Philosophy of Existence #60
PFR	Philosophical Faith and Revelation #56
PG	Der philosophische Glaube #26
PGO	Der philosophische Glaube angesichts der Offenbarung #25
PH I	Philosophie. I, Philosophische Weltorientierung #22
PH II	Philosophie. II, Existenzerhellung #22
PH III	Philosophie. III, Metaphysik #22
PHT I	Philosophy. I, Philosophical World Orientation #57
PHT II	Philosophy. II, Existential Elucidation #57
PHT III	Philosophy. III, Metaphysics #57
PS	"Philosophy and Science" #90
PSP	The Perennial Scope of Philosophy #54
PW	Philosophie und Welt #23
PWT	Philosophy and the World #58

```
QGG          The Question of German Guilt   #61
RA           Rechenschaft und Ausblick   #29
RAT          Reason and Anti-Reason in Our Time   #62
RE           Reason and Existenz   #63
Schilpp (ed.)   The Philosophy of Karl Jaspers   #124
SchW         Schicksal und Wille   #31
TS           Truth and Symbol   #65
UZG          Vom Ursprung und Ziel der Geschichte   #37
VE           Vernunft und Existenz   #34
VW           Von der Wahrheit   #38
VWZ          Vernunft und Widervernunft in unserer Zeit #35
WW           Way to Wisdom   #66
```

ABOUT THE AUTHOR

Gregory J. Walters is Assistant Professor of Theology at Saint Mary's University, San Antonio, Texas. He has published articles on the psychospiritual impact of the threat of nuclear war on children and adolescents and the ethics of war and peace.

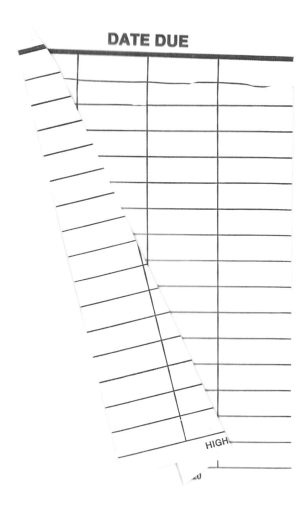

DATE DUE

HIGH